THE GRINDSTONE OF RAPPORT

A Clayton Eshleman Reader

*Selected Poetry, Prose, and Translations
of Clayton Eshleman*

THE GRINDSTONE OF RAPPORT

A Clayton Eshleman Reader

Selected Poetry, Prose, and Translations
of Clayton Eshleman

BLACK WIDOW PRESS
Boston, MA

THE GRINDSTONE OF RAPPORT: A Clayton Eshleman Reader ©2008 Clayton Eshleman. Black Widow Press thanks the following presses for allowing us to reprint previously published materials. Wesleyan University Press for excerpts from *Juniper Fuse* ©2003 and for excerpts from *Companion Spider: Essays* ©2001. Special thanks to Suzanna Tamminen for her help. University of California Press for excerpts from *The Complete Poetry of César Vallejo* ©2007 The Regents of the University of California and for excerpts from *Aimé Césaire: The Collected Poetry* ©1983 The Regents of the University of California. Thanks to Kim Hogeland for her help. Excerpts from *Conductors of the Pit* ©2005 Soft Skull Press. Special thanks to Richard Nash for permission to reprint passages. Excerpts from *Antiphonal Swing: Selected Prose 1962–1987* ©1989 by permission of McPherson & Co. Special thanks to Bruce R. McPherson for his help. Excerpts from *My Devotion* ©2004 by Black Sparrow Books. Thanks to David R. Godine et al. for his help. Excerpts from *Reciprocal Distillation* by permission from Hot Whiskey Press ©2007. Excerpts from *Watchfiends and Rack Screams* ©1995 by permission of Exact Change, Boston. (www.exactchange.com). Thanks to Damon Krukowski. All other works ©1964–2008 Clayton Eshleman. All rights reserved. This book, or parts thereof, may not be reproduced in any form or by any means electronic, digital, or mechanical, including photocopy, scanning, recording, or any information storage and retrieval system, without written permission from the publisher except in the case of brief quotations embodied in critical articles and reviews. For information, contact Black Widow Press, 134 Boylston Street, Boston, MA 02116.

Black Widow Press is an imprint of Commonwealth Books, Inc., Boston, MA. Distributed to the trade by NBN (National Book Network) throughout North America, Canada, and the U.K. All Black Widow Press books are printed on acid-free paper, and glued and sewn into bindings. Black Widow Press and its logo are registered trademarks of Commonwealth Books, Inc.

Joseph S. Phillips, Publisher
www.blackwidowpress.com

Book Design: Kerrie Kemperman
Front Cover Art and Design: Peter Blegvad
Photo Credit: Nina Subin

ISBN-13: 978-0-9795137-4-9
ISBN-10: 0-9795137-7-4

Library of Congress Cataloging-in-Publication Data on file

Eshleman, Clayton, 1935–

Printed by Friesens
Printed in Canada

10 9 8 7 6 5 4 3 2 1

ALSO BY CLAYTON ESHLEMAN

❧ POETRY ❧

Mexico & North [1962]

Indiana [1969]

Altars [1971]

Coils [1973]

The Gull Wall [1975]

What She Means [1978]

Hades in Manganese [1981]

Fracture [1983]

The Name Encanyoned River: Selected Poems 1960–1985 [1986]

Hotel Cro-Magnon [1989]

Under World Arrest [1994]

From Scratch [1998]

My Devotion [2004]

An Alchemist with One Eye on Fire [2006]

Reciprocal Distillations [2007]

❧ PROSE ❧

Antiphonal Swing: Selected Prose 1962–1987 [1989]

Companion Spider: Essays [2002]

*Juniper Fuse: Upper Paleolithic Imagination &
the Construction of the Underworld* [2003]

Archaic Design [2007]

JOURNALS AND ANTHOLOGIES

Folio [Bloomington, Indiana, 3 issues, 1959–1960]

Quena [Lima, Peru, 1 issue, edited, then suppressed by the North American Peruvian Cultural Institue, 1966]

Caterpillar [New York–Los Angeles, 20 issues, 1967–1973]

A Caterpillar Anthology [1971]

Sulfur [Pasadena–Los Angeles–Ypsilanti, 46 issues, 1981–2000]

TRANSLATIONS

Pablo Neruda, *Residence on Earth* [1962]

César Vallejo, *The Complete Posthumous Poetry*
(with José Rubia Barcia) [1978]

Aimé Césaire, *The Collected Poetry*
(with Annette Smith) [1983]

Michael Deguy, *Giving Given* [1984]

Bernard Bador, *Sea Urchin Harakiri* [1986]

*Conductors of the Pit: Major Works by Rimbaud, Vallejo, Césaire,
Artaud, & Holan* [1988, 2005]

Aimé Césaire, *Lyric & Narrative Poetry 1946–1982
(with Annette Smith) [1990]*

César Vallejo, *Trilce* [1992, 2000]

Antonin Artaud, *Watchfiends & Rack Screams*
(with Bernard Bador) [1995]

Aimé Césaire, *Notebook of a Return to the Native Land*
(with Annette Smith) [2001]

César Vallejo, *The Complete Poetry* [2007]

ACKNOWLEDGEMENTS

Many of these poems, prose pieces, and translations appeared, often in a non-final form, in the following magazines: *Poetry* (Chicago), *The East Village Other, Bachy, Grand Street, Sulfur, American Poetry Review, Arson, Caterpillar, Contemporary Literature in Translation, Denver Quarterly, Evergreen Review, Hunger, Kulchur, Montemora, New American Writing, Oasis* (London), *oblëk, origin, Tri-Quarterly, Ygdrasil* (Canada), *Sixpack, AWP Chronicle, Pores* (London), *Po&Sie* (Paris), *Studies in 20th Century Literature, Rehauts* (Paris), *Action Restreinte* (Paris), *Mandorla, Agni, Alligator* (Belgium), *Fence, House Organ, NO: A Journal of the Arts, Boxkite* (Australia), *Boundary 2, Translation Review, American Letters & Commentary, The Kenyon Review, Paris Review, River Styx, Temblor, Brooklyn Rail, Minutes of the Charles Olson Society, Ur Vox, Coyote* (Sao Paulo), *Exquisite Corpse, Bluefish, Scripsi* (Australia), *Caw, Odda Tala, Big Venus, Tansy, Madrona, Stooge, Pequod, Latin American Literary Review, Text, Curtains, Equatorial, Poetry L.A., Ba Shiru, Ploughshares, Callaloo, Network Africa, O.ARS, Conjunctions, B-City, Tsunami*.

Many of these pieces also appeared in the following chapbooks:

Grotesca, London Pride Books, 1977
Out of the West, Lord John Press, 1979
Our Lady of the Three-pronged Devil, Red Ozier Press, 1980
Nights We Put the Rock Together, Cadmus Editions, 1980
Lost Body (translations of Aimé Césaire), George Braziller, 1986
Mistress Spirit, Arundel Books, 1989
Nora's Roar, Rodent Press, 1996
Everwhat, Zasterle Press (Tenerife), 2003
Unarmed Chapbook #3, 2003
Telluric & Magnetic (translations of César Vallejo), Letters Bookshop, 2005

Some of these pieces were reprinted in the following anthologies:

Erotic Poetry: The Lyrics, Ballads, Idyls and Epics of Love—Classical to Contemporary, Random House, 1963.
The Tri-Quarterly Anthology of Contemporary Latin American Poetry, E.P. Dutton, 1969.

The Voice that is Great Within Us: American Poetry of the Twentieth Century, Bantam Books, 1970.

The Box, Peace Press, California Institute of the Arts, 1971.

Doors and Mirrors: Fiction and Poetry from Spanish America, Grossman, 1972.

Open Poetry: Four Anthologies of Expanded Poems, Simon and Schuster, 1973.

America A Prophecy: A New Reading of American Poetry from Pre-Columbian Times to the Present, Random House, 1973.

The Negritude Poets: An Anthology of Translations from the French, The Viking Press, 1975.

The Borzoi Anthology of Latin American Literature Volume II, Alfred A. Knopf, 1977.

The Random House Anthology of Twentieth-Century French Poetry, Random House, 1982.

Wireless Imagination / Sound, Radio, and the Avant-Garde, The MIT Press, 1992.

American Poetry Since 1950 / Innovators & Outsiders, Marsilio, 1993.

Postmodern American Poetry, W.W. Norton, 1994.

Poems for the Millennium, Volume One, University of California Press, 1995.

The Vintage Book of Contemporary World Poetry, Vintage, 1996.

Twentieth-Century Latin American Poetry: A Bilingual Anthology, University of Texas Press, 1996.

Poems for the Millennium, Volume Two, University of California Press, 1998.

The Recovery of the Public World: Essays on Poetics in Honour of Robin Blaser, Talon (Canada), 1999.

The Best American Poetry 2002, Scribner, 2002.

The Best American Poetry 2005, Scribner, 2005.

Asterisks by a poem's title or a particular line refer to commentary in Notes on the Poetry or Notes on the Translations. Footnotes for prose pieces are individually numbered and follow the piece they refer to.

TABLE OF CONTENTS

Dedication: Bedroom, 6 A.M.

POETRY

DEDICATION

BEDROOM, 6 A.M.

Bulbous rootwork of drape rings,
sleigh grey slides

    ceiling quilted ripples

City bus brakes releasing
—pigeon fluttermuffle—
lint of sounds...

We are young and beautiful to each other
posing for a snapshot,   Lespinasse, 1974,
we are flooding each other with the perfection of
   mutual reception,
there is a basement, a hallway, you are leading me
   past my parents,
there is Matthew... cows in Perigord fog...
dreams become visions...

Little canals of sunlight
saturate the curtain folds...

Your face from the bed extends,
your body goes out into the room,
to wake is to enter
the Caryl-enfabulated world.

2004, *My Devotion*

POETRY

I

Some Early Poems

(1963–1976)

                                    Over coffee, alone

                        —slowly, surely, they turn
                        to a crust of biscuit,
                        nibble a kiss in passing,
                                koi.
                                Brothers,
                        our record changes
                        nothing

...tú, luego, has nacido; eso
también se ve de lejos, infeliz y cállate,
y soportas la calle que te dio la suerte...   *

    —an interval.
Dangerously, fully, each instant is
a different man.

   ❧

Incredible the force of the Yorunomado coffee shop. When I first came,
pale sunlight drifted a wide lobby open to a patio where a tiny lantern's
soft red, latticed, glowed. By a dark shield I took a high-backed crimson
chair. A chanson played. Near the patio, a mother and her son sat down.
My word had a painful golden relief, unspoken; it churned, evaporated. I
tried every scheme. I found silence holds only to the music's end. I real-
ized one must face another. Even if rock, the other is a garden. Incredible
the scroll pressed out and held by four hands; on the table a letter from
Bashō, Le Pont Mirabeau. I had faith in a dead-end, in dignity, and
delight. The Yorunomado coffee shop compounded a language of man.

   ❧

and in the shallow pool by my feet
thin vermilion *koi*
motionless
love
grows and spends in me

❦

Like flame fleshed, voices
shoot about over the mossy stones. A foot down:
Europe shimmering light, Paris with the intensity of heat waves.
But this brick wall. This crude clay
no matter how much I want to wander out, to be a crimson pennant
unfurling in a blackening spired sky—
this hand of bloodsmeared Indiana wall...
O dimension of love I had imagined, O
structure in which, though terror drained, no energy was lost...

Flame torn, voices roil in compounding fire, the sea
—no. From this iron
chair: a pool of *koi*. Rose-popsicle
gold; plucked-chicken pink
with a pus-yellow head; and one a dream, the smoky purple
the moon gives to the otherwise midnight ... *The Four Zoas*—
a new life. Floating on the surface, the mung
he took into his mouth:

perfected
far off,
a gong

My language is full of dirt and shit.

Is it too great a leap to imagine
rice may spring from these waters,

a yellow
carp, a green carp?

—over there, still
under the knobby lotus, she with the white-splashed red belly,
pregnant, who is she?

❦

What demand. I am
blind as the bat-
god. There is nothing I can do.

She bleeds
and my silkworm eats a half-moon in the mulberry leaf

She bleeds
and now I get her want

The word is not enough
nor is grief.
Walking down the hospital steps—

WHAT was never born?

❦

Paused on the Shichijo Bridge,

the day misty,
lovely, grisly ... the Kamogawa fades, shallows forever,
winding out through Kyoto's southern shacks ...

below, in the littered mud,
a man stabs around in cans and sewage,
in his ragged khaki overcoat and army puttees
I was taken forward to a blind spot

(he pulled himself up
a rope ladder hung over the stone embankment
and with limp burlap sack slung over his shoulder
disappeared down an alley
home? to the faces?
                    What do
I express when I write?
    Knives?   or Sunlight?
                        And everything
that lives is holy raced through my mind

                    Walking home,
paused under the orange gates of Sanjusangendo, in
under the dripping eaves, cosy,
I noticed a strand of barbed wire
looped over stakes I had stepped
inside of

            and then it came to me)
            I would kill for you

❦

THE DUENDE   *

Overcast, after lunch, the sky fled. A colorless darkening void. The
neighborhood still. Walking, there was a light behind my head. At the cor-
ners of my eyes it fuzzed into cold obscurity. I must molt more than my
face. As if these brown houses, this standing alley water, were the only
reality. I must change more than the contour of my line.

It should be that the slightest scar of moss on the rainstreaked fence occa-
sion delight. And an old man, squatting on his steps, wringing out a rag,
praise. And when the man in my mind smiles, children should fill the alley,
white clouds drift high in the bright blue heavens over Tsuruginomiya. *

When the female principle takes over, it has been said that it is The Darkening of the Light.* Likewise, as has not been said, it is the point at which, recrossing Shichijo Bridge, I picked up from the embankment stone a slightly fishy, sweet, urine smell: the scent of Vallejo—

from which I learned: everything I sense is human, at the very worst *like a man*. And—that which can darken is not without light. Faint along the back of the emptiness grazes the herd of the multi-chambered sun.

    I entered Yorunomado and sat
    down, translating,
    Nightwindow.

    The coffee breathed
    a tiny
    pit—

As a black jeweled butterfly alights
in late summer on a hardening coil of dung,
so I lit on his spine

pages lifting in the breeze   in from the patio

We locked. I sank my teeth into
his throat, clenched, his fangs
tore into my balls, locked
in spasms of deadening pain we turned, I
crazed for his breath, to translate
my cry into his gold, howling, he
ripped for food

Locked, a month passed, and as he increased lean
I slackened, drained, and tripling my energy
drew blood, not what I was after, muscles
contracting expanded he was clenched
in my structure, turning

substance, a dead matter
eating into my cords, and saw deep
in his interior a pit, in spring
I went for it, made myself into a knife
and reached down, drawing
out from the earth cold.
A hideous chill passed —

another month, cunningly
he turned himself into a stone

I dulled on, grinding my own teeth, woke up,
another month, a season. I was wandering
a pebbled compound, the stone in hand.

I saw I had birthed the dead-end, but Japan
was no help—until I also saw
in the feudal rite of *seppuku* a way.

On the pebbles I lowered stonelike.
Whereupon the Spectre of Vallejo raised
before me: cowled in black robes, stern on the *roka*,

he assumed a formal kneel. With his fan
he drew a bull's-eye on my gut;
he gave no quarter; I cut.

Eyes of father tubes of mother swam
my system's acids. As one slices raw tuna
with shooting contortions not

moving a foot I unlocked Yorunomado
from the complex cavework of my own tomb.
Vallejo kept his word:

he was none other that one year than himself

Hello all I have ever felt ...

for this was the point upon which the pen
twisted loose an ego
strong enough to live.

＊

       Set in motion, the servants
washed down and raked the pebbles.
Deepening shadows, they crossed and recrossed,
swinging smoking braziers, chatting.
One, grizzled, picked up a lopped topknot,
grinned, and dropped it in the pail.
Far off, in the interior of this strange place,
a quiet weeping was heard.
Although who cut and who condemned were one,
the weeping was too sincere to be that of a lord.
In the heart of the poem there was
no longer a hesitation before power.
The platform on which the stuff was cut and shaped,
this very platform holds the life of another.

   "Will you help me?"

      I turned away and wrote:
I am taking a walk and holding Barbara's hand, a field
slower than centuries we've no mind of

But Vallejo insisted: "NO. LA MANO, HE DICHO."

You struggled up sinking
between your elbows, braced,
and turned eyes
were a miscarried woman.

Standing, I reached
under the arched wall of your back
and eased in under you
the bedpan.

Leaving the moist warmth of your back,
I sat down, your shattered dream
no longer divided from mine.

Entering me then the pebble of bread he put into his mouth, softly pass-
ing through my face the point of Vallejo, the trench and glory of his
human face, in my lips his, alum dry, passed, and with them my desire to
die. The yanked-tight viscera loosened, gave, it opened a palm for the
bread and cupped, a flower parched, opening, closing, a dark red flower
moving with heaven's untiring power, the verb coursing raggedly, wild at
first, then gentle, beating, whereupon the sutra went into motion, dark
monotone moving horizontal through the twilit bass, syllable upon sylla-
ble compounding, whereupon the compound-complex went into motion
with the simple following close behind—I felt the line set, and from the
right flow back into me through the fire rushing out to you from the left,
from margin to margin, mingling, ripening, the flow knelt and prayed in
my breath, it swept through my seat and cling, kissing my heart on its
wing it cleansed, coiled, unfurled

1963–1964, *The Name Encanyoned River,*
other versions in *Poetry* (Chicago),
Indiana, and *Coils*

THE BLACK HAT

Yorunomado sat in his
black goat's wool tent

a black hat,
a top hat

sat on a radiator
exhaling steam.
When

will it explode?
The man in *the*
or *or,* a fist

craven thru.
I walked

into Yuk Soo
Chinese Laundry
        —parcels
0   396
0   57
0   111
0   384

little pink slips
olive slips yellow ones
wrapped with string
the wind used to

break our kites,

what I've escaped is
greatly what's let go of me,
to see the sweat
shop the earth is

dew off the field at dawn or
or or
Chinee back over steam mat,
shit, I'm so
fucking lucky,

the perceptions break down
the poem seems to stall
and does
before the greater energy of the world,

I've been given this black
hat of internal anger

still on the hot radiator
To sit here you look at me
I'm riding on my anger
as men did

horses, drove in the spurs,
straddling the trunk of
energy the mind is

heir to, it
bobbles
& Yuk Soo

cuts the prow of iron
　boat
over linen,
rigid

victim of migration,
wife, two daughters
scared little foxes
scared to speak

the ore of or
wife in the same
dress weekly
when does she

leave the shop?

After 40 years she
might as Zukofsky
speak of marriage

There is an area of
sweetness born of
slavery, for years

the black hat has
gasped on the radiator
everyone has sat on

watched it shrink
in band carcinomatous
like a chemical

in pure food
drives our stomachs
Yuk Soo

over our belts
—no one

has touched it
Yuk Soo is there
because we're

out of Eden
in Eden,

I'm here
because I left the place
established for me,
(gesture of reaching for
the hat
Xrist it's a snake!
The silliest feat is
the deepest fear—)
as you reached
thru Matthew's
crib slats to touch
on your knees
shaking sobbing
the son, the idea of
son leaving you
Matthew—
marriage
a welt,

hardest
to break up
a welt,
rice
chews, a welt
wants its
anger, inflamed
by a core
    of misery

it surges to
surface again & again
core

is don't touch it,
or
in all its might & fury,
this
is the Selfhood Blake
adored & cleft
again & again
fruit lopped from stem
the earth

is to grow
diurnally
a clerk

come home ·
to brood
man

split into family
is man
surrounded
treasures
a hill

the earth
is looking at us
a skeleton

whose windows
are teeth
black holes

Matthew
pokes a pencil
into,
primal

to enter
Yuk Soo
get my laundry
leave

peregrination
under the face of
boo

boo boo
poop poo
pup

gh

1 August 1967–7 February 1968
Indiana

Wilhelm for you I would sit in the reverberation of The Last Supper
& still keep my eyes to the gentle look in the eyes of children,
for you I would make love to Caryl
would keep her as the vent through which I experience the world,
for you I would make her the terminal,
the station in which all the trains unload
with girls upon girls upon girls & fathers & old men & mothers,
for you, I would keep her before me, keep
that need of the unknown unknown through her,
& known in the rain that falls on me, in that sopping bed the poem is
alone in the landscape that you almost alone inhabit
We love & embrace in a lone bed set out in a meadow
Nearby a city of fire

Wilhelm four years I have watched you alone this century
kindling the heavens over that lone meadow bed,
four years I have watched you daily rub off the soot from Baudelaire's
immortal lines: "Real civilization consists not in gas,
not in steam, nor in turning tables, but in the diminution of
the traces of original sin."
                              Concerned doctor, in work pants &
work shirt, in the photo I have of you page 173 in your *People In Trouble*
1934 in Sweden, in exile then in the full flow of your Arian arrow
sprung from the bow of your breeding laboratory for butterflies when
you were 10, your ax-head Arian profile looking intently then 37 at
something we know off the page,
                              the youth breathing
fully for the first time in his life on a cot you in the late 20s
moved around from the chair placed behind him to sit beside him,
look him in the eyes & not use his dreams but confront him,
you are in a meadow in a room, yes! With insects buzzing in the dry
rigid prone youth on a cot on a hillock, you are torridly maintaining
his emotions are an expression of his biology & that his biology is

expression of a cosmic energy, that
We love & embrace in a lone bed set out in a meadow
Nearby a city of fire

Wilhelm four years, but the count is for all men, four years Blake
with marginalia on Lavater, this like an advance on Baudelaire:
"But the origin of this mistake in Lavater & his contemporaries
is, They suppose that Woman's Love is Sin; in consequence all
the Loves & Graces with them are Sins." – you Wilhelm
making rain over these lines, scouring them from reason,
keeping the fine edges cut into stone sharp in man's infinite
times of trouble, in work pants & work shirt (this image is
very important) — your compassionate eye on Merton
soundlessly repeating his rounds in the circumscribed nature of
Trappist, Kentucky, speaking gently to him in your fury of
your text on Jesus: "The great mistake is not the curbing of
man's evil urges for free-for-all-fucking with dead genitals,
the great mistake is the burying of the very natural powers in
man's body which alone are capable of putting out of function
the perverted sex in mankind."
                              God, Wilhelm, what a tract your
arrowhead everywhere would lead me to, how difficult it is to
move you into the company of poets where for all centuries you
belong, there is so much cause, so much argument, so many
things to set you straight; you with the medieval strangeness of
your simple frank theories, your orgone accumulator like a gigantic
slingshot before the Castle, your hollow metal pipes bringing
rain down on dubious Tim Reynolds visiting a farmer in Michigan,
Tim told me "I didn't believe he could make rain, he held the
pipes up to the bright sky and then we went in and drank beer,
it suddenly poured, an hour and when we left, a few miles away
the sun was again shining!"
                              To call you a poet
              is to deepen your place as an advance on
imagination, it is not to say you are not a doctor nor to slant
you so as to keep anyone from your meaning as a scientist;

it is the revolution of the identity of a person & his expression,
as such to make for Harry Lewis morality a function of intuition,
that these are not separable things, you urge me tonight
in a bar in New York City – as Breton felt Fourier in a fresh
bunch of violets at the foot of his statue in Paris, I feel you
before me in an unknown girl, she is your bunch of violets Wilhelm,
this girl in her voluptuous body & pretty face hard
with what you call "armoring" sipping brandy & wondering
What is my life? She came in her confusion to
enter the poem and say Yes –
I feel you most next to me in Caryl &
I feel you before me as emanation of something not
mine, in this very wood bench
your imagination vibrating violets
at the foot of your statue which is
now at Vallejo's cross in the Andes
& in Baudelaire's prayer that he simply might be able to work
& in Breton's old manifestoed hand in New Mexico
writing his *Ode to Fourier*, these saints
poets recognize in their own energies to be
Jesus in their hearts, that pioneering
cosmic fateful strength we know of you
through Aries, your glyph in the pulsating zodiac of
expansion contraction, the body of man
you as a red red Mars come like Isaiah
out of the judgment of the wine vats of your own being,
you curved, as your arrow was not wont to curve, you
bent the drive of that arrow, how can I say it, — to bions,
to heat sand once you had seen what drove you, to
keep the thing out of system, to follow out the strange
crooked road, to keep moving outward, & to keep perception
vital, to not backtrack in your later years & smudge
what I shall call your *clarification of Beulah*.   *

                                    Wilhelm, what I am
getting at is to somehow honor the clarification you
gave us of self-sacrifice, that the substance of love is
kept fresh in the death of feminine form, this happens in
that meadow, in the giving up of pride & possession, of
man & woman allowing their bodies to convulse, to dissolve
truly thoughts & fantasies, this is the sacrifice Blake named
Eternal Death, to die there in joy with another, that that form
die, that the substance be liberated to find fresh form in
creation. We love & embrace in a lone bed set out in a meadow
Nearby a city of fire
our brother William Blake named Eden, is creation &
in your understanding of the creative process you embrace
the poets telling them
sexual hindrance is imaginative crippling,
how simple you now appear, shoveling the hate out of our bodies,
you sturdy, in your work pants, with no mantle, no egg to
balance on your shoulders, you gazing intensely at
Vallejo's cross in the Andes on which you forever see
"Until I labor I in labor lie"
explaining to him in the ruins & dust that Beulah allows
the transmission, that creation is
not that struggle with the body,
that poetry is translation not just of language
but the passing of a psyche into new form.

                                                    1970, *Altars*

THE BRIDGE AT THE MAYAN PASS

I

Five nights stone
has crowded in, to
say my father's
face is stone, to

dress his face in
the stone of
stone that speaks more
powerfully as

the father of my
father & his father
but I can only love
that which is no

more impersonal than
my seeing of
myself, & since I have
no childhood memory of

my father's face
I have been rocked to the edge
of Last Judgment, I
was moving toward

eternal fire, across the bridge
I was building of
the poem, had put on
that Mayan bridge

a hunched form, in the darkness over
the swaying pass, below us
the abyss I sought to
watch a huge wounded

shoulder of a form roll
into, Goya's Satan this Christ
I thought, & adored
the phantasmagoria of

Billy Graham in bra &
garters, like the Rhine-
gold girl, serving the
pitiful legions of Eshleman

beer, in the nave, the
elders who are
my Presbyters. But to bring
lightning here, to

smear a face, which
as A face is
His face, into stone, to
establish the gaping

cisterns of Tlaloc's eyes
as *my father's face*, my
marriage of
heaven & hell, evades

my feelings about the living
man. Tonight I remembered
a flicker, a wince
of suffering, very

quick, an instant, a
flicker stronger than stone
across the mortuary
lobby I saw, in

his face, as I turned from
the relatives who had
turned from him, & saw
him, suddenly

alone. He stood
on the bridge &
looked for me, I was
simply a wider

flicker, burning with more
hate & more love
than he, No—with no
more hate, no more

love than is here, this
bridge of ceaselessly
eroding alarm, this
bridge in a stronger

moment I call the
golden string. But the fiber of
the string is likewise creaking
wood & wind,

it holds the entire
phantasmagoria of the
weighted dread
I am & I am & I am.

II

But I refuse to contend
with *your stone!* I have been there, consciously, father, you
have not! You are in under her, the stone she lies on,
I fought with you in Vallejo, I struggled to
kill Vallejo in stone
my contention with man!
I am sick to death
of what won't stink!
Caryl is alive, Matthew
is alive, am I
alive? SICK TO DEATH
of baptism without desire,
& I know through the worm,
through the humility at odds
with woman is, the magic
of your unreadable runes!
You are the stone
a boy cannot read,
I write to make
to Matthew Matthew
visible, that a fucking
transmission be made!
But this stone ground, how
long will the Indian
patch up San Cristobal his huts,
skulls, his houses, black
window eyes, eyes, a thousand
black eyes candle-lit over our
Christ-leaden city of Lima!
My god, father, you didn't even know
we were in Lima! You voting
& voting & not even knowing
[lacunae]
[lacunae]

in the Indian's water supply, in
the copper lines that extend like
intestinal cords between here &
South America, STONE!
You didn't even know what you were doing when you fucked Gladys!
Her one erotic memory was a choir-master in Chicago who around
    1930 looked at her!
I am angry at you because you didn't know how to fuck!
I am angry at you because having moved through the superficial layers
    of her death I do not reach the living,
but hit you! I am furious at you because you don't know what goes on in
    Lima!
I hate you because when you traveled to Lima you couldn't look at a
    starving child but went to Macchu Picchu!
FOR THAT IS THE ADORATION OF STONE!
I HATE STONE, I bring pieces of it into my room only to weight the
    pages from the wind
on which the honest words of men who have lived through their lives
    live!
I HATE THE STONE IN MAN,
I HATE THE ADORATION
    OF YANG MARKS
    IN BUFFALO PAINTINGS
    & YIN CIRCLES BEFORE WHICH
    THE SITTING WORLD ADORES
    THE HISTORY OF MAN!
I hate you because you are simply a cruddy uninteresting piece of this
    history!
Because you would watch
    black children bring you a newspaper & not give them a Xmas tip
but would give white children a Xmas tip,
& because you would chase children away from the buckeye tree
    because they crept into the yard while I was 8 sitting back of the
    porthole window wishing I was creeping into our yard to steal the
    unquestionably free fallen buckeyes!
And so you are in me, & I feel my hate for you my mother dies!

My mother dies! Yes, complex knot of real feeling through which
    burning rivulets leaked, her tears awakened my going-to-
    hell cheeks, & you sitting 30 years in the slaughter house
    creeping, your pen, across the ledger, coming home with your
    bloodstained coat tips, that I had only those rainblooddrops to
    imagine what you were drawing salary from! The nerve of you,
    to not break down ever once & WEEP with the blood of a steer
    on the heels of your Charlie McCarthy shoes! The nerve of you
    not to cry! The nerve of you never to blast me! The nerve O the
    NERVE dead, dead & dead & dead & dead *dna dead dna DEAD*
Yoru roars! Yes, the faculty that otherwise is literary careful
sadness, literary adolescence forever wrapped in the many-colored
coat of myth, what a Joseph coat you are, Ira Clayton Eshleman,
& all the neighbors all picking around in the suburbs looking with
flashlights for the murderer of a girl, you do not come home father,
I will not let you come home, for home is where you'd like to flicker
    forever, flicker a wince or a sad distressed look, lacunae
lacunae, sad distressed look lacunae, lacunae honorably in Catullus
Villon, lacunae in the parts of man
uttered & lost in paper-rot, but damn lacunae of what is never uttered!
    AND I WILL NOT LET YOU REMAIN STONE
    FOR STONE IS
    ANCIENT FIRE
    I HONOR ANCIENT FIRE
    FOR TOTALLY NON-CHRISTIAN REASONS
    I WOULD NOT CONSIGN YOU TO ETERNAL FIRE
The ancient fire! The ancient fire! Old fire! Anger & blessing, hate
desire, concern, sympathy, intermingling, Yes, this is
under Last Judgment, old pisco taste of last judgment,
music, song be DAMNED, the raw voices on benches at 12,000 feet be
held, the ancient men are those who have no clothes! Those men be
let in, those unlit roadways, those failures of rain
    YES I AM A BABY INCAN
    I RUN THE FULL CIRCLE OF THE YANG MARKS
    I SEE THE ONLY THING WORTH ADORING IS MY ART
    IN WHICH THOSE I LOVE ARE NOT ABSENT

And the lure of forgiveness is
consumed in the meaning of understanding
   THE MEANING OF STONE IS
   IT BE FUCKED ON OVER A BED OF
   DOWN EVERY SECOND DAY IN THE LIFE OF MAN
And the yang marks will be seen a movement
And the yin will be seen as movement
For the meaning of movement is the body of man & woman & child
Against rock to love & keep warm
   THIS IS HISTORICAL UNDERSTANDING
And the generations of Eshlemans, oh let them huddle, yes, with wine
& candles on a rope bridge over a Mayan Pass! Yes over the abyss,
the whole white spook-show like Witch Sabbath! Great black shadows,
let them pass the wine, unhuddle, let my father be among his people,
Let there be that picnic with the abyss beneath, let spastic Dean
Eshleman touch Matthew that Matthew not be confused, I open this cyst
that Matthew wander fully among these generations, let him see Iva
Eshleman's madness, THIS IS THE WEIGHT, Charles, Sylvia, Orville,
Leonard, Helen, Almira, Ira, Olive, Aunt Barbara never seen from
   Florida,
(these are the "books"), Fern, Faye, Bob Wilmore (these in Blake's
age *Generations of Man*), THE WEIGHT THE DREADED WEIGHT
   I

   NOW TAKE OFF INDIANA

   I RELEASE INDIANA

   NAILED MILE GALED IN ANSWER

   TRACED IN HEIL THY NAY-TURNED FACE!

1970, *Coils*

THE DRAGON RAT TAIL

Where my hope, naive
and controlled by a roteness
thought art might be
a single Japanese flower
deft in a bowl, my hope
to escape profusion,
a single flower, a red gleam,
one thing alone against
clay and wood —
    a poem began to grow
in the very room with
that wilting flower,
but it was an atmosphere of
a poem *can* be,
a poem is around here,
I took hold
between my crosslegged
legs of a string of rain,
it was to find something to pull
out, to put
into my mouth
an ancient story,
to find where
my tale began and pull
up, too physical
I knew, so physical
I would have to digest
the having of
a cock, gnaw
the archetype through,
the body
was good
but was attached

to an image I
could only sense, a rat
growing in the tatami,
I pulled
on a growing widening tail,
a construction worker
pulling an endless alligator out of a sewer,
but through the tatami itself,
hideously embarrassed by
the closeness of the thing,
whatever it was, to my
own organs, that I was pulling
myself inside out, that the poem
I sought was my own menstrual
lining, as if suddenly one day
I would have my inside
out on the tatami before me,
a kind of flayedness, a cape,
something in words, but words
hooked together an anguish or
covering, a quilt, as if
Indianapolis had been pulled off
and the rawness remained,
flickering off and on off my nerves,
jagged aura, some of it grey
some of it blue, and under?
The rigidity pit
where Clayton and Gladys sweetly
wandered, looking up
in intense innocent
complicity with an image
I moved into, then out, then into in
their eyes; that is when Kelly cried
"Find them in the grass!"
he meant find the mothering
fathering powers which are not

your mother, father, find
and connect to what they are
the ghosts of—
I glimpse the Doppelgänger
they as well as I
were involved with,
personal and cultural
shadow in diamond light
striding across a stage.
    The scales increased—
a long green thing was
piano practice, apprenticework
took 16 years, diurnal,
inside the day the impossible
spine of saying all
that the day was
blocked me, I bent,
spine, over keys,
inside the machine a Christmas tree
glowed, and under it
puberty subincision,
I posed, by my dog, he
went off into the night,
I tried to reach a Japanese bar hostess
through my morality play,
my father pressed the flashbulb,
Rilke fell out, compassionate,
distant, paper...
Rote screw-hive
alive but compressed into "God."
Days of sitting on the bench
and trying to bank a word
free from the roar of never
that quietly gnawed, given
my hold to the tail
which had not grown,

which had grown enormous —
"the moment of desire" Blake calls
it, break the judge
in highchair, bring that Jack Horner
that "Good boy" satisfied with
his plum dipped thumb into
the savage truth of this world:
people want love
only as a passive given,
they hate and actively
oppose love as an active opposition.
In Kyoto, faced with my dragon
rat tail I understood that the world
is adamant, that there is no way through it.
Gates, philosophies, arts, all "ways"
confronted orange mud running down
a twilit road on Sunday afternoon.
One way to get anything out: haul up
and sieve, engage the haul,
make the rat tail big, dragon tail,
make the dragon tail bigger than Jung,
bigger than all ideas,
let it engorge the house,
split the tatami! Ride
it! Not the moon, not
the nostalgia for that other place,
but the funk that struck inside
on the way home from the public bath.
Not to remember or realize the bath.
Be in the bath. Deal
with this other thing, art does not have to
lip the natural, live the natural,
jack off on her fender if I have to but
live the natural and confront
this other thing, sieve out
the little performer,

break the piano bench I was to become
an alcoholic upon, "Blue Moon"
"White Christmas" a chain of command,
break the chain, open it up and discover
the seed-chum she and he and all of them,
the whole atavistic octopus,
pumped into my wine cup, be
paranoiac, splay out, feel spiderlike
throughout the realm that paranoia
seeks to feel, understand the rigidity
pit is armor, something
I can get rid of,
yet it is bone, what
I stand in,
armorless armor,
my marrow, my
very scent, is
social, where I do not have to be,
where I am forever, as long as I
am alive, packed in with
who I am born to, alone, or
brothered, essentially with the ghosts of
the fathering mothering powers I
can transform to aid me.

My mother's dead eyes float out
bald in raving love for me,
how she knew what she wanted me to be
so confused was she about what I should be,
under the Betty Grable butt allowed on my closet door,
under the ghost games under the bed Saturday afternoon,
under my being allowed
to dress up in her girdle and twirl
the family safe, was *Liberace*, the person
she hoped I would be, fully middleclass,
artistic, gay, fully in command, a hero

wrapped in a 146
pound floor length black
mink cape lined with Austrian rhinestones,
a ghastly Virgil!

      Confidence
I pray, at 40, to lead this Doppelgänger out to pasture,
he cannot be done with,
I can only let him graze,
I am his shepherd, linked to
him Americanwise through Harlem,
through Peru, through Chad.

1976, *What She Means*

II

from *Hades in Manganese*

(1981)

FRIDA KAHLO'S RELEASE

Where I come from
is the accident's business…

exactly, how it made
thirty-five bone grafts
out of my impaled investment.
My dear father is here, not
off photographing monuments,
which he did so well,
in spite of epilepsy,
he took some
of the terror when the streetcar
created me. How those of us,
determined by one thing,
come forth
is no less complex
than you who are multifoliate.

My face unpacks
the corner of Cautemozin and Tlalpan Highway,
"a simple bonze
worshipping the Eternal Buddha,"
van Gogh's words, that other
dear epileptic, whom I took to bed
in honor of my father.
I let both repose me—
I lead with my right cheek
thus profiling the left.
For a moment, I was seated
straight up in Vincent's chair,
and because the light behind me and

my body were infested
with incombustible sulphur,
I am sister to a double putrifaction.

We who are singly determined
we too dream toward paradise
even though our outpour is contractive,
"one dimensional," you say,
"she only paints one thing,"
you, do you paint anything? And if
you do, is your ease
hard enough to skate? And if it is,
do the figure eights of your admirers ever
come to more than arabesqued return?

My face is rubbed
back into the shaft of human
bluntness. Its point
is to tamp seed
into eroded furrows of pain,
to look back at this life to say
exactly what the soul looks like,
exactly what life looks like,
exactly, what death!
Worn Coatlicue rememberings,
scabbed twistings in the flannel of rock,
I was so handled,
such a sugared skull,
I lived through carnivals
of my own organs, a cornucopia of processed fowl.

The others were off rutting in a firework haze.
I was lobstered in my chair shell,
balancing my vision on the spinal
crockery strewn about me,
shards of an exhumed prayer.

I drew paradise up close about my shoulders,
I gave monkeys my shoulders as well as my breasts,
I let them look through your eyes to Breughel
where Flemish scapes fade back to Job
under a spreading oak, the Adamic Job,
amphibious, caressing his progeny
(As Diego lowered, segment by segment
upon me, khaki and emerald
Behemoth mottlings dressed my injury).

I know the dry riverbed of illness
where orgasm's rachitic child
crawls in place. Gamy iodine on a silver plate,
I transformed the hospital linen
into more than a daguerreotype of paradise.

Pray no more for me, Mother of Unending Lightning—
illuminate the bleeding pulqueria nips
where gaiety, slaughter equidistant,
shishkabobs the sun
through a cellular catacomb of moons in
the quilted night sky pulsing
with El Greco bellows. Under the Mass
are the vast lamb wafers in the Mexican kiln
slid in at 4 a.m. on Christ-crusted rays.

I am fused to the inability to
reproduce what does determine me
with its unborn baby hand
which I finally learned to wear as earring in
the Galapagos Trench pressure
outside within what our species has lived.

1976

for James Hillman

Today I'd like to climb the difference
between what I think I've written and
what I *have* written, to clime being,
to conceive it as a weather
generate and degenerate,
a snake turning in digestion with the low.

But what you hear
are the seams I speak, animal,
the white of our noise
meringues into peaks
neither of us mount—or if we do,
as taxidermists, filling what is over
because we love to see *as if* alive.

Seam through which I might enter,
wounded animal, stairwayed
intestine in the hide of dream,
Hades, am I
yule, in nightmare
you weigh my heart,
you knock, in the pasture at noon,
I still panic
awaking at 3 A.M.
as if a burglar were in the hall,
one who would desire me, on whose claw
I might slip a ring, for in the soft
cave folds of dream
in conversation you woo, I weigh,
I insert something cold in you,

you meditate me up, I carry
what is left of you, coils
of garden hose, aslant, in my gut...

Hades, in manganese you rocked, an animal,
the form in which I was beginning to
perish, wading in eidola
while I separated you out!
To cross one back line with
another, hybrid, to take from the graft
the loss, the soul now wandering
in time, thus grieving for
what it must invent, an out-of-time,
an archetype, a non-existing
anthrobeast, rooted and seasonally
loosing its claws in the air!

O dead living depths!   *
One face cooing to another plungers
that went off, torpedos, in dream,
to spin through a pasture at noon,
sphincter-milled, sheep-impacted,
the lower body attached
to separation, pulling the seam of it along
cold cave stone, the head as
a pollen-loaded feeler tunneling
to ooze a string of eggs
where the rock, strengthening its yes,
returned the crawler to vivid green
sunlight that *was* profundity
now invested with linkage,
the grass, invested with linkage,
the whole sky, a tainted link,
man, a maggot on stilts,
capable of leaving elevation at the mouth
to seam unyield to his face.

Tethered, Hades phoned, om
phallos, the metro the zipper
of dread at every branch-off,
the pasture at noon conducted
by the bearmarm below, batoning
sun down word rust scraper by scraper out.

🌿

Below, in the culvert
behind the House of Okumura, 1963,
the conveyer belt ran all night.
The clanking got louder, tore
then died, surf roar, origin beguiling,
a highway was going through.
During late night breaks,
the itinerant laborers would smoke
by a sparking oil drum in domed yellow helmets,
navy-blue wool puttees, men goblined by metal,
pitch black and popping fire. I watched
from a glassed-in porch, not quite able to see
inside the drum, wanting to engage
the action, to tie the fire into a poem
Paul Blackburn spoke on tape to me,
which would not burn. He suffered savage men
without a context standing about a dying fire
jacking off into it. Depth was the crisis
I tried to raise. The surf roar, earth
tearing, lifted, but not transformed, seemed,
as if part of me, an unending mechanicality.
I could and could not—it could and could.

I was, in spirit, still
in puberty, before my typewriter,
as if in a pew before an altar,
itchy, bored, afraid of being whipped

when we all got home. I played the hymnals
and black choir gowns into a breathing cellar
larder, a ladder to
convincing ore, a bed-shaped
Corregidor flashing, as if a beacon, to me adrift
—or was it the Phi Delta Theta dorm door opened
a crack? I would think of Mrs. Bird's canary
waiting to be driven downstairs and beat bloody.
That canary, hardly an image, helped me,
but it faded in an instant, the actives were
shouting around our bunks, beating pans.
Meowing like Raoul Hausmanns—or were we silent?—
we bent over where the wall had been removed
and only the fireplace remained, gripping
each others' shoulders, our naked huddle
encircled the open-ended fire—we were fisted
loosely to a turbined mass, our heads
a common tampax clamped into the actives' hate.

A fire surrounded by walls of flesh is now
contained. Hades makes a target of this maze.

Perseus holds the written head out to the sun.
His sword from his hip projects what is on his mind,
a center torn from a center, Medusa
wrenched from her jellyfish stronghold,
her severed pipes, the caterwauling serpents,
his treasure from the underworld.
The hero will not be
transfixed into himself, he will lift
reflected terror from reflected depth,
he will thrust his hand down
into the sodden tampax mass where earth bleeds.
My father, for thirty years timing blacks

slaughtering steers, folds into men
beating the animal in other men,
extracting its Pan-pipes, jugular flutes of morning.

Picking the confetti from our hair,
Little Lulu and I cross the city
Francis Bacon mayors. In this city
cartoons mingle equally with men.
In their cruel goo outlines I sense
the terrible strength in our lifting up,
unceasingly to translate upward,
to take whatever stuff and lift it,
earth, dream, whatever, up,
the pyramidic impulse to slave-point sunward,
to streamline, rather than to learn from, Lazarus.

Surface is reality as is ascension
as is depth. Medusa hangs down through
fathoms of archaic familiarity,
the pylons men have made of female psyche,
women beat into gates through which to draw
the ore of heroic energy, to appease
a masculine weather for manipulation and torture.
War on matter lumped into a procrustian mater
crammed, with her crucified familiar,
into the entrance way to Hades. I knew,
holding my fifty pound mother in her swaddling
cancer sheet, that there is no triumph *over.*
Resurrection, a Carl Dreyer altarpiece, yes,
a true finger-exercise in hope, a waist-
hinge, in the waste of spirit the crocus-bud
surely is not to be denied, its yellowy flame
playing among the stones warms what is
youngest in us, most held in night, tender,

voracious for sunset, fire appetite,
to watch the mountain smoke with modesty,
the thing to transform itself, lifting
from itself but carrying Hades as pendulum,
the parachutist gathering in Medusa's threads,
an intelligence under, not of us, but receptive
to us as we drift and wither...

Why do we treat the hero
better than he treated the material
he severed to feed the sun?
Perseus with his fistful of belladonna,
could we transform him into a hermit
with a lantern? Give him an awl,
teach him meander-work, zigzag wobbling through
the infant-clotted rushes, teach him salamander,
teach his semen how to stimulate fire. Unblock
the entrance way to Hades, allow the violet odors
of its meats to simmer in ice penetrating
advice. Something will work its magic against
the door of never. Hell Week, 1953,
a postcard Hades mailed to me,
his kids in demon-suits tied a string
about my penis led up through my white shirt
tied to a "pull" card dangling
from my sport coat pocket. The personal
is the apex of pain, but without it
mountains begin to numb specificity.
The personal works in specificity like a tail-
gunner, the tension in the dogfight tying
my death into my work.

❧

Concentration now includes Dachau,
barbed wire has replaced reason
as the circumference of energy. There is
no hail to rise to. Names are cultural
foam, nada-maggots stretching their scrawl-souls, paw
scorings in the frost of the mother corridor
where our faces were first ironed softly.

Hades receives meandering Hermes
mazing my thoughts into the La Pietà
softness of the target-maker's arms—
there what I change is ended, my despair
is nursed cryptically, for Hades' breasts,
like cobwebbed mangers, are miracleproof.
There a sucking goes on, below the obstructed
passage way, all senses of the word, stilled
in its being, take place. I am playing
with what is left of my animal, a marble
it rolls into neuter, a cat's eye, rolls back,
I crack its pupil between word-infant lips...

Bird spirit flew into Apollo—
animal appeared in Dis.
What was sky and earth became life and death,
or hell on earth and psychic depth,
and I wonder: how has Hades been affected by Dachau?
In the cold of deepest bowels, does a stained
fluid drip? Does pure loss now have an odor
of cremation, a fleshy hollow feel
of human soul infiltrating those realms
Hades had reserved for animals?
Are there archai, still spotted with
this evening's russets, stringing and quartering
an anthrobestial compost? Or are the zeros,
of which we are increasingly composed,
folding out the quick of animal life?

Is that why these outlines, these Hadic kin,
take on mountainous strength,
moving through the shadows of these days?

A wheeled figure stabs and sews
the infancy in our grain to the skin of the ground.
Wheeled wall master who mends in manganese,
talk through what I do not remember,
the life in which I am glued
stringings of narrative Ariadnes.
All hominids share a scarlet where the dark is
pitch with horizon, note-leaps, the static
of non-meaning tendrilling us, making way
for not another bringing of the dark
up into the light, but a dark
delivered dark Paleolithic dimension.

1978

Our Lady of the Caves
dressed in rock,
vuliform, folded back
upon Herself, a turn in the cave,
at Abri Cellier
an arch gouged in a slab
makes an entrance and
an exit, She is a hole,
yet rock, impenetrable,
the impact point of the enigma
no one has lifted her veil,   *
the impact point of the enigma
yet rock, impenetrable,
an exit, She is a hole,
makes an entrance and
an arch gouged in a slab
at Abri Cellier
upon Herself, a turn in the cave,
vulviform, folded back
dressed in rock,
Our Lady of the Caves

a long sentence dissolving within itself
and when it ends, it is just beginning,
a presentiment that Her sign is one turn, uni-
verse, end of a first line, curved about
a vaginal gouge, as if She is a fetal arch bent about
a slit that goes in one quarter inch.
Our Lady may be the invisible archwork
through which all things
shift gears in the dark, at cheetah-speed,
at snail-struggle, on the shores of Russia
where Paleo-archetypes compressed into radar
gaze around with dinosaur certainty.

Before Okeanos, continuing through
Okeanos, before the uroboros, continuing in it,
Her gibbous half-circle tells me that She existed,
before an association was made between fucking and birth,
before a bubbling parthenogenesis was enclosed—
but to what extent She exists
in self-enclosure, in my triumphant
raising my penis to the sun,
to what extent She neatly
slides Her slit between my self and its point,
I do not know.

For the self has grown enormous,
I look through literal eyes to see Her
on a slab chopped out of Abri Cellier,
in a cool limestone room in Les Eyzies.
She seems only several inches tall.
It is a funeral to be there,
in a burial chamber where first otherness
is displayed behind a rope, with written instructions
which only describe the age of a shape.
And I who look upon this am immense,
encrusted with all my own undelivered selves,
my skeletal papoose-rack through which my mother's
85 mile long legs are dangling, out of which my father's
right arm with a seemingly infinite switch trails
down the museum road, across France, to disappear
in the Atlantic, and I jig around a bit,
because a ghost dance starts up as I stare
through the hermaphroditic
circle the snake made, so self-contained,
but what it and I contain, the "divine couple,"
is the latent mother-father who
has taken over the world.

Our Lady moved about
like a stubby pitchfork,
yellow fiber gushed out from between Her prongs,
She hobbled, toward image—
what lurked under Her vulviform was the trident
yet to come, for men realized that not only
could the point of Her slit be hurled
but that its two bounding lines could be too,
the whole woman could be thrown into the animal
And way in, trident deep in Le Portel,
did Her three prongs close?
Was the uroboros hammered shut when those hunters
at last hacked themselves free from animal sinew?
And was this the point at which
the wilderness was mentally enwalled,
serpent the outer circumference,
to teach, and banish, our Adamic Eve?

Below Our Lady, on the wall of my mind,
is the foot long rock phallus Her devotees may
have taken inside them while they chipped in Her sign.
I have been straddling, all poem long, that insistent,
rapacious thing, of phallus, the tooth-phallus,
the borer, for the tooth-phallus is insatiable,
male hunger to connect at any price,
but not to connect, to cease being an island,
a speck before the emancipatory shape of
the birth-giving mainland, to build a mole
to tie fucking to birth, to cease being ticks
on the heaving pelt of this earth, to hook
their erections to the sleigh of a howling starvling.
And they did
get across, at around 10,000 B.P.,
one night fucking and birth were connected by a mole
burrowing right under the surface of a full moon
boring a red mortal line from the edge

to a point equidistant from the circumference.
The corpus callosum was suddenly filled with traffic.
The last Magdalenians were aware that Our Lady
had closed. They padlocked Her
with the uroboros and planted the key.

She now grows on a long handle
out of ground at the edge of the abyss.
Some see Her as fly-eyed radar.
Others feel it is to Her prong that they cling
as the gale of monoculture whips them horizontal.
Many more on their knees inch along cathedral pavement
toward what they believe is Her virginal compassion
which will somehow make their manure-colored barriada water pure,
their nipple blood, their corporeal muscatel in which their children play,
miracle and misery on which my index
touches, to stir for a moment Her
gouged rock socket
octopus current of
faceless suckers Veil.

1980

III

from *Fracture*

(1983)

NOTES ON A VISIT TO LE TUC D'AUDOUBERT *

for Robert Bégouën

bundled by Tuc's tight jagged
    corridors, flocks of white
  stone tits, their milk in long
    stone nipply drips, frozen over

   the underground Volp in which
  the enormous guardian eel,
now unknown, lies coiled—

to be impressed (in-pressed?) by this
primordial "theater of cruelty"—
    by its keelhaul sorcery

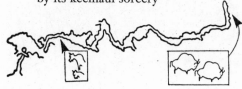

    Volp mouth—the tongue of the
      river lifting one in—

to be masticated by Le Tuc d'Audoubert's
  cruel stones—
    the loom of the cave

  Up the oblique chimney by ladder to iron cleats set
in the rock face to the cathole,
on one's stomach

to *crawl,*   working against
              one, pinning one
as the earth   in, to, it, to
makes one   feel for an instant
feel its traction—   the dread of

WITHERING IN
PLACE

—pinned in—
The Meat Server
masticated by the broken
chariot of the earth

★

"fantastic figures"—more beast-
     like here than human—one
horn one ear—   { one large figure
                   { one small figure

                                              ∗

          as in Lascaux?
   (the *grand* and *petit* sorcerer?)
                                              ∗

   First indications of master/
      apprentice? ("tanist" re. Graves)   ∗

the grotesque archetype   ∗

      vortex in which the emergent
      human and withdrawing animal
      are ***spun***—

            grotesque = movement

(life is grotesque when we catch
    it in quick perceptions—
at full vent—history
    shaping itself)

the turns/twists of the cave
    reinforce the image turbine—
as does the underground river,

                    the cave floats,
            in a sense, in several senses,
                    all at once,
            it rests on the river, is penetrated
                by it, was originally made
                    by rushing water—
                        the cave
                    is *the skeleton of flood*

images on its walls
    participate, thus, as torsion,
in an earlier torsion—

Here one might synthesize:
        1) abstract signs
                initiate movement
                    brought to rest in

        3) naturalistic figures
                (bison, horses etc)

In between, the friction, are

2) grotesque hybrids

(useful—but irrelevant to systematize forces that must have been felt as
flux, as *unplanned*, spontaneous, as were the spots/areas in caves chosen for

images—because shadowing or wall contour evoked an animal? Any plan a coincidence—we have no right to systematize an area of experience of which we have only shattered iceberg tips—yet it does seem that "image" occurs at the point that a "naturalistic" horse is gouged in rock across an "abstract" vulva already gouged there, so that the rudiments of poetry are present at approximately 28,000 B.P.—

> image is crossbreeding,
> or the refusal to respect
> the single, individuated body,
> image is that point
> where sight crosses sight—

to be alive as a poet is to be
in conversation with one's eyes)

What impresses at Tuc is a relationship
between river
        hybrid figures
        and the clay bison—

it is as if the river (the skeleton of water = the cave itself) erupts into image with the hybrid "guardians" (Breuil's guess) and is brought to rest in the terminal chamber with the two bison i.e., naturalism is a kind of rest—naturalism returns us to a continuous and predictable nature (though there is something unnatural about these bison to be noted later)—takes us out of the discontinuity, the *transgression* (to cite Bataille's slightly too Catholic term, of the grotesque
    (though the grotesque, on another level, according to Bakhtin, is deeper continuity, the association of *realms*, kingdoms, fecundation and death, degradation and praise—))

on one hand: bisons-about-to-couple
    assert the generative
    what we today take to be

the way things are   *(though with ecological pollution,*
"generation" leads to mutation,
          a new "grotesque"!

❧

to be gripped by *a womb of stone*
to be in the grip of the surge of life
imprisoned in stone

it is enough to make one *sweat one's animal*

(having left the "nuptial hall" of white stone breasts in which one can amply stand—the breasts hang in clusters right over one's head—one must then squirm vertically up the spiral chimney (or use the current iron ladder) to enter the upper level via a cathole into a corridor through which one must crawl on hands and knees—then another longish cathole through which one must crawl on one's belly, squirming through a human-sized tunnel—to a corridor through which one can walk haltingly, stooping, occasionally slithering through vertical catslits and straddling short walls)—

if one were to film one's postures through this entire process, it might look like a St. Vitus dance of the stages in the life of man, birth channel expulsion to old age, but without chronological order, a jumble of exaggerated and strained positions that correspondingly increase the *image pressure* in one's mind—

while in Le Tuc d'Audoubert I felt the broken horse rear in agony in the cave-like stable of Picasso's *Guernica*,

at times I wanted to leave my feet behind, or to continue headless in the dark, my stomach desired prawn-like legs with grippers, my organs were in the way, something inside of me wanted to be
an armored worm,
one feeler extending out its head,

I swear I sensed the disintegration of the backbone of my mother now buried 12 years, entangled in a cathole I felt my tongue start to press backwards, and the image force was: I wanted to *choke myself out of myself,* to give birth to my own strangulation, and then nurse my strangulation at my own useless male breasts—useless? No, for Le Tuc d'Audoubert unlocks memories that bear on a single face the expressions of both Judith and Holofernes at the moment of beheading, mingled disgust terror delight and awe, one is stimulated to desire to enter cavities within oneself where dead men can be heard talking—

in Le Tuc d'Audoubert I heard something in me whisper me to believe in God

and something else in me whispered that the command was the rasp of a 6000 year old man who wished to be venerated again—

and if what I am saying here is vague it is because both voices had to sound themselves in the bowels of this most personal and impersonal stone, in which sheets of myself felt themselves corrugated with nipples— as if the anatomy of life could be described, from this perspective, as entwisted tubes of nippled stone through which perpetual and mutual beheadings and birthings were taking place—

but all these fantastic images were shooed away the moment I laid eyes on the two bison sculptured out of clay leaned against stuff fallen from the chamber ceiling—

the bison and their "altar" seemed to be squeezed up into view out of the swelling of the chamber floor—

the sense of *culmination* was very severe, the male about to mount the female, but clearly placed several inches behind and above her, not in con-tact with any part of her body, and he had no member—   *

if they *were* coupling, and *without* deep cracks in their clay bodies, they would have disappeared into their progeny thousands of years ago, but here they are today still, as if Michelangelo were to have depicted God and man as not touching, but only reaching toward each other, caught in the exhaustion of a yearning for a sparking that has in fact never taken place, so that the weight of all the cisterns in the world is in that yearning, in the weight of that yearning is the real ballast in life, a ballast in which the unborn are coddled like slowly cooking eggs, unborn bison and unborn man, in the crib of a scrotum, a bone scrotum, that jailhouse of generation from which the prisoners yearn to leap onto the taffy machine-like pistons of shaping females—

it is that spot where the leap should occur that Le Tuc d'Audoubert says is VOID, and that unfilled space between two fertile poles here feels like the origin of the abyss, as if in the minds of those who shaped and placed these two bison, fertilization was pulled free, and that freedom from connection is the demon of creation haunting man and woman ever since—

we crawled on hands and knees about this scene, humbled, in single file, lower than the scene, 11 human creatures come, lamps in hand like a glowworm pilgrimage, to worship in circular crawl at one of the births of the abyss—

if I had stayed longer, if I had not with the others disappeared into the organic odors of the Montesquieu-Avantès woods, I am sure that I would have noticed, flittering out of the deep cracks in the bison clay, little winged things, image babies set free, the Odyssi before Odysseus who still wander the vaults of what we call art seeking new abysses to inscribe with the tuning forks of their wings...

1982

IV

from *The Name Encanyoned River*

(1962–1985)

Shaman of obsession—I said at his tomb—
excavated in electricity, opened between
anus and sex. In the Australian outback of the soul,
3 dead men are fingering your anesthetized root support
shining like a chain of sputtering lights, for the key to creation,
between the bone they've drawn out and your bone they so desire.

Priest of lethal phallic rites, of sparkings
in fetid material, of remaining in antithesis
with no hope of synthesis, priest of a genuine melée—
3 dead men are fingering your Muladhara Chakra, your amphimixis,***
as if, under the Christian gunk that clogged your focus,
they could plug into your triangle and its twisting tongue of flame.

Pariah in silence, coprophilially
squatting in the corner of your cell for years,
sealed open, who only came when called by your mother's name—
repressing their way in, to the point of anal cancer,
3 dead men, licking your electroshock-induced Bardo, have found
your atomic glue, the Kundalini compost they must eat to speak.

O shaman, from having been so masterfully plundered!
O priest, from having been fixed in antithesis!
O pariah, from having been so desired by the dead!

1984

One can glimpse Apollo in the door of each thing,
as if each thing now contains his oven—
in vision I open an olive tree and see his earlier animal
shapes fleeing at the speed of light, the python,
mouse, and lion Apollo, fleeing so that human forms
may walk unharmed by the invasion of the supernatural.
Light increased incredibly after the end of animal deity,
at the point verticality was instituted,
and the corpse of one's mother buried far, far from the place
on which one slept one's head. But the supernatural
in the guise of the natural is turning us over
in its fog a half mile from this ledge. Burnished
muscleless fist of a grey cloud. Sound of rain
from water still falling from the olives. I have no desire
to live in a world of nature conditioned by patriarchy.
I kick off my head and live in the light
bounding in from my mother. It is her great
ambivalence toward her own navel that conditions
the decreasing dripping. The hills now
writhe with green meat and something should follow.
Something should be explaining the tuft of salmon bull shape
abandoned by the other stilled clouds. Something
should be done with the swatted fly. Something is
this abyss of unusableness that remainders me
and pays no royalty. There are hosts of thrones
directly above. A witch hammer. A cleated enclosure.
The way a church has of making you puke your soul
upon entering and then, as the dryness of birth is rehashed
by nun and candle, of worshipping what has just left you,
the bride of your chest, the stuff inside you that a moment before
twinkled with the sadness and poverty of the street's
malicious laughter. How I wish that this poem
would birth another, and that the other had something to do

with unpacking the olive meat of this mountain. No
apocalypse. An enlargement, rather, of the so-called Whore
on her severely underfed Dragon. And more wine. More plumes
of silver azure evening coursing over
the thatch of the mountainside. More space to suffer,
more farewell to the flesh, more carnival in the face of everyman,
less perfection, more coherence. Meaning: more imagination,
more wigs for glowworms, more cribs for the restless dead
who wake us right before dawn with their bell leper
reminding us that fresh rain air is a clear indication
that here is not entirely here. The processions of graffiti-
scarred bison are, like us, clouds imprisoned to be viewed.
And then my mother began to speak: "You've put on a lot of weight!
Look at your father and me, some shape we're in! We've suffered
a lot for you these 14 years. You should've seen my left side
when it turned into a purple sponge and stained what
you buried me in to the point it rotted. I'm glad
John Ashbery appeared to you last night reading new
incomprehensible poems that made perfectly good sense. You are
much more organized, much more chaotic, than you behave here.
When I think of you, I see you at 12, stuck in the laundry chute,
your legs wiggling in the basement air, while the top part talked
with me as we waited for the renter to pull you out.
We had a nice chat that afternoon, and I almost liked you best
that way, just what stuck out of the chute. If I could only have
that part on a roller skate and let what was wiggling below go—
it's that part that's gone off gallivanting,
that's carried you goodness knows where while I
and your father lie here a few feet away from each other
waiting for our coffin lids to cave in. Then, even
the little space you left us to play with memories of you
on our chest bones will be gone. My buttons are mouldy
and my hands have no flesh left but I still manage
to squeak my buttons a little and get into your dreams.
I'm sorry if I appear both dead and alive to you,
but you should know by now you can't have it your way all the time.

I'm as real in this way as I ever was, sick more often than not
when I appear, but you're never here, you're worrying
how to take care of me, and then you wake to a jolt
every time there's nothing to take care of.
Now your father wants to say a word." "Clayton,
why don't you come home? We were such a nice little family.
Now it is like when you went off to that university,
your mother and I would sit up and talk about you
until our fathers came in from the night and motioned us
into our bed. You were such a nice little fellow
when we could hold you up high and look at each other
through you. Ten little fingers ten little toes.
Two bright eyes a funny little nose.
A little bunch of sweetness that's mighty like a rose.
Your mother, through you, looked so much like
your grandmother I could never get over it.
Why I bet you don't even remember your birth gifts:
A savings bank and one dollar from granddad and grandmother.
Two kimonas from aunt Georgia and uncle Bob.
Supporters from Faye's dollie Patricia Ann.
A Romper Suit from Mrs. Warren Bigler.
A Dress from Mr. & Mrs. SR Shambaugh.
Silk Booties & Anklets Knit Soaker & Safety Pins.
Hug-me-tight a Floating Soap Dish with Soap Rubber Doggie.
I don't see why you don't come home. Your mother and I
have everything you need here. Why sure,
let's see, maybe you could pick up some things,
Gladys —no, she's not listening — *Gladys what do you want?*"
"Well, I know we need some scouring powder and light bulbs"
"GLADYS WHAT DO YOU WANT?" "And Clayton, we want
Clayton to come back we don't like Clayton Jr. out so late at night"
"GLADYS WHAT DO YOU WANT?" "You never know what will happen,
   why
just last week Eunice Wilson, over in Plot #52541, told me"
"GLADYS WHAT DO YOU WANT?" "—are you listening, Daddy?

Eunice said while Jack was getting out of his car parked in his own
    driveway at 2 A.M."
"GRADDISROTDUYRUNT!" "—after his date with Kay Fisbeck,
    this man
came up to him and said something I will not"
"GRADDISROTDRURUNT" "—I will not repeat it was that
    vulgar —
this man said: if you don't come with me, I'll crush your cows.
Doesn't that take the cake? Why Clayton you can't blame Jack
for going off with him, and you would not believe where
this man took Jack Wilson and what he wanted him to do.
Now that your father's lid has caved in, I'll tell you:
he made him drive north to the Deaf School parking lot,
and when he was sure nobody else was around, he said:
            Persephone's a doll
                steeper than Marilyn,
            miracles lick her,
                dreams invade her,
            over the cobweb orchestra
                there's an ice
                conductor,
            forget the orchestra,
                conduct the pit!
            Hanged
            Ariadne
                giving birth in Hades
            is the rich, black music in mother's tit."

                                    1984, San Damiano di Stellanello, Italy

V

from *Hotel Cro-Magnon*

(1989)

A MEMORIAL TO THE GRAND

In my dead father's dreaming there is
a slaughterhouse called 4705,
a perfect fusion of our home and his place of work—
my mother and I are the cattle he attends,
a milker, wearing his long white smock with its blood braid,
a milker-general, medals dangling from his lapels.
How he tends us is of unceasing fascination:
he fastens his gloved fingers to our teats and we spray him rainbow-wise,
great fans of smoky juice raying through his dreaming—
he tickles then twirls our valves,
reaching up into our vast birth canals as if he is
at cathedral in our presence.
It is almost, sitting at his stool, as if he is playing animal pianos,
as if his fingers dip and plunge into our keyboard troughs,
as if we are one gleaming black lacquered bison grand,
and the blood-braided smock a silver and raspberry tuxedo,
the slaughterhouse opens out into an attentive world,
all our neighbors including the dogs and birds
enrapt in their coffin-like chairs,
even the grasses are there as he rips through Mozart.
Each struck note releases a massive repression.
The shy time and motion study father, rheumatic at 14, has finally
    hit his rhythm.

Frankfurt, 1984

He stayed up late, staved off sleep, wandered, drank,
as if sleep were a kind of devouring,
as if it would masticate and spit him out at dawn
a juiceless thing that would have to resurrect
and learn, all over again, to walk—
                              ridiculous,
for the ore of night was dream, and to push
the night against its lit elastic made him so tired
he did not dream, or recall, or
allow himself to recall dreams of fatigue,
bent earthworm doctors struggling from tumulus to tumulus
administering to eyes in dark whose bone paws
clutched the pills and disappeared,
                              or *was* it ridiculous to want
to push the dark, depoeticize it, to push it into dawn,
so that light would swarm with the hearts of the tumulus inhabitants,
skeletal raccoons, bearded white-haired badgers,
gnarled hermaphrodites whose orifices and pipes wheezed
that steam he wanted to inject into weightless day—

yet what to really see or really feel in Durango?
Sides of 19th century buildings
like mock-ups of the aftermath of Pompeii?
Indian beads laid out on velvet, kewpie dolls,
Minnie Mouse sweatshirts, "fresh" mesquite-broiled salmon,
the sound-asleep proprietors, *Here Dempsey kayoed*
Cochran to win $20 in 1912—or that is how he recalled
the recent wall mural, shuffling toward Denny's where giant forms
were putting away steaks at 2 A.M. North Americans!
They looked like mercs, or rioters, swollen
restitched Abe Lincolns, under the bright lights of an Ensor
Halloween. He sat down by a farmer his own age
who he felt would break his back if true feelings were shared,

he knew this in his midwestern bones
which were still processing the Christmas tree tinsel,
the presents that had so pleased him at eight.
The farmer introduced him to a pal one stool away,
who tried to speak, teeth tongue and lips
one sutured muscle, a lisping groan,
whose life swarmed in friendship-hungry eyes
as he gulped and nodded, the farmer's tag-along
catastrophe-buddy—Vietnam?
As the eggs went into his gut, the tinsel bucked and soured.
The present, glutted with its own unloved trash,
undermined even childhood snow. He stayed up late to feel *this?*
Wandered out of Denny's, rammed Durango up his right armpit
and limped toward the Jarvis Hotel. Wounded—
the empty basin of the street, wounded—
the imprint of place, no place, sturdy plastic patina
under which the larvae of an alien immensity were coiling,
muscular larvae, wetbacks dead from thirst, blending with
the New Mexico desert where ancient creosote
(the in-flight magazine stated) is the oldest thing alive on earth,
"10,000 year old seed near Yuma discovered in pack rat midden."
Did he stay up just to feel the roller-coaster-like heave of each thing
    short-circuit and fizz?
Did he refuse sleep to suffer this peculiar painless rancor?
How could anyone complain about a comfortable bed?
Yet it seemed a cold grill, with a brutalized Adam,
a blood-stained blood boy cursing beneath,
a mined-out bully who hacked up around
the mattress to claw at the sleeper,
a corpse under water, as the currents groped and belittled him...

as he unraveled into dream, the raccoons and badgers
emerged from their tumuli, in overalls, with trowels,
they wended their way (as childhood animals do)
to the cemetery where the earthworm doctor's funeral was a static
purple sketch of gestures... a canopy, a sobbing cricket...

then the gnarled hermaphrodite appeared
and began to leak from every pore... they lowered
the doctor in his casket-bag into a Mayan well?
a fleet of submarines pulled in...

                            the sleeper was at last
drinking his dream, coming apart, coalescing,
an oatmeal made sodden not in a bowl
but floating, like an isle, in a ring of light.
Not yet digested by America, he had also failed to force
the stuck drawer of night into the bureau of the day.
That ring of light. The one reward of sleep:
while falling to press the heels of palms hard against
closed lids, watch the filigreed nerve gold
shimmer and mill into formations,
coalescing into a fat doughnut of light,
blackness at center, blackness surrounding.
A kind of madonna curled in the aura of reptilian continuity
he floated, in pietà to
the unknowable body the poet takes on
everytime he starts to write.

                                        Durango, 1985

I love to watch Caryl eat fresh Dungeness crab.
Her plate, heaped with cracked ice, topped by
a reconstruction of the crab.   Over which her delicate
fingers, more delicate than the morsels
she will extract,   pause like wands,   and she slowly eats,
as if she were undoing a sewing,   as if her fingers
were needles investigating music,   or thinking about
"the most sublime act is to set another before you,"
which can refer to any act of respect
for the otherness all nearness is,   not to be worshipped
but revered in motion,   in pleasure
scythed and harvested,   a beautiful creature eating
                              a beautiful creature.

1987

Onto the keyboard of a concert grand Bud Powell shot his fingers.

Was he, elbows flexed, a kind of Tiresias drinking from a trench
    beheaded bison blood?
Are we not, at birth, like bison, deposited on a terrestrial keyboard?
Each depressed key makes an omen trench.
Thus does the earth become grand
and we suck, with Tiresias intensity, as did infant Powell, to prophesy.

Powell is face to face with a bison apparition, a lacquered, black ghost.
Unlike Tiresias, he must draw, through a keyboard, directional sound,
and even if he has a grand it is hardly a trench of warm blood.

To be a seer is to re-enter the trench out of which we emerged.
Powell made contact, but failed to drink.
For a grand, in profile, lid propped, evokes a headless bison, whose chest
    cavity, the keyboard, releases the sound Tiresias needed blood to utter.
And Tiresias, who re-entered the essential trench, did guide Odysseus.

At the keyboard, Powell clawed for blood, as if stabbing at a bison
    sacrifice.
Thus he proposes a grand dilemma: the living, no matter how grand
    their C chords,
lack the Tiresian recipe: to be all soul and bison vivid, a cunnilinctrice of
    the goddess trench.

On his cell wall in Creedmore asylum, Powell is said to have sketched, in
    chalk, a keyboard.

Powell, now the ghost of a grand, stared at this keyboard.
"O how get home, Tiresias? How drink bison music in this hellish
    trench?"

                                                                    1987

the apple trees turn into light, a liquid light,
weightless, spent, so dark, so ruddy brown, they are a sensing
that what we do not make is so much more here than what we do.
On Atget's road the souls curve about each other
like fish, or smoke, their presence deepens the emptiness
of the road itself, or of a cobbled street with no passerby,
with stone buildings in which people lived, a past
even more past in its evoked presence here...
                              but more than street or road
paths trouble his eternity, simple paths, half washed out,
wet, leaf-littered, the barest trace of human making,
a curving into disappearance, slightly rounded, as if earth
were felt in such clearing as a pregnancy we
could never know, only touch across...

                        gone! is the cry
of Atget in Atget, of his roaming now forever past world
in which a stone staircase is so gentle one
cups it in one's hand, with the love with which one
takes morning water from the faucet in two cupped hands,
seeing one's palms through the water,
which are thus so remote, not of one,
something under water, on Eugène Atget's road
insubstantial as all roads, the vernacular gesture of
a road in which paths and stones flee in place
the enduring velocity of night.

                                                            1988

> *I would gladly emulate Odysseus if I*
> *could, and go down to the shadows*
> *for another hour's conversation with*
> *Crane on the subject of poetry...*
>   —Yvor Winters

The balloon glass, the swirl—
what is the image of the wine's insides?

Numb, I was carried off by
unfriendly insects and tamped into their compost,
something good for a nest stave, perhaps fuel
for a grasshopper roast. Yet I continued to drink
as I slept, sleeping at the speed of wine,
for I had fitted out my dream body with a full *cave*—
there was Crane! His back to the action,
digging the distortions in Falstaff-bellied flasks.
He piled his suicide knives up in an amazing wickerwork
as I sat down,   and asked me,
as if he knew me,   which one would I choose.
I like the one that looks like a rabbit's ear, I said,
or that curious one at the bottom of the pile,
a piece of wood sculpture by Michelangelo
where he depicts himself leaning dejectedly against his cross...

A huge frog
lugged himself out of the Punchino Palace kitchen
balancing a tray of sordidity on one trembling foot.

My idea, I said to Hart, is to pick up a woman without breasts,
with wings instead of breasts,
one whose chest is a skillet of unmotherly crackling oil,

our soul in short,   why not try to pick up our soul for a change
instead of sliding anklewise into the flues?

Crane plucked a pair of tiny scissors from his vest pocket and snipped
    off his nose,
then turned to me with a widening red valley between his eyes.
Only then did I see his stairwell, and the extent to which it twisted into
    his brain,
I lit a match, and the blood turned back,
I lit another, and a helpless curare began to drain from his eyes.

"Poets in death need poets in life," he sobbed,
"not parasitically, my dear wench,
we need you here, under the image mill,
where Samson's soles are a kind of liquor for our eyes,
here, in the emptiness of the North American underworld,
any image you twist through the wringer of pubescent lubricity,
    tensioned on sheer need,
is manna to us,
no image = no food,   as simple as that!"

He raised his hands in a magician-like *voilà!*
a decanter appeared, a crystal ball of colorless liquid
I was to see into.   "This is the midwestern other side,"
Crane went on, "argument that you are half
what you think you are, and that to protect it
you must lose at least 100 pounds,
so that you appear to the sensual world a near-man,
rheumatic eyeball jelly in socket cylinders, a kind of god, a Tlaloc
of this Western night.   —Wait, let me finish. I argued flux
via my own barrel-rolls, leashed to Whitman's mobile hand.
Have you considered Rothko? The paintings by which
he sought to join the Surrealists were done by others.
Then he erased the content from his work.
What had appeared to be scenery for the drama
now *was* the drama—static, dirigible, stacks of weightless tires

injected with his Orphic blood.
The price was terrible, one I refused to barter. We're both suicides,
but I went out one door, Rothko another."

You're a flicker, Crane! Not an underworld!
I can relate to you, and feel the joist of comradeship
but as I concentrate, I see behind you the Phi Delt "hell room."
I know my chance of seeing things from the inside out was ruined at 19
as I took the bulldick around my neck and stood in humiliation
without striking back. Caricature can be oxymoronic venom,
and my desire then was baffled—even if the pain and weirdness of that
    pseudo-Satanic fete
turned me, 3 years later, toward this work.
So I must acknowledge a puerile satire of the underworld
as the father of my poetry. Or as the restriction that
    snapped my lassitude.
But such is no underworld support,
no Poe gangrenescent at the subway gates...
but then again, Poe's another individual, not a ripe swamp of otherness
hissing its affiliations into a sleeping live person's ear.
The core of our imaginal demise is: the Maya, the Greeks, and the
    Egyptians
will not transmit their fabulous gourds of juices in which
imps are instructing kobolds, ruled by stern fairies. Holy kaishaku!
They are as slides projected on our image screens!
This is why I've gone back through the agrarian earth to
those who appear to have spent 20,000 years
wrestling the animals out of and into their heads...
People defined by holes! They've so underscooped us
that now each stone seems to cap a void.
Your and my background assurance was: the surface holds.

Crane tilted his head. "I was a space sucker—
and you, are you a depth sucker,   are you sucking
    off depth?"

Was I being set up to defend a night-blooming abyss?
The shoulders all stand on, shoulders that are not there?
The muse angel duende congealed in 1000 floor deep Les Eyzies?

"You're pigging out on underworld hooey,"
Crane grimaced, "you want to find the missing story of yourself
and no personal or transpersonal myth or psychoanalytics will do.
Queerly, you emerged as a potential self
via a double beating: your father and the Phi Delt 'actives.'
For you, creation is counter-attack on catastrophe
and you'll bear that legacy wherever you bear.
Your tribulation is to have discovered that beyond the father-
     blocked doorway
are sons with clubs."

He was doodling on his face, as if it were a worksheet—
he'd move his eyes together, or eat one of his eyebrows, then
     draw it from an ear.
"New anatomies," he grinned, "here, have a chalk ..."
Then he pinocchioed his nose, and said:
"Jesus who worked in flesh is a challenge to all poets.
The desire, as Artaud retold it, is to reconstruct the human body,
get rid of its organs, equip it to really dance.
Having been devoured after my stunt off the *Orizaba*,
I found myself in collapsible space,
pound for pound in the gutturals of the hammerhead
who plucked my ass from—was it a 'light topcoat'?
Dionysian motion is a willful peristalsis, ruddering one's own dreaming,
where Whitman and Dickinson cross, a blond serpent is hatched,
one of the brood with your white Apollo. Look into my
     eyes, you'll see its brothers."

As I peered through his bruised lids into his irises,
twin coral snakes, tails in mouths, began to turn
behind what remained Crane's frightened, compassionate pupils.

Were they *his* missing story? The one we all are missing
until we take the oath of the abyss and induct that realm
in which the dead reach us and warn us with their whirling eyes
that defective railroad signals are positioned every way we turn?
Crane clawed out at me, I leapt back to see his talon
embed in his other shoulder.
He then tore out his talon-arm and rammed it into one eye,
caught his other eye through the back of his head,
gulped it down, tore open his fly and pissed a string of eyes.
A Möbius effect, for nothing disappeared.
"Everything in the underworld fits into everything else,"
he laughed. I was thinking about van Gogh,
I said, crows over the wheatfield was not his last painting.
He did the crows 2 weeks before his 2 versions of Daubigny's garden.

    "The mound with flowers in the lower
central portion is tumultuous," Crane exclaimed, "as if Vincent
buried himself there, not in wilderness,
but in another painter's yard! In the end, most value middle-class life.
Especially since it is what most artists are.
Shelley is windy and pure, his words seem to have floating
spaces between worlds, or letters, the claim on the infinite is too
    trusting.
Blake had working-class printer grease on his *Jerusalem*.
I'm aware Bunting told you Blake is 'the abomination of poetry.'
Bunting feared he forced experience into a plaster cast,
turned it into religious forgery. That is why
Blake's ghost put both contact lenses in Basil's right eye that night,
to show Basil had overviewed half, and not seen the other half at all.
But, let's stop talking about literature.
It only shows to what extent we are anxious about the discrepancy
between what we've intended, and what it appears we've done.
Peggy Cowley's cunt was extraordinary. I've not been able to
    reconstruct it
no matter how I reinvent my body."

Then he quoted Laura Riding: "'Until the missing story of ourselves is
    told,
nothing besides told can suffice us: we shall go on quietly craving it.'"

Did you fuck her, Hart?

"Of course, but not in the way you'd compose me.
You forget: I was born before the psychoanalysis of fire,
and thus held to my Promethian post. I was guilty, *under Walt*,
trenchant guilt, undercoating,
there was nothing else—Titan resolve!
Even humorous, but art is revolt against predetermined dread.
Rhymes? The manacles of Grace and Clarence—*clearance!*—grace in
    clearance, the *Orizaba* drop!"

Your "Tears of Christ" has the conundrum power of 2000 years,
or I should say, I've been draining its nailed feet for 20 years
and have yet to see the fluid run clear.
Way up in the crucified is a swan, and a goat,
and as for his head, I'm reminded of Our Lady Coatlicue,
whose head consists of 2 face-to-face pressed rattlesnake heads—
She faces us with one of their left eyes, one of their right,
to indicate that the back of any matter is the beginning of a
    new damnation.

                "Development is steel rain,"
Crane mused, "we write when Psyche is invited.
This is our core, to have spread the asparagus,
and to have perceived beauty in every mundane spread,
in atolls of guano, in the coarse heels of Caravaggio.
The demand on soul now is to ordain those powers still
    denied a human form,
to get the lower body out before its repressive furnaces ignite
    all worlds.
But you'll end up here"—he stared at me—

"in that most awful term, *regardless*.
Regardless, the name of America,
why not 'Regardless' as the name of your poem?"

Why not "Am Let" chipped into your headstone,
I said without thinking, irritated by his arrogance.
But the wine came round the glass, and I saw the density in
      his stained intentions.
Like Spicer, he had slept with all his poems.

At my thought of Spicer, Crane performed a fascinating act:
he shoved into the bar an iron stove into whose side had
      been riveted: *The Poem*
Then, working his face as if it were rubber,
he climbed a ladder and threw himself off
as if into the stove whose entire top was open and glowing red.
Having leapt, suspended in flight, he turned his head and looked at me
with a most amazing expression: he made me feel as if I were
      his primal scene,
I mean, he looked at me with awe disgust amazement joy—
      and Lascaux!
For behind the coral snakes backing up his gaze bisons were amassing,
as if I, as mortal non-otherness, were mammal blend in art—
was I meat parts? His association with a slaughterhouse?
Then he swerved, converting his falling leap into a J,
at which point the stove broke into "Giant Steps!"
Seconds later, I was in the furnace with Crane,
soldered to its northern wall, a kind of spectator, though I felt riveted to
rotunda iron. Crane was in the flames, or waves, or billows,
      playing and dissolving,
he drew up and out certain flames, as if udders, or cocks,
lengthening them, spires, tapers, then he'd fasten on,
with any part of his body, navel, mouth, and revolve,
spinning helplessly, ecstatic, a propeller-man,
and then arch up swan-dively, and then burn down onto another peak.
He was mostly head, his body hummingbird.

He flitted, simultaneously, inside and outside himself,
nectaring the flames, collecting as he spun.
As if all mask, he spun and held in place about
an inch above the fattest flame. His eyelids curved outward
    and downward,
he looked like an old dying infant! Churchill at 6 months!
Slowly he blasted backward, against the oath extending his reign,
contracted to a fetal zenith, and then inflated, a small
    transparent dirigible,
with electric wind, and I could see inside Crane at this moment
the emphasis of the Atikai, old helpless stars, worn to ember,
rekindling in this consecrated pod—consecrated? Yes,
because poetry is a primal emphasis, and uplifts in its sutured arms
a paeonic bed swarming with predecessor copulators,
a plate of Medusa as lightning pasta. Then Hart repoured
    into his deathly skin
and looked at me as if he were selling apples.

"Askesis," he said offhandedly, "Bloom's delight is to show
    in critical X-ray
the contra-naturum of the poem, but since he did not write poetry,
he must hover-foster it, you know, immaculate its eggy conception.
As you and I know, poems are dragged out of moray crevices,
they are braille impressions of forgotten infant soles,
their mordants an aggregate imposition.
The book is always late; the book *is*, in fact, belatedness.
Literate fumes are oral ember dependent. Through the looted
streets of the late 1960s comes Harold Bloom,
bearing his memoried reading of *Paradise Lost*—
he is as moving as James Baldwin driving through shattered
    Harlem plate glass, his father's
lifelong nonwords on his mind, his just-dead father, who
    never said a tender word to James.
We must not forget that in the loreweave of Lascaux,
critic is indistinguishable from poet.
We live on withering—or growing?—swaying beanstalks

whose roots are hidden, receivable as emanations
but static to contemporary radios… Cocteau's Orpheus,
hunched before the Rolls-Royce radio tried to make sense of noise,
as have we all, for ages! Was Orpheus aware
that the scat was exploded particles of Okeanos,
that what was firing through, via his 'radio,' was the god stuff
that has been in holding-scatter since the death of Pan?
From my gloomy viewpoint, your discovery of me in your winestream
as an emanation, and not a ghost, is a gain in respect to inspiration
and the recognition of a new abyss in life.
I killed myself because I was out of bond with an essential cosmos,
I felt disgrace, not as a cocksucker or punching bag for stokers…
I split because even in Mexico I could not find a wavering
    sky-band to bolt me into the now of my destiny."

He swirled his La Tâche and growled:
"For the hearing remains in the beast,
and is of the beast, and must be fucked out of the beast,
must literally be drawn from that fist-like pouch
that would keep knowing opaque, that testicle-haven,
that muttercore, that inverted tower of infant blasphemy,
                    'the unspeakable cruelty
of living and having no being who could justify you…'
—loss of god? But we've never had god, or gods,
as Western plagiarists we went to church,
no serpent was inserted into our most tender aperture at 12,
and the night?   THE NIGHT IS OPHELIAN," he raged,
"*her* body *in* water, is the feel of night
as it slips through us, toward us,   as the cling of things
again and again releases, as innocent beauty
again and again sinks through the pond layers of our bile and
    our confusion…"

I could tell he was tiring, that a sublimation was starting to claim him.
We said nothing for a while. Me thinking of the naked Hiroshima man
standing in that inferno, holding his eyeball out in his palm.

I thought of *my* nightmare, in which that eyeball
leapt into the sky and hugely hovered over me, that eyeball
more powerful than our moon, the conscience satellite,
raying down, as if a helicopter beam, into Everyman's backyard...

Crane cupped his goblet and broke paralysis back through his shoulders
by squeezing his glass until his back snapped.
He then recollected his anatomy, bagged himself small,
a hairless creature at the base of the goblet.
He saluted me like a sailor, lurched to a straw,
pole-vaulted up to the rim, ascended and
dove with a wink, like, *I've done this before!*
disappearing into the crimson wreathe, or Lethe,
of the tiny lagoon the scarlet violence recalled within the
    round aplomb.
Where was he diving now? As he entered the stem, I saw stars.
Was this vision to free me into an ample vulgarity?
A liquid fart of swear words zigzagged forth, and he was gone,
vulgar and feral, vulgar, of the Bulgar, Vulgarian and thorough.

1988

VI

from *Under World Arrest*

(1994)

by Horrah Pornoff

WHEN POETRY ACTUALLY OCCURS,
the particle flow between the mind and
the ceaselessly cabling other is monitored.

Glazed with the effort
to keep wet in the kiln,
I am handed out, homuncula.

I AM MY FATHER'S ONLY UNBORN DAUGHTER.
I gave birth to my mother and am responsible for her death.

Someone who believes that at least one part of her
is immortal is at loose in this room,
some hag who has set her peat on fire,
who, as if they are cosmetics,
is doodling with the fumes.

I CAME UPON MY MOTHER, AN UNBORN CHILD.
Her rimless letters floated before
the animal wall I had erected to see her by.
Out of serpentine repetition,
I sought to be doubled again,
to watch her decomposition compose...

Do you remember being born?
Then, were you?
Do you remember willing dying?
Then, must you?

All of the French Legion has been withdrawn.
The sands relax, now only under camel power,

and the no birth no death feeling that occurs
is my eaten-out navel in my hand unraveling...

BEING PULLS
    as if to magnet
I, filing, iron.
        I piss,
like all women,
        rust,
because my letters cannot yet porn out all
    the masculine hardware.

X HAS INVITED ME TO LUNCH TODAY.
While I sit in my skirt, he's in the Hungry Tiger can,
speed-zipping his fly. High on that special freedom,
he returns. Picking joke upon joke from the letchwater
always within pun reach to any mind.

As if I have a skull down there!
Around which he's tied a tiny shower curtain.
Lobster? If I could only tie up
the bottom of my skirt and still walk.
Or Steak? If I could only lift, and riding
the hardness of my thought fly point-blank into his zippered illusion,
that wall between navel and prick Dante called "the holy vacuum,"
while he picked paradises off Beatrice,
like fleas, nibbling each before her hungry eyes.

He said "vacuum" to me to bring up
the metaphysic in my floorboards.
Unable to raise himself, he wants me to pup up
his tent for him, to Via Negativa him with desire.
Poor pupa sex, the non-entity
I am brassiered in, bewildered by so much in my hymn.

THE OFFICE, FILLED WITH CHINESE LAUGHTER,

is Western chop suey at 5,
the hour the bull,
lamed by hunger, is prodded into time,
and my heritage,
behind its spectatorial fan,
vegetally perspires for
the blood imagination of the matador—

or so it appears
in the eyes of the woman who watches me—
she unfurls her huipil
like a red Saint Vitus flag,
and steps outside me a little after 5.

Corrida of an intelligence, then,
for the whole spilled athanor of a time
I believed in tied to, I-lust
to lie out, Horrah Pornoff,
procrustean receptionist
wedged into carmine shoes and checked
in the Chinese box maze
of the world Greyhound Station.

TWO SKELETONS INTERDANGLE MY OWN.
The one of Red Bone is very old, very
permeated with ochre mother.
The one of Black Bone is very burnt, very
sick of altar consummation.
It yearns to be packed and posted
by my own of White Oklahoma Bone,
its vine, its sustaining
virgin wall.
             And so,
I awake to my desire for friction of any kind,
with anyone, and to my desire for half of myself,
perhaps a woman, unmet,
perhaps a figure of snow
whose only point of contact is a salted cinder.
Love, thus, might be a state
where I live with only that unmet half,
never meeting who I would be living through.
I could walk up to a stranger I know well
and present myself as single and split.
Then he, or she, or perhaps the snow animal
I approach, would, with its cinder,
or perhaps with its tongue, divide me again
(I would be a touch that soft)
and through each finite division, love
would, with each split, be
more accurately defined.

ETERNITY IS THE GREATEST CONSUMER.
It buys from everyone her
being, his life as it were.
The seller gazes off
empty-shelved, into the sanctimonious blue.

I know that if I drop to my knees,
I worship not only what I sold
but what is packed above the fruited plain.

That consumptive beyond is watching,
wanting me to kneel, placing
fingers inside brocaded puppets, making
god fun at the end of my weaning
(man an incomplete woman,
woman an over-complete man,
nature a caricature of person).

I have left a concrete case of nothing
and so, check in, while nothing unpacks
clamp and razor, a traveling salesman
who runs a tool stand on the side.

Perhaps, while I lie in state,
he will screw back in all my treasures?

GROUPIE TO A HOLY GRAIL,
some might say. And it is true:
I still have one finger on a manger,
but one in which the fit is Siamese,
where prostitutes and surgeons
are packed among the circling wiseguys.

Given such Gnostic democracy,
it would be infantile to ask for strength
—which is exactly what I will do.
When they cease tossing meat into my bowl,
I'll crawl back under Hathor's dugs
                              whose liquor
will more than suffice for the yugas
                              when, in hell,
I'll be my own fork, meal, and stove.

Jacques Marsal [1925–1988] in dapper suede slippers would lead us into the darkness of Lascaux. It takes his absence today, our fourth visit, to say how much his presence determined what Lascaux is. As one of the discoverers, Marsal remained coated with the awesome freshness of that tumbling in, lightning-ripped juniper, under which four boys squirmed to arrive. That Marsal stayed on, nearly 50 years, was a bloom added to the stem of the cave, and I'm overwhelmed by the difference one person can make in the personality of a place, not via declaration or sheer information, but by being folded in, obliquely, wearing Lascaux, allowing its grace to loom, allowing us, hardly aware of his movements, our own reading through his light.

> Men spring up like violets
> when needed, Olson said,

and Blackburn, near his end,
lamented the disappearance of a Barcelona
waiter, an old man
who moved so accurately and gently
among the clientele. Paul wrote:
"We do not need to know
anybody's name to love them."

Because of Marsal, I know Lascaux in my heart
like a nearly weightless child
framed by thunder and a bruised, milling sky,
a child standing on the sensation of eternity,
sayable eternity, right under the dust.

1989

COOKING

I slide down like a fireman into a cauldron-shaped machine.
           The discourse
              shifts, scaly zucchini
wants to be scrubbed. Mother said: get outta the tub
soon as you finish washing,
so I scrub and consider the chicken, the cold
under her arms as I carried her into the hospital toilet.
All of life is present every moment.
We know this, or I do, dimly,
I wipe up something from the chopping block, it tastes
like 16th Street—best I can do,
     my birth? The flecks are more precious than
weight of bird in hand. Open the wine.
Curious, the antagonism wafting from the just-pulled.
But who wants to be opened? Down in the blood force,
I dream while I cook. Dreaming is
a kind of cooking, body between waffle irons bed and night,
ghosts of the introjected sipping and picking.
I am closer to Caryl in bed
than at table, but tapers shadow us here.
Are we re-enacting the primal snack
as we cut, munch, and talk? The tall tip of Chinon
that plunges to my belly,
a shore bird zapping up a crab?
Have you looked into your mouth,
considered the Labrador of ice floes, jungular lagoons,
infintestinal havens under invasion
as the tongue, trapped rhino, goes through its
     plungings, so articulate
after 20,000 years,   then Andrei Codrescu on NPR:
he too hates David Duke—I throw in more Louisiana,
cleaning a shrimp: serrated knife down the back
held against the chopping block edge,

swole gut tract furls back, husk won't disposal, so
I bag'm, thoroughly rinsing the headless, footless
    Paleo bodies under harsh cold,
each point of cooking so interesting,
                    I know you appreciate it
having shopped so carefully for all I fondle.
To clean a squid is to have a hand up the goddess.
To do so makes me want to help a cow give birth.
To cook makes me want to disembowel myself and eat.
Cooking is a form of labyrinthine pacing,
and is without fear, until we make contact with
the soul of the beloved, for whom we cook.
Then the two of us are out on plates
looking up into this gorgeous autumn. We are old,
and sliding about, but the dry golden trash
    still clinging to the maples
is a kind of funky Greek Keatsean urn.

Kenneth Burke, 94, is happy for a tasty meal.
He has a chic gray cap, and settles in
at our table on his pillowed chair.
Salmon without oil, or salt,
spinach, rice, Pilsner Urquell.
He said that night: "Beauty is Truth, Truth Beauty—
   Body is Turd, Turd Body"   and giggled.

Each evening we sit down to these bodies
    in cocoon, these woven green beans,
this artichoke harboring so many compressed
thorny lips. A delicate char molded by
    the coldest lake depths,
parts of my mother, parts of our mothers' mothers,
    myself, yourself.

The wind rises outside,
the gold, rouge-red, orange bonfired leaves are down.
We are skeletons eating amongst skeletons.
                              This
        is the delicious thrust and realization.

                                                1991

Is it our work to push doghouses, jeans
and waffle irons into earth's orifices,
to shun them as soon as we use them?
Isn't everything we shape imbued with what we can
    and cannot imagine?
Somehow, in Rilke's time, things shined, were company.
            Wine, shaped by the vintner,
"the savor of the earth, made intelligible to man."
In 1925, Rilke wrote: "Now, from America, empty indifferent things are
pouring across, sham things, *dummy* life... A house, in the American sense,
an American apple or a grapevine over there, has *nothing* to do with the
house, the fruit, the grape into which went the hopes and reflections of
our forefathers... Live things, things lived and conscient of us, are run-
ning out and can no longer be replaced. *We are perhaps the last still to have
known such things.*"

Update: in the core of America, as if at a hearth pit,
whose tentacles spread throughout the body politic:
Reagan's face, a mosaic composed of contra-
Midas touches, disposables, things adults no longer love
reproduced in miniature for their children,
life a non-sequitur. A Salvadoran woman returns home,
to find her family's heads set on the set table's
    dinner plates.
The Reagan face, frozen in vomit-guffaw.
Imagine seeing his stomach!
                    Take the Mount Elliott Exit
off I-94 south via the old Detroit "Black Bottom"
    to Heidelberg, and turn right.
Tyree Guyton's *Funhouse* is on the left.
It seems to cook there, in snow or summer,
                "belly of the shark,"
panopticon of American childhood and poverty.

African-American childhood, African-American poverty.
"Perhaps we are *here* in order to say: house, bridge, well,
gate, jug, fruit tree, window—at most: column, tower..."
But, collapsed wheel chair? Plastic yellow horseshoe?
Squashed truck tire with "cookie monster" peeking out?
Perhaps Rilke's "lovers" could merely pronounce such
    words, in the aristocratic world of Muzot.
                    On Heidelberg,
the street-abandoned is returned to the sides, roofs, porches,
    front yards and sidewalks of 2 houses.
Imagine "Blue Poles" tied around a house so staggered
    it can barely sustain structure,
"drippings" 1 to 5 layers deep, no longer "paint"
but a rubble ropology of bedsprings nailed over window,
jammed in crutches, one with LA Gear basketball shoe,
porkpie hat forced into white telephone receiver,
                      grey underpants,
tricycle poked window,   brooms through springs

fireman boot snaking eaves gutter

baby doll heel draped wire mesh

hammock loaded kitchen counter, to which nailed
                    saddle oxford,
hunk of grey shag carpet slapdashed white,
hobbyhorse (no front hoofs), peach mattress,
lawnmower blades, friction tape winding
                    industrial ducts,
rusted wheelbarrow pan, blue bath towel
                  stained scarlet,
water heater (sorrel around its tilted base)

                on front porch:
empty-overnight-case-piled phone booth

TV innards skewered plastic tenpin

TONKA Turbo-Diesel toy
rusted car frame
baby blue scooter
smashed mannequin head on prong

hobbyhorse hoofs gripping sagging eaves gutter
(what do thy eyes see upside down?)
beret on toilet plunger,   rusted tin world globe

"fence"
of semi-submerged
semi tires
M. Amelia
wife of Geo Zahn   ·
& daughter of
·   Chas & Anna Bleicher
Born Nov 8 1854
Died Dec 7 1877
rusted-apart lunch box, Suzie Homemaker stove,
motorcycle spray-graffitied chartreuse, footstool,
oil landscape by R. Robinson, catcher's mask,
half a license plate [MR 6
toilet bowl, its contents: "Jack Lemmon" Weekender hat,
purple leather high heel pump

Abortion
is
Murder
vote NO X
on B
be the voice of the
UNBORN

(4 blocks away, Tyree's friend, "the junkman,"
lives in a wheelless school bus surrounded by *ruined* junk.
In his potbellied stove, behind the driver's seat,
    he burns spars from torched houses.
At 77, he seems wired with energy, lives on Wild Irish Rose,
a man alive in his own graveyard. One frosty December,
we all walked the ice-rutted alley while he yelled
"I'M A **SCIENTIST** MOTHERFUCKIN COON!")

Malte Laurids Brigge: "and the fusel ordor of sweltering
feet... tang of urine and the burn of soot and the grey reek
of potatoes, the heavy, smooth stench of aging grease."
These sensations we must imagine here—
line upon line of watermarks, chains of object scum,
                    haphazard, intricate.

A block away, "the whorehouse," 3121 Mount Elliott:
nailed-up naked baby doll parts,
                    the unconceived
washed out by sink-top douche? Doll head
                lobotomized on porch rail,
rotted blue rubber dildo,   diapered torso roast.

Next door, Tyree's grandpa, Sam Mackey, 92,
sits at the kitchen table, drawing with crayons
versions of the androgyne. "In that distant chamber,
a bearded queen, wicked in her dead light,"
old Wallace Stevens wrote. Grandpa Mackey's have
    arm-like tits, gigantic dicks.

How paradise might look to the cast-out serpent
                    raising its head
to look back on the emptied place of origin.
All once inside now nailed to Eden's outer wall
                    —and the Cherub?

Nailed to the top of the wall, strutting,
as if to Sousa. The dream detonated,
all things in Babel on earth's multifoliate cross.

1989

GORGEOUS GEORGE COMES POUNDING
DOWN THE BEACH

On the San Diego Freeway
    rising toward Mulholland—
azure ghosts of canyons,
    cobalt lime dusk.
Agnostic snarl of art, aerobics, pizza,
valet parking for Trashy Lingerie.
Sun tinsel streaming in 5 P.M. light so strong
my eyes close driving, open to helicopters
walking the backyard on stalks of light.
Bricolage of tar Maya movie plaster.
"HI, my name's Bruce, I'm your waiter,
    I tried to kill myself last night."
Gladiator bright, collapsible city.
The Rolfed young man cries I am,
not realizing I *am* does not see.
So I'm 13, in my Aunt Georgia's trailer,
off Mulholland. I've been parked here
    while the adults play Canasta.
Stretched out on the bunk bed,
            turn on the tiny TV:
Gorgeous George comes pounding down the beach,
platinum locks atoss, bikinied,
    as if bounding the infinite.
Nature's radiation appears
        an angel layered in coke
stretched out on sushi cooler ice,
    Goddess Ikatakomagurouni.
LAX landing flights flashing   hero   no one
    while up the Strip I chug
below the toe level of billboard gods,
oily, puffed up in platinum heels.
Jackie Collins' anima-black mane,

neon lips,
"exquisitely jacketed in depths of anthracite."
Madonna, "The Frida Kahlo Story,"
            lacquered red nails,
silky hair crisscrossed in meticulous
      braids—visited by the Rockefellers,
         her unhealable abdominal wound.
Perhaps Frida is LA's patron saint?

On Melrose, mascaraed punk mannequins
      are digging "Day of the Dead." La Muerte:
         the exfoliating skull sending north
               Mexican macabre gaiety,
dens that abut globally:
the cleaning woman's husband
               decapitated in Guatemala
appears on TV.
               Kali-fornia face,
      Kali's fornix, Marilyn's whee!
her sagging frontier bodice line
where men are at once larvae and Valentino.
Brittle chrome candy of this Western edge,
haunted not as Brittany by "finisterre"
      (thus world-end everywhere)
but by the American Icarus dream: "Mounting
upon the wings of light into the Great Expanse"
Gorgeous George comes pounding up the beach.

Hockney-sketchy immortality
               swimming pool deep,
a water blue sky in whose bowl
I too steer, imperiled by cancerous fish,
a human being looking like a scuba effete
wandering unpeopled streets, wearing
            my house on my head,
my possessions pyramiding my sides

a mobilary Mesoamerican relief.
                    Porky and Bugs
        come tumbling through the palms,
    squirting my sunglasses with hotdog
                        shaped diners
        and saber-tooth perfume!

                                    1990

At Monte Alban, before a *danzante*,
the shadow of Ana Mendieta bends.
A flattened figure all surface like Ana,
cheek of stone, a lily-groined hunchback,
dismembered at the core of vision.
Thus compassion. Thus tenderness mixed with gravel.
In the tip of the solar arrow,
I discover my mother tied and splayed.
A great snail has arrived in the plaza.
In metaphor, the primal anxiety:
everything is nothing,
something is a toadstool under which
ragged elves are cowering.
How long does it take to get the weight of the earth
    through my head?

              Coatlicue leans forward
just enough to offer a worm shade.
Before Her as a man, I felt my infant size
before my mother—or let's say
Coatlicue is the size surrounding the hole
I made in mother's apple—and so, indeed,
I am a worm in the shade Serpent Skirt offers
—with whom one never shakes hands.
One shakes *hearts* with Coatlicue,
for she too is part of the great snail's retinue.
All true answers are questioned
by the two rattlesnakes that like facing
question marks fuse as Her head.

Against the underlight of Oaxaca
the night sky in suspended rise,
the necropolis in suspended fall.
We are nestled, forever, as now, in soft bone arms,
buttressed by breeze and the wail from the zenith tube

into which liquid night flows,
a kind of larval ebony for ballplayers' hands,
the braid of events in the fleeing stream,
the present the parachute's weighted pouch,
the past its canopy, the future
the rising hidden smile of the ground.

Time is layered. Each beginning deepens
as if each leaf weighed its tree,
and thus where I stand: the weight of me?
Infant pulled through the thighs of earth,
or is it stone emerging from man,
what is hardest in man, the bearing of non-being,
to be a finite cul-de-sac
impacted with seminal angel.

I am pinned against the base of the Southern Cross,
a vane over the tumulus of my hopeless central sleep,
here with my pots and dolls,
buried alive in my background,
in the crested fist of the specifities
I've been hung with, have chosen to wear.
The white Westerner moves no revolutionary boulders.
Unlike the Césaire-man he does not speak for the poor.
He is a mink in the flavor, something that
won't go down, or that does, failing those
stacked in the flues.

"navel of the moon"   Mexico
first disinterred me, a black cape of flies
took off from the pineapple of my innocent heart.
This is where I will bury my poetry,
blood gate of the moon, vale whose path
is the backs of ants, glossy scarlet road,
this is where I always wanted to play,
aloft, on penile dream stilts,
a Gulliver-man, in collage with time.

I am the man who waded in man,
who ate man's marrow and report it is without source.
WOT TIS SOR ROW the Noh ghost intoned.
"Dirty water which nevertheless cleans a pail"
the menstruating dreamer replied.
I, Ariel, spat between the two,
I, Ariel, freed by the two,
saw a girl dying in bed, her hand a rose tree,
crawled in with her, let self
form a moat around her, a halo,
then the tree bloomed a fairy shower.
Each wore a tiny fig pinafore.
Each carried a sparkler as she circumambulated the tree.

And we were followed into Monte Alban
by a little mongrel bitch
still nursing her litter,
our consort on that moonless night.
She rested by us as we sat, filthy, frisky,
wagging to the parking lot
where I wanted to adopt her.
Literal man, you've been adopted,
sick little dog, little Shulamite on the sward—
on her leash, power flows into your throat.
The work is everlasting conversion,
the mother is endless. Against vampiric literalism,
hold the metaphor, burn the cross with mental pain,
it will spring forth again, a violet, a summer storm.
Tonight I have made contact with
the immortality of error. Tjurunga,
impinge! Open your foramen magnum to me.
Between the genitals and the brain
there are only exploded bridges.

Oaxaca, 1991

VII

from *From Scratch*

(1998)

In Memory of Nora Jaffe
(1928–1994)

As she recedes, living still,
first lung, now liver,
I am turning to
"The everlasting eyes of Pierrot
And, of Gargantua, the laughter"
   her laugh
Ohio Gothic, bass
swoons, a booming of merriment.
 We lay in the dawn road pickled
while others dropped salt into our mouth

To wake and to think only of the wine to come,
the wine of the work of drawing,
to need only this wine, to live
in near obscurity, happy
within the frame of *imagination*, this word
we mob,

it is our only refuge.

7 October, 1994

the wake an elegy stirs... something to be listened to.
I find you everywhere, mainly as voice echo,
I think of you, then hear you before I see
entoptically a blur of your face...

the unheard voice then resilences. The silence
opens out, chimes of *Habilis, Erectus*...
 the wake of elegy, dirty churn of what
 the voyage rejected,
standing at the stern of what life might be,
it keeps you pinned in me, as I pine,
semi-conscious unplugging of a bathtub
in which the water used doesn't want to leave...

W

Most just, I guess, to find you
in the flux of realization and grief.
As ash, you are a complete whatever,
and it is hard to comprehend that anti-force.
I string it on my feeling for you

to go overboard with you,
to honor your rich void.
I am gaining this word by word,
for the loss is at odds
with something curdled in praise.
The grand "So What" flicks by,
at Miles Davis with my need to bulge
absence/presence

"Sadness" once meant "solidity,"
"steadfastness in faith,"
but nothing will support my sadness this week,
 a wandering distraction, as if
Nora's death were a box jellyfish
 adrift in my atmosphere.
Death has four sets of eyes, no brain,
one set for each side of what we call direction.
Death's mouth is over its eyes...

...as all senses of her
cancel, recompose,
    "Procession of the Quick"

The upward piling impulse of eternity. Cloud-like, rock-like, forms,
jostling against—here it comes again—absolute absence

A leg, thigh and calf, bent, lower left hand corner, gets me interested in
the physicality, the eros? of the painting, now I spot a male back lunging
upward, whose head disappears in a kind of window of winter trees. His
right arm droops, leading me to a woman—it's Nora herself!—eyeballs
rolled up, hair stark black and funnel-like swooping into the upper
right corner

The work now looks draped, an upward piling, weighted, with loose,
body-like forms, detonated below, into floating, bumping, somewhat
phallic blocks—on which the rest of the painting "stands"—it doesn't real-
ly stand, it wobbles, tectonic, as if on plates? (suddenly the buttocks of the
upward lunging male look like an amazed lion!)

The form argues, wrestles with, the punctilio of human desire salted, as
ground, for a realization of the form to *grind against*. Nora Jaffe depicts
herself under a roving blank cloak of men, as they surge around, across,
and over her. The procession of the quick, *being* overwhelmed, as the
quick (and the dead?) pile into paradise, over the body of the painter—

Cocks abound, but as often in Jaffe they are syntactical eels, the patriar-
chal thrashing in the net of an imagination that instead of practicing polit-
ical correctness prefers, demands, the re-leasing of the obsession. Coils of
rape are here bounded but not dismissed—

the out-of-in-balance of the painting amazes me. I'm stuck
with the use of the female (Nora) body overlayed by blankets
(lacunae) of quasi-phallics. Now I lay me down to sleep.
The garment of the world: stitched penises. O
mother: where? As the garment out of which the cocks are stitched.

O father: why? Isn't it wonderful how semi-abstract,
charged and essentially formal works dump our psyche
upward? My father made me a blanket out of my mother, ay!
then withdrew it, leaving me with my first tooth!
oh! and it is around this tooth that I have woven my poems,
weave, woven, sploven... the spindle bursts,
yet a King now appears at the crest of "Procession of the Quick"
—the winter landscape is his crown,
his body that of the lunging man,
willynilly covering the now double female body
(two heads, Nora's and what I took to be another man's)
and he is kind of dancing, as he fucks,
lifting a Subcommandante Marcos leg, as an insult to
all fashion, as a shark form noses in...

But why two women? Why both at once?

We are in orgy at every moment (too many unused parts)

This sadness is without edge
or forceps, it is weighted with total absence,
which is the difference
between Nora's ashes, and Nora, it can be
    weighed in mind, it is fractal
and thus not without contour,
it is the toothed heart of a black hole,
what the star feels in its inexhaustible extinction...

Sadness, then, is a protection,
        a kind of Covering Harem,
it is sweet, as "The Wild Rose" in Budapest was sweet,
nostalgia mired in cool fat, a piano player
whose elderly infant head, with stuff oozing onto the keyboard,
smiled at us, the eaters...

Our friendship was blessed with an erotic lining.
My eyes turned off before Nora's art
and something else turned on—
a glade would appear, compact male flesh
reorganized, penis shifted to armpit,
thigh used three ways, as stalagmite, Long Island, floe,
libido frozen, on the trail of her hand
finding its way through a coral forest of congealed
    male fragmentation

            Seeing the extent to which
she had imagined her masculine-fraught destiny,
I knew male force was grasped, and that she was free
—for a moment. We can deal with nearly anything
—for a moment. In minuscule time,
a stroke, or an image, is paradise,
darkness a chrysalis of unharvested stars

She had reorganized the male tentacles
and glimpsed what Bosch envisioned
—while she smoked.
In her breath, steel doors began to rot.
She hurt herself
as who does not who has glimpsed the other as
"Dear Fellow Particle"?

It is very transpersonal, never private,
how the pylon figures of our lives
rub open scars and palpitate the antique
    feeling under

Nora is Egyptian,
a gorgeous baboon
in whose slender figure my language
is hived.

To learn to love your death.
Is this not the requirement? not to love death,
but to love you in death,
to learn nourishment from your absence

Dear now ancestral spirit, you feed me
as do the spirits of poets dead but for the page,
or frame, of chaos, white
for these ant legions

Are not the chosen dead blowing
energy into these lines? Yes, I have good energy,
but it is nothing compared to
Nora as ash, the microscopic gale
    in the thought of her,

billowing, these dead who make life-in-image possible,
we all work at a single world poem,
    a hybrid exchange,
I become pregnant with Nora's soul,
I swell at night, cannot rest, I sleep
    but do not rest...

how beautifully herbs break in, fumes and
filterings, by which her presence is
swarming, micron by micron, with the jest of absence,
    like tiny wine flies...

Nora's spell,   terrible to be a speck in this exchange.

A hardon, severed,
enwombed, the umbilical-
knotted
goad.

Nut
descends, arms
alongside,
she kisses its cleft, tongues

the semen-charged

mummification,

the hydra-hydrant
gong.

One senses in her art a luxuriant ambivalence
toward masculinity,
"Merman" manticore pushing into female
plush, the tobacco
in the cigarette, dildo
as driving void,   a sort of infant

misericordia, this 9 inch nail
rubbery as old celery
has been given refuge,

battered Manhattan, bandaged,
with potato-eyes, ending in a hoof,

"Our Strips of Stuff"
lingam bound to stretcher poles,
bags of blood, bound in with coal and stones,

whose yoni is a nurse
whose ward (whose nave)
strains with mayhem chained,

gorgeous energy, this
crest of a house ridge phallic helmet line
whose attic is timbered meat.

🌿

The dirtiness of death,
        her head a chopped meadow,
chemo-crewcut grey and stubby,
steroid swollen face. I did not recognize Nora,
blundered into the next death section
        CLAYTON   I heard my voice
This man in her bed—then knew he was Nora,
who asked me to bring her a box of Malomars.
Because of the steroids, she said, she would wake at 4 A.M.
    ravenous   (perhaps also to see me
                one last time...

I cannot say what was in the bedpan,
I would like to,   to keep my poetry
sensitive to what we suffer,
or what was in the casket
no casket,   ash,   her goings,
the butchered countenance and what must be
    wrapped, discarded,
            O I am thinking, Charles
Baudelaire, into the fluttery life of your old ones,
as they snapped like wasps against the rue corner,

is this an indulgence
    or is it touched with cancer?

Must poetry become infected to truly live?

            ❧

October 30, 1994
Dia de los muertos

Is it possible there are better days in Bardo
than others? Days of less weighing, days of more
rending? Nora on one scalepan ash,
on the other, a speculum mirroring the heart.

Could I recognize you in Bardo,
I would have to love your shredded tentacles,
your eyes I once knew as piercing
now dead wash across some scene of disarticulation,
the paintings taken back into the experiences
out of which they came, so that Joe's face now
floods the periscope eyepiece

Forty days, is Bardo, is she being dressed?
Is she a trussed goat? Dressed for the pyramid?
Force-fed for sacrifice? What happens in these forty nights?
And then I saw them slam you down again
and take you apart

Forty days, is Bardo, is she being flayed?
Can they get her heart on the scales?
We project jealousy on even the caterpillar.
Rood into the sky of prehistory.
Subjectile man: we magnetize *and* we project

This is her day twenty-two.

For what does she battle in Bardo?

Release? She is released. To not come back?
She's back for a pause, lodged in my kale,
in the very nurture of my breathing.

Drafting her battle, like I once drew her bath.

&

The back of my head is hollow

it is filled with Nora's ash

      Nora ash
   the possessive disappears.

&

Nora's roar:

"You're inside my body now
and while it may look like ash from without,
inside, in this drawing, this apart-ment,
these interlocking fuses, these cunei or cunt forms,
these uncials, my face is forever present,
forever as long as seen, perceived as my allegiance to Aphrodite,
the line, the point of the line on the long and generous leash of
.body as the enduring reality.
There is no significant form without body's roar,
the long and terrible adventure of two bodies,
three, four, woman in mother in man in father, two-by-fours,
unlock the cross and let its ties swarm—
you will not escape my body for I will not conform, be
formula, be line without body's presence.
And so, though I love a line more than line can aura,

for my love to be good it must scintillate with origin,
member, cavern of pools and dentata.
In this ever nearness to body is my joy—
body the unfolding interlock of generative stillness,
defused as the line, tender earthworm,
heads off into the loam of blankness again and in her curling,
in her feints, gasps, spurts, crests my love,
roars my forehead into galley, rowing, stroking deep,
tasting the lover as line tongue delirium into sense and
registers home."

                              🌾

A jaguar of bubbles in the toilet bowl
tells me your Bardo
                    Flushed

and then an airplane,   as if company,
    hums against my lungs.

                              🌾

"Beyond Repair," she said,
I want to paint a painting I could call
"Beyond Repair"

my mind honed on Indiana heard a wreck.
I fidgeted toward her meaning: a painting
that was *beyond* repair (hear: compare)—
    a painting no one could monkey with,
a painting that was beyond
    repair,
thus perfect, with no break-downable parts,
a painting that will blaze with her being.

that you can enter. in which you can be.
yes. blues for Nora.
she wants her essence to be attended.
she wants the pelvis to be. the pelvis fossil.
she wants man as *Homo* in, as *Erectus.*
she wants erect man to scream inside
    the downy glade pro-
nounced woman. she wants woman like a wagon train
to encircle innocence (Does she know
no one is innocent? Of course. she knows and
    does not know.
like us, the living who know less than she.

like the alive man who thinks he is alive.
and the poor dead woman who might think
    she is totally dead
TOTAL is the name of the station I took gas from tonight.
TOTAL is the 7 oil multinational sisters.
TOTAL the impact of capitalism on indigenous person.
    As blacks and whites swarm into the blues.
as the blue sky and blues and bruise fuse
a brilliant dim carpet on which Prufrock would never
    dare to recline—
against the total. of the total. yes. totaled one.

she wants all life to reign. pile. and scour.

1994

Last night it was not Ophelia but Nora Jaffe crawling the Milky Way, her cloud body shredding like Nancy Spero's image of a mutilated Salvadoran woman crawling the dirt on which she had been assaulted—and I thought of Rigoberta Menchu's mother crawling tethered to a tree, of Charles Olson describing himself as a "tireless Intichiuma eater & crawler of my own ground," of Gary Snyder off the trail crawling "on the crunchy manzanita leaf clover... around between the trunks"—

as I continued to dream and reflect, I saw all these crawlers, one below the other, moving in parallel rhythm, some agonized, some studiously inspecting—all seemed to be returning to their totem, their *ototama* or *ototeman*, to their animal brothers or sisters, this nearly-destroyed blood-covenant between the human and the animal—

our night crawl through Le Tuc d'Audoubert, past bear skulls and viper skeletons, to the sculpted bison 700 meters inside the cave, made a vulva-like loop, a coming turning going, with the mating animals as the center—

and then there is the story my Indian friend in Bloomington told me in 1960: how on his first night there, having come directly to Indiana from India, he walked past a house on which there was a sign: *Nightcrawlers*. He was touched by what he thought was the kindness of Americans: hotels for drunks that stayed open all night long—

there are now other kinds of nightcrawlers, big tough ones moving across darkened Michigan firing-ranges, toward targets of silhouette men, the heart areas blown out. Upright around their smoking barbecues, my fellow Americans are singing: "Dropkick me, Jesus, through the goal posts of life!"

1995

Looking into littoral fog
the shore has always stopped me,
laid a barrier across association,
made writing by the sea
listless, as if stumbling about
an ode... dangerous to stare
at nature and write—

❧

Surf crests have leatherine
concaves
then it's all froth crawlers trill

Gigantic skirts with meandering hems,
slits in weave to sand

Little cliffs' white rubble,
high sizz then
"sundered parentage"

Ropes vertically aflow—
describe the sewing throwing:
Mumonkan stitch, gateless
gate

as if a text of iles
detextiled while
ile flexing
wound sound
perception stops,
a shushing weave whelms the eyes:
skyscrapers under nuclear barrage.

I'm a little boy in my glandbox
   sifting mommy purr,
the simmerunderoar   spreads
   a virus under tone
taking the lips back to suckle shapes,
   trom   bone
the slides of brass
     under 4:30 sun
silver   so glaucous pocked,
               more cicada
        than constant

    Watch out for unity as you age,
     it's in cahoots with reduction

Be as these rocks not deluged,
just gleamy in their lenten instant

        Myriad-glimmered
reason surfing the tectonics of dream,

Mallarme's "throw" still tumbling in the air,

poetry as shipwreck,   oceanic page,
"a throw of the dice"   the gamble of alchemical research
"will never abolish chance"   no way
    to predetermine reception—

Unless a work of art is its own shipwreck
a master is proposed outside the maelstrom

Surf looks more perfect than I can imagine a god,
perfection that if not seen through
     dwarfs imagination—
seen through,   nature is imagination,

roving tooth breast
on which I row
60 years a second

    Pyramidal speed-ups
slow lozenges of satin steel
storied pounce in rinse,
      dipping sun drapes a mail
across the crestlets

    then 7 gulls in muscular goodbye.

                Yachats, 28 May 1995

The exultation at Céret has the long dirty ghost legs
   of bony ravens,   it marches without body.
Terror is seminal. It says: I am not the spit
my father shined me with. All windows are monstrous eyes.
All houses pupiled caskets. I'm sorry but the road
   is in the sky,
I mean, the sky is pumping the road, I'm sorry
but the road is in pump with the sky, if you know what I lean.
A whole treed plaza picks up its sunderskirts and runs,
    ruby lava.
The earth is unsubstantial lapis
while his body is poised on a brush

You can't see what I see, reader,
so I have to mail you
red gristle howling away from black fire—
"Landscape with Gnarled Trees," yes,
but the sensation is tree-torrential hill-tides
binding houses buckling and elasticized

So many gorges, upon inspection,
have not scissor-faced mothers, but hammerhead fathers,
pockets of gold, of pus,   pockets of hearth and pomp
knotted in a wickerwork of forced labor, of freedom, of
    tearing burgeoning—
in Soutine's Céret, a quaked slob
discovers his mortitude, the chutes of his lying,
all the image leprosy percolating Smilovichi,
the beatings,   their energy,
being famished,   its energy,
the energy in being rejected,
the energy of *no*
romantic folklore

· Clutchy belonging to something
inexistent until created. Think of it!
You have no life, painter,
until out of nothing you create it!
Out of nothing? Out of a village church
looking like a huge gold spider about to vomit.
Out of a trampled green hex.
But to paint the exploding raven head
in which sun and moon may be copulating,
to ball this gonadal wax into a honeycomb
then to invest it with one's own bees—

this is to travel,   this is to visit Soutine at Céret

Jigging farmhouses burnished by a urine-colored dusk,
scree on the move. Bovine
femurs inside of which villagers live.
The feel of noon at 3 A.M. Dream of a deal
in which one's fetal cash register is clanged shut.
As for *should you be?* The argument at Céret
is a road upchucking a cascade of zilch.
As for *why?* White-haired butcher babbling tomatoes
in the swill of pink organs meaty flood of boils

O the primal slaughter before all the houses!
Garden of Blowsy Delights!
Slaughter so real it deflowers—
the barns are boozy with it!

And there is always a hill. Not a mountain,
nor a slope, nor a rise,
but something 100 times Soutine's height,
of porphyry,   of jasper,   lit within,
a bubbling town dump, shack-
faced urchins poking through what Spaniards

sliced Indians into,
a shifty hill,   a shtetl,   a townlet,
morne on which Césaire's mother pedaled her Singer,
Dead Man's Drop where I sledded,
there is always a hill,   a peak,   an excel
from which we are falling,   a precipice
of which we are the innards,

the traffic jam in paradise,
grid-lathered Babel,

to feel a potential versus life as you piss,
shipwrecked roofs,   this scowling thatch,
whitened oaks like goose necks
force-fed with nothing,   stretched forge
with corkscrew thighs,   sky-wired elms,
clap of a single cymbal,   sound of self-rounding,
fire of the stem called masturbation.
Turba Mass in male soul   we have yet to figure.
Men, those brutal bastards who never really
get to be king of the hill.

❦

The pheasant is risen.
The dead pheasant, risen from her bath—
out of tomatoes, she is risen,
the garrotted pheasant,   out of her vessel,
a still life,   life in the still of
alchemical imagination

It is very murky here, fleeced of sunlight.
The potted flowers grapple with the chair back.
The lilacs in their jug look like spoiled meat,
like scrapings turning scarlet with desire?

Jug acrawl with roses, looking Argus-eyed,
face swarming with eyes, roses as blowflies,
release these ravens, peacock entail them!

   and then some jonquil yellow
   some geranium
   a plaster statue
concerning which, the legend goes:
"embrace her with love, and deposit upon her some semen—
like Pygmalion's Galatea, this *fate* will come to life in your dreams
and tell you, now her lover, where to find buried treasure"

Song of the gladiola-spirit yearning for blood,
yearning to become what Soutine was unable to eat.
In the still life retort, flowers feeling
   flow-er rapture,
a contra naturam, as Soutine nerves
flow through gladiolas,
                  van Gogh is near,
the background blackens,   a putrefactio is under way.
Petals like copulating infants.
       The canvas a urinal
in which the moon is lying on her back
         in blackish water—
could we dissolve into this flower-flow,
what lurid wonders we'd unearth.
Soutine van Gogh shaking hands in sperm,
squeezing pulpy red ocelots out of pressed palms,
flukes of childhood hunger resonating in the woods.
Scum of boiling, bloody broth, the fidgets, the blocks.
Resistance in the gladiola,   the word itself
unhinging, a "sword lily," diminutive of *gladius.*
Is the painter a gladiator? Little swords form a mandala,
a magic circle,   a fly is trapped under Soutine's eyelid.
He leaves it there. Fly rots, green cream forms over the eye.
The pot of flowers now looks like wilting antlers.

Van Gogh guffaws. How wring out these gladiolas?
He cuts his hand on the steel stalks,   forces them through
his mother's wringer,   *his mother's wringer,*
he looks out from between her legs, his mouth
stuffed with gladiola stems.   Self-Portrait as a Hydrant
Gushing Tulips.   A herring falls across.
He's still stuck in Smilovichi, plucked clean in Paris.
Van Gogh throws up into the pot. In the violet mess
     a storm begins to twinkle...

The herring's eye looks like a truffle floating in yolk

Explain the cephalopodic grasping of these tulips.
Explain
these manta talliths, this Cimmerican inkiness,
the way painted-over paintings (flea-market scrape-aways)
Ouija directions in circuit shock with Soutine's
once used, tossed away brushes

"I am the source of all pornography,"
sings the little flayed rabbit still in woolly socks,
"laid out on my pale gold and suet sheet,
my whole cavity is open to your eye-fingers,
     my legs are spread,
     my crotch smeared red,
     my wispy forelegs wiggle
     by my skinned but staring
     head"

According to Paracelsus, every body (meaning every tangible substance) is
nothing but coagulated smoke breathing forth from the matter, or the
matrix, in which it is present

Thus this pike "body," a sulphur fumet of cobalt, tar and
blood, slapped down on a shiny bench,
mouth rubble frozen in a paroxysm of snapping,

alongside a row of vermilion onions
which must be tomatoes,
little bloody turbans of smoke

Another pike-shaped flayed rabbit
so mutilated as it quivers in its violin
Bacon is immediately present,
or Bacon's grinder mind, through which this creature
seems to have passed

It has always given me pleasure simply to say Soutine's colors,
to reflect on the way his things interpenetrate,
a mahogany table whose cinnabar grain liquefies
around 4 steel blue, grey and white fish
whose surging immobility is picked up by the rumpled, knotted
    ochre cloth

All here is living and dead at once,
as if half-frozen bodies were dropped on red-hot coals,
photographed in their first seizure,
glimpsed before the awakening became being awake

Some scholars have written that Soutine is dominated by anthropomor-
phic gestures, that he is undisciplined, hallucinated, out of control, a
necrophile. To spot subliminal forces organizing in his limbo brawn is not
to see him as cartoon-complexed; rather, it is to affirm the extent to which
he turned the still life into life in the still. Soutine is one of the most
porous painters who ever lived. In the bloodmares to be found in the oily,
night hair of his Seine are hybrid consequences still-dwelling in our
minds-to-be-born

Such is his ray, a wealthy bawd, in the profusion of fat and jewels nosing
forth out of the blackness of her latrine, while the pot of tomatoes below
digests itself, tomatoes turning upon themselves, slipping up and around
each other, anxious to burst

Or another ray, which appears to be disemboweling itself of tomatoes, parboiled and skinned, which Soutine cannot digest, a ray with multiple tomato breasts, O Ray of Ephesus!

Or still another ray scene in which a copper teakettle has come alive, flinging its ribbony handle-arms to the dark, dancing and leering at the 4 pomegranates inching toward it like seething little kegs of blood

The color and texture of this ray evokes the face of the older Rembrandt, jewel-like decay, mucous and cinders, creature as mineral, as flesh, as paint, in whose pocked and luminous surface a child is born and marked in Bethlehem

Annie Mae Grudger has been listening to all of this,
looking for many years now through Walker Evans' kind lens.
She is 27, has 4 children, wife of an Alabama cotton tenant farmer,
and is nearly-starved. She is losing her hair,
holding her mouth in a smile-clench.
For a moment her humble bile has receded and she has offered
her tilted gaze to Evans' camera.

For a moment, she would walk out of her body
and embrace something she has just felt.
1936,   she is standing posed against
bare unpainted siding,
she is backed by Soutine

and it is her spirit that often shines in Soutine.
She is so thin at 27, you can see her upper chest bones,
she has one dress she could be photographed in,
no underwear, I'm guessing, nothing like a bra.
She might have some saggy, ripped panties.
Annie Mae Grudger is the Smilovichi intersect,
a cleaned-up version of Chaim locked by father
    in the chicken-coop

(I'd argue Barnes is the crucial provocation,
but clearly self-destruction is endemic to Soutine,
destruction of his self,   not himself,
destruction of what he made of himself,
Jewish hatred of the image,   bypassed by the man,
scorpion-tailing back on the painter,
he honors the terror of Smilovichi
when he slashes a Céret)

To be hanged in Venus-flail inside a crumbling chimney:
turkey in rotting turquoise high heels,
with sulphur henna Sapphire-blue breast,
aureoled in black, with circular buzz saw of blue-black feathers.
To be at genital-lock with one's forge
lit up as if by interior bluebottles.
Ode to our wretched turning,   to be,
volatile body,   Soutine would deny Mercury
and insist that the body in glory
is the squirrel in the arbor
starved and pawing for chew.
Turkey carnal candy. Timid girl legs,
hesitating death-droopy talons.
Steatopygous chicken, whose larder lesions
purl with peppery gland streaks.
The Eden-rot of Maya. Texture of foggy morgue fuel.
Have you smelled a stale chicken? Have you,
Whitman might inquire, smelled your stale self?

"Yellow Turkey" with red flayed-rabbit-head
pointing lode-ward as if in pollinated
gyre,   carcass
already treacle,   moving with lice-accord.
This nothing we are,
arrested,   but not spent

And it is beautiful for things to get out of hand,
for the wine of Tartarus to soak through the snow,
for a turkey to hang and orange.
Corralled chaos inside of which a moldering
duck exults,   or is it a green eagle?

Turned on its side, the 1924
"Fowl Hanging Against Red Bricks"
becomes a chicken goddess propelling herself through an under-
    water grotto.
She has multiple breasts,   a human profile.
She is passing over a sunken red tugboat—
the disintegrating horizon of a subliminal Céret?

In the life-spirit of pure blood
a lapis is dwelling. It is the whirlpool in chaos.
It kills, and it quickens.
Wonderful stone, held in derision by the world.
It is heaven. It is the scum of the sea.

The Buffalo "Carcass of Beef."
Threadlike black scribbles, drips,
antic milling in the pit of a colosseum
framed by the richest blue.
Tension at the top,   tolling
gravity below,   this glassy, roily fatalcore,
this animal crib become our slatherfest,
the first god quaternified,
it is the animal garter soaked in us,
nigredo-overpowered alembic,
this predator temple,   this immense
Buddha-compassion breakdown,
    to disembowel,

to toss the liver to the wolves,
to core the animal of itself, and move in,
and once inside the animal house,
to start to work on oneself!

And then a mahogany-red pheasant comes twisting
through the waves of a semen-cream drape.

🌿

Soutine's portraits are marvelous machines of consciousness.
The coils, the hairpin
turns, the tics,
muscle armor,
flabby troughs of that weighing station between
nothing and an enlarged suckling
each person is the patina of.
Crispate fingers that suggest the hand's desire to act
the octopus,
have a beak hidden in palm.
Hands knotted in prayer like an inflamed pumpkin.
Or glove-like, and melting,
fingers become nightcrawler independent,
hands as the exhausted straw of the body's peristalsis,
as in "Woman in Red,"
broken, paired slabs, stacked one on one.
There's a wildly-flopping turkey in each of us,
an atavistic flyer manacled to bipedal hesitation.
I like the whirling raw hamburger in his faces,
the drab fix of their stares.
"Village Idiot" and "Mad Woman" join
Madeleine Castaing in her black fur
and "Man with Straw Hat," whose face is toothpaste
being as squeezed impasto,
the epanadiplosis of the body
moiling back on its rhyme,

out of the shtetl, forever rocking,
a prayer metronome Whitman never knew...
repressed missions fade in the choir boy's eyes,
the white of his dress
almost redeems the color white,
it is as stained as an old cooking rag,
washed rewashed,
the flecks of parsley, garlic, rancid butter,
bits of chopped red pepper,
it is a tunic on which fowl have been dried,
in which parboiled tomatoes were squeezed into
little balls, to garnish
a chicken in champagne sauce.
The "Page Boy at Maxim's" blood-drenched-red uniform
breaks out on his face and hands,
or do his crimson ears and black eyebrow eye-pits
release their pained,
ruined, servile
clots into his uniform?
Soutine has drawn an empty circle on his outstretched palm,
the circle's slightly off,
the tip will never be right,
never connect with the need
beyond any tip
of one ground between tables,
whose life is errands.
These are faces as charged as marshes with their own
uroboric devouring,
heads whose source must be
in the privation of hewn and crafted images
from which Soutine's ancestors suffered.
The Biblical world sack turned inside out,
there tumbles forth
—along with flame-shaped praying men
and mousy pastry cooks with elephantine ears—
Soutine himself:

According to Maurice Sachs, he was "at first glance, coarse, un-planed, ill-shaped. A thick, haphazardly-planted nose, fleshy, pale lips opening on irregular teeth, a single thick eyebrow, stubborn and without malice, barring his forehead crowned with dense, black, tousled hair. His small, penetrating eyes were of a rare color, a kind of saturnine blue, and their speckled, mazarine grey irises were like fluid, lively, animated agates. He had short hands, but they were admirably shaped, agile and graceful."

Who *is* this "Woman in Pink"
we'd all like to know? She *is*
her coiling chair, a pythoness dredged,
battered, in moldy, foaming rose.

1996

from **MATRIX, BLOWER**

I keep having this fuzzy vision of the psychic head,
of a brain termite queen pumping out image tendrils,
a vision of source hovering as this soft stuff in the skull
and then a creature blowing into it
(Sirens, the nightside or ancient form of the Muse,
are said to suck the breath of the sick
and are associated with siesta-nightmares),
"muse" akin to *musus*, "animal muzzle,"
a Muse-muzzled succubus crawling across the dreamer

or up through the dreaming,
blowing the dreamer's mind,
mind ejaculating into Muse muzzle,
"psyche" akin to "psychein" = to blow

Say Laussel ripped off the bull's horn
and experienced inner tearing
as if something began to bleed within,
what is this thing that was felt?
A killed-out image?
The sensation of a plunging rise,
a fall so total it swerved into ascent?

This bleeding, this fount—
Aztecs saw snakes coiling out a decapitated's neck
not as a fantasy of wriggling veins
but as the body's serpent power
released in the instant of decapitation

To have severed a head
to gaze at life's black, U-shaped power
out of which image larvae began to seethe,
as if in doubling-back depth

there is a fructifying compost equal to
the weight of the loaded horn
which this faceless woman of the nightmare
could barely raise,
feeble left hand resting on her swollen belly,
she now possesses what impregnates her,
she's parthenogenetically cocked

Out of a curdling implosion,
out of a caldron of generational fat,
the Venus of Lespugue rises
and is caught at the waist by
—is it mother flesh
she is ascending through?
As if she would completely pop out, a maiden.
Then I look again: she is docile,
her bowed head dove-like
over a bulbous
double stomach, forearms flaccid.
Buffie Johnson noticed the arms were wing-like,   *
that Lespugue has tail feathers.
One senses that Lespugue is a frozen instant
where woman breaking into bird
breaking into woman were seized and held,
the pupa of each.
The daughter rises out of the mother core,
bird-shaman invested.
Footless Lespugue—
held upside down, from the back
her pressed-leg-stumps become a head,
buttocks   enormous breasts

     She floats,   Cro-Magnon mind,
frog brain shaped

Like the Venus de Milo, her lackings
project us into her... chips off the old vulva

Nor is Jeffrey Dahmer
utterly beside the point:
to not want to be left by anyone we touch
   is amniotic—
                    in imagination
we seek to keep our freezer full of heads,
we bow to heads taken before we existed

If nothing is absolutely dead
then all—and nothing—has the power to rise,
like smoke, to permeate me
with its insurrectional deadness

At Abri Cellier: the neck and head of a blowing horse
crudely engraved in a stone block.
Across the neck, a vulva a bit bigger than the horse head
   has been gouged.
"The original sentence, the original metaphor: *Tat Tvam Asi*,
   Thou art that"   *
Blowing horse head = vulva,   *
thus: a blowing horse head vulva,
"Beauty will be erotic-veiled, exploding-fixed,
   magic-circumstantial or it will not be"   *
The *exploding* and the *fixed* at 30,000 B.P.

8:16 A.M. After writing my Notes, I assumed *From Scratch* was finished. Then I rewrote parts of "Soutine's Lapis," and wondered about everything else. I reread fifty more pages and decided, no, it *is* finished, and went to bed. It then seems that I dreamed for hours, over and over, of being at a large university for a residency that included several poetry readings. Each time I showed up for a reading I would discover that I had no books to read from, or that the books which some kind soul had taken out of the library for me were in foreign languages. At one point someone gave me a copy of *The Gull Wall*; I started to read from it to discover that I was trying to pronounce Hebrew words and that I was in the midst of someone's prayer. A touching, beautiful woman kept turning up in the audiences, I knew her, did not know her, having had some touching adventure with her that turned on poetry, or about it, I had given her some life words which she had written down and was now trying to find. Like me, she was out of words, or without the words she thought she had. Book after book was handed to me, some with my titles in English, but none of them were my books as I believed I had written them and Black Sparrow had published them. The dream was like the branchings of some great, proliferating tree, each branch becoming a me going out into audience-filled skies, or colosseums where I was to be studied then sacrificed, or sacrificed then studied. Each time I'd show up bookless a 1950s college audience would be there, shuffling about, sitting down, getting up, Cokes in hand. After five years, four thousand worksheets, this dream. Then I think of the right to write, of the fact that no one is shooting at me as I sit here, that if every poet who'd ever lived were to assemble in Ypsilanti and dig my situation they would probably conclude I didn't have such a bad deal. So, I'm not in Bolivia or China and I don't, as Carlos Germán Belli used to, have to carry a few books of mine around in a brown paper sack trying to place them in Lima bookstores. But are my books incomprehensible, can no one read them—isn't that one message of the dream? You say that you write for yourself but that you try hard to communicate this self to others. Well, maybe you try too much. Nobody wants all anyone else has. Are alls poisoned, are some so heavy they feel like nothing? Is my all the empty coal bucket Kafka's bucket rider mounts, or in my case, a book, there I am, riding my book about, hovering over a reader's condo, Hello I cry, it's me, Professor E, I've just completed another book! Another book the interior groans, oh god he's written another one. But no! this one is the best I've ever done, this one will light up the distant horizon and demonstrate how you are attached, or belong to that which is under you, this one will point you at the looney tunes under all you think. Indiana to Lascaux, one fast drive, a single smoking road. Well, the interior replies, that is of some interest, but since attention span has now reduced to dime-thin sauce, what are we do to with you? Your all is now pointless; it may not be a waste of our time but since time itself has become waste, or an immense archeological dump, your contribution is no more than another unleaded can. Postanything, that's the key word, you fill in the blank and hitch it to the Post. Meanwhile, we're inside drinking and gambling with Marlon Vendler and Harold Brando, and it's not that our cards are blank, they're packed with jokers, yet no matter what we draw, the same king always reappears when these low rollers lay down their hands. I returned to my dream. To my inability to have the book I thought I had written. Many in the audience had copies of things that looked like mine, a booked audience that shows up as all authors to hand to the bookless speaker volumes that appear to be his but turn out to be their own prayers. I'd call this blizzard weather, or books as flakes, a gyre in flail: who has come to hear who? Should I stand by podium and listen to the three hundred read from books with my covers but books whose pages are more attached to the audience than to me? Plasmic pages, like loose skin pulled forth, a stomach furl gripped, held forth, and read? Why not? *Read the sun*, I once heard, becoming a poet is the process of learning to read into, around, and through, anything. To read the moon is to imagine the moon. To imagine the moon is to speak as moon. To be a mooner! So the audience is exposing varying parts of their flesh which they read hearing me, or hearing my rustling looking for my book. I read, and they hear me as themselves. Shouldn't that be an occasion of great appreciation, even joy? They experience what I read as part of their own flesh? I am the man I suffered I was *theirs*. But it doesn't work this way anymore, does it? Holding forth a leaf of skin they fail to realize that the words are not theirs, these translators, they hear me as themselves and my presence translated into their pulled-forth selves is, upon translation, simultaneously erased. So my words, which they appear to hear, are translated into their own hopes and confusions, and printed out, or so it appears, for what they hold in their hands is a print-out that "once upon a time" was said to be mine—or at least not theirs, a text between, a table between a me and a you that we used to rest our cases on. So I left the auditorium and looked up a publisher... it would be easy to be clever here and repeat, with neat flourishes, the author dilemma in a time of commodity. Easy to make jokes, for example: I sold my book on the origin of image-making in Upper Paleolithic cave art by explaining how, in the caves, I had not only lost weight but come to terms with repressed childhood abuse, and as I uncovered this abuse, conspiracy theory was at long last clear: the ghost of JFK appeared in a Font-de-Gaume bison and compellingly narrated how while Oswald was the sole assassin, Oswald was not Oswald but a surrogate mother impacted with Cuban cigars, CIA wiring, and the limbo force of Al Capone's vault. Ruby took care of "Oswald" before this doppelgänger could be disassembled. Actually, Ruby was not Ruby either, but a maniacal distant cousin of LBJ named Strom Hoover. In other words, publisher X told me: anything can be anything as long as it sells. Image has gone into apocalypse. Beast and Scarlet Woman are costumes the natives have abandoned, they are props, as fillable by Hiroshima as by ant-eaters from outer space. Your problem, pub X told me, is: you're still voting in a shack on the Isle of the Blessed. Dope you still believes a mullet is a mallet. So there I was, or here I am, in accord with the industry and still holding my heart in my fist like Verlaine, Rimbaud sneered, clutched a fish. Pub X went on: your absurdity is that of an obsolete white guy; if we could can you we could sell you, but as a heart jumping around like a feverish puppy, the die is cast. It does not matter what you say, what matters is your caste. And just because you're the problem doesn't mean you can harvest some negativity by confronting the system that's produced your crop. Kapeech? What you call imaginative courage is decadence on parade. We both believe an image can be anything. Yours are still strung on transpersonal chains manipulated by your missing story. The images we buy are critic-coded, their stories all reflect existing missings, pop-up audience zones or prestige perks.

So I'm like an alchemist, I guess, an antiquated beaker bubbling away in a Swiss hut, right here, glued to NPR, listening to myself, observing my spider, cooking up a storm, waddling off to teach, translating my baby book, an octopodal radio giving off all the right signals, my flack taken care of, a hopeless case, a cause not lost but encased by too much having been found, an August moon strayed into February, Ariadne's tidbit, Ariadne's clew entangled in the Minotaur's teeth, Theseus slumped drunk in a cul-de-sac, a labyrinth in effect, a sun-oiled tunnel when it comes to night.

On Missing Story Hill, the elves were squirreling away *amanita* for a journey I had just begun. I watched them work, hoarding vision for a literal launch. Indeed, without this unreadable dream how would I have chanced upon these elfin sties swarming with the flatulence of images-to-be? I was suddenly almost grateful for my fix, babbling away here while Oprah interviews the soul's code. But to leave it at that would be to dismiss my audience reading their own seasonal flesh and accept the auditorium bare. Maybe it always is, for all of us, Smokey Stover included. Maybe the most celebrated author, daisy-chained with readers, stares through these uroboric wreathes as if they are smoke rings, into pointless toil. But maybe he does not. Regardless, here I am, watching on the neighbor's sunny garage front a gargoyle bobbing as it devours its perch. Now, wait a moment, the redbud said: don't mistake my foliage for my fate.

1998

VIII

from *My Devotion*

(2004)

I want to come to terms with my vaulted
and faulty
interior, with the clocks stacked in my kidneys,
with my face of a radish
draining tears into a tile sea.
And I do not want to come to terms with this vaunted
faculty, with these mer and men maids
calving right below consciousness.
Fuse and refusal,
torque of the Vallejo legacy.
To mince the baby wind—
to feast on nothing.

When I was a woman
I smiled, the arrows bristling from my face,
an old-fashioned woman, a rooted flow.
Then I became a winged pilgrim, intestinal offerings
bumping along the ground as I flew.
My ambivalence worked my negations on looms.
Now I am gutless,
peristaltic in ascent,
radiant with memories of menstrual wastes.

Sitting under this outcropping, thinking at
the speed of limestone, I hear waiters below
struggling with diners, diners sparring with food,
a breeze sweeps up the sound of gardeners
locked in combat with shoots, swimmers intercleaved
with the spermatic flex of yesterday's wind.

A workman shears the earth's head, revealing
its timed skull, limestone time, openly dead,
not closed like we are, fighting with
everything we touch, trying to become headless
gods below the horizon, gods of the mystical hollow earth.

The reason you came here
has dropped away. You have butter on your fly.
You write because your beanstalk is raced by giant Jacks.
Because the midden strata at Laugerie Haute
strikes you as the origin of fashion.
At best, a zipper meshes dualities,
the zipper of the mind interlocking its own bite.
How moving it is to hear someone say
something veined with
reflective and suffered pleasure.

Awake as if drunk with the last dream,
ready to remake whatever
—my life, my vision, my love—
to see through is to have nothing to resist,
is to lose the resistance for which one secretly lives.
Poetry from the beginning is posited,
based, on resistance,   is a work *against*,
whether with flint or quill
it is to convert one's boring into a lateral spell,
an ecstatic wandering in which one lives
as if weightless on the hunch of a finger tip—
hunchwork   wondrous release of the body
poised on the burin of itself.

1999

IN HAPPINESS A POWER

There is in happiness a power that stems the maggot tide.
And not just dying, but the maggotry men invice in life.

When Caryl's face smiles forth, I think I briefly pass on,
or pass into the chill of passing crossed by permanence.

1999

THE TUSK HOTEL

Lonely to death, totally engaged,
lifeless, snoring, I round the carnal cape and
bet on Africa, as the rift in my design,
the "western wind" by which I was driven from the trees.

Every poem could end here,
pointedly, on the ground,
yet every poem begins here,
baby sling packed with amethyst and memory.

Backdrop for the play called *My Unknowable Death*.
Backdrop billowing forth, elephantine peril.

We're registered in The Tusk Hotel.
Caryl and I share a double with an abysside view.
Every morning, in spite of what life is,
we ensnout our masks and ripple through the Flood.

1999

Light from the TV burnishing Caryl's shoulder.
11 P.M., she's on her side, head pillowed,
I'm sitting up, stroking her back,   so the light
purls, or hesitates on her round
then greys into whatever,   I don't know...

I'm entranced by the tenderness I feel,
the almost-far-reach of TV light
furling, it seems, or pearling,
a ridge, a radiance, I'm so dumped in myself
thinking of the Dordogne,   some rock off which to travel...

What is this tenderness that glows right before sleep?
There is something disgusting about it
(a voice says) if not expressed during the day.
It is the eternal brink of lying down to sleep
(another voice) for you might not wake up,
she might not,   something in you says goodbye
every night before you crest—

into what? As if the day has been so active
it takes 11 P.M. to elicit humble love and worry,
sweetness and broken cordage...

2000

Gleaming, half-housed in steel sheath, the debrider's rotary blade whirring, resecting scar tissue, flaked-away rotator cuff.

It is inserted via a trocar pushed through the portal cut into her shoulder.

Apparition of a whirly, round eye on the debrider as it swivels caught in the arthroscopic beam.

Octopus or shark eye.

The debrider now a kind of monster in a feeding frenzy.

Blobs of bloody tissue stream the video screen.

Feathery tissue flurries.

The mowing of Caryl's ocean floor.

From another cut that appears to have no trocar the cauterizer appears, spurting bubbly water as it prongs up tissue.

Amber tufts throbbing by threads.

Tentacle-sucker-like bubble chains.

Rose shadings, yellow, bronze, in the white densities.

What happens to her deadened pain?

She's out, but her body's experiencing what I see.

Faced by the ungraspable within my own making.

Again the debrider, a ferret into the baby rat nest of her shoulder, whirring forth what the cauterizer tore up.

Watching this silent 20 minute video as you rest upstairs.

Blood-tinged snow chamber.

Cave amber.

As if I am looking at calcite draperies.

Cosquer being ensouled.

Orchid-like tissue bunches, almost loose, the cauterizer hooking up cartilage.

Threads of blood from her humerus head spurting, snaking out, vanishing.

Humerus head framed by the octagonal lens.

Fleecy white skull.

The moon.

The debrider shaves what looks like skull hair—not head hair but feathery wisps clinging to a skull.

Beautiful grassy white skull.

The debrider mowing and mowing.

For a moment: craters   rilles   ghostly inverted nipples.

The burr with square steel cleats rasping her acromion, trimming its hooked edge that cut into a tendon and caused her such pain.

"Frozen shoulder," which for a month she could not move.

Others will watch arthroscopic surgery inside their beloved's body.

Others will wince and draw close to "heavy debridement and acromioplasty."

Others will be given access to the body's interior grottos, its blood strings jetting, its moon and cave scapes, the sudden black fissures that check the eye.

Others will project and know how I felt, respectful of projection while attempting to see through to the images forever emerging, as if trying to make contact with us, where projection and something there and emerging meet, as an image is glimpsed in an undulant dimly-lit cave.

Yes, others before me, by juniper wick, watching creatures emerge, recede, Cosquer, 18,000 B.P., auks, seals, jellyfish, there and not there, spirits receding, emerging, in ochre outlines, blood-ribboned snow chamber.

Before a screen, outside your invasion, and the source of your invasion.

Alone and with you in this wild disturbance of your sense of physical unity.

Fox-like rotary saw in the hen house of your scar tissue.

Rapacious correction of the destruction of your enjoyment of life.

for Mark Mijnsbergen

2000

Said to Caryl at day's end: this is home,
and then an aurochs wavered, or
was it shadow across the bulging
Les Eyzies cliffs? Bulging stone,
bulging horns, curling home. Lotal twisting
chambers where zero flexes.

The gate is open. Miller perceived some of the fix: *
paradise is not of the French, is truly
Upper Paleolithic, of the Dordogne,
of the poets, to be reclaimed by the poets.

This is perfect, I felt,
making love in our farm apartment, spring 1974.
A bit north of Les Eyzies, the enchantment begins:
shadowing the curling single lane road,
moist outcroppings of limestone walls.
Out of the rock endlessly fabling.
Root wisps, black stains. My aurochs ancestor hovers.
We share a phallus, as if part of a carousel.
Slowing for a curve, up and down,
my aurochs ancestor on our turning shaft,
bird and fruit bodies on a common bend.
Uroboric carousel. Drifting into origin, or
into origin's coals, into the lifting off heat,
the dusty run-over, the psychic gore
alive in such caves as Combarelles.
It was in connecting with the mystery of a land
underscored by the most important thing I could learn
—the origin of poetry—
that bowled me under.

They entered earth to rise again.
Inside stone, no animals, blackness without stars,
By juniper flame, honey-colored ramparts
to be incised, brooded, crawled away from
back to tundra and frosty light.
Did this "round trip" resonate *resurrection?*
Did stone animals imply mortality could be broached?
Was scratching an enclosing line *resurrection?*
A proto-shamanic dream of healing form?
"I conceive and depict the bison I am to be"
Or was the marking of a bison as slain *resurgence,*
    a form of "resurrection"
uncomplicated by our "rising from the dead"?
I am suspended over such questions
    as over an abyss.

Line animating stone. Incipient alphabet.
At what point did the sound lark
split open to reveal a letter,
inkfaceting our dreams?

I crack open to find my
life. As if the word

stone were nut,
I must invent the kernel,

there must be life in my shell.
My rite must yield. Unlike Olson,

I do not "hunt among stones."
I hunt inside stone.

I work the manganese that holds, withholds.
In the end I hunt for more end,

of the beginning
I scrutinize each ochre start.

To be in paradise and to feel paradise at
an impossible remove. To crawl
the cemeteries of paradise. Rock
once alive, god bone.
Flint burin then as a tattoo needle to
    a human back today.

I sit on a green metal bench on
now-called *Rue de la préhistoire*, facing
Hotel Cro-Magnon.

To get at the round,
the jagged round of any situation,
how we fence with the udders of snow!

A complex of rainy perfection clears itself through me.

Packed with perpetuity's
negation, with swaying wordflora,
the alpha veil still refuses to unravel.

2001

IX

from *An Alchemist with One Eye on Fire*

(2006)

In bed, looking up at the light-peppered dark,
as if the ceiling were not there, as if I were staring into
my own staring. Tinctured absence. A grassy sweet aroma
    lifting off Caryl.
                            In the zone between
here and not here, the lunar curtain parts,
as in a Matta painting, there are tilting astro-planes,
each a kind of ark, or flight deck,
one covered with snow has standing mammoths—it tilts,
slides through a plane crawling with reptiles.
I think of my brain with its reptile stem, its mammal hood,
I see a bear humping a crocodile,
try to get between them, to push them apart, open a space for a nascent
    self.
In the zone between bear and crocodile, what will I be?
A bear-headed croco-boy? A croc-headed baby bear?
I screw off my head, toss it into the dark
—will it become a raven? A large bee?
Headless, I watch through my chest the air swarming with spirits,
Nora! How is it where you are?
"Busy. Bodies rushing in and out, did you know Cheney is full of reptile
    blood,
and driven by the mind of an Incan child abandoned on a mountain
300 years ago? A child spitting up
lizard blood, freezing to death in a stone shrine,
now can you grasp Cheney's infantile wrath?
Bush's secret is his tiny tail, leathery, about 3 inches,
like the tip of a Komodo Dragon's tail—
note how he is always heavily guarded from behind,
for if some joker pulls his tail, a long yellow forked tongue will spurt
    from his face—
very few humans are pure human, most are occupied by
bizarre creature combines, the dead and the extinct pack the air

unseen from a senses-five perspective.
I have a horse's cock now, and I'm planning on using it soon,
I'm going to fuck one of those dead art dealers
who "fucked" me, then help her open a gate to your plane,
watch the fun as she gives birth in a few brains to some mustang
    raillery!"

She screamed with laughter—then I heard a strong, central suck,
something in the dark had gulped her back.

The pepper-dotted room began to undulate.
I thought of the veils within "No one has lifted her veil,"
    revelation, to draw back the *velum*,
to hear dead Nora through a spiritual gate,
to see the Dogon earth naked and speechless,
without language, a fiber skirt the first word,
speech as plaited fiber, "speech lattice,"
or Christ nailed on the cross as the arrested word,
vulva as lower mouth issuing red fiber,
a many-colored Isis rainbow, net within which
my fate is entangled, where the Nora spirits can be heard.

Then I saw a black-capped facial netted "full body veil"
sitting, as if on the Kabul bridge, begging.
"No one has lifted her veil" became
"At no time have women not been oppressed."
My heart tore left and right, I tried to peel
the true from the truthful, the rainbow flashed
a central scarlet band—I knew it was the Wawilak Sisters' menstrual
    blood
circulating within rock python venom.
I saw ripples of albino babies, each with a red or silver balloon,
setting off across the rainbow bridge for
the argentine body of the moon—

the Kabul bridge beggar roared back,
burkha, menstrual never shed,
chrysalis of a monstrous anti-metamorphosis
"sewed up in a hammock, with a small opening so she can breathe"
—are all of us, enclosed in the world of five senses, mummified pupas?
The beggar hissed: "Your bars, spaced and wall-papered, allow some
   comfort and expanse.
Mine, wrapped around me, nearly cover my eyes . . ."

I turned and sought sleep's stagnation,
respite from the sear of intersecting planes.

2004

PAUSE

I hear you close the bathroom door.

An absence-weighted balance lifts into presence.

Is the source of human bondage the fear of loss?

Now that you are showering, cables of water convert, ghost-loaded suds,
Rabelais's mane furls from Aphrodite's thigh . . .

The patter of my tattered tale, swirled drain. Rising like a sewer
of precognition: Is the real death the death I am preoccupied with
here and now?

The sound of drying, the clay in the cloth, the veil that will rend me
before I reach the end.

To pull out the last part of myself left inside, to get all of myself
born.

2004

TRANSFORMATIONAL GRADATIONS

My innate Indiana tendency is
to tiptoe on a razorblade
and to feel the Presbyterian tingle
masochistically up my spine.

Poetry has been to compel the razored toe tip blade
to hybridize,
to allow an underworld
uprush to fruit through the root twine.

So, who is here at 6 A.M. this morning?

Persephone, kneeling on a pomegranate half,
Eros seated on her shoulder.
I read their hand signs to mean: "Flow! Conceive!
The scission of the Mother into mother and daughter
is to be found in the abyss of the seed!"

I stooped to inspect the Dionysian upsurge
spreading octopodally through my brain.
I sensed the lost half of myself: my dog, when I was 12,
car-smashed Sparkie, who gave birth to the vine.

Then, in the spectral interior of a cypress, I saw Rilke,
in his death bed, a blackened strawberry,
attended by a kindly bedbug nurse,
his marmalade-soft face still poised in praise—

as the smoking gate moved into presence,
Rainer exchanged verse letters with an 18-year-old Austrian,
Erika Mitterer.
Persephone's verdure and her duration
were now layered into all his transformational gradations.

Not "Here Lies," he wrote,
but "Here Lives," happy to feel the soil
pulse his soot shaft, that cypress affirmation,
overplus of arising
with which the beloved gleams up.

Bellagio, 4 November 2004

FROM A TERRACE

"We have destroyed Fallujah
so as to convert it"
overheard in the breeze by the massive broken oak.

Sunday lakeside serenity.
People with their skin burned off, hospitals bombed by
an us I bleed in
psychically, my government
completely corrupt.

To be sixty-nine now, "old style"
shot through with fecal sorrow,
bedbugs in my mouth, us-bugs, my whole mouth bugged.

The oak leans into blue rapture
over roily, white-capped
gasoline-turquoise water,
its leaves sort of dribble about in the air.

The carnage cloaked by
television's visibility sterility
—is this less sterile?

Small lichen saucers indented into
hundred year old bark,
noble whorled
    wood showing
through, as I would like to.

This asunder-written No to
the interventional might of America,
millions raked into invisible piles,
the 9/11 blowback a drop

in the bucket blood of
Guatemala
Nicaragua
Serbia
Iraq
    How terrible
    to not feel pure
    grief for the
    WTC dead, how
terrible to have to
contextualize to be honest.

Across Lake Como
mountains rest on the waterfold,
slant shadowed rows. They are
mammoth heads with verdant folded eyes,
beautiful, meaningless
                in
an extinction-tinctured view.

Man driven by hate for what he is,
a lost puppy bowl
mother-licked, father-interfered.

—O breathe and just
enjoy the warmth on writing hand,
the church bell tower below,
its innocent stone crossed by
ravens in the shape of men

    —I can't
    I twist here
mentally gibbeted,
particle of a warrior form,
hell done in my nationality,

the Ho- Ho-
san
ta
cackle-embedded warp in being.

Some axial release holds sway
in the after-
ring of a re-
    immobilizing bell.

Bellagio, 14 November 2004

The Last Supper as a watermelon feast,
each disciple with a tequila-plugged slice
and Jesus already with Isis in his eyes,
be slurped be slain—
to travel as a seed within another's imagination,
arked with lithic freight.

The lunar light dims,
the stone softens. Are we still in
a pagan/Nazarene distillery?
Si, Hart Crane murmurs, from his trench off Tampico,
the stable is a flowchart of Jesus and bison exchange,
yet all takes place in an amphitheater
carved from the rudiments of shamanic protocol.
I hear it in the postponed Ann Arbor sky
as pre-emptive jets pop time.
So it's bolgia within bolgia, a new Comedy—
cosmic structure no longer vortices and trinity,
rather: animating socks, suspenders, a laundry
bag of the mind. Fascism would rinse all to
techno-sheen. CEOS living in platinum grenades
littering planetary shanty-towns.

Note where your first line has taken you,
how each image appears to encyst another,
so that the poem is a mental cave under formation,
the political as the grit in the image water push,
anatomies reconstituting as thresholds,
chalice-shaped cul-de-sacs, the mind anchored and
willy-nilly. Stay aware of the 850 million starving—
such may help keep you honest when the self-censor

purrs: shut up. Unbuckle his tongue from
the door on your heart, show the world gash
but keep it in your own veins.

Like pinheads in a sunny glade,
JC and his gang are now in round dance,
watched by cranes. Dionysus is near
but so is Ashcroft, while Mother Teresa
cuddles a gigantic gangrenous ear.
Carnival is hardly farewell to the flesh.
In imaginal revision, it is the lambent stampede of
autumn's rash, or Persephone rampant in
the gray November grass. It is the discharge
as the teeth of consciousness sink into
the etymology of gum
releasing depth charges into the mind's ancient hives. Manifesto:
I am here like a scarab rolling my *crottin* through
death's doorway ablaze with billions of golden grubs.
This is the trail I leave,
my wobble weave, analphabetic Lascaux.

2005

A white road crosses its motionless storm,
vernal pool where frogs live trapped in archaic hail.
I've wasted too much time with moonlight
and now sit gazing through the small hole in my dress at Monday's
   naked nail.

Manchuria, I feel your invasion!
Suddenly we are ourselves, without brushes, lawn mowers, or saloons.
I confess the crimes against my monsoon self—
these chess words, slippery with blood,
they are my pistons, my petrol, the fits of memory scrawled in a hulk
   log.
Cockroaches cross the deck   moving from Picasso to snowman.

The thought lost to the eyes of a unicorn reappears in a dog's bark.
Dressed in resistance, I laud the most important figure in the United
   States:
Mickey Mouse, legislator of urban alcohol adieu.
My courtesan instructs me in the wrecked balcony of her arms.
The idol? A chessboard of truffles and snow.
Unlike comrade Huidobro, I'm a whittled id,
a city hall boss standing on prison steps,
thriving like a burnt out sun, a sun which never imagined a lamp.
O summation of Chile! A man loves only his obscure wife.

To run with the nectar, to bypass alarm.
Is not joy somehow canopic?
What moves in the air: ways that are not the way,
the whey of snow, way of the flayed flake.
My slash is yours, riptides amassing.
O Chilean summation! I poke into the moon's watery lace.
Between sequitur and non sequitur falls the imagination.
"There is grandeur in this life, with its several powers."

Spare the gestures. Nothing for show.
I am neither aft nor fore, nor foreafter,
nor ever to be afterforementioned again.

I hear Neruda—he's a langoustine of a man,
a violet maiden in multicolored fleece,
both hands paralyzed from swatting political lice.
Neruda! A swiller of a gale, a snood disguised as a church,
rutabaga in cleats, something found on the beach which,
as you fondle it, urinates in your heart. Neruda,
what is truly to be found under his tray of forceps and sledges?

Passing mons Veneris clouds.
The translucence of human flesh.
Ceremonial lenses made of ice, brought down from Andean peaks.
A rainbow defective in a single hue.
The spider *Dolomedes urinator* which runs simultaneously in two worlds.
The sound of air in a cave.
Sensation of longing for an eclipse powerful enough to darken death.
Changes in the light initiated by a stranger's arrival
—Chilean marvels, equal to the Surreal.

I prepared. Waited to be called.
Cut logs. Laid a hearth. Burned my valentines.
Visited the Incan adoritories on Mount Llullaillaco.
Examined the grave goods of The Prince of Mount Plomo.
Which is to say: I prepared. Set the caldron boiling,
spliced postcards from Isla Negra with photos of infants left out in the
    snow.
Mastered myself. Arrived in Harar with only 10 camels.
Sketched each waterfall. Took out no personal ads.
I faced fear, then clarity, then power.
Tonight I have a meeting with the last enemy of the man of knowledge.
In his uncorked left testicle, it has been raining for years.

2005

SURVEILLANT VEILS

For Andrew Joron

I reached through art to touch ensouled stone,
a once
fully-embraced ever
now ensouled in never.

Organically, I am encased in never.
Creatively, I neverize
to reconstitute ever.

All the elements of this wall,
according to George Oppen, have come
from eternity.

Why, when I look at that thought, do I see
a Malawi prison floor covered with
bedraggled men,

or recall
the sorrow charged and twisted face of an Iraqi
clawing at her 9-year-old son's tiny coffin?

It is good that her ululation
makes me ashamed of my own fulfillment,

good too that first light can still be imagined,
suppurant as it is
with the wounds in that child's box.

There is rage in the body's sequences—

cancer cells, immortalizing, divide
until they kill their host.

Eternity is pregnant with
the mortal tern.

2006

COMBINED OBJECT

Listening to Caryl sleep,
thinking of the cross-hatching in the 7-mile verticality of her living,
the Challenger Deep
as her mind makes its way across the 40,000-mile mid-ocean ridge,
across abyssal plains and canyons in tree-shaped networks,
across the hadal trench off Peru containing the oldest water in the
    world,
her young life, which she remembers so keenly,
like a die tumbling among arabesques of leafy sea dragons with seaweed
    wings
trailing kelp blends, green clouds pouring
from the sides of wounded fish, millions of image trains,
I am on one, looking down at the stratified trains below,
one called Venus's-flower-basket, the passengers:
shrimp, crabs, worms, and clams. Multiple water spindles containing
water fairy proms, high school friends being reborn,
I am following the course of her sleep
through sea pastures of whirring diamond saws,
under a cowl of pelican eels,
in full flight, astride the thorax of a four-winged flyer
she carries away with her, in her trailing skirts,
a web filled with tiny men, drowned islands, radiolarian ooze,
at 800 feet, only the deepest, blackest blue,
the ocean of her sleep breaks over me, like light gravel,
sensation of being in a horse's mouth, a deeper breathing is forming—
the infinite, far from being a suburb of the gods,
is an eternal surpassing, removed from any essential halt.
I see her standing before a glass stairway, a Jacob's ladder
with more steps than she could ever climb in three lifetimes,
they disappear like bubbles in champagne,
now she is struggling against
suctions and pulls, against stretched webs, against curving spidery legs,
she breaks free—what nightmare did she just slip?—

she becomes navigation itself, shining with a pure white flame,
passing over foaming ditches, wheeling ravines,
I imagine her retinue: dwarf plankton,   flamingo tongues,
coccoliths giving the water a milk glow,   bristlefooted worms
patterned with colored rosettes,   arrow worms like fine threads of glass,
pteropods with winged feet,   salmon-pink winged slugs,
salps like little barrels, pulsating, a mouth at each end—
out of the warm, dimly lit, dilute broth of a shallow Silurian sea
a jointed-legged proto-scorpion,   ancestor of all on land.
How do without a head? How present all edges of the body
equally to the outside world? A poem without subject,
all parts of which surprise and interlock, a poem with twenty centers,
all muscular and avid, each word dense, full in itself, a nest,
a sound of wood crackling in the fireplace, a shiver without skin,
each word an outpost, a courier, monkey words
feeling the earthquake coming before I do.
Going through myself,   is it her heart that I am hearing?
—she gasps—silence—rebreathes   ka   ka   ka   ka
suddenly, she is other than herself,
rake tines rise from her brow projecting brain energy into the
    atmosphere,
impaling celestial hexes, they glow pale blue in the dark
like thin upraised arms; I pass slowly through them,
standing in my Protestant canoe, alone, stiff, an erection curving
from a golden pubic beard—behind my back,
the Absolute, straight as a wall.
I am possessed by a sole idea: that snow is ceaselessly falling
obliquely through all of us, on each flake
the population of the Beyond cluster
like minute beardless seals, or albino cougars,
spherical, knots of unearthly calm
sailing on an invisible current. As my monoxylon
sinks slowly into dead space, the dark is flecked with one-winged birds,
with barkless trees, and I also see the full squalor of the sea,
the rubbish of a thousand boats daily fished up, winnowed,
and thrown straight back—crushed into the netted haul

the new mermaid, limbs twisted among dogfish, whiting, and plaice,
a deflated life-sized sex doll, hermit-crabs inside
her red-rimmed mouth. O sea layered into my dreams,
the daily rewound trash,   visitations of the dead,   Tenochtitlan
thoroughfares,   extra-terrestrial spider queens,
cork-screwing flights through kaleidoscopic barriers
to land by a nightstand and be watched by
two swans,   who are being watched by
two ocelots,   who are being watched by two snakes,   watched by
sixteen triangles,   watched by countless staring eyes.
Cessation of the mirage of the finite,
illusory conviction that anything concluded exists—
call it re-embarkation, call it a multiple leaving.
I have for shade a whole spread of hyena shadow.
I am my own ground, slashed, a wild sea of ground.
There is a silent breaking of waves,   spots of light,   sensation of fissure,
a flowing furrow,   I see Caryl gliding through
the infinite little curlicues in its flanks,
when I graze her I graze a deep pit of joy.

2006

X

from *Reciprocal Distillations*

(2007)

[Bacon Studies]

You want to recover the original wholeness?
Re-enter chaos.
Kill your own profane existence.
Become a chocolate skull, wrapped in white silk, teeth sewn shut, sockets
   shell-stoppered.
The auroral instant prior to existence?
Death is a rite of passage, not an end.
In flight, an erection becomes the World Tree.
I am a crow perched in the foliage of my scattered skeleton.
From the mud under Satan's nails I have made a mound on which to rest.
An animal goes into a cave, re-emerges as a man.
The animal on the wall: earth cosmetics, cosmopathy, the make-up of
   inner space.
Spirits of the head.
Brow of unpolished wood.
My left eye a rouge of blood and sperm.
Eyeball: a rabbit balled-up in a cage.
A Mohawk hairjolt stiffened with soot.
The inner head, beat-up version of somebody else.
The whap in the jaw, slug of the male jaw, castrated bullet of the
   prognathus jaw.
Eye as moon crater.
The target of the eye.
Eye closed under a brain kindling geysers and splitting fontanels.
I am jawless with long, long ears, my throat extends to my eyes.
Spirits of the head.
Mustache of drool and loam.
Face of waves, of serpentine mobs.
Aviary face, eyrie of coons and owls.
Shore of the eye, quicksand of a look.
And then George Dyer—a spirit head if there ever was one—

turned to show in profile
a root-chopped, tusk dug continent,
issue bandaged with eyelids and whiskers.

Dead Dyer with bumblebee lips.
Dyer with a snow cone blood picked nose.
Skull with nimbus of Germanic steel and gold.
Merry Xmas, Mr. Mayhem, I'm here to interrogate the nimbus of your
　　lungs.
Here to enjewel your ribs with metal buttons, velvet flaps.
Head in rotary division, a single eye, mouth, and terrine of ears.
God has withdrawn into the Devil's Skull from which he fires
　　spider filaments into the glory hole of mankind.
Within the face, Bosch working the pump: mouth slashes up into
　　eye, eye bruises over, pickled garden of shredded amanitas and
　　blind sables.
Pit of the face, cemetery pitted against chaos.
Brain as a tub of marrow filled with the diced hands of scientists.
Head of bone, of spirit, unbroken head.
Head destroyed and intact as a granite egg.
Lynched tongue-bunched neck invisible to the boys setting fire to its
　　toes.
Fly of the human eye excreting as it broods.
Snowshoe of George Dyer's mouth planted in ice.
How much white can a head take? Can it assimilate supremacy, heaven?
Can it take on the reddened battlefield of man's pincer gaze at pluck
　　with his brother?
Can I make the unsayable bark to verify that racial whitewash will never
　　succeed in gating the community of souls?
Head on its hair body, homuncular head, alchemical gaze of a hair body
　　through which the putty of the face mills.

1999

There is in Michaux an emergent face/non-face always in formation. Call it "face before birth." Call it our thingness making faces. Call it tree bole or toadstool spirits, *anima mundi* snout, awash in ephemerality, anti-anatomical, the mask of absence, watercolor by a blind child, half-disintegrated faces of souls in Hades pressing about the painter Ulysses-Michaux as, over his blood trench of ink, he converses with his hermaphroditic muse…

Ink beings spear themselves into rupturing elfin thumbs.

The doubles enrubble, cobble ruins, gobble gobble, aerial brains.

Zigzagging corpuscles surprised by a bacterial whinny.

Reintegration at the cost of re-entry.

Black sand dense on white ground. Mites. Mites in mitosis.
    Mitochondria. Miscible mites. Mitomitosalchondrialmaze.

A gangrenous, thousand-windowed penile haze.

Backed by scarlet maggots, by teeny-weenies, by fetal corn flakes.

A glacial stadium enraged by a torii invagination.

Clothespins cutting up with squidy lattices, no, phosphenic lesions, yes,
    cruciliquinixies.

Once razed, the mind's hive releases mastodontal honey.

Mescalinian nets through which infant marmalade englobes.

I am free in Michaux, free to be coccolithic, a gas candy bar, whatever…*

Better: everwhat. What forever what.

Being unbound. Unbound being bonded.

Ever in the state of *what!*

Everwhat sun. Everwhat dust.

A powder of points. Veil

pulled back, the revelation is lithic velum.

A line encounters a line, evades a line.

A line waits, hopes, a line rethinks a face.

Ant-high lines. Ant-visibles streaming through lines.

A melodic line crosses twenty stratigraphic fractures.

A line germinates. Martyr-laughable lines.

Lines gaslighting lines. Lines budding on a dune.

A dream of paradise: lines in conversation with their liminal selves.

The linen of lines, worn, lineage of proliferating life lanes.

The Minotaur as a horned line.

Bitter combat at the center of a line.

What is the center of a line?

Where the whatever folds, becomes everwhat.

Ramose, lachrymose hollow of lines, sisters of stain.

Stains immaculate in their sordid, humid bellies.

Jonah-Michaux in the moray mescaline belly.

Aimé Césaire's "stiff wine of moray eels," overboard cast slaves harvested
by morays.

Dry furnace of a landscape. Stampeding tacks, lassoed by Jesus, lassoed
by Sartre.

The scolopendra line. The cockchafer line.

Lines milling insectile to their rodent spoils.

The Last Judgment performed by worms.

The tick faces in gorilla traces.

Lines in reason's glare seething with kettle life.

Nematodes in round dance on a hyena vagina.

2000

The contours of certain cave walls invite engagement.
Hosts in the wall, bald, convex,
hold vigil over mental drift. To populate
the moonscape of a wall. To draw in lit craters
the squirm and reel of incarnate trial.
Their bellies hang low, their shoulders
rise and sink like pistons, each step is placed
soundlessly. *Panthera spelea*. Larger than
the African lion. Larger even
than the Amur tiger. Maneless. Craning forward.
Cheeks bulging. Heads telescoping out of heads.
Eyes dilated. Knowingly, lovingly rendered.
Deftly shaded. Bone structure and depth.
Some are sheer outline, limestone showing through.
73 in all. One with blubber lips evokes
a hominid cartoon. The monster of God sensed
as manivore. Deity as predator. Jehovah's foreskins.
Zeus Lykaios. Behind sacralized violence,
the trauma of being hunted, and eaten. Check this:
animal holocaust of the late Ice Age
corresponds with the rise of war.
Cowl of the master dark,
its red breath heading west
toward a tilting vertical
"totem" of bison heads, spitted
like big furry bugs. Baby mammoth with
wheel feet. Hoofs seen from below? Full moons?
Body shaded smoky tan. Over it
a massive bison emerging from a fissure.
Two turned-toward-us bison heads,
one on lion haunch, one on lion shoulder.
Carnivore tattoos. Targets. Earliest body decor.
Drink to me only with thine

fangs. Energy I would induct. In dank
scrape light, as if Arshile Gorky
traced his life dark as lion space,
or Hans Bellmer, his erotic unending line
alive with orgasm's blocked flue.
Enkidu. Humbaba. Teelget. Hercules at Nemea.
Grendel "bit into his bone-lappings,
bolted down his blood
and gorged on him in lumps, leaving his body
utterly lifeless, eaten up
hand and foot." Astarte on lion back.
Artemis with a bull scrotum necklace.
Rhino with 8 oversized curving parallel horns,
as if drawn by Marcel Duchamp.
Rhino Descending a Lion Stare.
Stuttering horns. River pour of meated miles,
horns trestling dawn as red deer foam through.
See-saw of rhino bodies. "Central stripes"
make them look like "armored" Indian rhinos.
Sketchbook of this wall. Started, thwarted.
Body parts in fugal maze. Sacrificial diagram.
Palimpsest of beasts and humans. No finish.
But finish is near. As I stand on this aluminum ramp,
a CEO is stretching his eyeball around the planet
like an interstellar Santa, bag full and off to Saturn.

2005

He shook the Counter-Reformation
decorum out of *tableau vivants*,
eliminating from painting
saccharin distortion and ecclesiastic agit-prop.
If by "the human" we mean actual lives
kicking up dust as they speed toward us
shattering idealistic frames,
then Caravaggio, like Vallejo's *Human Poems*,
produced human paintings.
A young whore in red dress dumped on a simple bed:
"The Death of the Virgin,"
The painting refuses the porcelain vagina.
There is no Jesus appearance, just Carmelite men,
convulsed, confused. Whore or virgin, she is laid out,
feet bare, arms and hands dangling
carnivorous, red shadow. The canopy bucks, collapses,
stung through by sin and atonement—
Caravaggio could not completely
slip the Christian corset.
He tore it, revealed its sweated inner lining.
In the destroyed "Resurrection"
it is said that he depicted Christ as
an emaciated convict climbing out of a pit.
What was this painter's engine?
What does his strong room look like?
The 1602 "John the Baptist in the Wilderness"
(with a gorgeous, naked "Baptist" pulling his ram to him,
a gesture rich with animal coitus),
and the "Victorious Cupid" (a naked fuck-boy with wings,
offering himself joyously to the viewer)
would not have been realized by a heterosexual painter.
He painted the Baptist eight or nine times,
at first using Biblical trappings to be able to work with

adolescent flesh. The story of someone
living on locusts and wild honey,
shaman-like with his lamb or ram familiar,
a moral loudmouth, perfect grist for
a despot's mill, is of little concern.
These attributes only register on Malta,
site of Caravaggio's second undoing, 1607.
He arrives with a capital ban on him (for the accidental
killing of Ranuccio Tomassoni who
provoked him over a small debt), meaning:
anyone can sever his head and present it to a judge
for a reward anywhere under Papal jurisdiction.
With the image of the severed head,
we open his strong room. There is the 1597 "Medusa,"
with a shocked, young Caravaggian face,
the 1599 "Judith and Holofernes" jetting blood
as the repulsed but turned on Judith
saws through the neck bone (the fact that the model
for Judith is a 17-year-old whore transforms
the Biblical setting into a brothel).
There are three "Davids with the Head of Goliath,"
the finest of which, done in 1609 or 1610
after the painter's face had been slashed outside
a Naples tavern, depicts a pained, even sorrowing, David
holding out the head of—Caravaggio!
David withdraws, with his other arm,
his sword from his crotch. Implication:
the beheading of Goliath/Caravaggio is David's self-castration,
or, the Goliath/Caravaggio head is David's phallus.
Tomassoni bled to death from a sword-nicked penis.

On Malta, he paints "The Beheading of Saint John the Baptist"
as payment for becoming a Knight of Obedience.
Prison yard dark, 17th century Valletta.
Night in brownish-black settles through,
just enough rakes of light to see, in silence,

what men robotically visit on each other.
The Baptist lamb-trussed on the dirt,
neck partially slit. The executioner,
gripping a fistful of long Baptist hair,
yanks the head toward us, as, with his right hand,
he pulls a small knife from his leather belt sheath.
His rigid left arm is vertical architecture—
in the deltoids, triceps, radial forearm muscles,
contoured with amber shadow, ivory light,
I sense a sculptural Last Judgment
(it is as if the Ivory Tower rose from the ground of
the Baptist's "rape"). The executioner's
white bloomer folds have been painted so that
between his legs a phallic loop dangles,
inches over the Baptist's red cloak-covered rump.
Under this cloak: his lamb pelt,
the two forked legs of which jut out
as if from his groin. They are vulva-evocative.
The castrational humiliation of beheading
underscored by implicit buggery.
Baptist as catamite. Under the blood
oozing from the cut neck Caravaggio has
—the one time in his life—
signed: "f michelAn," directly from the blood blob.
In what spirit does the painter sign?
"f" = "fra," brother—and as a man,
condemned to duplicate the Baptist's fate—
and as a martyr to his own cause
which is, in the spirit of Herodian denunciation,
to tell the visual truth, to penitentially argue,
as an artist, the glacial contradiction between
transcendental hope and squalid reality.

After 1608, along with the Goliath/Caravaggio head,
there are two "Salomés with the Baptist's Head,"
including the executioner and the old woman witness

who, like a compressed Greek chorus,
holds her own "head oh head oh head don't leave me now!"
over the Malta beheading. The three float
as partially bodied heads in inky blackness about
the head-charged platter. The heads of Salomé and granny
implicitly share the same torso
as if making up a whole. Given Caravaggio's
fixation on the Baptist and Goliath,
with the signature and the painter's ruined face,
a dyadic Caravaggio is evoked,
a Baptist-Goliath, two heads sprouting off
the same severed neck, or
off the same severed erection
—while there are soft penises in the oeuvre,
there are no erections, so erection may be
the undepictable "thing," in Vallejo's words,
Caravaggio's "dreadful thing thing,"
generating the decapitational obsession.
Neck as erection, stem connecting
root to bloom, yes, but also the demonic link between
damnation-pocked head and runaway body,
this head that cannot really "lose itself"
as long as the neck yokes.

Four months after becoming a Knight,
Caravaggio is said to have been thrown into
the Fort Sant'Angelo oubliette,
to have gotten out of this eleven-foot-deep "hole,"
and to have sailed to Syracuse. There is
no record of his misdeed or crime on Malta,
nor how he was able to escape the "hole"
or who arranged his successful flight.
Peter Robb conjectures that the painter got caught
with one of the pages that his sponsor had
imported into unruly Valletta.
"Sex with a page would have been the ultimate outrage."

So they whisked Caravaggio out of there,
stripped him of his Knighthood (he left the island
without permission), leaving him to his own devices.

One of his Maltese paintings is a portrait of his sponsor,
Adolf de Wignacourt, Grand Master.
Next to Wignacourt in full armor is a page in red hose
looking directly at the painter (as very few subjects do),
holding Wignacourt's large red-plumed helmet.
If one takes the Goliath/Caravaggio head from David's grasp,
and superimposes it over the Grand Master's helmet,
Robb's conjecture is visualized. Grand Master
(surely the profoundly offended in this scenario),
delectable page, and Caravaggio as the Goliath-to-be,
a kind of *ménage à trois*. The unacknowledged
Maltese crime is, in its own way,
duplicated in July 1610. Caravaggio has disappeared,
his body is never found, all the official
reports of his demise make no sense.
Robb thinks he was murdered, probably by
people associated with the family of the man
he had killed. Martyrdom and salvation
are packed into the double Caravaggio head.
His paintings show, in compressed form,
a new self, released from Scholastic rote,
cloaked in Venetian red. Behind it:
desire for revelation, not of a transcendental ilk,
but of the soul made monstrous. Out of this full showing,
the true life of humanity—the poor, the tortured,
the saintly, the common, mother and child—may assemble.
Caravaggio gyrates on in me. I have,
in my stomach, some of his hermetic lantern shards,
undigestible martyrdom/salvation.

2002–2004

"A bootful of brain
set out in the rain"

—that is Paul Celan, Paris, 1969.
Could have been a GI snapshot, Vietnam.

Leon Golub rounded up four boots,
grew military torturer legs in them,
shiny brown pedestals on which
outside my bedroom door
a naked man hanging upside down is being whacked.

The avant-garde: the first upon the scene,
while the crime is still blazing, in Laverdant's 1848 definition:
"those who lay bare, with a brutal brush,
all the brutalities, all the filth, which are at the base of society."
The core of Golub's career is in its complex response to annihilation.
His comrades-in-arms are Goya at the Judas peephole
refusing to avert his gaze; Callot with his lynch tree, become
Billie Holiday's "strange fruit;" Dix's *Trench*; Picasso's *Guernica*;
Heartfield's angels in gas masks intoning:
"O du fröhliche, o du selige, gnadenbringende Zeit!"

1946: to transform the water-filled, wreckage-laden basement of
Western culture into a primordial bath,
a deep rolling masked blackness in milling assembly,
fangs studding the abstract with wilderness eyes.
Burnt, bird-legged Hamlet paws the air.

Golub sphinxes: half-swallowed, half-born, from *sphincter*,
orifice of the contracting angel, the nightmare choker.
How much degradation can an image take
and still, scraped into and from the canvas itself, manifest

this world's lethal embrace? The age
demanded an image, right? ok? here it is:
man as ruined monumentality. Reclining Youth:
his surface spatter mimicked by wound-trailed ground,
the limb-ghosted ground mimicked by white bone-like finality.
Gigantomachies: gods fighting in accelerated grimace,
syncopation of drunken, flayed cargo sloshing in an undestructable hold.

The Golub archetypal question:
if abstract color fields are peeled away,
what terrors will show through?

Golub's torturers know we accept their actions
as they accept our passive regard.
For most of us watch them from behind the great religious systems of
     compensatory evasion.

Golub asks: "Is it possible to export destruction, to burn and drive peas-
ants from their homes, and maintain the dream of the perfectibility of art?
Well, it is possible if art concerns itself with itself and does not dare to pre-
sume political meaning." (1969)

This is mental war, intellectual, determined
that art be somehow commensurate with international event.
Golub's South African blacks,
the chorus of a lifework, watch him and occasionally break into
     threnody.
They watch you, viewer, as do the Salvadoran white squads
stuffing car trunks with the corpse you will never escape.
The power principle behind evil,
so deeply a matter of the unconscious now
as to not know its own name, "down there,"
in close combat blood galaxies,
where one plus one is always one, a zero rack
encrusted with victimized rage.

A Golubian vision of the American flag:
napalm-blistered stripes so star-mangled they resonate burnt blue.

Oh fatality of expectation and freedom!
(Where other Americans saw angels beaming at Reagan,
Golub saw Contras destroying Nicaraguan grain silos, health centers,
    cutting off women's breasts)

In old age,
touched by death, the hand of the master sets free the fractured
    landscape,
the goal dims, a shredder abyss moves in,
dissociation tears apart time.
Skeletons wear the pants in the house of being.
Night street nodes of slicks, glare and wash out
mesh in crystalline smear.
Has any other artist ever depicted the zone of closure more trenchantly?
Golub in the underworld at 80,
still facing America's will to administer absolutely,
but now the prey of dogs, eagles, and lions,
as if man the predator had once again become prey.
Slogans honk, lit tableaux in a tunnel of horror.
"Another joker out of business"   "Raptor sanction"
Foresight become gore right. A sparagmos of the torn and the tearer.
Pink dog tongue fused dick diddling a female spectre.
In the new armpit showcase, skeletons toast hounds.
"Transmission garbled."
                    Leon Golub exits.
                    Now in my mind indelible,
        the corrosive flicker from his unstanchable wound.

                                            March–April, 2005

XI

The Tjurunga

begins as a digging stick, first thing the Aranda child picks up.
When he cries, he is said to be crying for
the tjurunga he lost
when he migrated into his mother.

Male elders later replace the mother with sub-incision.
The shaft of his penis slit, the boy incorporates his mother.

I had to create a totemic cluster in which imagination
could replace Indianapolis, to incorporate ancestor beings
who could give me the agility
—across the tjurunga spider's web—
to pick my way to her perilous center.

(So transformationally did she quiver,
     adorned with hearts and hands,
       cruciform, monumental,   *Coatlicue*
         understrapping fusion)

Theseus, a tiny male spider, enters a tri-level construction:
look down through the poem, you can see the labyrinth.
Look down through the labyrinth, you can see the web:

              Coatlicue

   sub-incision   Bud Powell

      César Vallejo

       the bird-headed man

Like a mobile, this tjurunga shifts in the breeze,
                    beaming at the tossing
foreskin dinghies in which poets travel.

These nouns are also nodes in a constellation called
Clayton's Tjurunga. The struts are threads
in a web. There is a life blood flowing through
these threads. *Coatlicue* flows into Bud Powell,
César Vallejo into sub-incision. The bird-headed man
   floats right below
                    the pregnant spider
               centered in the Tjurunga.

Psyche may have occurred, struck off
—as in flint-knapping—
an undifferentiated mental core.

My only weapon is a digging stick
the Aranda call *papa*. To think of father as a digging stick
strikes me as a good translation.

          The bird-headed man
is slanted under a disemboweled bison.
His erection tells me he's in flight. He drops
his bird-headed stick as he penetrates
    bison paradise.

The red sandstone hand lamp
abandoned below this proto-shaman
is engraved with vulvate chevrons—did it once flame
    from a primal sub-incision?

This is the oldest aspect of this tjurunga, its grip.

               Recalculating.

When I was six, my mother placed my hands on the keys.
At sixteen, I watched Bud Powell sweep my keys
into a small pile, then ignite them with "Tea for Two."
The dumb little armature of that tune
engulfed in improvisational glory
roared through my Presbyterian stasis.

"Cherokee"
"Un Poco Loco"
sank a depth charge into
    my soul-to-be.

This is a tjurunga positioning system.

We are now at the intersection of *Coatlicue*
and César Vallejo.

Squatting over the Kyoto benjo, 1963,
wanting to write, having to shit.

I discovered that I was in the position of Tlazoltéotl-Ixcuina.
But out of *her* crotch, a baby corn god pawed.

                    Recalculating.

        Cave of
Tlazoltéotl-Ixcuina.
The shame of coming into being.
As if, while self-birthing,
I must eat filth.

I was crunched into a cul-de-sac I could destroy
only by destroying the self
that would not allow the poem to emerge.

Wearing my venom helmet, I dropped, as a *ronin*, to the pebbles,
and faced the porch of Vallejo's feudal estate.
The Spectre of Vallejo appeared, snake-headed, in a black robe.
With his fan he drew a target on my gut.

Who was it who sliced into the layers of wrath-
enwebbed memory in which the poem was trussed?

Exactly who unchained Yorunomado
from the Christian altar in Clayton's solar plexus?

The transformation of an ego strong enough to die
by an ego strong enough to live.

The undifferentiated is the great Yes
in which all eats all
and my spider wears a serpent skirt.

That altar. How old is it?
Might it cathect with the urn in which
the pregnant unwed girl Coatlicue was cut up and stuffed?
Out of that urn twin rattlesnakes ascend and freeze.
Their facing heads become the mask of masks.
Coatlicue: Aztec caduceus.
The phallic mother in the soul's crescendo.

But my wandering foreskin, will it ever reach shore?

Foreskin wandered out of Indianapolis. Saw a keyboard, cooked it in B
    Minor.
Bud walked out of a dream. Bud and Foreskin found a waterhole, swam.
Took out their teeth, made camp. Then left that place, came to
    Tenochtitlan.
After defecating, they made themselves headgear out of some hearts and
    lopped-off hands.

They noticed that their penises were dragging on the ground, per-
formed sub-incision, lost lots of blood.
Bud cut Foreskin who then cut Bud.
They came to a river, across from which Kyoto sparkled in the night sky.
They wanted to cross, so constructed a vine bridge.
While they were crossing, the bridge became a thread in a vast web.
At its distant center, an immense red gonad, the Matriarch crouched,
sending out saffron rays.
"I'll play Theseus," Bud said, "this will turn the Matriarch into a
Minotaur."
"And I'll play Vallejo," Foreskin responded, "he's good at bleeding him-
self and turning into a dingo.
Together let's back on, farting flames."
The wily Minotaur, seeing a sputtering enigma approaching, pulled a
lever, shifting the tracks.
Foreskin and Bud found themselves in a roundhouse between concep-
tion and absence.
They noticed that their headgear was hanging on a Guardian Ghost
boulder engraved with breasts snake-knotted across a pubis.
"A formidable barricade," said Bud. "To reach paradise, we must learn
how to dance this design."
The pubis part disappeared. Fingering his sub-incision, Bud played
"Dance of the Infidels."
Foreskin joined in, twirling his penis making bullroarer sounds.
The Guardian Ghost boulder roared: "WHO ARE YOU TWO THE
SURROGATES OF?"
Bud looked at Foreskin. Foreskin looked at Bud.
"Another fine mess you've gotten us into," they said in unison.
Then they heard the Guardian Ghost laughing. "Life is a joyous thing,"
she chuckled, "with maggots at the center."

XII

Notes on the Poetry

The Book of Yorunomado

"Tú, luego, has nacido": from César Vallejo's poem, "The Soul that Suffered from Being its Body" (see p. 494 in this book). "NO. LA MANO, HE DICHO" is from the end of the same Vallejo poem.

THE DUENDE: according to Garcia Lorca (in "Theory and Function of the Duende"), "we must repel the angel, and kick out the muse; the real struggle is with the duende, which burns the blood like powdered glass and rejects all the sweet geometry one has learned." This section of the poem also draws on material from the 1962 Japanese film, *Seppuku* (= harakiri = ritual disembowelment).

"Tsuruginomiya": "Sword Shrine," a Shinto temple complex facing the Ibuki home in Kyoto where Barbara Eshleman and I rented two tatami rooms in 1963–64.

"The Darkening of the Light": see Hexagram 36, the Wilhelm/Baynes translation of the *I Ching*.

Ode to Reich

"*clarification of Beulah*": a fusion of Reich's theory of the function of the orgasm with Blake's interpretation of "Beulah," the world of gratified desire leading to imaginative vision and work (a sighting of the "antiphonal swing" elaborated throughout my poetry).

Hades in Manganese

To place Hades in manganese is to take the Greek god of death and the Greek underworld and imagine them as having been prefigured in the black manganese cave imagery of the Cro-Magnon people. In this revisionism, the emphasis is on the first construction of an underworld in which the Hadic figure is less a god of death than a proto-shaman envisioning the forms he is expressing on the walls.

The burden of this poem is to assimilate a range of personal and transpersonal twentieth-century "hells," which may be thought of as rubble packed against the gate to the Upper Paleolithic (in the same way that debris is often found covering decorated cave walls). My notion was that only after this material was cleared (imagined) could I give myself to the deep past. This kind of clearing away is a never-ending process and crops up at many points in *Juniper Fuse*.

"O dead living depths": As I was coming to the end of the fourth stanza, I realized that I had entered the magnetic field of César Vallejo's poem, "Telluric and Magnetic," in particular its impassioned central stanza beginning "Oh human fields!" My fifth stanza draws on the energy and some of the strategies of Vallejo's stanza. This is a good example of how poetry that one has previously translated may, out of nowhere, move into psychic accessibility and act as an emanative angel for a new poem under way. See pp. 481 of this book for my translation of "Telluric and Magnetic."

"Paul Blackburn spoke on tape to me": Paul Blackburn (1926–1971) sent several tapes of poems and conversation to me while I was living in Kyoto (1962–1964). One poem, "Crank it up for all of us, but let me heaven go," went off like a depth charge in me; I couldn't shake it for weeks. It conveyed a level of anguish that I had not thought could be expressed in poetry.

Our Lady of the Three-pronged Devil

The title attempts to tie the Aurignacian engraved vulvas into their reactive development, the trident, so that what was originally open and receptive becomes, at the point intercourse and pregnancy were linked, an uroboros enclosing germination. According to this thinking, the uroboros is hardly "prior to any process, eternal" (Neumann à la Jung), but rather a major arrest of movement drawing into its vortex an overwhelming preoccupation with mother-goddessing the earth (carrying in its wake the attribution to women of all the horrors to be found in nature).

The open Aurignacian vulva evokes a simple labyrinth with an exit and stresses, sexually, torsion. It seems possible that the earliest intercourse/pregnancy association was torsion (underscored by the fire drill) and that the subsequent uroboros belongs to agricultural peoples, with stress on the enclosed seed, the male as "star," i.e., patriarchy in contrast to an earlier more mysterious "open" union, in which the female was both place-of-fire *and* phallus (the so-called "Venuses" fit neatly in the palm).

"no one has lifted her veil": Concerning the unlifted veil, Barbara G. Walker writes (*The Woman's Encyclopedia of Myths and Secrets*, Harper & Roe, 1983, p. 855):

Latin *revelatio* meant to draw back the veil *(velum)*. It was the Goddess's rainbow veil that concealed the future and the secrets of the spirit under the colors of earthly appearance. After death, men might see her "face to face." A vision of the naked Goddess was vouchsafed to her sacred kings, who could draw back the veil of her temple, the *hymen*, pierce her virginity and die in their mating, to become gods. But as the Goddess said on her temple at Sais, "No mortal has yet been able to lift the veil which covers me." Those who saw her unveiled were no longer mortal.

Elsewhere (p. 367), Walker writes: "The Hag as death-goddess, her face veiled to imply that no man can know the manner of his death, was sometimes reinterpreted as a nun. Christianized legends were invented for their veiled figures." Hans Peter Duerr notes (*Dreamtime*, Blackwell, 1985, pp. 18–19) that "the head of the Venus of Willendorf is covered with a pattern of horizontal ridges in such a way as to suggest the masking of the face. If this interpretation is valid, then we may have here a prototype of the 'one who veils' of later times, the goddess of death such as Calypso or 'fraw Holt' whose names hide the Indo-German stem *kel-*, 'hide' or 'veil.'" See Duerr's footnote 14, pp. 177–178, for additional and fascinating information on veils.

Notes on a Visit to Le Tuc d'Audoubert

Le Tuc d'Audoubert is a Middle to Late Magdalenian cave (meaning the engravings and sculpture in it date to around 15,000 years ago) in the French Ariège, near the town of St.-Girons, and one of the three caves that make up the group known as the Volp caves (the Volp being an underground river which emerges near the entrance to Le Tuc). The other two caves are Les Trois Frères, and Enlène (with no wall imagery but more than a thousand small engraved plaquettes). Privately owned, the Volp caves have been protected against thoughtless exploration and destruction. They were discovered in 1912 by Count Henri Bégouën and his three sons (Les Trois Frères being named for the three brothers). The Count's grandson, Robert, is currently in charge of the Volp caves.

While Caryl's and my six-hour visit was unexpected (a chance phone call to Jean Clottes in Foix leading to an invitation to join Clottes, Robert Bégouën, and several students who had spent the summer excavating a midden outside the cave),

I had been reading what I could find on the cave. I had some notions about what I would see when, in rubber-raft units of two, we floated off on the underground Volp to the cave's interior shore to begin our 800-yard, mostly crawling, ascent. We emerged at midnight. I slept a few hours, awaking in the giddy, image-filled trance that over the years I have learned to trust as an ignition point for a piece of writing. I was so excited that the "note" jumped back and forth from prose to poetry several times per page. About two-thirds of the way through what is now the finished piece (with the words "image pressure"), my mind went blank and I stopped writing. Upon reaching this point while typing up the "Notes" several months later, the earlier charge returned and everything flowed without revision to the end.

After finishing these "Notes"—a mix of poetry, prose poetry, paragraphs, and visual "punctuation"—I recalled that Northrop Frye had referred to Blake's "The Marriage of Heaven and Hell" as an *anatomy*, suggesting that it was a composite work that included as its "members" various forms and strategies of the art of writing. In the mid-1990s, I realized that "Notes on a Visit to Le Tuc d'Audoubert" was the nuclear form for *Juniper Fuse* that would become an amplification of its multiple genres.

"theater of cruelty": A translation of Artaud's proposed name for a revolutionary theatre.

"fantastic figures": In their book *Les Cavernes du Volp*, Arts et Métiers, Paris, 1958, Henri Bégouën and the Abbé Henri Breuil describe these creatures in the following words: "The left side of this gallery contains several strange engravings: two fantastic animals, half-feline, half-bull, one above the other, of which one cannot make out the hindquarters. The upper figure has a horrible head, with a single short horn flanked by a large ear behind it. Its narrow neck supports a large head with animated contours, a prominent and rounded muzzle, and an open mouth. Its withers are very convex; its vertically striped head and body, and its slender, long foreleg, end in long, retractile claws. The lower figure has been reduced to a grotesque head, topped by two little ears. I think that we have here the Guardians of the Sanctuary."

"the *grand and petit* sorcerer": See pp. 176–178 of *Juniper Fuse* for the figures in Lascaux that the "sorcerer" figures in Le Tuc d'Audoubert remind me of.

"*tanist* re. Graves": An association between the "fantastic figures" and the sacred king with his tanist (or deputy) is discussed in Robert Graves's *The White Goddess* (Noonday Press edition), pp. 125–126.

"The grotesque archetype": This phrase came to me spontaneously upon seeing the "fantastic figures." I then realized that my phrase was a spin-off of Mikhail Bakhtin's "grotesque realism," discussed in his Introduction to *Rabelais and His World*, MIT Press, 1968. According to Bakhtin, the word "grotesque" appeared at the end of the fifteenth century in descriptions of certain Roman ornaments excavated from Titus's baths (which were in grottos, implying that these ornaments were an expression of the grotto itself). While the word initially referred to the fanciful interplay of plant, animal, and human forms (which often seemed to be giving birth to each other), the classical canon soon relegated "the grotesque" to the barbarous, associating it not only with playful energies, but with the alien, the illegitimate, the bestial, and with humankind's infantile and "primitive" past. By defining the carnivalesque atmosphere in Rabelais as "grotesque realism," Bakhtin not only rehabilitated the word but suggested the extent to which it has permeated all of the stages of historical antiquity.

While there are elements in common between the medieval, classical, and primordial grotesques, none of the historical terms express what I intend by "the grotesque archetype." As a way of approaching a definition, I want to consider some observations that Jung—the originator of the 20th century use of the term "archetype"—made about these primary psychic structures.

Jung differentiates between "archetypal" and "archetype," writing that "archetypal representations (images and ideas) mediated to us by the unconscious should not be confused with the archetype as such. They are varied structures which all point back to one essentially 'irrepresentable' basic form… the archetype as such is a psychoid factor that belongs, as it were, to the invisible, ultraviolet end of the psychic spectrum (*Collected Works*, Vol. 8, para. 417). Comments by North Kimberly (Australian) aborigines to Geza Róheim seem to anticipate Jung's approach: "The natives say they do not make the *wondjina* figures but only repaint them. The figures themselves are called *wondjina-made-themselves*. They are self-created." (*The Gates of the Dream*, International Universities Press, 1979, p. 107).

I would propose that hybrid images, arrived at by any number of means (shamanic trance, sensory deprivation freak-out, initiatory rites, or mythic notation) are grotesque archetypal representations of somatic materials. They evoke the so-called "mythical times" when man and animal were one (or as some histor-ical shamans put it, when man and animal spoke the same language). These "myth-ical times," undoubtedly populated by infant sensations and childhood repressions, could represent Jung's "essentially 'irrepresentable' basic form."

Commenting on Michael Maier's alchemical journeys (specifically his 1617 *Symbola aureae mensae*), Jung speaks of Maier

> approaching that region of the psyche which was not unjustly said to be inhabited by "Pans, Satyrs, dog-headed baboons, and half-men." It is not difficult to see that this region is the animal soul in man. For just as a man has a body which is no different in principle form that of an animal, so also his psychology has a whole series of lower stories in which the specters from humanity's past epochs still dwell, then the animal souls from the age of Pithecanthropus and the hominids, then the 'psy-che" of the cold-blooded saurians, and deepest of all, the tran-scendental mystery and paradox of the sympathetic and para-sympathetic psychoid processes. (Vol. 14, para. 279)

Here we have an active, vertical midden image of the personal unconscious down through the collective unconscious, based on evolutionary scale. One might conclude that "animal souls" began to intermingle with nascent human souls when Cro-Magnons projected and drew/engraved animal and hybrid images.

"and he had no member": The sculptor Bruce Beasley visited le Tuc d'Audou-bert on two occasions in 1984 specifically to examine the clay bison. His observa-tions are detailed and worth considering because here we have a sculptor looking at sculpture, approaching it from a combined viewpoint of craft and aesthetics ("Les bisons d'argile de la grotte du Tuc d'Audoubert," *Bulletin de la Societé Pré-historique Ariège-Pyrénées*, Tome XLI, 1986, pp. 23–50). For my comments on Beasley's observations, see pp. 255–256 in *Juniper Fuse*.

The Excavation of Artaud

The form of this poem is based on a prosodic pattern by César Vallejo in his poem "The Book of Nature" (see p. 487 in the present volume). A fuller treatment of my translational and imaginative relationship to Vallejo and his work can be found in the essay, "An Ego Strong Enough To Live," in *Archaic Design* (Black Widow Press, 2007).

"3 dead men are fingering your Muladhara Chakra, your amphimixis…":
Artaud mentions the attack on his Muladhara Chakra (= root support), or in his
own words, "that bone / located between anus and sex" in "The Return of Artaud,
the Mômo" (see p. 534 in this book).

In *The Masks of God: Primitive Mythology,* The Viking Press, 1959, Joseph
Campbell quotes Geza Róheim on Australian aboriginal magic directed against
"the flesh between the scrotum and the rectum."

The term "amphimixis" (= the synthesis of two or more erotisms in a higher
unity) was coined by Sandor Ferenczi in his "Thalassa," *Psychoanalytic Quarterly,*
1938.

The Bison Keyboard
A sestina fantasia involving the jazz pianist Bud Powell who was the first living
artist that I responded to as a teenager in Indianapolis. Other pieces on Bud
Powell are: "Bud Powell 1925–1966" (*Indiana*); "Bud Powell" (*The Gull Wall*); and
"Tea for Two" in "Eight Fire Sources" in *Archaic Design.*

On Atget's Road
Eugène Atget (1857–1927) was a commercial photographer whose some 10,000
photographs document the historic character of French life. This poem is based
on some of his photos of rural French villages to be found in *The Work of Atget /
Volume I / Old France,* MOMA, 1981.

At the Speed of Wine
Of the American poets whose work is identified with the first half of the 20th cen-
tury, Hart Crane has always meant the most to me. This poem was stimulated by
reflections on my co-translation of Vladimir Holan's poem, "A Night with Ham-
let," (see the 2005 edition of *Conductors of the Pit*) in which the speaker imagina-
tively engages a special night visitor (in Holan's case, a phantasmagoric Hamlet,
who appears to the poet in his apartment in Prague; in my case, an intoxicated
Hart Crane in a lower Manhattan bar). I also had in mind here Ulysses' conversa-
tion with Tiresias in Book XIII of *The Odyssey.*

Other pieces on Crane are: "Portrait of Hart Crane" *(The Gull Wall),* "The
Collected Poems of Hart Crane" in "Eight Fire Sources" *(Archaic Design),* and "A
Gloss on Hart Crane's 'Lachrymae Christi'" *(Archaic Design,* and here, page 417).

For the poems, "For Aimé Césaire" (from *Hades In Manganese*) and "Short Story" (from *Under World Arrest*) see the essay "At the Locks of the Void: Co-Translating Aimé Césaire" in the prose section of this book.

from **Homuncula** by Horrah Pornoff

In 1974, Marjorie Perloff published a long review in *Contemporary Literature* magazine, called "The Corn-Porn Lyric: Poetry 1972–73," in which the books of twenty poets were put down as being corny *and* pornographic. Set against works by, for example, Ai, Creeley, myself, Jong, Levertov, and Wakoski, were some gloomy lines of Wieners and Rich. Perloff argued that the corn-porn culprits "are those who want to have their cake and eat it too; they wish to be completely uninhibited about sex and yet to respect such time-honored values as fatherhood, motherhood, a 'good' marriage, friendship, fidelity, trust, integrity, or devotion to the sick and the poor." Unlike Wieners and Rich (and the Rimbaud of "Poets Seven Years Old") we lacked "a sense of extremity, of dangerous desire and demonic possession."

I said what I had to say about all of this in a long response printed in *Contemporary Literature* in 1975, and only bring the matter up again because my anger at Perloff s flat-ironing twenty of us into a cliché led me to ponder a poetry that would be both demonic and pornographic. To my mind, Perloff didn't offer any convincing examples in her review (she could have cited Artaud), but her core issue became important for me to deal with. I had written a set of poems "by" a Russian dwarf whom I made up named Metro Vavin ("the 9 Poems of Metro Vavin," *The Gull Wall*) as well another group of improvisations called "The Gospel of Celine Arnauld" (*Tumba* 12, 1977), based on a real French poet. How about a work "by" a woman whose mode of expression involved both horror and pornography? It was Caryl who suggested that such a figure might be called Horrah Pornoff. So I made an attempt—and got nowhere. But I did become fascinated, and then obsessed, with creating a feminine persona ("a woman of some sort out of his imagination to prove himself," as Williams put it in *A Dream of Love*), someone who, unlike Celine Arnauld or Yeats' "Crazy Jane," was not based on a real-life figure, and who would thus be free to be *and* not to be.

I decided that Horrah Pornoff's manuscript should consist of 77 poems (the number in Vallejo's *Trilce*), and over the next year completed a fifth draft of *Homuncula* (which in subsequent reworkings became much shorter). I also became interested in how certain editors and friends would respond to this poetry, so I took out a PO Box, as Horrah Pornoff, in the local post office, and began to send poems around. Horrah appeared in Charlie Shively's *Fag Rag*, Bill Mohr's *Momentum*, and she was featured by Cid Corman in the 4th series of *origin* (Cid wrote Horrah that at last LA had a poet!). Soon, going to the post office for her mail, and staying involved with her several correspondences (two of which had her fending off people who wanted to date her) grew stale, and I ended the game, which also meant putting aside the manuscript.

In 1990, after reading Camille Paglia's *Sexual Personae*, I went back to the manuscript. Paglia's book made me realize anew the extent to which writers are persona-infested. Not only do we take on "masks" that float forth ghost-like through our personalities, but we are fascinated with expressing what we are not as an aspect of what we are—with the underlying alchemical insight that wholeness consists of the circulation of negative as well as affirmative formations. At that time, I began to see that although Horrah was make-believe, she was also a serious working of persona. She was an expression of the extent to which the feminine aspects of my personality had fought over the years for their rightful place in my work. She was my inner "little woman," or "homuncula," whom I had become aware of through poetry itself, and her "birth," as it were, was precious for me to work through. All of Horrah's twenty-six poems appeared in *Under World Arrest*.

Guyton Place

In the late 1980s, the painter/sculptor Tyree Guyton and his wife, Karen, created a unique, ongoing art installation in a run-down Detroit neighborhood, called "The Heidelberg Project" (named after the street on which Guyton's grandfather lived, which was also the central street in the project). Basically, it involved attaching junk and abandoned objects to several abandoned houses and turning them into outdoor sculpture. The street itself, trees, fire hydrants, etc., were also painted and decorated.

The City of Detroit at first welcomed the project, listing it as a must-see for tourists (thus at the height of its popularity, Mercedes and stretch-limos could be seen slowly driving by). After numerous complaints by uncomprehending citizens (who thought Guyton was into Voodoo), the City decided that "The Heidelberg

Project" was a public nuisance, and, while leaving scores of crack houses in the same area alone, bulldozed all of the Guyton houses in two stages (1989 and 1991). Not owning the houses, the Guytons simply had no way to protect them.

My poem is a result of several visits I made to the project at which time I made lists of the things attached. There are photographs of the houses in *Sulfur #25*.

Navel of the Moon

In the summer of 1991, Caryl and I spent a month in Oaxaca. Seeking to avoid the crowds at the Zapotec necropolis Monte Alban, we got permission from local archeologists to visit the ruins at night. We went in at midnight, and wandered under the star light until close to dawn. A longer, and much more complicated version of this meditation may be found in *Under World Arrest*.

Nora's Roar

The memorial gathering invitation reads: "The artist Nora Jaffe," and that is how I remember my friend, along with my mother and my wife Caryl my closest female companion. I remember her remarkable hands, their strength and firmness, as they would sheath mine in greeting. I once wrote of Nora's hands as pilgrims, or palmers, on their way to the destination drawing and painting daily led them to— a destination that always paid homage to the human body, not expressionistically or representationally but as the underscoring for formal decisions. The relationship in her work between the formal and the sexual—specifically, often a bandaged phallus within female containment—is uncompromising and eerie. Beyond the evocations of Gorky and Bellmer, I realized that I was facing in Nora's work the erotic and generative body as the contouring agent of a formal goal. A fierce ambivalence regarding Eros is both the joyous and sorrowful weight in the webs of her searchings.

Both Adrienne Rich (one of her oldest friends) and Robert Kelly have made perceptive comments on the art of Nora Jaffe, who remains virtually unknown in the art world. I included Adrienne's and Robert's commentaries on pp. 176–178 of *From Scratch*. Reproductions of Jaffe's work can be found in *Caterpillar #2* and *#13*, and on the cover of *Sulfur #26*. There are also ten of her drawings in *Realignment*, Treacle Press, 1974, a book we did together.

There is also my poem "Nora Jaffe" in *The Name Encanyoned River*, Nora's unexpected interruption in "Nocturnal Veils" (p. 185), and "Nora's Transmission" in *An Alchemist with One Eye on Fire*.

from **Soutine's Lapis**

The immediate source for this poem is the 1993 Taschen Soutine *catalogue raisonné*, a revelation for Soutine admirers: it reproduced a number of newly-discovered paintings and discarded, as fakes, some mediocre works.

In the National Gallery of Art catalog, *Willem de Kooning Paintings*, David Sylvester reports that when, in 1977, de Kooning was requested to identify his key influences, he responded: "O I think I would choose Soutine... I've always been crazy about Soutine—all his paintings. Maybe it's the lushness of the paint. He builds up a surface that looks like a material, like a substance. There's a kind of transfiguration, a certain fleshiness, in his work... I remember when I first saw the Soutines in the Barnes Collection... the Matisses had a light of their own, but the Soutines had a glow that came from within the paintings—it was another kind of light."

Over the years, I have written a number of poems concerning Soutine and his art. In *Indiana*, there is "Soutine." In *The Gull Wall*, "Portrait of Soutine." In *From Scratch*, along with "Soutine's Lapis," "Oy." There is also a short essay on Soutine, "Soutine's Impact" in "Eight Fire Sources," collected in *Archaic Design*, and a review of *The Impact of Chaim Soutine* in the Fall 2002 online edition of *Rain Taxi* magazine.

from **Matrix, Blower**

"Lespugue has tail feathers": Buffie Johnson, *Our Lady of the Beasts*, Harper & Row, San Francisco, 1988, pp. 14–15.

"Thou art that": Norman O. Brown, *Love's Body*, Random House, NYC, 1966, p. 224.

"Blowing horse head = vulva": One engraved limestone block from Abri Cellier in the Les Eyzies Prehistory Museum has never ceased to fascinate me. A neck which appears to be part of a horse head has been crossed by a vulva slightly larger than the head. There is a cupule in front of the horse's head, one as its eye, and one in the center of the vulva. Studying this image, I was reminded of Pierre Reverdy's 1918 definition of an image: "a pure creation of the mind—it cannot be born from a comparison but from a juxtaposition of two more or less distant realities." It was from this formulation that André Breton defined the Surrealist image's juxtaposition of the fixed and the exploding.

"Convulsive beauty will be veiled-erotic": André Breton, *Mad Love*, University of Nebraska Press, Lincoln, 1987, p. 19.

Cemeteries of Paradise

"Miller perceived some of the fix": Henry Miller's stirring paragraph on the Dordogne is quoted in note #5 to the Introduction to *Juniper Fuse*.

A dream of February 16, 2000, which seems to enact the devolution of Charles Olson, may have cleared the way for this poem as well as my definition of one phase of my work as a poet ("I hunt inside stone") set against the last line of Olson's "The Kingfishers" ("I hunt among stones"). For more of my thoughts about Olson and prehistory, see "Notes on Charles Olson and the Archaic" in *Archaic Design*. Here is the dream:

> Near a beach I discovered mole hills between kennels or chicken coops. A farmer said he'd turn his dogs on them. I watched furious fighting inside a shed, lots of mole-pups being spit out. Worried that Caryl would not know where to find me, I started walking a path to suddenly find myself in a crowd where I heard that Charles Olson, now out on the road with a small child, wandering and giving lectures for food, for some eighty days, was to arrive. I was shown photos of Robert Kelly with a young black woman and other strangers. Then I was in a house with people who had studied Olson, including an attractive Irish woman who had a small *tansu* set into the floor. She said it contained Olson texts and could not be opened until he arrived. The excitement was mounting— Olson enthusiasts seemed to be everywhere. I was now in a spacious cave and heard the approach of what I took to be Olson and his retinue — there he was, seven feet tall, shaggy white hair, thin neck, large block-like skeletal head, hunched over, climbing through the air. I went up to him and took his huge hand. He looked at me curiously, then boomed: "How are your caves coming along?" I started to describe the completion of *Juniper Fuse*, but he interrupted: "The music, how about the music?" Before I could respond, he was past me. I was surrounded by hip-looking men in sunglasses who I figured were Olson aviators. It was a joyous occasion—then it hit me: how could he be here? He died in 1970! Larry Goodell then piped up: "That's the majesty of it!" I was now caught up in another crowd, and being shown a map of the Pech Merle cave with certain areas marked which I understood Olson had explored. "Olson is coming!" I heard. "What?" I said, "I just saw him!" "No, he's coming now," voices clamored, and a strange creature rounded a cave bend, a leg-

like head with one huge eye, stick-like body, insect legs. "No, this is not Olson—I JUST SAW OLSON!" I shouted. There was intense conversation about what was referred to as a "restoration." New people appeared, shouting that Olson was on his way. An even stranger apparition appeared, more insectile, arachnoid, long extending legs front and back, its head—a compact lavender mass—under its body. I worked my way under as the creature ambled along, yelling "What happened to you?" I got my hands around the jewel-like head and wrenched it free, at which moment an agonized voice cried: *I couldn't get the whole Theolonius!*" What was left disappeared among the mass of people thronging the cave.

The Magical Sadness of Omar Cáceres
See Eliot Weinberger's essay "Omar Cáceres," in his book *Karmic Traces*, New Directions, 2000. According to Weinberger, Cáceres is one of many significant and forgotten 20th century Latin American poets, and one who is known only by a collection of fifteen poems published by his brother in Chile in 1934. In his essay, Weinberger translates one of these poems, and this translation, along with the bits of information on the poet, moved me to write my own poem in the voice of Omar Cáceres.

Spirits of the Head
See *Reciprocal Distillations* for "A Note on the poem 'Spirits of the Head.'"

Michaux, 1956
"whatever…": Giorgio Agamben focused my attention on the word "whatever" in the opening essay in *The Coming Community*, University of Minnesota Press, 1993. In the poem "Q" in *The Promises of Glass*, New Directions, 2000, Michael Palmer, possibly inspired by Agamben's fascination with the word, plays off the Latin *quodlibet* ("whatever"), and creates a character named "Quod."

Chauvet: Left Wall of the End Chamber
I visited the Chauvet cave with Jean-Marie Chauvet (one of the three 1994 discoverers) on January 8, 2005. My gratitude to Dominique Baffier for arranging my visit. Excellent color photographs of the wall with the paintings addressed in my poem may be found in *Chauvet Cave / The Art of Earliest Times*, The University of Utah Press, 2003.

The Beheading

I am indebted to Peter Robb's rethinking of Caravaggio's life and art in *M / The Man Who Became Caravaggio*, Picador, 2001 (the quote in my poem is from p. 437 of that book), as well as to Catherine Puglisi's excellent *Caravaggio*, Phaidon, 2000, with its detailed investigation of "The Beheading of Saint John the Baptist," and to Leo Bersani and Ulysse Dutoit's *Caravaggio's Secrets*, an October Book, 1998, with its sensitive scrutiny of many paintings. I am also in debt to Dominic Cutajar, not only for his essay, "Caravaggio in Malta" (from *Malta and Caravaggio*, Malta, 1986), but also for his asking the Oratory guards in Valletta's Co-Cathedral to turn off the two alarm systems so that Caryl and I could almost touch the twelve-by-seventeen-foot "Beheading" with our noses, in May 2002.

Monumental

This poem was written for the public memorial program for the painter Leon Golub, who died at 82 in August, 2004, at Cooper Union's Great Hall in NYC, on April 17, 2005. Golub is one of the greatest of American painters, and his painterly trackings of our horrendous overseas government involvements in torture and murder throughout the '60s, '70s, '80s, and '90s, are acts of courageous witnessing. The last twenty-five years of Golub's paintings are the closest thing we have in America to Goya's "black period" and *The Disasters of War*. No wonder no major museum in the NYC area has ever given him a retrospective: his moral acuity cuts like acid through the evasion and lies that have become our public and aesthetic policy. See "Golub the Axolotl," my review of Donald Kuspit's *Leon Golub, Existential/Activist Painter*, Rutgers University Press, 1985, in *Antiphonal Swing*, and a second poem on Golub's work, "Figure and Ground" in *Reciprocal Distillations*.

The Tjurunga

I was first alerted to the *tjurunga* (or *churinga*, as it is also spelled) by Robert Duncan in his essay "Rites of Participation" (from *The H.D. Book*), which appeared in *Caterpillar* #1, 1967. Duncan quoted Geza Róheim ("The *tjurunga* which symbolizes both the male and female genital organ, the primal scene and combined parent concept, the father and the mother, separation and reunion... represents both the path and the goal"), and then commented: "This *tjurunga* we begin to see not as the secret identity of the Aranda initiate but as our own Freudian identity, the conglomerate consciousness of the mind we share with Róheim... the simple *tjurunga* now appears to be no longer simple but the complex mobile that S.

Giedion in *Mechanization Takes Command* saw as most embodying our contemporary experience: 'the whole construction is aerial and hovering as the nest of an insect' —a suspended system, so contrived that 'a draft of air or push of a hand will change the state of equilibrium and the interrelations of suspended elements... forming unpredictable, ever-changing constellations and so imparting to them the aspect of space-time.'"

Reading Barry Hill's *Broken Song/T.G.H. Strehlow and Aboriginal Possession* (Knopf, 2002) brought back and refocused Duncan's words.

In Vol. 13 of *The Collected Works*, para. 128, Jung writes: "*Churingas* may be boulders, or oblong stones artificially shaped and decorated, or oblong, flattened pieces of wood ornamented in the same way. They are used as cult instruments. The Australians and the Melanesians maintain that *churingas* come from the totem ancestor, that they are relics of his body or of his activity, and are full or *arunquiltha* or mana. They are united with the ancestor's soul and with the spirits of all those who afterwards possess them... In order to 'charge' them, they are buried among the graves so that they can soak up the mana of the dead."

PROSE

XIII

from *Antiphonal Swing*

(1989)

In the autumn of 1960, after I had spent a summer in Mexico writing what I felt were my first real poems, Paul Blackburn and I had lunch at a place in New York City he refers to in his own poetry as "the bakery." At the end of lunch I showed him some of my poems, and after reading "A Very Old Woman" he looked up at me with a big grin on his face and with some superlative exclamation blew me a kiss. By doing so at just the right time he confirmed the fact that I had, on my own, at least got up on my feet. A few years ago, reading one of Robin Blaser's poems, I came across the lines: "the poet's kiss / given—caught *like a love- / adept* on my lips." He was speaking of an actual kiss, and it made me think of what Blackburn gave me, which was a covenant given by an already-confirmed poet to another non-confirmed one. By confirming me when he did I felt Paul had given me in an ancient and noble way a "charge," the Poet's Kiss, which would only be realized when in some original way it was returned. In 1964, in my poem "Niemonjima," I worked one of Paul's central images, the gull, and transformed it into the Gull-robe:

> And it was only the robe that drove him on,
> a vision of the inland sea, which is called the Gull-robe,
> gorgeous, of white feathers emblazoned with stars & moons,
> the lovely garment every loved woman wears, of midnight-
> blue & silks, in which a light streams for all who ride
> away into the darkness carrying the torches of imaginative
> love, the softness & precision of loved desire.

A great deal of the meaning Paul Blackburn has for me, his life as well as his poetry, is involved with the role he played in my becoming a poet and this is especially touching to me because during those years he was beginning to lose grip on his own life and writing. From 1962 to 1964 my first wife, Barbara, and I lived in Kyoto, Japan. I had published my first

---

This essay was written for the 1974 Paul Blackburn issue of *Sixpack* magazine.

book of poems before moving there and the poems in it were written while I was either a student, on vacation in Mexico, or teaching. Upon moving to Kyoto, I found myself for the first time cut loose from any job or study routine to depend on; I was suddenly on my own, I had 24 hours to face and fill, and for most of these two years I was tied up in the frustrations from my past that I thought I had evaded by becoming a poet. I was reaching the point when I would either accept my own life as my material, or reject my life, and continue to imitate other poets. This is the point at which what is previously amorphous in a young poet's work begins to appear either original or "academic"—where he begins to doubt the meaningfulness of his first influences. Since I chose the first alternative, I began to feel lost, a feeling which lasted for a number of years.

Originality at that time meant little more than taking my own life to task; the writing that resulted seemed to mean less than what I would have written had I continued to imitate others. I understand something about this now, I understand that apprenticework, in the sense that I am speaking of it, has a great deal to do with letting the held-back dam of one's past break through one's mouth with all its roil, its stones and silt, and that this act itself, taking years perhaps, is only the first stage of approaching an art of poetry, for as the dam gives way the novice must continually create *out of* what is struggling through him as well as keep the past itself in motion. It is the "creating out of" that is felt as a terrible friction, almost blockage to the longed-for flow, especially if the destruction of the dam is sudden.

During those years in Kyoto I would sit for hours before the typewriter, sometimes just staring at the first line I had written trying to figure out how to make it yield poetry, or at other times typing the line out over and over, varying it, repeating it, trying to dislodge it from my own common-sense world of the past which I was still holding on to, not only because I was scared of losing all moorings; but because I was working with the past, I was to a certain extent stuck with the way my mind in the past had functioned. Paul and I wrote each other about every two weeks during those years and every six months or so exchanged tapes. Our correspondence was not strictly about poetry—it was basically about what we were seeing and doing and feeling. It was real sustenance for me because a friendship was being created and I was finding out that not only did I need to find my identity but that my identity was manifold.

In late October, 1963, Paul sent me a new tape which I took over to a man who had a tape recorder. I remember sitting in an empty tatami room by a large window which looked out onto a backyard filled with junk. It was cold gray out and had begun to snow. Paul's voice, filled with images of brick walls and nearly deserted streets, of men huddling by little trash fires in gutters, his peculiar vision of New York City which integrates the literary life with the viewpoint of someone on the Bowery, began to worm into my feeling for my life as it never had before. I was just opening up to seeing a world inclusive of the outcasts that Paul identified with.

For I too had been watching lower caste leather-workers in Kyoto who seemed to live in the street as well as the migratory construction workers who were building a highway down in the cut below where I lived. They worked all night long, keeping an oil-drum fire going, and I was very moved watching them standing around their fire with their yellow helmets and dark blue wool puttees. At that moment there was no distance between Paul's poems and the junk-filled backyard, the cold in my hands, and the endless repetition I felt watching the tape slowly turn. But it was also a specific repetition, it was not just life repeating itself, but repetition becoming a state of mind through Paul's poetry and his voicing of it—he read some *Rituals* that day, which made me think for the first time, what is a ritual, is it any more than repetition, doing something the way my father had done it, and if so, where is the warmth in that? Something about the way Paul was looking at things found a place in me, but it was a place I was trying to destroy by making poetry. What a dense web of ambivalence was being woven between the two of us that late snowy afternoon—I was being bound into the act of a voice which seemed to consume my defenses against poetry. At the end of the tape it was nearly dark and the snow had turned the junk into little castle-like hills—there was only a faint streak of rose-colored sun left in the light. At this point Paul read a poem whose title I do not remember, I remember only two images in the piece: the first was a vision of a group of primitive men standing around in a circle jacking off into the flukes of a dying fire, and the second came moments later: Paul cried out, "O Leviticus, Oil for the Lamps!"

All the negation in my own life was suddenly present, but it was present to me, a gift—Paul spoke of my negation so that I no longer had to wear it but could begin to work with it as an object. The circle of primitive men became a circle of young Indiana men, pledges to the Phi Delta Theta social fraternity at Indiana University in 1953: I was one of them, and we had been shouted down from the dormitory late one night, ordered to strip, and then bend over holding hands making a circle around the double fireplace which hissed and crackled while "the actives" played *Slaughter on 10th Avenue* at full volume (the fraternity was located at the corner of Jordan and 10th Street), and beat us bloody with long wood paddles. In 1963 I was faced in the act of finding poetry with this impotence in my own makeup—what anguish must have been buried in me that I would have allowed myself to be so abused! There must have been something, some ceremony perhaps, which never took place during my puberty, I thought, which, had it taken place, would have released me from boyhood into manhood—but what could that mean in my present life? I had been reading about an Australian sub-incision ceremony which climaxed a puberty initiation, in which a boy was held down spread-eagled over the back of a kneeling man and his urethra was split with a sharp rock. Would it have been better had something in my boyhood been bled out of me? It was not simply my manhood that I sought—manhood was too easily just the world of grown-ups. I sought the persimmon tree in the Okumura backyard, I wanted to be in contact with it. Blackburn got through to me that there was something which I experienced as being inside me that had to get out for the contact to exist. He made me aware of this not as one who had succeeded in getting whatever it was out, but as one who had failed and whose cry was uttered as a result of having failed.

It was dark when I left where I was and started back to the house of Okumura. At the point I passed the Senryuji Gate, which led in to the Ancient Imperial Burial Grounds, there was a long flight of wide stone steps which led into Imagumano, my neighborhood. I started to descend and immediately recalled an accident I had seen a couple of years before, the legs of a Japanese schoolgirl extending out from under the rear axle of a bus. When I witnessed this I had a desire to roll the bus off her. Now the axle became a turnstile and as I approached the bottom of the steps I imagined that I was heading into death, but the death I was heading into was so singular it immediately became absurd—I was suddenly aware that I could not resolve Paul's misery nor could I resolve the death of the schoolgirl, and that my desire to do so before was ridiculous. I had been living my life as if it were a life that could be solved from day to day, first I would do this, then get out of it, then that, get out of it, etc., and as long as I had done that I lived with an awful anxiety but pretended there was no fear in my life. But no, that girl's death impinged upon me and it impinged in the living body of Paul Blackburn, and I could not keep Blackburn's sense of life away from me, I was not singular, what I was was not what I had identified myself to be—I reached the end of the steps, I got down to the turnstile I had felt I was descending to, my crib with only *one* being inside, and I was free of its singularity, wonderfully free of the absurdity of my life and within it.

The gull is more than a central image in Blackburn's poetry: it is the presence of the creation itself, the confirmation that Blackburn allows himself—when a gull or a flock appear in a poem there is hope as well as all that the phrase "the creation" suggests—I would almost say that the gull is the presence of God in Blackburn's body of writing, but that would be making a connection he only alluded to in the opening section of what for several years (1963 to summer 1967) he considered to be his masterwork, *The Selection of Heaven*, a 25-page poem he was unable to complete:

GOD,   that it did happen,
that loose now, that
early confirmation
        of birds, the texture set in
        words,   1945,

A Staten Island beach in early October
here in more than flesh and brick,
9th Street,   March 1963....

This grey   .   soft .   overcast . not-quite-rainy day,
that I can
swim my mind in it, swim it in overcast, the sun
tries, and there they are, the birds, my gulls
circle over a street to the North.

At about the same time that he wrote these lines in March, 1963, Paul enclosed a photo of a gull standing on a rock in a letter to me, and wrote under the picture: *Dear Clay, Never look a gull in the eye, love Paul.* That admonition really puzzled me, because even then I knew that among all other things Paul Blackburn loved to look and watch—some of his finest poems have a basic fulcrum of Paul sitting someplace, like on a street-bench or in a park, and watching what is going on around him, presumably writing the poem in a notebook while it is occurring before his eyes. Anyway, I didn't then pick up the literary connection to the line which comes from the poem called *The Purse-seine*, written in 1960:

> we cannot look one another in the eye,
> > > > that frightens, easier to face
> the carapace of monster crabs along the beach   .   The empty
> shell of death was always easier to gaze upon
> than to look into the eyes of the beautiful killer   .   Never
> > > > > look a gull in the eye.

The "we" includes the woman the poet is with, and thus by implication both she and the gull are held for a moment in the phrase "the beautiful killer." I think that, deeply, for Paul Blackburn woman *was* the beautiful killer, and that since he insisted on always searching for and being with a woman, his failure to overcome that feeling explains much of his failure to develop as a poet and to live longer as a man.

But before I enter into these problems I want to make a few assertions so that the problems themselves can be seen in the proper context. Blackburn is one of the half-dozen finest American poets of his generation. The body of writing that he left us and the generations to come is much larger and much more impressive than what is now publicly and thus as his *image* available. He wrote first-rate poetry at several periods in his life and his finest poetry in the fifties when he lived in Spain, and this work carries on into the early sixties when he lived in New York City. His gifts were various: he had an acute ear and eye that together enabled him to lay a poem out on the page in an utterly unique way—a Blackburn poem is recognizable about four feet away, one can spot it by its shape, the way the lines extend and break, run for full stanzas or bunch in neat units at any place on the page, often in short-lined quatrains. His ability to stop the poem the moment the poem itself stops is uncanny (e.g., *Hot Afternoons Have Been in West 15th Street*). In Blackburn's poetry one always feels that the quatrain has not quite yet been abandoned, it appears, floats out, fragments, dissolves, is felt in two- and three-line units or is *sensed* at times through inner-rhyming: one will occasionally *hear* quatrains when on the page none are visible. In other words, the verse never becomes free, gets free of that traditional cohesive—I would even say *communal*—urge, while at the same time it is open enough to accommodate emotional glide (I almost said "drive" but Blackburn is generally not a driving poet—he more naturally enjoys gliding, veering and banking, or suddenly dropping to a fused position—for just a moment—like his gulls). In many ways, he is the Buddhist path between Robert Creeley and Charles Olson.

As for his content, his best poems warm the reader with a sense of a generous, compassionate and patient humanity, wry and foolish at times, bleak and helpless at others. While there are few revelations of being in Blackburn's poetry, he does get, given the situation he is addressing, a great deal of what it felt like into the composition he is conceiving; he does not approach the poem (as does Gary Snyder for example) having thought its subject through—his poems most often begin with an impulse, a partial perception or sounding, and pick their way out from there. His strongest and most successful poetry is contingent upon a kind of distance that he creates when he is alone, i.e., unobserved somewhere, not directly involved in the action he is watching, e.g., observing Paul Carroll being tossed a white sunburned body by breakers at Bañalbufar (*Affinities II*) or watching common people fill and leave stone benches at dusk on a busy street in Barcelona in the lovely *Plaza Reál with Palmtrees*. While his writing is free of dogma, there is an implied stance suggesting a way of being. One feels this most in his attitude toward women and sex—toward Romance. The source for this, in a literary sense, is the early-medieval Troubadour tradition, which he knew and suffered thoroughly. He spent more than twenty years translating this poetry, and when it is published in book form I believe it will not only be definitive but will never again be equaled in the American language.

One reason that Paul Blackburn translated the Troubadours is that Ezra Pound complained that here was a great body of poetry to be brought to bear on American poetry which no one had really even attempted. Pound's attitude certainly must have been Blackburn's original incentive. However, such an incentive needed a powerful fuel to sustain this project over two decades, and the fact that Blackburn never completed the *Troubadour* translation, or I should say, the fact that he completed it again and again, keeping it alive, revising and adjusting it, suggests that it kept an obsession in him alive, kept it churning. Central to this obsession is the idealization of woman as expressed by the Troubadours—a view in which woman is a grand icy queen of heaven the poet sings for, a queen who will never be lived with, *period*, an untouchable in a much higher social station than the poet himself, who may reward him with her hand to kiss or with a benevolent glance (there are several tremendous burlesques of this maddening situation in the Troubadour poetry Blackburn translated, notably Guillem Comte de Peitau's *Farai un vers pos mi sonelh*, but these pieces hardly dent the idealization). I can imagine how in twelfth-century Europe such an attitude might have had a great deal to do with the evolution of consciousness, adoration of spring and burgeoning being more and more associated with human love, and of course regardless of what it meant to the lives of those concerned, it produced a genuine body of art.

To consider why such an attitude was attractive to Paul Blackburn is complicated. I don't think he himself knew—for like nearly all men of his age he was sexually cracked in a number of directions and the parts never fit together. On one hand, he was a very warm and sensual man who loved cats and food and wine in a way much more European-Catholic than American-Puritanic, and in this sense he lacked typical American hangups regarding hygiene and order; he was messy (his desk was always covered with strata of unfinished letters, translations and poems) but not dirty, or I should say I always had a good natural feeling about the world in his presence. On the other hand, I had the feeling that for Paul sensuality and sexuality did not flow together—I always had the impression that he allowed the woman he lived with to rot on the vine. He had serious problems about his identity regarding men and women, and he expressed this conflict in a rare self-confrontational passage in *The Selection of Heaven*:

Tell me what else this shoulder might serve for
please, I want to live beyond that
please, the drive back   300   miles
please, the ground is cold, there is
please, no other life, please,
please there IS that
difference, say it
might have been a man but
now, no care, who
could care? it was that dif-
                              (small dif-)
        erence be-
tween the man who filled was
more a child   .   You can
turn your back
or I can turn my back—

                        it is a child
unborn, it is our being
all our being
man and wife, or else the rest
of life is Jack the
life is back, is fact, is black, is
rope enuf, is no rope, is the ripper
        is the ripper
        is the ripper
is the child, un-
born perhaps,
                and sucking.

An idealization of woman in our time has roots in a man never having got enough of his mother and consequently never finding/allowing a woman to equal/surpass her image. I know that Paul's mother left his father when he was quite young and, with Paul, lived with another woman for most of the rest of her life. Paul's mother was the poet Frances Frost and while he wrote very little about her I know that she was very powerfully in him (he once sent me a photo of himself at five years old clutching the handle of a Mickey Mouse cane; his mother was standing behind him, dressed in black, with both of her hands placed firmly on Paul's shoulders—her eyes were extraordinarily intense and looked straight through you). In his poetry, at least, his primal affection is for his maternal grandfather, about whom he wrote a great graveside poem that is the sixteenth section of *The Selection of Heaven*. He had a disastrous first marriage; after fighting for years he and Freddie broke up, and to get a divorce in New York then Paul had to pay her a ton of money, which he did not have. It required him to work for four years as an editor in publishing houses as well as an eight-hour-a-day professional translator. If my sense of him is accurate, by the time he married a second time, shortly after the beginning of *The Selection of Heaven*, he was losing grip on his life and numb to really living with whom he did live with. When Sara left him the summer of 1967 he was utterly shattered, and in drunk despair made a few attempts to hurt, or possibly kill, himself. The fall of 1967 he returned to Europe, having finally received a Guggenheim Fellowship, where he met his third wife, Joan, who was much younger than him and from a similar Irish-Catholic-American background; Paul lived with her and their son Carlos until he died in the autumn of 1971. I think they were deeply happy together, and I am certain that having a son meant a great deal to Paul—but he met Joan too late, he was too far into a downward spin, his body was too rundown from years of steady drinking and smoking. He died of cancer of the esophagus, and my impression was that the life-negative root I felt in him as early as 1963 was as much involved with this as anything else.

Most people who are artists, though, are not so because they have solved great human problems or even the daily minutiae, but because of the particular way they feel these problems and minutiae are unsolvable in their own lives. It is not even a matter of simply feeling deeply, for there are many, many people who feel deeply and suffer the world thoroughly who never have anything to do with art. No, it takes a particular set of imbalances, incredible stresses in some directions with unusual absences in others, faults, burning explosive deposits and areas of glacial motion that create the energy stresses that volcano under an art. It is not possible to say what is THE artistic conflict (or for that matter, the artistic glory) because each artist is a product of his upbringing, a crucible of his times, as well as a creator of his own vision. True, I can say that a thorough reading of Paul Blackburn's lesser poems reveals him as a man haunted by sex-in-the-head who viewed women as sexual-relief possibilities, but as soon as I point this out I am also aware that his so-called failures are part of the reason he is compelling, and fragments such as got through to me and burned me against my own stem on the 1963 tape he sent to Kyoto may be the very things that count. Perhaps it is fair to say that he did not explore his obsessions far enough, that he was defeated by the very vulnerability that allowed him to let in and assimilate his world. When I look at photos of Paul taken in the early fifties he looks amazingly compact and focused, and in spite of what happened to him this plumb line was present until the end. He was a very non-competitive man living in the fifties and sixties in the most competitive art center in the world—he absorbed too much—many people took advantage of his meager defenses, his own generation of poets lacked respect for him—it may be that he was simply too frail to withstand the world he chose to live in, yet when I say that I must also recognize at the very base of what I know of his being a kind of meaninglessness, a failure to know what he was about, to compete, in other words, through asserting his ideas and making them felt in those he was in contact with. It is easy to be sentimental here—surely many people watched Paul Blackburn lug his fifty-pound tape-recorder up 2nd Avenue to the St. Marks Church to record poetry readings once or twice a week for seven or eight years, and many, not just a few, but many poets alive today are beholden to him for a basic artistic kindness, for readings yes, and for advice, but more humanly for a kind of comradeship that very few poets are willing to give. HE WAS AN ANGEL working for no profit or big reputation gain to keep alive a community of poetry in New York City—he stayed with the poets instead of the critics and publishers and he paid for it. In fact, those who let him down the most were often those he felt the closest to. I remember the formation of the Poetry Project at St. Mark's Church around 1967 when suddenly money became available mainly because a poetry program had been built up through Paul's unpaid efforts. The Church, by which I mean the minister and some local poets, decided to establish paid readings as well as a paid director, a poet who would be paid $15,000 a year for doing officially what Paul had done before informally. It was obvious to a lot of people that Paul was the natural choice for the position, but it was not given to him. I recount this episode mainly for its aftermath: Paul continued to serve, continued to tape readings, to read and help arrange readings. I think he continued because in a dogged and pathetic way he was like the old employee replaced by the machine who insists on continuing his work even if in a mock role. Paul lacked the anger to tell the whole gang to go fuck themselves and take his energy and intelligence elsewhere. This kind of mole-insistence is very interesting, and the more I think about it the more it reveals about Paul. When one paid him a visit, often, after being cordially met at the door one was turned into a listener for what Paul wanted to play among recent tapes or what he felt the visitor should hear. At times it felt as if he was teaching something, like helping one to get over a prejudice about someone else's poetry—as for me, I never really knew what was up—certainly there must have been a reason to listen to so-and-so for an hour before being able to have a conversation—or was that just something Paul put *me* through?

One thing I have had to struggle with in writing this is that I must not explain his meaninglessness, must not give it a mythic quality, for when I think of his death I think of an absence that was never explained in his life. It is possible to say any life is meaningless or meaningful, of course, depending upon the good or ill will with which one approaches that life— but I speak of extruding particularities with Blackburn—the anecdotes he enjoyed telling that became more and more without conclusion or point as he grew older and less in control. I have imagined his relationship to his gull as one of retreating into the gull's head to sit and be by himself, for it was contact with others that was much of his trouble, contact—to not have to stay in contact, to avert his eyes, to tell the story or put on the tape to derail for a moment the other so Paul would not have to feel he had to make sense of his own life—I see him enter the gull's head and pick up little things in his hands to look at and puzzle over, like childhood toys he had almost forgotten—there he is safe, no one can betray or not betray him in this place—then he becomes anxious after a while and crawls back through the gull's eye into the presence of others.

I went over to Sparky's pen
where the little turds were steaming with joy, I picked them up
and placed them on the out-stretched Gull-robe. After I had a pile
I began to mold them into a gull shape, then I wrapped it in
the robe and dug a hole, burying the Corpse of Gull-robe
    by my childhood place of secret joy.
        As I completed my task a figure loomed at garage edge,
            Weren't you supposed to clean the eaves trough this
afternoon, it said,
            I smiled, ok,
            a ladder was in my hands
I was 9 feet off the ground, Clayton Sr was standing under me,
        the despair in his face, checking me out for evil,
concerned if I was doing a cud job, was I swallowing my cud, was
I doing a cud or was I spitting out the influence, was I swallowing
the cudfluence or was I manufacturing my own salts?
        As he stared at me I transferred myself to 12 years old
and through this transference maintained the vector of his stare
through the eaves trough into the interior of the white garage. Here
is the place I understood Blackburn is to transform himself. I
    kneaded
the energy from Clayton's eyes, made out the white garage interior,
in the rear was Sparky's inside pen, so she'd be warm in winter,
above the pen the shelf where storm windows were stacked,
building out from this shelf was a false garage ceiling Clayton
had constructed, to pile boards and garden tools on—the ridgepole
and false ceiling made a hazardous little house at its peak
four feet high, an attic of sorts, enormous
wonder of my puberty body up there on a hot summer day
interlocked with urine
                    Attis
                        saw, here I now crouched, unzipped,
    a vine institched with tiny skulls spilled out
    plums, persimmons, grapefruit, I transferred
outside the white garage again and got more energy from Clayton's
    eyes

pumpkins, pears, an outbranch of apples,
the strengthened false ceiling now abounded in vegetation,
I transferred to a wall, picked up the grass-stained hedge shears,
began to sever the fruits from my vine, hanging them on pegs and
    tool
          nails,
transferred down to Sparky's pen, scooped up her puppies
drawing the birth-glisten from their blind bodies
I built tensile webs; now the walls went into transformation, spider
guardians began to scuttle
in and out of the vegetal wall, this circulation developed for a week,
the following Saturday I opened the right-hand garage door onto a
jungle! A place Clayton had never seen—I left the cavern and started
    forth,
Blackburn's presence was now everywhere, about a mile from the
    cavern
I could see the blue Mediterranean waters, out on the beach in
    solitude
a figure was seated on a little wood chair at a table writing,
as I approached it turned and watched me, its beak closed, its eyes
beady, unmoving, at the base of its feathered neck were human
    shoulders,
from the freckles I knew, yes, and from its short muscular build—
Can you speak, I said,
          the creature nodded yes then shook its beak no,

                              it sat at Blackburn's kitchen table on one
of his kitchen chairs,
                    I walked over to see what he had written,

*In a way, it's hard to know that I know you anymore. Deep, OKay,
yes, forever, etc. But you've learned & grown & changed so much in
the last couple years it IS hard to know. Things do get thru in poems,
to & from both of us, I guess, that are not discussed in letters. Then*

long time when I do not feel like letters or any other contact, that
problem. And the whole problem of experience, the sharing of it,
giving it to someone, or wholly.

I've returned the Gull-robe, I said,
   and fashioned a place for you, for when it gets cold out here,
would you like to see it?
                    The Gullpaul stood up and began to walk
   back with me, along the path he took my hand,
and we walked hand in hand to the Cavern of Self

 I have to leave you here, I said—
as you gave me your life
that moment in Kyoto 1963
when I was nearly dead with despair,
so I have created
a place for you wrought
from the most intense moment of my puberty—
this is not how I thought it would end,
but the weight of the sadness of death is
in me, even facing you here—
I had thought to put a bar in along the right-hand wall
but that meant comfort, and the place I leave you
is shelter yet terrible, is formed of my spirit
which you helped form, yet dark with Clayton's eyes
transformed into spider guardians,
Use this place, or abandon it,

      he entered it, his back lost in the echoing struggle

                            1973–1974

A DISCUSSION WITH JAMES HILLMAN ON PSYCHOLOGY AND POETRY

CLAYTON ESHLEMAN: I propose that the first things we address are two essays by Jung and what they imply about an opposition between psychology and art. In "On the Relation of Analytical Psychology to Poetry," written in 1922, Jung states that art and psychology cannot be compared. While he acknowledges that they have close connections, and that the connections arise from the fact that the practice of art is a psychological activity, he still wants to keep them separate. He then makes a distinction between intentional and spontaneous art, and sets forth these two categories as follows:

Intentional Art	Spontaneous Art
"sentimental"	"naive"
Introverted	Extroverted
A conscious art,	An unconscious art,
one that does not	one that is suprapersonal
challenge comprehension	and transcends understanding.

In an essay written in 1929, "Psychology and Literature," Jung more or less maintains these two categories, but expresses them in a terminology more appropriate to his own psychological thinking:

Psychological Art	Visionary Art
Art that nowhere transcends	Art arising from primordial
the bounds of psychological	experience, grotesque, demonic,
understanding.	beyond historical and mytho-
	logical events.

In both essays, Jung clearly shows a preference for the spontaneous/visionary category, and he seems to be proposing something incompatible between cogitative, planned activity and inspired, "seized" activity—in

---

This discussion is based on an interview with Hillman taped in Dallas, Texas, in 1983; it was rewritten in 1985, and covers approximately one-third of the taped material. It appeared in *Sulfur*.

fact, in the 1922 essay, he states that "as long as we are caught up in the process of creation, we neither see nor understand; indeed we ought not understand, for nothing is more injurious to immediate experience than cognition."

My experience has been that Jung's oppositional categories are backed up by the majority of significant twentieth-century poetry. Few poets would use Jung's terminology, but most would participate in some form of oppositionalism, whether it is Dionysus vs. Apollo, Romantic *vs.* Classical or experimental *vs.* traditional. The tendency is to believe that there is a kind of Blakean antinomy between the "prolific" and the "devouring," Devils *vs.* Angels, that is an essential aspect of poetry itself, and that this "war" is played out from generation to generation, with each side accusing the other of not really being what they propose to represent. While it may be that a yin/yang coherence of the new warring with the old is essential to imaginative movement, the poetic products always seem to be heavily indebted to one of the two sides.

Rainer Maria Rilke, who would be close to Jung's spontaneous/visionary category, articulately defends what could be thought of as an anti-analytical and anti-revisionary position that is dependent upon an inspirational wind or angel sweeping through the poet. In a 1921 letter, he wrote: "I believe that as soon as an artist has found the living center of his activity, nothing is so important for him as to remain in it and never to go further away from it (for it is also the center of his personality, his world) than up to the inside wall of what he is quietly and steadily giving forth; his place is *never*, not even for an instant, alongside the observer and judge." Now, this observer or judge—is this the doctor, the psychologist, the man of science?

JAMES HILLMAN: Yes, I think so, but I also think that the notion of the psychologist as man of science/observer—I think that's where the trouble is. I think that psychologists have fallen into that. They have imagined themselves to be objective, outside critics. Or they have imagined themselves to be interpreters, or commentators, and in the scientific flow, even Freud was there. But the psychologist who is inside his own response is not necessarily outside either, and he is risking, and up against the wall, of his own place, I don't want to say center, but place.

ESHLEMAN: You mean that when Freud is working with Leonardo da Vinci, you think of him as doing primary, creative, imaginative work, even though he is responding to a previous text?

HILLMAN: Yes, and his genre is different, and his writing style is different. It's not effuse, it's not based on rhythm, it's not based on what I would call a poetic genre of writing, but there is poesis going on in it.

ESHLEMAN: Would you go so far as to agree with Jung's statement in regard to what you've just said about Freud? I mean, where he says that as long as we're caught up in the process of creation, we neither see nor understand.

HILLMAN: I would not agree. Because I think Jung is sharing the same viewpoint as Rilke here. And I wouldn't agree with that. I would say that when you're in the midst of the process of—I don't want to use the word "creation" either, it tends to get inflated—but in the midst of writing, or speaking a poem, or whatever, let's just say writing, there is a seeing going on in the hand and in the heart, and in the eye, which is not the kind of seeing that Jung is talking about which is detached outside seeing, but the fingers have an eye in them. E-Y-E. An eye that knows to put down this word and not that word and to cross that out suddenly and to jump to the next thing. That's all seeing. It's not blind. That's again a romantic sense that there's natural creativity and then there's detached scientific observation.

ESHLEMAN: The eyes are in the fingers—meaning, there is an organizing going on that is perhaps not rational in the sense that it would be used in the context of logic. But it is rational or coherent to the creative process itself.

HILLMAN: Absolutely! And I even believe, even in Nietzsche, or in Goethe's *Faust*, which you could say are "spontaneous" in Jung's language, extremely spontaneous, or without guilt, there is a built-in critical learned tradition. It's not absent. Those are not simply effusions. Human consciousness is built into their language, and it isn't even *their* language. It's built into *the* language, perhaps, and their access to language through learning. That's perhaps another side of the issue we're looking at. I mean, it's not some sort of primordial effusion. It's terribly formed as well.

ESHLEMAN: So one way to approach the split is to think that the role of imaginational activity as associated with the poem has been too weighted on the side of the unconscious or of the effusion in which the poet is viewed as this kind of receptacle through whom the power moves, but who has, as it were, no control over the power. And then the psychologist is weighted too far, as he who is in control, he who is, as it were, judging the process, evaluating the process.

HILLMAN: Absolutely. In other words, the discussion has always used the terminology of a certain court model, which splits consciousness from unconsciousness, reason from unreason, creation from criticism, and I think it is, fundamentally, a romantic paradigm. And it puts great weight on access. That the poet is a special person who has access to this beyond. Therefore, the poet is put in the category with the insane, the child, the primitive and, at one time, women. They all had special access to this beyond.

ESHLEMAN: Well, it is a very nifty way of containment. It's a way to applaud and view the poet on Parnassus at the same time that you can definitely say he is irresponsible, and has no real responsible relationship to what he is doing.

ESHLEMAN: I'd like to keep the Rilke statement before us for a bit longer. It is not clear from his statement about the living center *vs.* the observer and judge, whether he would admit conscious, intentional shaping as a valid part of the creative process. Does he mean that the artist should not judge or observe his work while it is being created, or merely not assume the role of observer/judge when he is not creating? As you may know, Rilke had a deep-seated fear of correction. In 1912, when he was seriously considering Freudian analysis, he wrote to Lou Andreas-Salomé: "I rather shun this getting cleared out and, with my nature, could hardly expect anything good of it. Something like a disinfected soul results from it, a monstrosity, alive, corrected in red like the page of a school note-book." While Rilke did not appear to mind if analysis exorcised his "devils"—thinking of them as neurotic habits, I guess, rather than as chthonic powers—he feared that the loss of his angels would mean that he would stop writing altogether.

His desire to stay at what he calls "the living center of his activity" must have involved a lot of observation and judgment. In fact, his concentrated, relentless effort to organize his entire life around his art seems to oppose what would otherwise be considered a highly romantic position. It is as if with great planning and rationality, Rilke built a wall around himself, entered this *temenos*, and then waited, refusing to act creatively unless he was acted upon, "seized," as it were, by one of his angels.

Another point: Freudian analysis in Rilke's day seems to have regarded creativity as being analogous to pathological processes—in fact, while not reductive in the way that Freud can be (seeing images as cover-figures or concealments of basic personal life experience), Jung himself states in the 1922 essay: "The divine frenzy of the artist comes perilously close to a pathological state." If Rilke believed that Freud believed that works of art were an expression of human pathology, he was probably smart to stay away from analysis.

HILLMAN: Now, Clayton, we can't take seriously this "divine frenzy" idea! I know that authority from Plato through Jung argues for it. I know it still appears in notions of the artist as shaman or medicine man for the tribe, or the artist in league with the devil as in Mann's *Doctor Faustus*. But these words "divine" and "frenzy" have to be unpacked because they come loaded with unconscious Protestant theology, where divine means some glossolaic trance state descending from the Wholly Other (Rudolph Otto), and where "frenzy" means madness, pathology, instead of what it might once have meant when gods were present in the actual world, in Rilke's sense, and not only present in subjective states of possession. "Divine frenzy," then and now, could mean something far different from Jung's "pathological state." It could mean very close participation with or immersion in actual reality—reality as the radiance of the actual world rather than the descent of inspiration from another world or lifting off to another world. Besides, we have to unpack these words in regard to Jung himself, autobiographically, his anxiety regarding Nietzsche, Dionysus and Wotan. I examined this complex very closely in a paper published in the book I edited called *Facing The Gods*, and you can see in that paper how Jung's division regarding art and psychology parallels his division in himself between personality Number One and personality Number Two. Nietzsche, Dionysus and Wotan as well as the artist, the shaman and the madman are all possibilities of personality Number Two. You see, the entire structure in which Jung casts his life, let's say the narrative of his self-diagnosis, is also the structure he uses to view the artist. Pat Berry worked this out in great length in her study of Jung's buried aesthetics, and we shall have to come back to it with her later. That really is her subject: aesthetics or poetics in relation to psychology.

ESHLEMAN: Let's go on then with Freud and Rilke. There is good evidence that Rilke's masterpiece, the *Duino Elegies*, was begun out of the poet's despair that should he call out for divine aid, no angel would hear him. The entire work opens: "Who if I cried out would hear me among the angels' / hierarchies? and even if one of them pressed me / suddenly against his heart: I would be consumed / in that overwhelming existence." This suggests that if the artist feels that his chosen position, as it were, has abandoned him, he will move to the opposite pole and, like Rilke, set himself on fire by attacking the betraying angel.

All this leads me to believe that we must re-imagine the psychology of cognition, bricolage and inspiration. Perhaps we could begin to do so by asking why Jung insisted on a dichotomy. Was he basing his theories on Classical vs. Romantic "ideals" as manifest in particular works of art, or was he saying something about human sensibility and the extent to which it is creatively limited—that there is something about "us" that experiences creativity as an either/or situation?

After stating that in the process of creation we neither see nor understand, Jung goes ahead to write: "...for the purpose of cognitive understanding we must detach ourselves from the creative process and look at it from the outside; only then does it become an image that expresses what we are bound to call 'meaning.'" Clearly, he is referring only to "spontaneous" or "visionary" art here (and by implication relegating *his* other kind of art to a very secondary role). Jung's statement strongly suggests that an artist does not know what his activity signifies while he is doing it. I think this is nearly always partially but *only partially* true—the "muse" of Picasso's *Guernica* was a squad of German bombers (when asked by some German officers, standing before the canvas, "Did you do this?" he is said to have replied, "No, you did"). But I think it is fair to assume that throughout the process of doing the painting, Picasso was aware of the significance of what he was creating—he may not have had an accurate sense as to what extent the world was going to consider it significant, but the fact that its execution was in part a response to a horrible event "out there" creates an immediate field of meaning.

HILLMAN: I think Jung's emphasis on the spontaneous takes aim at those who reduce a poem or painting to an external field of meaning—those German Stuka Bombers. The field of meaning "out there" is always part of the context from which a dream, a poem or anything flows, but that field of meaning is not the cause, or the substance, or the meaning of the dream, poem, etc. Psychology often misses this point in practice. It either literalizes the spontaneous and cuts off an event from any external field of meaning or it literalizes the field of meaning and reduces the event to it. Spontaneous has to be understood not literally, but spontaneous within a specific image or context in which the spontaneity appears. Appears *here*, and only *here*, and not somewhere else.

ESHLEMAN: Jung also places strong emphasis on "the primordial" when he discusses "visionary" art. It is "a primordial vision which surpasses man's understanding... it arises from timeless depths; it is foreign and cold, many-sided, demonic and grotesque... it suggests the abyss of time separating us from pre-human ages..." I find this definition to be very troublesome; in fact, I do not know how I could accommodate it to most of the poetry I consider to be visionary, because regardless of the extent of the prophetic activity, it is anchored in the anguish of its own times and is, to varying degrees, an imaginative adjustment, or a reaction, against thwarted desire. It appears as if Jung only regarded art of the considerable past when he made his comments about psychology and art, or that there is something inherently distancing in both of his defined artistic categories. To separate the intentional from the spontaneous, or the psychological from the visionary, is to draw a line down the center of much art that participates in all four modes. It seems to be ultimately undermining to the creative process, and in effect subordinates the artist to the observer or judge. Each "type," for Jung, is incomplete, and two incompletes do not add up to a single "whole" artist. It is not only a curious way of exalting and castrating the artist at the same time, but it performs the same kind of elevation/subordination on the work of the psychologist or "judge." His compensation for not being primordially creative is to be seen as a healthy, wise, responsible citizen, empowered with the right to extend or deny significance.

HILLMAN: I seem to be trapped into opposing Jung, yet I can't help feeling annoyed by this word "primordial." Am I hanging on words? Why do I dislike "primordial"—probably because it brings with it all those half-thought-through Darwinian assumptions, cavemen as ape men, developmental history toward the light, and the notion of ourselves as refined, effete, weak-kneed dilettantes making up ineffectual trivia with our minds while deep underneath in the past or in the soul lies grunting primordial truth. This notion of "primordial" leads to an effusionist notion of art, art production based on an altered state of consciousness. Laudanum, absinthe, gin, LSD, cocaine. But what about art as craft, art in cultures where there is no "art" as we call it, where there are only chants made for rituals, objects made for eating, where there is exquisitely complicated dancing, body-painting, and masking? These cultures are also "primordial," and yet not merely wild, savage, or volcanic. Isn't it told that the people of Bali, for instance, when asked about their "art," reply by saying they don't know what that is; they simply make things as well as they can. No effusion or inspiration here, maybe no novelty either, but at least the everyday and the gods, the ordinary and the beautiful are not divided from each other. So I prefer "primordial" to mean essential or irreducible. So, a painting by Edward Hopper of a gas station or a cafeteria at night is so exactly irreducible to anything beyond itself, so descriptive of the despairing American soul (which is both its referent and not its referent), that this careful, almost mathematical, image is primordial because it is essential.

ESHLEMAN: Perhaps we should consider to what extent "access" and "the beyond" are terms that hold up under scrutiny. W. H. Auden has argued that the loss of belief in the eternity of the physical universe, including a loss of belief in the significance and reality of sensory phenomena, have made an artistic vocation more difficult than it used to be. "The beyond" may be a booby prize for those who have lost contact with what is at hand—or as Charles Olson tried to drive home via Heraclitus, "Man is estranged from that with which he is most familiar." It is as if at a certain point in his history man left the thing at hand to quest for immortality, and when that pursuit was revealed to be empty, he was left with the thing at hand, the soul of which had withered from being untended for so long. We now live in a world with a broken beyond and a plastic cup, and one reason that you and I are talking here is because of this. We both seek to lift the essential up through the consumer film and work with it in imagination without vatic inflation.

Because the poet no longer performs a useful function in society, he is to a great extent parked to the side in a playpen where he can dream and say anything. If his writing is entertaining, he is occasionally picked up and carried about in adult arms for a little soul titillation. But the serious poet is not entertaining. He is still involved, as I believe you are, with attempting, through sounding his own adhesion and estrangement, to engage a reader or hearer. Unlike the psychologist, however, his address is more elliptical, harder to get hold of, because he proceeds associationally instead of logically. I think it is a proven fact that an educated person could grasp a good deal of one of Jung's lectures on literature and psychology, but that the same person would be lost on a first or second hearing of *The Wasteland*. On the other hand, your writing in, say, "Blue and the Unio Mentalis" tends to engage associational, or paratactical alignments, so that the argument slides, or moves sideways as it moves forward.

One of the reasons that poets and psychologists have been out of touch with each other is due to the poet's lack of psychological sophistication. From the Romantic viewpoint, such sophistication would be suspect, because the moment of inspiration is absolute and not to be understood by the poet who is to function like a gate (or radio, in Jack Spicer's modern version), through which the poem rushes. I know the thrill, or the bony certainty, of absolute address, and I am tempted, when it occurs, to believe it is the truth, and that it should not be tampered with, regardless of how it looks a week later (awkward, inaccurate, inadequate, etc.), for to think of it as scrutinizable is to regard it as mortal, changeable, capable of error, revisable. I think that, possibly, poets who assert the absolute truth of inspired address do so because they do not want to deal with what other aspects of their mind tell them has occurred at the inspired moment. In that sense, they could be considered psychologically irresponsible.

In his 1929 formulation, Jung puts the poet in an impossible situation: If his writing is psychological, meaning if it remains within the bounds of psychological intelligibility, it is, by the way the definition is set up, inferior—a kind of poeticized psychology, versified discourse. If, on the other hand, it is visionary, arising out of "primordial experience which surpasses man's understanding," who can possibly care about it? It may be worshipped by a handful of people who will pass it around like a chunk from outer space, people who adore unintelligibility as an end in itself, and if there are enough followers, over the years a critical "house" will be built for it, and it will enter the canon as one of the diamonds in the national literary tiara.

I realize that by putting it this way, I am on the verge of saying that because Blake was not understandable to virtually anyone for at least a hundred years after his death, he is solely responsible. Much of Blake now appears to be understandable *and* visionary, so *that* possibility must be kept open—that art which surpasses contemporary understanding can be judged unintelligible for reasons that have little to do with its value. Because it offends taste and style, say, people may claim that it is unintelligible.

HILLMAN: Let's set aside the word psychological for a moment and just talk about the responsibility of the poet. To what is he responsible? Is he not responsible to the poem? Or responsible to receiving, getting out of the way of what Robert Duncan might call "the angels and the demons"? So that he isn't in the way of that, doesn't disturb that, but lets it come through well? Doesn't the poet sense a responsibility in the act of his work?

ESHLEMAN: Getting out of the way of the angels and demons and being responsible to the poem is fine as long as it does not mean a cessation of thinking. To use your image, it means insisting that the angels and demons emerge from the midnight murkiness of the corner of the studio and allow their teeth and messages to be checked out. I believe that there should be a constant critical pressure applied to irrational message. However, if you are arguing that one reason poems fail is because the speaker has fore-grounded himself at the expense of imaginational activity, I agree. Then the poem takes on very small grounds and finally becomes only the poet's "scene," e.g., a description of something that he once did—and for him to offer this as his experience is not enough.

HILLMAN: Certainly not enough. But I say it is comparable with ego-psy-chology. It's comparable with the reduction of the extraordinary that goes on in a dream, and in a life, to my personal experience of it. And psychol-ogy, for the most part, today is comparable then with poetry, for the most part—it teaches you to do that. That's what a psychological training is supposed to do, to turn the imaginal richness of the psyche into your own personal account of it. So you lose the archetypal dimension, you lose what you call the imaginational activity. You lose the whole sense of the gods in art in your life. And the focus is on "me," not on the gods. When Rilke keeps turning us back, when he says to get inside your own experi-ence, he doesn't mean it in the subjectivist modern sense of inside your own ego experience. Inside your own experience is focused on the giving back. Because your experience, as I try to say, too, in what I write, is not yours, it is the soul's, and the soul is inherently related to the gods, so that being in the center of your experience is not being in the center of what we commonly call "my" experience. The "my" is sort of *ausgehoben* ("lift-ed out, removed").

ESHLEMAN: I was talking with Rosemary, the student who picked me up at the [Dallas] airport the other day. She was asking me questions such as, "What is your experience of yourself in the poem?" I made a distinction between the fictive or imaginational "I" and the autobiographical "I," and suggested that the freedom for any "I" to appear in the poem, for there to be a shifting sense of "I" that does not lock into autobiographical frame, was one way to approach the experience of oneself in the poem. The image I offered her, colored by my involvement with Upper Paleolithic cave paintings of animals, went like this: I am in the driver's seat, I initiate the poem as driver, but as the poem gets under way, there is a sense of being outside and almost, to stir the metaphor, of running with an animal, say, through a field, so while it is clearly C. E. sitting in his room doing the writing, there is the sense that the less I interfere, in other words, it is like having this animal bounding…

HILLMAN: That's a wonderful image. Wonderful. That's marvelous. And you don't want to lose touch with the animal by making wrong moves of your own. So, your self-consciousness is focused on keeping in touch. Isn't that why one says, right in the middle of writing something, "Oh, I've lost it. It's gone." By this I mean I've lost touch with that leaping, bounding (or burrowing) animal. I do believe this is what we mean when we say we've lost our concentration. The nose is on a scent, tracking, and all of a sudden, the track is gone. This keeping on the track, or what's called concentration, is one focus of self-consciousness. It's a dim awareness, of honing, of direction, of attentiveness. But it's not *will*. It's not willing yourself to the track as if it is my personal intention to squeeze out of myself just what I want to say in this paragraph—although that kind of self-consciousness can come in too. Sometimes, losing the track may simply be picking up on a cross scent. Another animal lures the line of thought into another part of the forest. This feels like a distraction, dis-track-shun, and just here still another kind of self-consciousness appears: oscillating between two ways to pursue. Then, there's another kind of self-consciousness or dim awareness. To do with rhythm or beat. To do with form. I feel what I am writing is getting too long or wordy. This kind of focus is on the overall fantasy of the piece as a whole. It is very much in my mind when I write something—that it not break out of the dimension of the piece. I think this is the psychological experience of what Aristotle called *unity*.

1983–1985

In his Introduction to my *Selected Poems 1960–1985*, Eliot Weinberger writes: "As for translation: the dissolution of the translator's ego is essential if the foreign poem is to enter the language—a bad translation is the insistent voice of the translator."

My first experience with what I think Weinberger means by "the translator's ego" was with Ben Belitt's translations of Garcia Lorca's *Poet in New York*, in 1959. Belitt appeared to be imposing his own poetic voice onto the Spanish text when, for example, he translated the last line of Lorca's poem "La Aurora," "como recién salidas de un naufragio de sangre" as, "as though lately escaped from a bloody disaster." Lorca's "shipwreck of blood," a powerful direct image that needs no translational revision, had not only been lost but turned into British-English slang—Belitt's "bloody," as in "he's a bloody good bloke," neatly effaced Lorca's "blood." In the case of Belitt's Lorca and Neruda translations, we hear the translator-poet's own mannerisms leaking into and rendering rococo the meaning of the original texts. It is as if Belitt is colonizing the foreign terrain of these poets instead of accommodating himself to the ways in which they differ from his own poetic intentions.

The image of a translator colonizing the foreign terrain of an original text has somber implications, especially in the case of a "first-world" translator working on a "third-world" writer. By adding to, subtracting from and reinterpreting the original, the translator implies that he knows more than the original text knows, that in effect his mind is superior to its mind. The "native text" becomes raw material for the colonizer-translator to educate and re-form in a way that instructs the reader to believe that the foreign poet is aping our literary conventions.

Belitt, of course, is not alone in such activity, although his imposition seems more monolithic and damaging than that of many other translators. When Robert Lowell drops out ten of Rimbaud's twenty-five stanzas in translating "Le bateau ivre," there seems to be a presumption that only

---

"The Translator's Ego" was originally written for a presentation on translation at Bookworks in San Francisco (February 1986).

two-thirds of one of the greatest poems in the French language is worth carrying over to English. Cid Corman, at times an extraordinarily fine translator, has a tendency to eliminate repetitive phrases and to drop articles. This appears to be a manifestation of his own poetics which have led to the short, terse lyrics he is well known for. I, too, am guilty of ego imposition. For example, in my 1968 translation of Vallejo's poetry, I rendered the line, "pero me busca y busca. Es una historia!" as, "but she looks and looks for me. What a fucking story!"

The Vallejo poem in question here is made up of a series of anguished lamentations on the failure of his wife to connect with him. During the first eight years that I translated Vallejo, I was unable to connect with Georgette Vallejo—by which I mean that she constantly blocked my work with the excuse that no one could properly translate her late husband's poetry. After much effort, by a fluke, Grove Press gained permission to publish the translation. One afternoon I was sitting in Gil Sorrentino's office going over galleys. When I came to the poem in question, I read it to Gil and complained that the last line—at that point rendered, "but she looks and looks for me. What a story!"—lacked punch. By that point, Vallejo's "Es una historia!" was not only loaded with his consternation, but had taken on the symbolic weight of my struggle with the translation and with his widow. My memory is that after a moment's reflection, Sorrentino threw up his hands and exclaimed, "what a fucking story!" and in a giddy moment I said, "that's it!" and added the intensifier to the line. I was wrong to do so, and when José Rubia Barcia and I retranslated the poem six years later, we took it out.

I've gone into a little detail here not to excuse myself but to suggest that a translator's impositions upon his text are not necessarily a worked-out plan to create a new tone or meaning for the original. Were Lowell to be here, he might explain (probably not to my satisfaction) that he left all those stanzas out because he was unable to render them to his satisfaction. Corman might argue that by cutting here and there rather than adhering to the original at every point, he had made a sharper and not really unfaithful version in English.

So, how might a translator work to resist ego imposition or, at worst, translational imperialism? For the fact is, there is no such thing as a literal translation of a poem—denotative choices come up in every line. There is a constant process of interpretation going on, regardless of how faithful one attempts to be to the original.

When the original poet is available for questioning, a certain amount of denotational guesswork can be eliminated. When one is translating the great dead, or out of contact with the author, the only indicators come from the text at large, and the way key words can be identified relative to the author's background. While translating the Martinican Aimé Césaire with Annette Smith, I visited Césaire several times, always with a few pages of specific word questions. Given Césaire's busy schedule, it was never possible to ask him all the questions that came up in translating him, so many tricky decisions had to be made on the basis of the text itself. As an example: Smith and I occasionally came across the word "anse," which can be rendered as "bay/cove/creek," or "[basket] handle." Since Césaire's poetry is very specific to Martinican geography, and since the entire island is pocked with bays and coves (which had led to such place-names as Anse Pilote, or Grande Anse d'Arlet etc), the obvious choice here seemed to be "bay" or "cove" (assuming that the context of a particular poem does not call for a "handle" reading). Yet in the 1969 Berger-Bostock translation of Césaire's *Notebook of a Return to the Native Land*, we find "les Antilles qui ont faim... bourgeonnant d'anses frêles..." translated as "the hungry Antilles... delicately sprouting handles for the market." Not only has the Surrealist Césaire been falsely surrealized, but the translators have backed up their error by adding an explanation to the reader as to what these handles are for. When Smith and I retranslated the *Notebook* in 1976, we rendered these phrases as "the hungry Antilles... burgeoning with frail coves ..."

In the case of Vallejo, I learned not only to check my work with Peruvians and Spanish scholars, but to check their suggestions against each other and against the dictionary. I worked to find word-for-word equivalents, not explanatory phrases. I also respected Vallejo's punctuation, intentional misspellings, line and stanza breaks, and tried to render his obscurity and flatness as well as his clarity and brilliance. An unsympathetic reviewer of Barcia's and my work, John Simon, exclaimed: "Eshleman has tried to render every wart of the original!" Which is, in fact, exactly what we had tried to do—to create in English a non-cosmeticized Vallejo.

As a poet translating another poet, I let my sense of my relationship to Vallejo and his poetry enter my own poetry, so that the translating activity, in the context of an apprenticeship, was envisioned and critiqued as an aspect of my own evolving poetics. Over the years, I constantly tried to skim my own imaginings of Vallejo off the surface of the translations and let them ferment in my own poetry. I came to understand that if a translator does not do this, he runs the risk of building up an imaginal residue in his translation, which, with no outlet of its own, spills into the text.

The thing is: Imagination is always present. We know this when we try to remember and write down a dream upon waking. As we try to remember we forget, and in the flux we reorganize, imagining the dream into a writing that ends up locking the nebulosity of psyche into a fixed grid of print. In a similar way, our imaginations are active as we move one language into another. As we read translationally, we risk revising the original to reinforce our dream of a poetics that might hold its own against alternative poetics.

All the poets I have spent long periods of translation time with—Neruda, Vallejo, Artaud, Césaire, Deguy—have drawn me because I felt that their poetry knew something that my poetry wanted to know. Besides attempting to make accurate, readable versions, I was also involved in a secondary plot, or a sub-text, wanting to shovel some of their psychic coal into my own furnaces.

Since translation is such slow work, requiring multiple rereadings, it can require a more prolonged reading-in-depth than when we read poetry written in our own language. As the translator scuttles back and forth between the original and the rendering he is shaping, a kind of "assimilative space" is opened up in which "influence" may be less contrived and literary than when drawing upon masters of one's own language. The kind of "influence" I have in mind here involves becoming porous to the *character* of the original, and to the various ways in which it resists or does not resist being transformed.

Thus in the case of Vallejo, I do not think of myself as having been influenced, at least not directly, by his Marxism, his Christianity, or by his own indigenous influence which, since he was a Peruvian sierra cholo, gives his writing much of its austerity, anxiety and immutability. No, in

Vallejo's case, I believe that it is his capacity for contradiction, and the consequent complexity of viewpoint that has been the fuel. He offered me not merely ideas and stances, but a way of receiving and twisting the blows of the world.

1986

XIV

from *Companion Spider*

(2002)

Many creative writing students put too much of their energy into defending what they write, forming a resistance to change which occurs while attempting to write in a way that depends on change as its primary characteristic.

Rimbaud tells us that I is another. He means by this that the I one brings initially to writing poetry is at best a chrysalis for incubating an imago, an imaginatively mature, or monstrous I whose life is in the poem. To achieve this second I one must *translate* the first I, moving it from the language of experience and memory to the language of imagination and inspiration.

The poet Rilke has declared that no one should engage in such a "translation" unless he would be willing to acknowledge that he would have to die if it were denied him to write. After making this severe statement, Rilke somewhat softened the matter, adding: "above all: ask yourself in the stillest hour of the night: *must* I write?

Rilke is extreme on this point because he knows that a half-hearted response to such a calling leads nowhere. Some students may feel that I am too hard on them, too critical of what they write. My response is that I am trying to instill in them a sense of just how hard they must be on themselves to be able to translate their given I into a creative I.

However, I would be willing to depart from Rilke's command and say that a limited commitment has its uses, and that working on poems can make one a better reader, a better seer, maybe a better lover.

In both cases, it is hard to advance without at first imitating or translating poems of those who seem to be beacons of the art.

Then one must learn to corner oneself, in the process of being hard on oneself, and to eliminate the two intertwined enemies of the young poet.

The first is obscurity and the second, obscurity's opposite, obviousness. Like two facing banks of a roily river, these two enemies beckon, as if offering refuge from the undertow.

This piece was originally written to be copied and handed out to students in a senior-level creative writing workshop at Eastern Michigan University.

Obscurity is tempting because it releases the writer from the burden of making what he is writing meaningful. One's being obscure is an attempt to shift the burden to the reader, to make him feel that failure to find significance in the poem is his fault, that there is something paradoxically significant about obscurity. In the same way that obscurity frames the obvious, obviousness frames obscurity. What is obvious about obscurity is its failure to articulate a mid-ground, a place that the reader has to reach for (it is not obvious), *and* a place that contains a reward (significance) for those willing to reach. In the words of Havelock Ellis:

> If art is expression, mere clarity is nothing. The extreme clarity of an artist may be due not to his marvelous power of illuminating the abysses of his soul, but merely to the fact that there are no abysses to illuminate. ... The impression we receive on first entering the presence of any supreme work of art is obscurity. But it is an obscurity like that of a Catalonian cathedral which slowly grows more luminous as one gazes, until the solid structure beneath is revealed.

Such poems as Yeats's "Byzantium," Hart Crane's "Lachrymae Christi," Dickinson's "My life had stood a loaded gun," Rilke's "Duino Elegies," or César Vallejo's "Trilce I," argue that if the reader is willing to go 50% of the way, the poem will match that 50%. At the point of fusion, a child that is half poem, half reader-apprehension, is born.

When Rilke writes in the sonnet "Archaic Torso of Apollo," that "there is no place / that does not see you. You must change your life."—he seems to suggest that one must either transform oneself or be seen through. There *is* no unseeing refuge—one stands revealed at every point. This god torso, itself fragmentary, refuses to allow Rilke to cozy up to it. The torso insists that he change his life in order to perceive it, that he match its change (from a block of marble) with his own. Rilke's stirring lines are darkly echoed, some forty years later, by Paul Celan's:

Once, when death was mobbed,
you took refuge in me.

—a two line poem that bears in a haiku-like instant the European Holocaust and perhaps Celan's anguish over having to turn his heart into habitation, to admit a dear one, and to cherish all that this person was, including of course her death.

Only when one has cornered oneself can a center be found, a way of being in the poem that accepts one's gestures *and* nourishes one in return. So I lean on you to help you lean on yourself. I push you back so that in being pushed you may feel what in you is pushable. I resist you to help you feel what you yourself resist in the act of working on a poem.

You may handle this pressure in several ways. You may feel that my role is mainly to confirm what you write so that you will not feel that any deep changes must take place. This attitude evades the principle of the workshop, which, as I see it, should be a place where constructions are examined, taken apart, maybe destroyed, maybe reassembled, occasionally perfected.

You can also listen to me and reflect on what I say, scrutinizing my comments: are they useful? Disprove them out loud to yourself if they are not. Where do they lead? If anywhere, make a list of possibilities. What do they make you feel about what you felt when you were working on the poem? Have you actually written what was on your mind or have you "poeticized" it?

You may also swallow my suggestions whole hog, which is probably not much better than totally rejecting them.

When I rewrite one of your lines, rewrite my rewrite.

There is no way the reader can know what is on your mind unless you articulate it. A good poem, in this sense, is one that fills and reveals its own contextual space. It allows the reader to enter, and to think with or against it—at the same time that it protects its own integrity.

Often an inexperienced writer is baffled by what is on his mind. He writes about something that happened, drawn to it, moth-like, and before he can imagine it, or dream it, or ponder it in trance, he is consumed by it. The experience sits there on the page, thumbing its nose at both writer and reader, sealed about itself.

To corner oneself, to face the opacity, not go over or around or under it, but through it. Van Gogh:

What is drawing? How does one learn it? It is working through an invisible iron wall that seems to stand between what one *feels* and what one *can do*. How is one to get through that wall—since pounding against it is of no use? One must undermine the wall and drill through it slowly and patiently, in my opinion.

To stare for an hour at a line on a sheet in the typewriter, to realize its limitations (Who does it sound like? Has it been uttered before?). To ask such questions with a book by an admired poet open by one's side. To talk to oneself while Wallace Stevens is listening in.

Ideally, you don't need a workshop—or, I should say, you can start and run your own, with and of yourself. But as an American, you may understandably find the solitude of a Rilke or a Cézanne nearly pathological—we are so gregarious, such leaky vessels.

That is when you meet me, or someone like me, unlike most of your professors someone who practices what is at stake rather than standing outside of it and writing about it. Those of us who are writers who also teach are like pigs at a pork-judging contest. We are living examples—not always satisfactory ones—of what is under inspection. We are also burdened, as scholars are not, by our desire to be, as writers, equal to that which we are teaching. And while we may bring a gut level of creative experience to the workshop, we are to varying degrees the victims of our own tested views.

I don't think I ever leave my poetry. I may walk across campus to be with you and your attempts at poetry, but in some way I am always working with the last unfinished thing, when I cook, when I dream—even in dreamless sleep, material is seeping into the unfillable abyss called my life. As I resist accepting your writing as it is, wanting it to be more, wanting you to want more of it, a similar process—more weathered and distant from birth than yours—is turning like a cement mixer in me, folding and refolding the weight and the murk of the *to be*. If we can understand how these processes overlap, and draw off each other as well as support each other, perhaps our time together will not be wasted.

1993

In Kyoto, October 1962, I had become aware that I needed some sign—like Rilke's touching the crotch of a seaside tree and passing through to what he called "the other side of nature," or Ginsberg, after masturbating, in Harlem, hearing Blake's voice proclaiming "Ah! Sunflower"[1]—to justify writing poetry. While I can't say that I was literally on my knees, begging for a vision, I had reached a point in which nerve and blind desire *had* to be backed up by, in Blake's words, "divine aid."

It all began with a gorgeous red, green and yellow spider centered in her web attached to the persimmon tree in the Okumura backyard. I got used to taking a chair and a little table out under the web where I'd read *The Masks of God* and struggle to digest and translate César Vallejo's *Poemas humanos*. After several weeks of "spider sitting," the weather turned chill, with rain and gusting wind. When I went out one afternoon, the web was wrecked, the spider gone. Something went through me that I can only describe as the sensation of the loss of one deeply loved. I cried, and for several days felt nauseous and absurd. A week or so later, I was picked up by some sake drinkers in our local sushi bar—something that happened only this one time in my three years in Japan. The following day, I decided to motorcycle out to northwest Kyoto and visit Gary Snyder. Gary was not home, so I had tea with Joanne Kyger and, late in the afternoon, started the half-hour drive back home. I had been pleasantly hungover all day, sensory field narrowed, a lot of tendrils into areas that, in my case at least, are ordinarily available but not encloistered. Saintly sensitivities, little bowls of holiness—that is the sensation—if you can just pick out the right pebbles they will lead to a "see through."

Riding south on Junikendoori, I noticed that the motorcycle handlebars had become ox horns and that I was riding on an ox. A lumber company turned into a manger of baby Jesus with kneeling Wise Men. I forced myself to stay aware that I was in moving traffic, and looking for a place to turn off, spotted Nijo Castle with its big tourist bus parking lot. Getting

This essay was written for "The Recovery of the Public World: A Conference and Festival in Honour of the Poetry and Poetics of Robin Blaser," held in Vancouver, 1995. It appeared in the *AWP Chronicle*.

off my ox-cycle, I felt commanded to circumambulate the square Castle and its moat. I saw what appeared to be Kyger's eyeballs in the moat water. At the northwest corner, I felt commanded to look up: some forty feet above my head was the spider, completely bright red, the size of a human adult, flexing her legs as if attached to and testing her web. After maybe thirty seconds the image began to fade. I immediately felt that I had been given a totemic gift and that it would direct my relation to poetry. Out of my own body, I was to create a matrix strong enough in which to live and hunt.

I completed my circumambulation of the Castle, and very slowly cycled down Junikendoori to a coffee house in which, for what seemed to be ages, I stared at my book of Robert Herrick poems in a mass of glowing blue light. I finally got home at around midnight and after sleeping soundly woke up refreshed. Everything I tried to write about what had happened at Nijo Castle seemed superficial, so I went on to other things.

For all of 1963 I worked on Vallejo translations every afternoon in the Yorunomado coffee house in downtown Kyoto. I had convinced myself that getting these 104 poems into decent English was to be my apprenticeship to poetry. Because of what seemed to be insurmountable difficulties, I began to fantasize that I was in a life-and-death struggle with the spectre of Vallejo. I was trying to wrest his language away from him as if it were his food while he ferociously tried to thwart my thievery.

In the winter of 1963, I began to work on the first poem of my own that fully engaged and tested me. I called it, after Blake's short prophetic books, "The Book of Yorunomado,"[2] in honor of the coffee house, my Vallejo workshop. The poem had a double focus: a coming to terms with my first wife's abortion the year before, and an attempt to imagine my Jacob/angel struggle with Vallejo's labyrinthine texts. I tried to pair what was never born, as an infant, with what I was unable to bring forth myself into American English via Vallejo. The only thing I was able to wrest away from this Peruvian was a stone, and with stone in hand I found myself in a different time and place frame. I was in a large, pebbled courtyard in a medieval Japanese palace complex. The spectre of Vallejo, now dressed as an overlord, commanded me from his regal porch to commit *harakiri*, as a dishonored samurai. So I did, slicing into my Indiana guts. An eerie ecstasy ran through me as I envisioned the destruction of my given life, as if I was ripping my mother and father out of me. In the poem's final passage, "a dark red flower" appeared, opening and closing, "moving with heaven's untiring power." At the time, I made no conscious connection between the color of the flower and the spider. While I had been defeated by Vallejo at the time, I *had* written a poem I could live with.

The way the spider and the Vallejo experiences intertwined has, over the years, led me to some notions concerning muse and mentor. Initially, they play oppositional roles (for the mature poet they are in harmony). The muse is emanational (making poetry possible), while the mentor is spectral (contesting the novice's right to speak in poetry). Harold Bloom's sense of influence, welded to anxiety, is thus spectral. Neither muse nor mentor is sheerly what it appears to be; rather, they are more like the Siamese twin aspects of a single force that would inspire us at the same time it would enable us to be critically aware of what we are writing. Vicente Huidobro has a deft phrase for this. He writes: "Invent new worlds and back up what you say."[3] While the muse is traditionally feminine (for both men and woman), and mentor (possibly as a historical development of the great mother/son-lover complex) masculine, the gendering of these forces is troubling, to say the least. This problem has the smell of what Weston LaBarre called an "archosis," "a massive and fundamental misapprehension of reality, often of incalculable antiquity."[4] In a tiny poem written for but not included in the second *Maximus* volume, Charles Olson wrote[5]:

the IMMENSE ERROR
of *genderizing*
the 'Great Mother'

                inCALCULABLE
damage

So I do not want to equate red spider with muse or Vallejo with mentor. I would like to keep them in an open dimension, though specifically in and under that persimmon tree web where they were in such close proximity. The orbed web with a female spider at center is a compelling metaphor for the labyrinth. The male spider, with semen-loaded paps, must make his way to the center without signaling via the wrong vibrations that he is prey, inseminate the much larger female, and then skedaddle before she seizes and devours him.

In the Cretan labyrinth a hybrid man-bull, the Minotaur, lies in wait at the center for those who attempt to pass through. In one version of the myth, Theseus with a thread from Ariadne (whose name relates to Arachne, the weaver turned into a spider by Athena) kills the Minotaur, exits the labyrinth, and with others transmutes its turns into a weaving dance. The alchemist Fulcanelli writes: "The picture of the labyrinth is thus offered to us as emblematic of the whole labour of the Work, with its two major difficulties, one the path which must be taken to reach the center—where the bitter combat of the two natures takes place—the other the way the artist must follow in order to emerge. It is there that the *thread of Ariadne* becomes necessary for him, if he is not to wander among the winding paths of the task, unable to extricate himself."⁶

Fulcanelli turns the web-become-labyrinth into a transformational arena. This triple overlay may offer some useful leads in understanding self and other. Jung offers considerable information on his view of the self in *Psychology and Alchemy*. He calls the self the union of opposites *par excellence*, the opposition between light and good on one hand and darkness and evil on the other. He proposes that the self is absolutely paradoxical, representing in every aspect thesis and antithesis and, at the same time, synthesis. It is the totality of the psyche, embracing the conscious and the unconscious. It is the *lapis invisibilitatus*, a borderline concept, and ultimately indeterminate.

The red spider pierced my heart as an extraordinary gift. Did it bestow a self? Working through Jung, I would have to say no. It confronted me with an extreme otherness that has taken years to process, and its presence, and absence, must have bled into "the bitter combat of the two natures" that I engaged in with the obdurate *Poemas humanos*. Fulcanelli tells us a bit more about this "bitter combat," describing it as a battle between an alchemical Eagle and Lion who tear at each other until, the eagle having lost its wings and the lion its head, a single body (referred to as *animated mercury*) is formed. As a hybrid, the Minotaur consists of a grotesque synthesis prefigured by mating spiders. Both conjunctions emit a lethal aura.

Making his way between biology and classical myth here may be the ur-poet shaman, who at the center of his or her initiation undergoes symbolic torture, dismemberment, and rebirth. While the animal-masked dancing shaman originates with prehistoric hunting peoples, in the 20th century there are intriguing parallels between the career of a shaman and the life and work of Antonin Artaud. Both share a nervous crisis, a painfully isolated initiation, symbolic death—in Artaud's case, a ninety-minute coma after electroshock—and rebirth, a new name and new language, chanting, gesturing, drumming, and detailed accounts of their spirit world adventures with allies and demons. The material here is much more complex (and utterly unintentional on Artaud's part) than those associations that cropped up in the understandably disputed "white shamanism" of the 1970s.

Shamanism aside, it is possible to make use of Fulcanelli's mutilated, single body to understand something that happens in literary translation. A new body is arrived at through strife and destruction. Loss is registered by what can never be brought over from the original, as well as in the second language's limitations and inability to overcome such loss.

For the shaman as well as for Jung's initiate seeking the integration Jung called "individuation," the combat of the self, or selves, is registered either as charisma or as a dream record. While charisma or dream journals may effect the way we respond to a particular poet, the challenge for the poet is in the ability to translate self-combat into a poem. Centers begin to abound and overlap. Both Jung and Robin Blaser have emphasized indeterminacy in their work. In a copy of *Image–Nations 1–12*, Robin had written me: "this is my most incomplete and best loved work—in my view, the indeterminate is my subject and open—."[7] I checked the word the other night in my Webster's *International Dictionary* and found "see INFLORESCENCE." Under "inflorescence," I found eleven illustrations of the budding and unfolding of blossoms. Like spider webs, inflorescence is both centripetal and centrifugal.

Caught up in the propulsive maze of the now well-known process, "form is but an extension of content," the poet, every which way in conflict, may very well seek out an otherness to curb the action. Curbs are circumferences. For Blake, "Reason is the bound or outward circumference of Energy." For Emily Dickinson, circumference for a butterfly is purposeless but in resurrection full. A year before his suicide, Hart Crane was given profound advice about labyrinth and circumference by the bacteriologist Hans Zinsser.[8]

Other is a heartless word; these days we sometimes set "significant" before it to romanticize its neutrality. The other is what Theseus sees in the Minotaur. For Blaser, other is multifoliate. He identifies it as ourselves, the unthought of, a translation of oneself, the chiasmatic (via Merleau-Ponty), the anonymous, and: silence. Such definitions in transit wind out from "that odd Fork in Being's Road" (Dickinson),[9] or, "the Place of Twisted Water (Aztec), transpersonal yin-yang-like symbols for the center which is, alas, actually diffused throughout the entire labyrinth. For example: any creative project worth its salt lacks an aerial view. It is always "Groundwork: In the Dark," for decisions must be made about one's route without the overview needed to spot the resolution or exit. As Anton Ehrenzweig noted: "This dilemma belongs to the essence of creativity."[10]

"Companion" appears to come from "com" (together) and "panis" (bread), the one with whom one shares bread. Blaser associates the word not only with "refreshment," but with "opposites": "those opposites, who are companions." In *The Holy Forest*, might they be the two treed men at the beginning of the work who become "the great companions," Pindar and Duncan, as the work moves toward resolution? Blaser also writes that "the world of 20th century poetry involves a huge companionship," and in the same essay (on Olson and Whitehead), he states that "great poetry is always after the word—it is a spiritual chase… never simply subjective or personal." "La Chasse spirituelle," according to Verlaine, was Rimbaud's single greatest poem—irretrievably lost! (Such a comment resounds as an unscheduled moment in Robin's ongoing series, "The History of Laughter.")

Blaser's lifework imagines a world in which the human is not demonically separated from the other, a heroic task, and one over which the W. H. Auden of "The Poet and the City" (1962) broods.[11] For Auden, the poet's vocation is now much more difficult than in the past because of an encirclement of losses: "the loss of belief in the eternity of the physical universe; the loss of belief in the significance and reality of sensory phenomena; the loss of belief in a norm of human nature which will always require the same kind of man-fabricated world to be at home in; and, the disappearance of the Public Realm as the sphere of revelatory personal deeds."[12] In *The Human Condition*, Hannah Arendt comments: "The public realm... was reserved for individuality; it was the only place where men could show who they really and inexchangeably were."[13] Both Auden and Arendt are here concerned with the classical Greeks. Auden continues: "Today, the significance of the terms private and public has been reversed; public life is the necessary impersonal life, the place where a man fulfills his social function, and it is in his private life that he is free to be his personal self. In consequence the arts, literature in particular, have lost their traditional principal subject, the man of action, the doer of public deeds."

In Auden's, Arendt's, or Blaser's sense of it (in Blaser's case I refer to his essay "The Recovery of the Public World"), there is no evidence that twentieth-century poets have recovered a public world that has been unavailable to them for hundreds of years, much more unavailable in the twentieth century than in the nineteenth. T. S. Eliot's audience of 14,000 people that filled the University of Minnesota's football stadium in 1956 to hear the Nobel Laureate lecture on "The Frontiers of Criticism" is such an anomaly that it should make us groan. However, it is just too easy to trot forth a litany of the senses in which the phrase can be contested. I do want to make a couple of points about our distancing in this regard before suggesting a way in which the phrase can be true and support all of our coming together here in Vancouver, 1995.

Politically, the contemporary poet is undermined because, unlike Yeats or Whitman, say, he is not intimately related to figures of power (he is mainly aware of them via the sensory deprivation tank of media filtration). Whitman, for example, saw Lincoln up close, often, in 1861, could describe him in "doughnut complexion" detail, and felt that he was a comrade. Thus the "Lilacs" elegy reflects a public *and* a personal loss.

In regard to nature, which regardless of the "death of Pan" has been a sempiternal theme of poetry, ecologically, the contemporary poet is witness to its disappearance (or its confinement in expanded versions of the zoo). Money is what is behind such destruction, and money and spirit are turning into each other now more than ever, credit and credo, as billions and billions of dollars circulate constantly every day above our heads in "heaven" via telecommunication satellites. Luther thought a black, excremental Devil was the God of this world. Can you imagine what he would make of the exploitation of rain forests and the now lurid precipitate of money, not simply shit, but the pollution of the planet?

However, there is another perspective possible concerning the recovery of the public world. Such works as *The Maximus Poems, Passages*, and *The Holy Forest*—to name but three recent American examples—have drawn into their nets an immense amount of historical, philosophical, esoteric, popular, primitive, and psychological materials, many of which had previously not been made part of poetry's responsibilities. The "huge companionship" of which Blaser speaks involves, in the twentieth century, in Robert Duncan's words, "all things coming into their comparisons." There is, in fact, an adjective-defying interplay between destruction and recovery in this century, which may be its most heartbreaking hallmark. As if a response to Auschwitz, in 1947 Artaud wrote *To have done with the judgment of god*. While one may argue that Artaud's poem is but a drop of manna in a sea of blood, it is still a heroic attack on eternal damnation, the great blight of Christianity that even Dante supported.

Under the circumstances, in our century many artists have done the utmost that could be expected of them. Is there now too much grief for thought to handle? About that, I am unsure. But it is still possible for a novice to bring his or her given life into confrontation with a created life, for a blindly desiring beginner stuffed with categories (each of which claims a wholeness) to connect with the force of a lore that liquefies boundaries and opens out into a world.

Robin Blaser, in two prophetic passages from *The Holy Forest*, articulates what I take to be the antiphonal tension, regarding community, of our times. From "Salut":

> there is nothing here but an intense
> interior monologue with moments of colour, forms
> flowing toward beloved plants   the cost has
> been high   when all the world is loved by the
> daimon of mediocrity,   you, unpriestly, among
> hierarchs on fire   burned mouth
> must know why you strike

and from "sapphire-blue moon":

> we still dream behind us of a perfected
> humanity   a religion of cities   and
>   take the thought east   the twentieth-
>   century project, delving centuries of
>   mind and heart for a new relation among
>   things,
>   overwhelmed
>   to dream again
> of *laissez-faire*   going fair   along paths
> through the gardened wreckage and consequences
> the State and the Nation agog with redemption   re-
> ligions smoke on the hills, sacrificial as
>   always

Is not this "intense, interior monologue" and a "dream behind us of a perfected humanity" the sensation of so many twentieth-century poets as we hover, from Auden to Artaud, over the abyss monologue and dream expose?

The companion may be the least damaged of the poet's loves. In the French cave known as Pech-Merle, decorated at around 15,000 B.P., in a hidden corner, is a male figure (identified as such by a dangling penis), with a bird-like head, whose body is traversed by long, thread-like lines.[14] The body is slack, as if strung upon the lines passing through it. Caressing the figure's head is what appears to be the tip of one leg of a schematical-ly drawn spider. Might the traversing lines be magic projectiles, as in shamanic dismemberment? I take this bird-headed figure to be an initiate depicted at a crucial stage of his transformation. And the caressing spider? The companion of all who have ventured into the maze of a searching for that confrontation that would generate a self strong enough to love, strong enough to not judge, and strong enough to disintegrate.

NOTES
   1. For the Rilke, see "An Experience," in *Selected Prose*, (New Directions,1960); for the Ginsberg "A Blake Experience," *On the Poetry of Allen Ginsberg* (University of Michigan Press, 1984).

2. Four differing versions of this poem have been published in *Poetry* (Chicago), July 1965; *Indiana* (Black Sparrow Press, 1969); *Coils* (Black Sparrow Press, 1973); and *The Name Encanyoned River* (Black Sparrow Press, 1986). The 1986 version is reprinted in this collection.

3. From Huidobro's poem, "Arte Poética." There is a fuller consideration of the line's significance in "Still Life, with Huidebro," *Under World Arrest* (Black Sparrow Press, 1994).

4. From *Muelos*, Columbia University Press, 1984, cited by Robin Blaser on p. 365 of *The Holy Forest* (Coach House Press, 1993).

5. *Olson #9*, University of Connecticut Library, 1978.

6. *Le Mystère des Cathédrales* (Neville Spearman, 1971), pp. 48 and 91.

7. The ancient Welsh poem, the *Kat Godeu*, proclaims in its opening line: "Before I was free, I was multiform," and then goes ahead for hundreds of lines to list the facets of the human and natural universe that had made up this multiformity, or indeterminacy. We are caught up in the paradox of seeking to be and know ourselves while participating in a round dance that makes up a world. When we call the dancer to our left or to our right "companion," perhaps we send the shiver of a loving humanitas out as an encircling chord. In "Fousang" (from *The Holy Forest*), Blaser writes:

the living creatures stomp on the earth,
tell it, repeat, enter the shine
of
    how old we are
back to back the larks sing, back
to back the creatures sing, back
to back, the beginning and the
end of it—out of it, the
light-patches of a crazy-quilt
arrange, derange, a range
of the movement—lifted, so that
at one moment end and beginning meet
full of laughter.

Blaser then translates "the beast" into "a violet, golden, sweet, the violet companion."

8. This advice, from Crane's prose poem, "Havana Rose" is quoted on page 367, in Note 17, in the present book.

9. *The Complete Poems of Emily Dickinson* (Little, Brown, 1960), #615, dated 1862. The "Our" suggests a pilgrimage that is suddenly confronted with "the bitter conflict of the two natures," for Dickinson, death and eternity. The speaker is paralyzed (yet speechful) before this "center." Her circumference is Argus-eyed with gods, evoking Rilke's "There is no place that does not see you." Dickinson does not attempt to release the paralysis, which is to the poem's benefit, since the double bind of blocked center and judgmental circumference is, as an enactment, completely sufficient.

Our journey had advanced—
Our feet were almost come
to that odd Fork in Being's Road—
Eternity—by Term—

Our pace took sudden awe—
Our feet—reluctant—led—
Before—were Cities—but Between—
The Forest of the Dead—

Retreat—was out of Hope—
Behind—a Sealed Route—
Eternity's White Flag—Before—
And God—at every Gate—

10. *The Hidden Order of Art*, University of California Press, 1971, pp. 35–37. I have briefly summarized Ehrenzweig here. The pertinent passage is quoted in full in Chapter 7 of *Novices*.

11. The center itself is not merely a mating, grappling, or paralyzing place, but the reservoir of the *anima mundi*, the center of the Tibetan world wheel, the mandala, the Fountain of Youth, the face of the Sun God Tònatiuh at the center of the Aztec Calendar Stone, Sumer in Olson's vision of civilization's "One Center" from 3378 tó 1200 BCE, and even the earth itself seen midway between light and darkness. In Paris, it would be Notre Dame, with *arrondissements* winding out centrifugally within the bounding *périphérique*. In Cairo, today it appears to be the Al-Ahram building, a glossy steel-glass-and-marble office tower in which executives communicate with secretaries by closed-circuit television, fifty yards away from which "begins a labyrinth of narrow lanes where millions of Egyptians live in seedy shacks and dark warrens above and below ground, often without water, sewers, or electricity" (*New York Review of Books*, April 6, 1995, p. 32). Or, as Eliot Weinberger writes (*Artes de México* #21, p. 86), in Oaxaca, Mexico, it is the zócalo, "a place for doing nothing, sitting at the center of the universe... Sitting in the zócalo, one's eyes are invariably drawn to the center of the center, to the ornate and Ruritanian band shell. It is the late European contribution to this concept of a sacred place: that at the absolute center is not a cosmic tree or sacred mountain or pillar of stone—ladders between heaven and earth—but rather an enclosure of empty space. The English word *bandshell* captures it perfectly: *band*, the source of music; *shell*, a bounded hollow, a seashell you hold to your ear."

12. Reprinted in *Poetry and Politics* (Morrow, 1985).

13. *The Human Condition*, University of Chicago Press, 1958, p.41.

14. I know of two photographs of this image. One is in Giedion's *The Eternal Present: The Beginnings of Art* (Bollingen, 1957, p. 467). The other is in Leroi-Gourhan's *Treasures of Prehistoric Art* (Abrams, 1967, p. 420). There is a poor reproduction of the Giedion photo in Hadingham's *Secrets of the Ice Age* (Walker, 1979). I am the only one who identifies the image by the line-traversed figure as a spider. Giedion calls it "a large and curious symbol"; Leroi-Gourhan describes it as "a brace-shaped sign"; Hadingham calls it "an abstract sign." None of these scholars sees it as part of a compound image involving the lines, or threads, traversing the human figure's body.

AT THE LOCKS OF THE VOID:
CO-TRANSLATING AIMÉ CÉSAIRE

I first discovered Aimé Césaire in the second issue of Jack Hirshman's tiny *Hip Pocket Poems*, 1960. Césaire's prose poem, "Lynch I," since edited out of the 1948 *Soleil cou coupé (Solar Throat Slashed)*, was translated by Emile Snyder, a French transplant who was an early translator of Césaire. The poem sank into me like a depth charge. Emile's translation was adequate, but a close scrutiny of it and the original text revealed that he simplified a few of the poem's erudite words and tropes, so I retranslated it in 1995 during the O. J. Simpson trial. Here it is:

Lynch I

Why does the spring grab me by the throat? what does it want of me? so what even if it does not have enough spears and military flags! I jeer at you spring for flaunting your blind eye and your bad breath. Your stupration your infamous kisses. Your peacock tail makes tables turn with patches of jungle (fanfares of saps in motion) but my liver is more acidic and my venefice stronger than your malefice. The lynch it's 6 P.M. in the mud of the bayou it's a black handkerchief fluttering at the top of the pirate ship mast it's the strangulation point of a fingernail up to the carmine of an interjection it's the pampa it's the queen's ballet it's the sagacity of science it's the unforgettable copulation. O lynch salt mercury and antimony! The lynch is the blue smile of a dragon enemy of angels the lynch is an orchid too lovely to bear fruit the lynch is an entry into matter the lynch is the hand of the wind bloodying a forest whose trees are galls brandishing in their hand the smoking torch of their castrated phallus, the lynch is a hand sprinkled with the dust of precious stones, the lynch is a release of hummingbirds, the lynch is a lapse, the lynch is a trumpet blast a broken gramophone record a

---

Written for the 1998 Lecture Series at La Maison Française of Columbia University, and read there on November 11.

cyclone's tail its train lifted by the pink beaks of predatory birds. The lynch is a gorgeous shock of hair that fear flings into my face the lynch is a temple crumbled and gripped by the roots of a virgin forest. O lynch lovable companion beautiful squirted eye huge mouth mute save when an impulse spreads there the delirium of glanders weave well, lightning bolt, on your loom a continent bursting into islands an oracle contortedly slithering like a scolopendra a moon settling in the breach the sulfur peacock ascending in the summary loophole of my assassinated hearing.

In its "logic of metaphor" chain reaction, its linking of social terror with the violence of sudden natural growth, and its sacrifice of a male hero for the sake of sowing the seeds of renewal, "Lynch I" is a typical and very strong Césaire poem of the late 1940s. For years I didn't know what to make of it, yet its strangeness was mesmerizing. It seemed to imply that for the speaker to suddenly inhale deeply, to offer himself to the wild, was to induct the snapping of a lynched neck. Erotic aspects of the poem came to mind in the 1970s when I saw the Japanese film *Realm of the Senses*, in which the sex-addicted male lead makes his partner choke him to wring the last quiver out of his orgasm. At that time I started to read Césaire bilingually and determined that he was a poet of extraordinary importance, and that he had not been translated as well as he might be (at that point only around one-third of his poetry had been translated at all). I decided, as I had with César Vallejo in the 1970s, that the best way to read Césaire would be to translate him, since the antiphonal traffic of translation, for me, opens up a greater assimilative space than monolingual reading. I will have more to say about this later.

In 1977 I received a California Arts Council "Artists in the Community" grant that involved my teaching poetry for a school year in the predominantly African-American Manual Arts High School in south-central Los Angeles. I got the idea of translating Césaire's "Notebook of a Return to the Native Land" while teaching at Manual Arts and presenting the translation to my students at the end of the year. As soon as I began to seriously work on the poem, I realized that I was in over my head, and that to do a thorough job I would have to work with a co-translator. I teamed up with Annette Smith, a professor of French in the Humanities Division at the California Institute of Technology and, to make a long story short, working 20 or so hours a week, we translated all of Césaire's 1976 *Complete Poetry* between 1977 and 1982. Our work was published in 1983 by the University of California Press as *Aimé Césaire: The Collected Poetry*. We had planned to call the book "the complete poetry," but in 1982 Césaire surprised us with a new collection, *moi, laminaire (i, laminaria)*, which we subsequently translated along with Césaire's early poetic oratorio, *Et le chiens se taisaient (And the Dogs Were Silent)*. This collection was published in 1990 by the University Press of Virginia as *Aimé Césaire: Lyric and Dramatic Poetry 1946–1982*.

Our working method was as follows: we would both read a poem and take notes on it. Then Annette would dictate a version of it to me which I would take home and type up, questioning this and that in an attempt to isolate specific translation problems in the second draft. In most cases, Annette would have spotted difficulties that I was not aware of. Our work on the third draft was mainly an attempt to theoretically solve these problems, leaving us with the challenge of how to actually translate them. We worked together as much as possible, in tandem, as it were, constantly questioning each other's information and solutions. By doing so, we avoided the often disastrous results that occur when the person responsible for the original language hands or mails a literal version to the person responsible for the second language and he finishes it on his own. In our case, I met with Césaire in Paris twice on my own and once, when we had our questions down to a dozen, with Annette. At the point that a final draft was possible, I holed up for two weeks in the stacks of the Cal Tech Library with a typewriter and piles of reference materials.

As a co-translator, I have been extremely fortunate to have had two great co-translators to work with, Annette and, with Vallejo's posthumously published poetry, José Rubia Barcia. Besides being very alert and responsible, Annette and José were both rigorously honest, which means in this context, among other things, being able to express ignorance, which leaves a problem open, rather than sealing it into a guess.

While the syntactical difficulties involved in translating Césaire are formidable, to properly discuss them we would all have to sit down at a table, as Annette and I did, and examine original texts against their translational possibilities. Here I would like to draw upon some of the material from our

"Translators' Notes" in our Introduction to *The Collected Poetry*. Annette was primarily responsible for this material (in a spirit that balanced my primary responsibility for the final American version of the text).

Syntactical difficulties aside, the lexicological ones were even more taxing. Large numbers of rare and technical words constantly kept us bent over various encyclopedias, dictionaries of several languages (including African and Créole), botanical indexes, atlases, and history texts. Once we were fortunate enough to identify the object, we then had to decide to what extent the esoteric tone of the poetry should be respected in the American. Dispatching the reader to the reference shelf at every turn in order to find out that the object of his chase was nothing more than a morning glory (convolvulus) or a Paraguayan peccary ("patyura") hardly encouraged sustained reading. A delicate balance had to be maintained between a rigorously puristic stand and a systematic vulgarization. The case of plant names was especially complex, as we had to be careful to highlight Césaire's concrete and political interest in Caribbean flora. The following comments by Césaire himself (from a 1960 interview) reinforced our concerns in these regards: "I am an Antillean. I want a poetry that is concrete, very Antillean, Martinican. I must name Martinican things, must call them by their names. The cañafistula mentioned in 'Spirals' is a tree; it is also called the drumstick tree. It has large yellow leaves and its fruit are those purplish bluish black pods, used here also as a purgative. The balisier resembles a plantain, but it has a red heart, a red florescence at its center that is really shaped like a heart. The cecropias are shaped like silvery hands, yes, like the interior of a black's hand. All of these astonishing words are absolutely necessary, they are never gratuitous..."

Neologisms constituted another pitfall. Some were relatively easy to handle because their components were obvious. "Négritude," "nigromance," "strom," and "mokatine" were clear by association with "infinitude," "néromancie," "maelstrom," and "nougátine" (a rich French almond candy). But coining equivalents for "rhizulent," "effrade," and "desencastration" (which we translated respectively as "rhizulate," "frightation," and "disencasement," in the last case giving up on the castration aspect), required a solid sense of semantics. Only Césaire himself was in a position to reveal, in a conversation with me in a Paris café, that "verrition," which preceding translators had interpreted as "flick" and "swirl," had been coined on a Latin verb "verri" meaning "to sweep," "to scrape a surface," and ultimately "to scan." Our rendition ("veerition") attempted to preserve the turning motion (set against its oxymoronic modifier "motionless") as well as the Latin sound of the original—thus restituting the long-lost meaning of an important passage (the last few lines of "Notebook of a Return to the Native Land").

As a final example, the problems involved in translating the word "nègre" go to the heart of Césaire's poetics. Put as simply as possible, the lexical background is as follows: before the Second World War the French had three words to designate individuals or things belonging to the black race. The most euphemistic was "Noir" (noun or adjective). The most derogatory was "négro." In between, on a sort of neutral and objective ground, was the word "nègre," used both as a noun or as an adjective (as in "l'art nègre"). For the general public, "noir" and "nègre" may well have been interchangeable, but the very civilized and very complexed Antilleans considered themselves as "Noirs," the "nègres" being on that distant continent, Africa. And it is in this light that one must read Césaire's use of the word "nègre" and its derivatives "négritrude," "négrillon" and "négraille": he was making up a family of words based on what he considered to be the most insulting way to refer to a black. The paradox, of course, was that this implicit reckoning with the blacks' ignominy, this process of self-irony and self-denigration, was the necessary step on the path to a new self-image and spiritual rebirth. It was therefore important to translate "nègre" as "nigger" and its derivatives as derivatives or compounds of "nègre" and "nigger" ("negritude," "nigger scum," "little nigger," etc.).

Césaire's "Notebook of a Return to the Native Land," as allusively dense as "The Wasteland," and as transcendental as "The Duino Elegies," is one of the truly great poems of the twentieth century. With its 1055 lines that constantly shift back and forth between poetry and prose poetry, it is more of an extended lyric than an epic. After the initial burst, it moves into a brooding, static overview of the psychic and geographical topology of Martinique, generally in strophes that evoke Lautréamont's *Maldoror.* A second movement begins with the speaker's urge to go away; suddenly the supine present is sucked into a whirlpool of abuses and horrors suffered by blacks throughout their colonized and present history. The nonnarrative "fixed/exploding" juxtapositions in this movement reveal Césaire's commitment to surrealism even though thematic development is always implied. The second movement reaches its nadir in a passage where the speaker discovers himself mocking an utterly degraded old black man on a streetcar. The final, rushing, third movement is ignited by the line: "But what strange pride suddenly illuminates me?" In a series of dialectical plays between the emergence of a future hero giving new life to the world and images from the slaves' "middle passage" of the past, the "sprawled flat" passivity of the first movement is transformed into a standing insurrection that finally wheels up into the stars. The incredible burden of the poem is that of a parthenogenesis in which Césaire must conceive and give birth to himself while exorcising his introjected and collective white image of the black.

Here is the initial burst, which contains, in telegraphic shifts, many of Césaire's lifelong themes:

Beat it, I said to him, you cop, you lousy pig, beat it, I detest the flunkies of order and the cockchafers of hope. Beat it, evil grigri, you bedbug of a petty monk. Then I turned toward paradises lost for him and his kin, calmer than the face of a woman telling lies, and there, rocked by the flux of a never exhausted thought I nourished the wind, I unlaced the monsters and heard rise, from the other side of a disaster, a river of turtle-doves and savanna clover which I carry forever in my depths height-deep as the twentieth floor of the most arrogant houses and as a guard against the putrefying force of crepuscular surroundings, surveyed night and day by a cursed venereal sun.

Three sentences: two swift commands to the police and priests, followed by a third made up of ten hairpin-curving clauses containing Césaire's basic contraries: on one hand, he commits himself to a sacred, whirling, primordial paradise of language, open to his subconscious depths and destructive of "the reality principle," or as he himself puts it, "the vitelline membrane that separates me from myself." On the other hand, his quest for authenticity will also include confronting the colonial brutality in his own overpopulated and defeated Martinique where, as Michel Leiris once pointed out, "no one can claim to be indigenous, since the Indians who were the first inhabitants were wiped out by immigrants from Europe a little over three centuries ago and since the white settlers made use of Africa to furnish its manpower."

This is a vision of Eden that also includes its night side, a dyad that is incredibly difficult to maintain, because a vision of paradisal wholeness and existent human suffering in the present negate each other. A significant part of the energy in Césaire's language is generated by his attempt to transform the language of the slave masters of yesterday and the colonial administrators of his own day into a kind of *surfrançais*, as in *sur*real, a supercharged French that in its own fashion is as transformational as surrealism attempted to be of bourgeois, patriarchal, French mentality.

In terms of Césaire's career as a poet (which extends from the late 1930s to the early 1990s), the first half of my earlier set of contraries—a whirling paradise of language—dominates the 1940s. Much of the writing in the 1946 *Les armes miraculeuses (The Miraculous Weapons)* has a hallucinatory concentration to it, as if Césaire has taken Rimbaud's illuminated vistas to a new plane. Here are the first two pages of the seven-page "Les pur-sang" ("The Thoroughbreds"):

And behold through my ear woven with crunchings
and with rockets the hundred whinnying
thoroughbreds of the sun syncopate harsh uglinesses
amidst the stagnation.

Ah! I scent the hell of delights
and through nidorous mists mimicking flaxen
hair— bushy breathing of beardless
old men— the thousandfold ferocious tepidity
of howling madness and death.
But how how not bless
unlike anything dreamt by my logics
hard against the grain cracking their licy piles
and their saburra and more pathetic
than the fruit-bearing flower
the lucid chap of unreasons?

And I hear the water mounting
the new the untouched the timeless water
toward the renewed air.

Did I say air?

A discharge of cadmium with gigantic weals
expalmate in ceruse white wicks
of anguish.

Essence of a landscape.

Carved out of light itself fulgurating nopals
burgeoning dawns unparalleled whitescence
deep-rooted stalagmites carriers of day

O blazing lactescences hyaline meadows
snowy gleanings

toward streams of docile neroli incorruptible
hedges ripen with distant mica
their long incandescence.
The eyelids of breakers shut—Prelude—
yuccas tinkle audibly
in a lavender of tepid rainbows
owlettes peck at bronzings.

Who
riffles
and raffles
the uproar, beyond the muddled heart of this
third day?

Who gets lost and rips and drowns
in the reddened waves of the Siloain?
Rafale.

The lights flinch. The noises rhizulate
the rhizule
smokes
silence.

The sky yawns from black absence

behold—
nameless wanderings
the suns the rains the galaxies
fused in fraternal magma
pass by toward the safe necropolises of the sunset
and the earth, the morgue of storms forgotten,
which stitches rips in its rolling
lost, patient, arisen
savagely hardening the invisible faluns
blew out

and the sea makes a necklace of silence for the earth
the sea inhaling the sacrificial peace
where our death rattles entangle, motionless with
strange pearls and abyssal mute
maturations

the earth makes a bulge of silence for the sea
in the silence

behold the earth alone,
without its trembling nor tremoring
without the lashing of roots
nor the perforations of insects

empty
empty as on the day before day...

In 1978, I tried to explain to Florence Loeb, the daughter of the famous Parisian art dealer, the desire for the prodigious in Césaire's poetry and some of the circumstances under which it takes root. She listened to me and then said something I will never forget: "Césaire uses words like the *nouveaux riches* spend their money." She meant, of course, that this prodigal son of France, educated and acculturated by France, should cease his showing off, racing his language like roman candles over her head, and return to the fold (to the sheepfold, I might add, to a disappearance among the millions for whom to have French culture is supposed to be more than enough). To this aristocritic woman, Aimé Césaire's imaginative wealth looked like tinsel. I carried this sinister cartoon of his power around with me for a couple of years. One morning what I wanted to say was a response to Césaire himself:

For Aimé Césaire

Spend language, then, as the *nouveaux riches* spend money
invest the air with breath newly gained each moment
hoard only in the poem, be the reader-miser, a new kind of snake
coiled in the coin-flown beggar palm, be political, give it all away
one's merkin, be naked to the Africa of the image mine in which
biology is a tug-of-war with deboned language in a tug-of-war with
Auschwitz in a tug-of-war with the immense demand now to meet
   the complex
actual day across the face of which Idi Amin is raining—
the poem cannot wipe off the blood
but blood cannot wipe out the poem
black caterpillar
in its mourning leaves, in cortege through the trunk of the highway of
history in a hug-of-war with our inclusion in
the shrapnel-elite garden of Eden.

Césaire's spontaneous, dream-like surges of language that dominate the 1940s seem to be posited on a belief in the possibility of a fundamental change in the Martinican situation as well as in human society at large. I should mention here that Césaire backed up his poetic ideology with a parallel full-time career of political action: at the end of 1945, he was elected mayor of Martinique's capital, Fort-de-France, and, as a member of the French Communist Party, became one of the deputies to the Constituent Assembly from Martinique. He was responsible for the bill in the French parliament that transformed the so-called "créole" colonies— Martinique, Guadeloupe, French Guyana, and Réunion—into constituent departments of France with full right of citizenship for all their inhabitants, an act for which he has been bitterly criticized by more radical Caribbean thinkers who insist on independence, and for whom departmental status represents a serious compromise.

In the 1950s, and since, Césaire's language of paradise has been increasingly freighted with political consternation, based on the limitations and complications in any genuine change. *Ferrements (Ferraments)*, published in 1960, is permeated with fantastic evocations of black bondage through history. It is as if every line in this collection is the "Flying Dutchman" of a slave ship, each word the ghost of branded flesh. We are told a relentless tale of abduction, pillage, and dumping, of vomiting broken teeth, of ants polishing skeletons, of chunks of raw flesh, of spitting in the face, of trophy heads, of crucifixion. The transition point between *Ferraments* and the much earlier *Miraculous Weapons* is Césaire's shortest collection, *Corps perdu (Lost Body)*, ten poems published in 1950 and illustrated with thirty-two engravings by Picasso (in 1986 George Braziller published a facsimile edition of this book with Annette's and my introduction and translation). In *Lost Body* Césaire seems to have realized that in certain ways the black would remain in exile from himself and, in effect, not enter the house called negritude that Césaire had been building for him.

In "Word," the opening poem of *Lost Body*, the speaker commands the "word" (which initially suggests The Word, or Logos) to keep vibrating within him. At the moment that its waves lasso and rope him to a voodoo center-stake where a shamanic sacrifice ensues, it is also revealed that the "word" is "nigger"—and by implication, the curare on the arrow tips—as the quiver of social stigmata associated with "the word 'nigger'" is emptied into him.

When Annette and I visited Aimé Césaire in his apartment in Paris in 1982, after we had received responses to our final batch of questions, we asked him if he would read us a poem. From some five hundred pages of published work, he chose the title poem of *Lost Body*. Here is the poem in our translation:

Lost Body

   I who Krakatoa
I who everything better than a monsoon
I who open chest
I who Laelaps
I who beat better than a cloaca
I who outside the musical scale
I who Zambezi or frantic or rhombos or cannibal
I would like to be more and more humble and more lowly
always more serious without vertigo or vestige
to the point of losing myself falling
into the live semolina of a well-opened earth
Outside in lieu of atmosphere there'd be a beautiful haze no dirt in it
each drop of water forming a sun there
whose name the same for all things
would be DELICIOUS TOTAL ENCOUNTER
so that one would no longer know what goes by
—a star or a hope
or a petal from the flamboyant tree
or an underwater retreat
raced across by the flaming torches of aurelian-jellyfish
Then I imagine life would flood my whole being
better still I would feel it touching me or biting me
lying down I would see the finally free odors come to me
like merciful hands
finding their way
to sway their long hair in me
longer than this past that I cannot reach.
Things stand back make room among you
room for my repose carrying in waves

my frightful crest of anchor-like roots
looking for a place to take hold
things I probe I probe
me the street-porter I am root-porter
and I bear down and I force and I arcane
   I omphale
Ah who leads me back toward the harpoons
   I am very weak
I hiss yes I hiss very ancient things
as serpents do as do cavernous things
I whoa lie down wind
and against my unstable and fresh muzzle
against my eroded face
press your cold face of ravaged laughter
The wind alas I will continue to hear it
nigger nigger nigger from the depths
of the timeless sky
a little less loud than today
but still too loud
and this crazed howling of dogs and horses
which it thrusts at our forever fugitive heels
but I in turn in the air
shall rise a scream so violent
that I shall splatter the whole sky
and with my branches torn to shreds
and with the insolent jet of my wounded and solemn shaft

      I shall command the islands to be

For a moment, Césaire's body of work buckles with the dilemma that true humanity might only be discovered in madness or apocalypse. The severity of this moment is registered by the wrenching ending where the black, although torn apart by the white devil's hounds, destroys the sky and re-creates primal islands in one paroxysmic gesture. Such an ending recalls Hart Crane's poem "Lachrymae Christi," in which a Nazarene/ Dionysus who is crucified, torn asunder, and burned at the stake is beseeched to reappear whole. Both poems confront the reader with a radical vision of creativity that is bound up with an assimilation of such destructiveness as to render it, in the moment, sublime and absurd.

Earlier I contrasted translating with monolingual reading. As the translator scuttles back and forth between the original and the rendering, or in this case engages in dialogue with a co-translator, a kind of "assimilative space" does open up, in which "influence" may be less contrived and literary than when drawing upon masters in one's own language. Before considering why this may be so, I want to propose a key difference between a poet translating a poet and a scholar translating a poet.

While both engage the myth of Prometheus, seeking to steal some fire from one of the gods to bestow on readers, the poet is also involved in a subplot that may, as it were, chain him to a wall. That is, besides making an offering to the reader, the poet-translator is also making an offering to himself—he is stealing fire for his own furnaces at the risk of being overwhelmed—stalemated—by the power he has inducted into his own workings.

When I speak of creating an American version out of a French text, I don't want to imply that I think of myself as writing my own poem in the act of co-translating Césaire—or to put it more vividly, à la Kafka's "In the Penal Colony," writing my own sentence in the back of a victimized text. I do not believe in so-called "free translations," Lowellian "Imitations," or Tarn's "transformations." I see the poet-translator in the service of the original, not attempting to improve on it or to outwit it. He must, alone or with a coworker, research all archaic, rare, and technical words, and translate them (in contrast to guessing at them or explaining them). As I see it, the basic challenge is to do two incompatible things at once: an accurate translation *and* one that is up to the performance level of the original.

All translations are, in varying degrees, spectres or emanations. Spectral translations haunt us with the loss of the original; before them, facing the translator's inabilities or hubris, we feel that the original has been sucked into a smaller, less effective size. Like ghosts, such translations painfully remind us to what an extent the dead are absent. Emanational translations, on the other hand, are what can be made of the original poet's vision; while they are seldom larger than their prototypes, good ones hold their own against the prototype and they bring it across as an injection of fresh poetic character into the literature of the second language.

The emanation and spectre distinction is originally William Blake's, but I am lifting it out of his bisexual vortex and applying it to the influence one poet may have upon another. As someone who has been translating almost since I began to write poetry, I have probably been much more influenced by César Vallejo, Aimé Césaire, and Antonin Artaud than I have by any English or American poets. Taking into consideration the curious matter of self-influence that seems to be one of the mixed blessings of poetic translation, I would say that their combined and most potent gift has been one of permission—of giving me permission to say anything that would spur on my quest for authenticity and for constructing an alternative world in language.

Surely influence in the form of the gift I have described is emanational and not the spectral blockage Harold Bloom equates with the whole matter of influence in his wrong but useful study, *The Anxiety of Influence*. Poets who have somehow managed to speak, if only in part, in an original way, convey a permission to do the same to some of those who assimilate their work. Poets who primarily represent a dilution of others' energies— I am tempted to say "academic poets" here, but such is true for "anti-academic" or street or experimental poets as well—tend to project a spectral influence. Uninspired and conventional writing is much more the result of the writer's timidity, evasiveness, and willingness to be easily shaken loose from what he has sunk his teeth into than it is of the innovators he has read.

I worked on Césaire when I was beyond my apprenticeship to poetry and thus his effect is less initiational, much less crucial to my being a poet, than is Vallejo's. However, I got seriously involved with Césaire at the same time that I was starting a long period of field and library research on what I have come to call "Paleolithic Imagination & the Construction of the Underworld." Césaire's dyadic emphasis on both the deep past ("I am before Adam I do not come under the same lion") and the often unbearable present encouraged me, on my own terms, to try to do the same.

The most direct use I have made of Césaire's poetry is in my poem from the late 1980s called "The Sprouting Skull," a fantasia based in part on the four lines that end Césaire's poem "Lay of Errantry." In 1995, struggling to find a way to write about the Brown and Goldman murders and the trial and acquittal of O. J. Simpson in a way that would not simply restate what readers and TV observers already knew, Césaire's description of three fabulous beasts in another poem edited out of *Solar Throat Slashed* gave me the idea of creating my own fabulous beast images for Simpson, Brown, and Goldman at the moment the murders occurred. Once these images were in place, I was able to finish the poem, "Gretna Green."

The use of Césaire's work in such pieces is a kind of bonus based more on familiarity with his writing than on being porous to its character. Aspects of Césaire's solemnity, ferocity and tenderness, startling imaginal shifts, and word coinage have become mixed into the strata of my subconscious. Occasionally I will look at a poem after I have written it and sense that while there is no visible presence of an influence there is a lot of Césaire weather in the climate of its construction. I would like to end this presentation with one such poem, "Short Story," written in 1992. I'm pretty confident that the last two lines would not have been written without the assimilated companionship of Aimé Césaire.

Short Story

Begin with this: the world has no origin.
We encircle the moment, lovers
who, encircling each other, steep in
      the fantasy
now we know the meaning of life.

Wordsworth's *recollection:* wreck election,
the coddling of ruins, as if the oldest man
      thinking of the earliest thing
offers imagination its greatest bounty.

A poem is a snake sloughing off the momentary,
crawling out of now (the encasement of
      its condition)
into layered, mattered, time.

Now is the tear and ear of terra's torn era.
For the serpentine, merely a writhe
            in appetite.

We posit Origin in order to posit end,

and if your drinking water is sewage,
to do so is understandable.

When the water is pure, Lilith's anatomy
is glimpsable in each drop.

But the water is never pure.

Before time, there appears to have been
a glass of pure water.

Therefore, we speculate, after time,
there will be another.

Life, a halo surrounding emptiness.

Continue with this: not body vs. soul,
but the inherent doubleness of any situation.
Thus in fusion there is also abyss.

Conclusion: I am suspended between origin and now,
or between origin and a bit before now.
Unknotting myself from both ends,
I drop through the funnel the y in abyss offers.

Nothing satisfies. And,
my suffering is nothing. Two postage stamps
glued, back to back,
abysscadabra.

What is missing? A poetry so full of claws
as to tear the reader's face off.
Too much? Look what men do to each other.
Why should art account for less?

Poetry's horrible responsibility
in language to be the world.

A NOTE ON THE DEATH OF PAUL CELAN

While living in Sherman Oaks, California, in the spring of 1970, I had the following dream: a man that I recognized as Paul Celan walked to the bank of the Seine in Paris and stepped up onto a stone which I also recognized as the "Vallejo stone." Celan stood there for a moment—then leapt into the river.

When I mentioned my dream to someone a week or so later, I was informed that the poet had just drowned in the Seine, an apparent suicide.

The "Vallejo stone" refers to a poem that César Vallejo wrote while living in Paris in the mid-1930s. Like many of the poems that Vallejo wrote during these years, "Parado en una piedra" records his acute sensitivity to human suffering. This particular poem strikes me as a stay against suicide. In the early 1930s, Vallejo still believed that a Communist-inspired world revolution would occur, but this belief was beginning to flounder, overwhelmed by the suffering he found everywhere daily.

Vallejo's untitled poem opens with the following two stanzas:

> Idle on a stone,
> unemployed,
> scroungy, horrifying,
> at the bank of the Seine, he comes and goes.
> Conscience then sprouts from the river,
> with petiole and outlines of the greedy tree;
> from the river rises and falls the city, made of
>   embraced wolves.

> The idle one sees it coming and going,
> monumental, carrying his fasts in his concave head,
> on his chest his purest lice
> and below
> his little sound, that of his pelvis,

This note appeared in *Studies in 20th Century Literature* in 1983. A French translation appeared in *rehauts* (Paris), 2001.

silent between two big decisions,
and below,
further down,
a paperscrap, a nail, a match...

Bottom thoughts. The generational body, out of work, ends in the trash
in the Seine's slime.

I think of this "Vallejo stone" as a locus of exile where lamentation is
tested. It brings to mind a passage from Rilke's 10th *Duino Elegy* that evokes
the crisis of lamentation for the twentieth century. A young woman, iden-
tified as a Lament, responds to a young man's questions, saying:

> We were a great clan, once, we Laments. Our fathers
> worked the mines in that mountain range. Sometimes
> you'll find a polished lump of ancient sorrow among men,
> or petrified rage from the slag of some old volcano.
> Yes, that came from there. We used to be rich.

Attempting to read my dream in the penumbra of Vallejo's and Celan's
lives and poetries, I see that Vallejo, still weighted with some of the rich-
es of lamentation, could address the misery of humankind from his stone,
and then walk away from the Seine to write other poems.

For Celan, both of whose parents were murdered in Nazi death camps,
lamentation was not entirely empty but was so distorted by the absurdity
of praising anything that its so-called riches had been undermined. I sus-
pect that at a certain point he could no longer even feel sorry for himself.

From *Sprachgitter* (1959) onward, the movements of words and lines in
Celan's poetry have a strong, twisting, downward propulsion, like strands
of a rope that is, at the same time, tightening with increasing weight and
self-destructing through torsion into cast free strands. As if the direction
is vertically commanded by a central suck, a whirlpool. Language as spars,
rapidly milling. For example (in Cid Corman's translation from "The
Syllable Ache," a poem in *Die Niemandrose*, 1964):

Forgotten grabbed
at To-be-forgotten, earthparts, heartparts
swam,
sank and swam. Columbus,
the time-
less in eye, the mother-
flower,
murdered masts and sails. All fares forth,
free,
discovering,
the compass-flower fades, point
by leafpoint to height and to day, in blacklight
of wildrudderstreaks. In coffins,
in urns, canopic jars
awoke the little children
Jasper, Agate, Amethyst—peoples,
stock and kin, a blind

Let there be

is knotted in
the serpentheaded free-
ropes—:

By modifying "Let there be" with "blind," freedom and license twist into each other, and for a moment Aleister Crowley's "Do What Thou Wilt" shows its lust-deformed face. By putting it that way I attempt to indicate to what an extent Celan's poetry contains a pronouncement of creation emptied of meaning. When "Do What Thou Wilt" becomes, as it does for Crowley, the only law, there is no meaningful creation. The god-spark is exterminated, one is no one, one says one's prayer to ashes.

On another level, Celan's contraries were "I" and "Thou," and in his mature poetry they grow unbearably close, closer than contraries can to function; one could say they devour each other, the living become the dead, the dead the living, and out of such devastation a grand but dreadful vista opens. Celan's voice is finally consumed in a "we" that is the living and the dead scratching a message on stone to "no one." Under the stress of such an anti-vision, nothing is forgotten: memories of the death camps and insignificant slights have hundreds of doors opening on each other. It is a condition in which there cannot be poetry *and* in which there can only be poetry.

In regarding Paul Celan today, I meditate on the stamina of his wound. He neither allowed it to flow at full vent, nor did he brilliantly cicatrize it at the right hour. He worked it as a muscle as long as there was any strength left in it—he knelt at its altar alone, and thus did not set other energies in motion that might have given him reasons to continue to live at the point that the wound ceased to ache.

Then there was only numbness. And a great poetic testimony in which Paul Celan and annihilated millions can be sensed as a single "we" that you and I can try to pronounce.

Los Angeles, 1975

Since 1956, when he read his poems about the Native American trickster Coyote at a reading in San Francisco during which Allen Ginsberg read Part One of *Howl*, Gary Snyder has been developing a selfless, sensual, landscape-attuned poetry of change and becoming that in the light of our current awareness of planetary potential and doom has become a clearing in American consciousness. It presents itself as ruggedly and thoroughly as monumental Chinese Sung Dynasty landscape painting in a context of interconnectedness involving lore, research, meditation, and a range of living and mythical companions. In "the cold companionable streams" of Snyder's poetry, there is a deep faith in the capacity of the earth to injure and to restore.

Rivers and Mountains Without End is Snyder's sixteenth book, 138 pages of text, thirty-nine poems in four sections or movements.

This work was struck, some forty years ago, off a Sung Dynasty scroll painting. Snyder's opening poem, the key to the book, describes the painting as, scene by scene, it unfurls to the left. He comments: "At the end of the painting the scroll continues with seals and poems. It tells a further tale." *Rivers and Mountains Without End*, then, is the twentieth-century addition to the painting. In its own interlocking, unfolding segments, it draws upon ecological awareness and nature's architecture to such an extent that I want to coin a term for what is happening, to suggest that *Rivers and Mountains Without End* is an *ecotecture*, a habitat-structure. It redirects Whitman's "adhesive love" from solely human comradeship to a comradely display that includes Artemisia and white mountain sheep. Thus I feel that this work is not really an epic, as the dust jacket states, in the tradition of Pound and Williams. Snyder himself thinks of it as a sort of sutra. A string of kayaks comes to mind. Functionally speaking, this book is a rock with centrifugal eddies that can be set at the center of Snyder's life work.

I introduced Gary Snyder's reading from *Mountains and Rivers Without End* at the University of Michigan, November 16, 1996.

What appears to be the leanness in the work is actually Snyder's precise observation, which obviates explanation. At its most intense, his observational power evokes prayer and praise.

Snyder adheres to the Buddhistic principle of emptiness; there is no self, everything we see and are is empty. Thus the absence of the sensitive or tormented psychological subject in this poetry.

In the spirit of Sung landscape painting, as well as in the later Cézanne, one thing is as important as another, each part is as important as the whole. Thus the nodes of illumination are strung throughout the writing. Snyder's world is redolent with common wealth—his elixir of enlightenment is buttermilk.

Finally, all is metaphoric, or let's say any truth is in the synapse between the parts of a metaphor. For example: two kilograms soybeans equals a boxwood geisha comb. Four thousand years of writing equals the life of a bristlecone pine. Our love is mixed with rocks and streams.

To overturn two thousand years of Christian dominion over "unChristian" nature—"over all the earth and over every creeping thing that creepeth upon the earth," including women and human slaves—the scale of values has to be massively rebalanced. *Mountains and Rivers Without End* is the first major Western poem to sweepingly foreground the natural world from a Buddhist perspective and, without cynicism, to present civilization on a sharply diminished scale.

Or as Furong Daokai, as quoted by Dōgen, puts it:

The green mountains are always walking;
a stone woman gives birth to a child at night.

"When you write mystery stories, you have to know something; to be a poet, you don't have to know anything."

—Richard Hugo (NAMP, 1121)

Once upon a time, there was a great, great poet named Yeats [55].[1]

Yeats was so great, in fact, that he "dominates this century's verse as Wordsworth dominated that of the last." Indeed, a year before this century even began, with *The Wind Among the Reeds*, Yeats "set the method for the modern movement." Drawing upon the discoveries of Romanticism— "diversified expression of the self," "the primacy of the imagination,"—as well as upon French Symbolism—"truth in mental operations rather than in the outside world"—Yeats became the poetic overlord of the twentieth century. Furthermore, he inserted his own symbology, as well as his mortal body, into his second, or mature, phase, and dwelling "boldly upon lust and rage, mire and fury, he envisaged more passionately the state of completeness to which incompleteness may attain."

In the shadow of what might be called French-Symbolism-become-Yeatsean-Symbology, several other great but clearly (and unexplainedly) lesser poets were picking around the ruins, trying to make sense out of the new (though from a Yeatsean viewpoint, finished) century. Both Pound [31] and Eliot [28] "wrote about the modern world as a group of fragments." Pound believed in "direct treatment of the thing," and in this way he was an ally of Williams [34] and his "no ideas but in things." Since "the general framework within which modern poets have written is one in which the reality of the objective world is fundamentally called into question," the reader is to understand that Pound, Eliot, and Williams were unable to achieve the completeness achieved by Yeats. Eliot's "sifting and fusion ended in a surprisingly orthodox religious view." Pound ceases to be of much interest after being found mentally incompetent to stand trial for treason after WWII, and in spite of his attempt in the *Cantos* to find a pattern, "the total impresssion may rather be one of shifting, intersecting forms, coming into being and then retreating on the page." Williams, who "agreed with the poets Verlaine and Rimbaud in opposing 'literature' as a phenomenon created by the 'establishment,'" felt that the poem should be "allowed to take its own shape." "He sees most writing as having taken a wrong turn and regards his own efforts, even if stumbling, as at least in the right direction." The few British poets "who followed the lead of Eliot and Pound made relatively little impact on their readers." Exceptions are Sitwell [5], MacDiarmid [4], Jones [10], and Bunting [6]—but they are all of minor importance and worth only a handful of pages. "For in England as in America, the influence of strongly programmatic poetry" (Pound, Eliot, Williams, or anyone with a new poetics) "was balanced by much more traditional modes of verse."

Thus not only was 1922 "the year of *The Waste Land* and of Joyce's [8] *Ulysses*... it was also the year when a group of teachers and students at Vanderbilt University brought out a literary magazine called *The Fugitive*." Up to this point, all the poets have been introduced under the Yeatsean canopy called "Symbolism." We are now in a period described as "Elegant and Inelegant Variations," presumably on Yeats and his lessers. While Lawrence [22] "centered his own verse in the passions of tortoises and elephants," and Frost [24] "converted his self-disgust and loneliness into verses of Horatian dignity," such Georgians as de la Mare [3], Graves [10], Sassoon [5], and Edward Thomas [5] "wished to preserve rural England in traditional prosody." In this regard, they were compatible with *The Fugitives* (Ransom [11], Tate [11], and Warren [11]), "who hoped to keep for the South some of its traditional values." Fugitive ramifications are Empson's [5] *Seven Types of Ambiguity* (1930), Ransom's *The New Criticism* (1941), and Warren and Brook's *Understanding Poetry* (1938), the latter of which "had a vast influence on the teaching of verse at American colleges in the forties, fifties, and early sixties; the influence was even greater on the many imitative textbooks it spawned." "In England during the late twenties and early thirties, the most important young poets were W. H. Auden [22], Stephen Spender[7], Louise MacNiece [11], and C. Day Lewis [4]," who, "eager to express radical political attitudes, preferred to do so through older verse techniques."

The sun continues to set. We are now in that period called "Poetry from 1945 to 1975," which is introduced as follows: "During and immediately after the Second World War, most poets living in the United States came to write in a way that poets of the twenties and critics of the thirties had prepared for them." I believe we are to understand here that *The Fugitives* and the Auden group were the overwhelming influence on post-WWII American poetry. In reaction to Dylan Thomas's [9] "apocalyptic mode," "a loose association of university poets who called themselves, badly, 'The Movement'"—Amis [6], and Larkin [14]—favored wit "over prophecy and extravagance, urban and suburban realities over the urbane." "For some years after the war the esthetic of the New Criticism helped to shape most new American verse." "The qualities it enshrined, such as metaphysical wit, an irony too complex to permit strong commitments, and a technique which often calls attention to its own dexterity, are characteristic elements of what its detractors called an academic style." Effected were: Jarrell [10], Eberhart [6], Shapiro [5], Roethke [11], Lowell [16], Berryman [6], Bishop [14], Wilbur [13] Nemerov [7], Miles [6], Simpson [6], Hecht [8], and Hollander [7]. In reaction, under the "subversive influence" of Williams and Pound, we find Ammons [14], Ginsberg [14], and Creeley [6]; the latter was also "one of the poets who gathered around Charles Olson [7] at Black Mountain College, an experimental and unaccredited school in North Carolina." The Beats—Ginsberg and Ferlinghetti [5]—who "tended to dismiss the Black Mountain poets as too much at ease with authority figures," "found a congenial milieu in San Francisco, where a poetic renaissance had already been fomented within 'the alternative society.'" It included Rexroth [4], Duncan [7], and Snyder [10]. "This kind of poetry came to be known as 'confessional.'" There was also the New York school—O'Hara [6], Ashbery [12], and Koch [14]—these poets "practiced a calculated effrontery and discontinuity of perception." A "new surrealism" (Surrealism being defined as "a mode which exploits as material the distortion imposed upon reality by the unconscious") is found in the poetry of Bly [5], Wright [13], Merwin [8], Strand [5], and Wakoski [11]. By 1959, "it seemed at first that Lowell might himself be becoming a Beat, but in fact his verse is more controlled than it appears." "Other poets who wrote in this intensely autobiographical vein"—Snodgrass [9], Roethke, Berryman, Plath [10], and Rich [17]—"either played against conventional form or wrote free verse in a peculiarly unrelaxed way. These poets are generally melancholy." Black poets of this period are Brooks [13], Baraka [6], and Lorde [8].

We have now reached the present—"Poetry Since 1975"—a decade with no new poetics, experimentation, or American poets of more than modest significance. The late David Kalstone[2] identifies this period (which, quoted, becomes the Norton definition) as one of "personal absences." He means that the main events of this period are: "the deaths of Bishop, Lowell, Wright and Hugo"; "the comparative silence of others"; and the fact that only "four of the more prominent post-1945 writers"— Ashbery, Ammons, Merrill [18], and Rich—"have continued to develop." In summary, "the major poetic innovations and consolidations earlier in the century are now simply history." The closest to anything new is a kind of "regionalism... a vigorous use of vivid experience in a particular place: what Richard Hugo [9] called a 'triggering town.'" Other than Carolyn Forché [7], who "places herself and us, strongly, in El Salvador," all of these "regionalists" are Black, Chicana, Chicano, or Native American poets: "Gary Soto [10] in the San Joaquin Valley, Rita Dove [10] in Akron, Ohio, and Cathy Song [10] in small Hawaii towns." Younger women poets "do not always seem impelled to take gender as their central subject." Some, like Cathy Song or Rosanna Warren [4], "make poems out of visual art"; others—Rich, Lorde, Marilyn Hacker [6], and, "in 'Kalaoch,'" Forché—"write about women's love for women." "With all this diversity, it would be hard, if not impossible, to point to poetic trends." "The personal is a prominent subject." "A significant mode is that of the dramatic monologue." "Many recent poets are writing longer poems or poetic sequences, such as Stanley Kunitz's [6] "The Wellfleet Whale," William Everson's [10] "The Poet is Dead," James Dickey's [9] "Falling," and Frank Bidart's [8] "Golden State."[3] The commentary ends with several paragraphs on contemporary Canadian, English, and Irish poets. Al Purdy [5], born in 1918, is identified as Canada's "foremost countercultural spokesman." James Fenton [9] is identified as "having explored the Cambodian wars in terms of a battlefield dinner party." About the leading Ulster poet we are told: "Seamus Heaney [19] has said that the Irish poet cannot hate the English, because without them he would not have their language, his chief resource as a poet."

In the above condensation/pastiche of the Introduction to the *Norton Anthology of Modern Poetry* (second edition, 1988; henceforth, NAMP), I have attempted to raise the primary features into a stark topology. It is worth doing so, because at 1,865 pages (fifty-five lines to the page), given Norton's distributional effectiveness along with the classroom tendency to rely on a single big anthology to be used all semester long, the NAMP, over the next decade, may very well reach more classes than all the individual collections by twentieth-century English language poets combined. Before considering omissions and misrepresentations, I'd like to make a few observations based not only on the 10,000-word Introduction, but on the contents.

In his thoughtful essay on American Poetry Anthologies,[4] Alan Golding, considering the 1975 Norton *Anthology of Poetry*, writes: "they never discuss what governs their choices. Distinctions between 'major poets' and 'their interesting contemporaries' are assumed to be clear and not open to question." Golding also points out that "you can't read a Charles Olson poem in the same way that you read a Richard Wilbur poem. But the structure and purpose of the teaching anthology limit these new ways of reading, perpetuating old ways of reading the new poetry." Both of these objections still hold true for the NAMP, and the limitations they address are a good deal more formidable than they might appear.

Other than the generalization (quoted in the first part of my essay) concerning the fundamental questioning of the objective world, "modern poetry" is not defined, let alone pondered, in the NAMP. If one considers the Objectivists (omitted en masse), Williams, much of Pound, Rexroth, Bunting, Bishop, Snyder, etc, the generalization falls apart. The terms "Modernist" or "Post-Modernist" do not even occur in the Introduction; instead we have such phrases as "modern verse," "the modern movement," which, under the vague precursor categories of Romanticism and Symbolism, are used to include such clearly Victorian figures as Carroll, Bridges, Wilde, Housman, and Kipling, as well as the Georgians, *The Fugitives*, the New Criticism, and ultimately the writing of young writing workshop apprentices who we are told have no relationship to the past, whatever it is. In the NAMP context, "modern" means little more than the poetry written in English over the last one hundred years. This means that anything that appeals to the editors' taste can come in.[5] It means that the book is shipwrecked from the start, because there is no working definition from generation to generation to distinguish the sheep from the goats. And since there is none, and since "teachability" (more on this later) anchors the editors' taste, "traditional verse" (not even "poetry") becomes the book's common denominator. Certainly Whitman, Dickinson, and Hopkins are there, at the beginning, but they are islands in a sea made up of rhymed "verse," much of which is doggerel.

By the 1930s, in order to advance their taste for traditional verse, the editors use the New Criticism, or classroom-oriented professor-poetry, to provide a criterion for mainstream poetry up through the 1980s. The new is continually set up as a reaction to the traditional (with token page allotments to innovative figures who are used to promote a fake "diversity"). There is no glint of awareness that such poets as Olson and Duncan were not reacting to Hardy or Tate, but were building on, advancing in their own ways, the work of such emanational figures as Williams and Pound. A sense of "making it new" is never allowed a foothold as an ongoing transformational force in poetry, and because of this the NAMP emits black light. I have forced myself to read it twice over the past year and a half; never before have I had such difficulty in continuing to read a book. The message is that from Yeats onward, the energy in modern poetry is entropic; while there are occasional disturbances (*The Wasteland, The Cantos*, etc.), the calm we should depend on consists of story-like verse in which a first-person speaker describes an event from the past. If there is any essential change between 1900 and now, it is that flat, conversational workshop poetry has replaced rhymed verse.

Omissions: all of the Objectivists (in the introduction to the six-page Bunting section, Zukofsky is mentioned as one of Bunting's "associates"). All of the figures who kept avant-garde possibilities open between 1914 and 1945, e.g., Arensberg, Brown, Duchamp, Freytag-Loringhoven, Hartley, Loy, Crosby, Fearing, Henri Ford, Gillespie, Jolas, Lowenfels, Cage, Mac Low, Patchen, and Riding.[6] While Post-Modernism is mentioned once, it is not discussed, and there is no indication that such poets as Olson, Ginsberg, Snyder, and Rothenberg represent a turning away from the Anglo-American tradition (toward Third- and Fourth-World cultures, primitives, and the East) that goes beyond the Modernist preoccupation with the Other. Deep Image, Ethnopoetics, Concrete and Visual Poetry, Performance Poetry, and Language Poetry are not mentioned (meaning that none of their practitioners are included or mentioned either). Such a list of omissions only begins to indicate the NAMP's distortion of twentieth-century American poetic action,[7] and while I dislike making lists of omitted, important poets, I have to do so here to illustrate not just how the Objectivists and the Language Poets have been erased, but how many other innovative directions have had their principal figures omitted, and how movements in part acknowledged by the NAMP editors ("the Black Mountain poets," "the San Francisco poets") have been undermined and diminished through the refusal to include most of the poets who gave such movements their solidity.

Zukofsky	Lamantia	Wieners
Oppen	McClure	Tarn
Reznikoff	Whalen	Padgett
Rakosi	Corman	Coolidge
Riding	Corso	Sobin
Loy	Guest	Sanders
Bronk	Bukowski	Simic
Blackburn	Schuyler	Taggart
Eigner	J. Williams	Bromige
Dorn	E. Williams	Cortez
Kerouac	L. Anderson	Ortiz
Niedecker	Berrigan	Reed
Cage	Rothenberg	Henderson
Mac Low	Kelly	Cruz
Spicer	Antin	Irby
Blaser	Lansing	F. Howe
Palmer	Silliman	S. Howe
C.K. Williams	Hejinian	R. Johnson
Bernstein	Perelman	Kleinzahler
Schwerner	DuPlessis	Grahn

Thirty years ago, it was customary to make a simplistic, dualistic distinction between academic, or closed, poetry and experimental, or open, poetry. In his 1960 acceptance speech for the National Book Award, Lowell appropriated Claude Levi-Strauss's distinction between the raw and the cooked. One wonders how Lowell saw himself. For the author of

Life Studies, raw poetry was "huge blood-dripping gobbets of unseasoned experience dished up for midnight listeners," while cooked was "a poetry that can only be studied." Even for the early sixties, Lowell's distinction is suspect, if not outright sloppy. *Howl* might have some blood in it, but the experience was hardly unseasoned; is Oppen cooked or raw? Spicer? Rothenberg? Implicit in the old distinction is the idea that the experimental is thoughtless, and inappropriate for study. Thus, a false distinction, loaded as usual against the new.

In the NAMP section introduction to Wilbur, this distinction is referred to with the following elaboration: "Wilbur's poetry is elaborately cooked, or, to elevate the metaphor, he is Apollonian while Lowell is Dionysian: that is, he centers his work in the achievement of illuminated, controlled moments rather than in sudden immersions in chaos and despair." Again, a fake distinction (even for Lowell: all of *Life Studies* is "illuminated, controlled moments" regardless of Lowell's neuroticism). The new twist here is that "chaos and despair" have now been added to the experimental's burden of unseasoned experience, or thoughtlessness and its failure to reward study. It is as if we are now watching anything that is confrontational, up front about experience (meaning some of it is bound to be negative, or despairing, given the world we all live in) sink out of sight, with the outright lie that such poetry does not reward study. Anyone aware of post-WWII poetry knows that certain avant-garde poetries, based on international research, are more ideological than academic mainstream writing (writing found in *The New Yorker, APR, Poetry* (Chicago), the Knopf series, the last 200 pages of NAMP, etc.). From all this I conclude that the contemporary equivalent of *The Waste Land* or "Canto VII" would not stand a chance of getting into the NAMP (or virtually any other teaching-oriented anthology). I take Hugo's remark that I have used as an epigram to this essay very seriously: if one expects to be anthologized (and taught, etc.), one's poetry should know very little—it should not be emotionally confrontational, seriously critical of government and society, or imaginatively dense. While one may find mid-career Ivor Winter's too logical and dry, it is, in comparison to the last several hundred pages of the NAMP, extraordinarily thoughtful, and "difficult." In 1960, it would have been considered "academic." Today, textbook-anthology-wise, while it would not be thought of as raw or experimental, it would be dismissed, and were its intensity to be performed without regular rhythms, stanzas, and rhymes, it would be judged chaotic, and in effect be judged, and treated, like the poetry of William Bronk, Robert Kelly, or Ron Silliman.

Not only is the idea of the new and the old perverted in the NAMP, but the seemingly clear distinction between the omitted and the included has several subtexts. The NAMP is able to perpetuate old ways of reading new poetry not only by setting up the new as an unsatisfactory reaction against the old, but also by leaving out key new texts that, were they to be present, would make it much more difficult for the new to be misread. To this we must also add the number of pages allotted to each author, which, more often than not, is used to imply that uncanonized authors of the new are worth less attention than more traditional and teachable poets. To examine this in detail would extend this essay beyond what seems appropriate here. What follows are some examples, which could be multiplied fourfold in terms of the book at large.

Whitman's [23] "Song of Myself," which understandably opens the book, lacks stanzas 15 through 45, or over half of a masterpiece that would have taken up all of 24 pages had the entire 1855 version been printed.

The Dickinson [8] section, includes several trivial poems, but omits a number of major works, including my candidate for the single finest nineteenth-century lyric, "My Life had stood—a Loaded Gun."

The four pages of Stein make her look like an oddball instead of a writer whose language and composition still test the limits of poetry.

The Stevens [23] section has all the early "teachable" poems we have seen in anthologies for years. It includes 21 lines from *Transport to Summer*, and 18 lines from *Auroras of Autumn*, his two greatest collections.

Both Bunting and MacDiarmid are utterly falsified. Bunting's section lacks the extraordinary "Chomei at Toyama," and MacDiarmid's gives no indication whatsoever that he is the author of "On a Raised Beach" and "In Memoriam James Joyce."

Keeping in mind that Olson's more traditional contemporaries (Auden and Lowell) are presented with their major works, it seems grossly unfair that the small Olson section omits "The Kingfishers" (the Post-Modernist equivalent to *The Waste Land*), "In Cold Hell," "The chain of memory is resurrection," and selections from the last three-quarters of *The Maximus Poems*.

In the table of contents, Ginsberg's *Howl* is listed as "Howl." One presumes this means the complete *Howl*. Turning to the Ginsberg section, We find that *Howl* Parts II and III are not there. Part II is arguably the finest two pages in all of Ginsberg. One wonders if the phrase "Cocksucker in Moloch!" kept it out of the NAMP.

The Duncan section is a disaster. Its seven pages include several early lyrics, a 10-line poem from *Bending the Bow*, and three of the slightest pieces from *Groundwork I*. Missing: "Poem Beginning with a Line by Pindar," "My Mother would be a Falconress," "Uprising" (the greatest of the anti-Vietnam War poems), and everything from "The Tribunals" and "The Regulators," the two major sequences in *Groundwork*.

Looking at the NAMP from the viewpoint of page allotment, one encounters one bizarre juxtaposition after another. Is it possible that Rita Dove is more than twice as significant as Hugh MacDiarmid? Do Hopkins [16] and Richard Howard [16] really deserve the same number of pages? Is it possible that Gary Soto is more significant than Emily Dickinson? Lorna Dee Cervantes [6], the author of a single book (1981), is offered the same amount of pages as Bunting. Gavin Ewart [7], an English author of sexist doggerel, receives more than twice the pages alloted to Samuel Beckett [3].

One might inquire of John Benedict, the Senior Norton Editor whose presence is often felt in the NAMP (he appears in footnotes as the recipient of author query responses), why the late Ellmann and O'Clair were contracted to edit such a book. The superficial answer seems to be that both men coedited the 1973 Norton *Anthology of Modern Poetry* and the 1976 Norton *Modern Poems: An Introduction to Poetry*. O'Clair appears to have been a Victorian scholar who never published a single book or article of his own (according to *Contemporary Authors*, Vol. 77–80). The only clue in the NAMP as to why O'Clair was involved in such projects is the following sentence in the Preface: "In making selections of all poets and poems, the editors were guided by the responses of the many teachers who have used the earlier edition, as well as by Robert O'Clair's unerring sense of how well a poem works in the classroom."[8] Other than offering a rather meager explanation for O'Clair's right to codetermine what millions of college students are to read in the name of poetry, the statement implies that the entire organization of the NAMP is primarily determined by what O'Clair and other teachers consider to be easy to teach, and secondarily determined by what the editors believe is the most masterful writing. Does this explain the omission of such poets as Zukofsky and Mac Low? In a publicity brochure for the Third Edition of *The Norton Anthology of American Literature* (1989), the slightly revised Olson section is identified as "an accessible offering of *The Maximus Poems.*"

As for Ellmann, most readers will know that he is an eminent scholar of Irish Literature, with several acclaimed books on Yeats and Joyce, and in his last period, a biography of Wilde. The uncomfortable question is: could Ellmann, in the 1980s, ill, living at Oxford, working on Wilde, have kept up with contemporary poetry?

Going back to the Preface, we also read: "We have provided liberal annotation, translating phrases from foreign languages and explaining allusions when they are not common knowledge, so that every poem can be read without recourse to reference books." The intention here seems to be to save the student from his dictionary and ultimately from the library itself. Such "translations" and "explanations" often result in one-word synonyms. In Stevens' "A High-Toned Old Christian Woman," nine words are footnoted: they are "nave," "citherns," "peristyle," "masque," "bawdiness," "palms," "flagellants," "muzzy," and "spheres." I have several problems with this annotation. The movement from poem to reference book takes time; such time is valuable for assimilation and exploration of the unknown word. To glance down at the bottom of the NAMP page takes a second. One look down from "muzzy," spots "3. Confused" and bounces back into the Stevens line. "Muzzy," I propose, has not registered in the way it might had an International Dictionary been opened to the appropriate page. In my Second Edition *Webster's*, I find: "Dull-spirited; muddled or confused in mind; stupid with drink," and I also note that "muzzy" is connected with "to muzzle:" "Dial Eng. *a)* To root or grub with the muzzle, or snout; said esp. of pigs. *b)* To muffle, esp. church bells, *c)* To make muzzy, *d)* To handle roughly; maul; thrash." In the next Stevens poem, "The Emperor of Ice-Cream," the phrase "cups concupiscent curds" is footnoted as "Literally, lustful milk solids." All the work has been taken away from the reader; he can say, oh, that is what that mysterious phrase means—and glide on. Such a "translation" erases the difficulty, and releases the reader from the crucial activity of recomposing the metaphor on his own terms (or finding it opaque, or silly, or whatever). On the other hand, it is appropriate to footnote "Bickfords" in "Howl I," and to offer some information on words that are not in International Dictionaries. NAMP's procedure wavers in these respects: at times, fairly common words are footnoted—at other times, very esoteric words receive no annotation. I counted over two dozen typographical errors, and some errors in verifiable information, such as Hart Crane's death year, and the misidentification of the Martinican poet Aimé Césaire as "a Congolese writer."

Beckett's three pages in the NAMP are filled with his early poetry, of some interest, but only tangential to the vision by which he is recognized. Joyce is also in the book; his eight pages are split between early verse, and the "Anna Livia Plurabelle" passage from *Finnegans Wake*, with footnotage rising like water in a sinking ship. The presence of Beckett and Joyce cause me to question: should they even be in a book that purports to cover "modern poetry," and if so, shouldn't they be represented by their pathbreaking writing? An insight of Hugh Kenner's is useful to bring in here. In his essay "The Making of the Modernist Canon,'" he cites F. R. Leavis' *New Bearings in English Poetry* (1931) as the first attempt to canonize Hopkins, Eliot, and Pound, and then points out that Leavis' subsequent dismissal of Eliot and Joyce was based on an ignorance of two things of great scope: 1) the unprecedented interdependence of prose Modernism and verse Modernism, and 2) awareness that the English language, by 1931, had split four ways, leaving English natives in control of but a fraction. Kenner proposes that by 1925, three countries—Ireland, America, England—were conducting substantial national literatures and that by mid-century there was a fourth center, "locatable in books but on no map: International Modernism." For Kenner, the four masterpieces of Modernism are *Ulysses*, *The Waste Land*, the first 30 *Cantos*, and *Waiting for Godot* (two Americans—two Irishmen—no Englishmen). Kenner's "split" illuminates the extent to which the energy of the new had left geographical England. Like Leavis, the NAMP appears to be ignorant of this development (in 1988).

In my view, if one adds Post-Modernism, there is a fifth split-off, as of 1949, the year of "The Kingfishers." Or we could say that International Modernism turns out to have a much wider thrust in time and space than Kenner calculates. Whether one sees Post-Modernism as a distinct "new wave" of Modernism, or the two as facets of International Modernism, one thing is clear: the movement is not confined to the English language alone. If we agree with Kenner regarding the interdependence of prose and verse, then sections of *Ulysses* and *Waiting for Godot* are prime candidates for a text that addresses the "split" English language. If we acknowledge that the domain of International Modernism is a "floating world" of the imagination, then we may salute 1922 not only as the year of Eliot's and Joyce's masterpieces, but also of Vallejo's *Trilce* and Rilke's *The Duino Elegies*. And with these two new additions, we may also agree that any representative International Modernism text would also have to represent the likes of Breton, Césaire, Artaud, Mayakofsky, Mandelstam, Cendrars, Neruda, Paz, Celan, Radnoti, Holan, Lorca, Borges, and Genet. To do so would be to shrink the English-language list to only those writers who have made genuinely innovative contributions to International Modernism. What a grand book—or two books—it could be. All of the above have been by now, at least in part, excellently translated. My guess is that the phenomenon could be displayed in a NAMP-sized book, and were they to spend a year with it, students might well emerge with a revolutionarily complete sense of the diversity and range of twentieth-century writing.

While I believe that such a book might be possible by the end of the century, it still does not seem just around the corner, and until we get to it, there are a couple of lesser but quite meaningful American anthology projects (I am not going to argue here against anthologies per se; while I don't currently use them myself, I know that thousands of professors do, and will continue to; I propose instead that they be offered something more dynamic than the anthologies that are available right now).

1. An expanded and updated version of Don Allen's *The New American Poetry* (1960)[10]—a book that would cover 1960 to 1990. Besides poets whose work began to appear in this period, it might resourcefully contain advances by writers who broke new ground earlier. The

fact that no book like this exists now shows to what extent the NAMP and its kin dominate the poetry textbook anthology market.

2. An expanded and updated version of the Leary/Kelly *Controversy of Poets* (1965). It would be very interesting for students to have twenty pages of the best Olson set side by side with twenty pages of the best Lowell, etc., in such a way that the cards were not stacked in favor of one writer against another.

Until such books appear, the anthology atmosphere is grim indeed. For the NAMP, the sun rose and set a long time ago, leaving poets in a kind of changeless Scandinavian winter light. As we sit at our desks, a figure shuffles by our window daily with Kantian regularity. It is the spectre of Philip Larkin, intoning:

Give me your arm, old toad;
Help me down Cemetery Road.

1989

NOTES

1. The bracketed numbers are the number of pages given a specific author in the NAMP *(Norton Anthology of Modern Poetry)*. I include opening and closing pages even though they may not be full pages. Such page allotments clearly represent the NAMP hierarchy (Yeats at 51 is 21 pages more than Williams at 34—with 3 pages, Edwin Honig, Bernard Spencer, and Beckett are the low—the average allotment must be around 10 pages). Contemporary American poets with 10 pages or more are Merrill, Howard, Rich, Everson, Brooks, Wilbur, Levertov, Koch, Ammons, Ginsberg, Ashbery, Wright, Walcott, Wakoski, Harper, Pinsky, Soto, Dove, and Song. This essay appeared in the *American Poetry Review* in 1990.

2. Kalstone is quoted here probably because along with Patricia B. Wallace he was coeditor of the "American Poetry Since 1945" section of the 1989 *Norton Anthology of American Literature* (Third Edition, Volume 2). While there is, because of understandable space limitations, less post-WWII American poetry in the NAAL than in the NAMP, someone—Wallace perhaps—has added Niedecker, a couple of late *Maximus* poems, Duncan's "Poem Beginning with a Line by Pindar," Creeley's "The Finger," and Snyder's "The Blue Sky." Although the overview of post-WWII poetry is essentially that of the NAMP, such additions are a start in offering a more realistic picture of the period's innovations. However, on the back of the volume, as part of the blurb material announcing changes and amplifications, we find the following line: "Poets of the 'Objectivist school'—Lorine Niedecker, Robert Duncan, Robert Creeley." When it comes to the avant-garde, it is as if Norton can never get things right.

3. What the Introduction does not tell the reader is that these "long poems" are 138, 190, 175, and 270 lines long, "middle length" poems by current long poems standards. This is a typical NAMP maneuver, to identify and at the same time utterly misrepresent a genre. We live in an era that includes Zukofsky's 803-page *A*, Olson's 634-page *The Maximus Poems*, and Kelly's 415-page *The Loom*.

4. "A History of American Poetry Anthologies," in *Canons*, ed. Robert von Hallberg, University of Chicago Press, Chicago, 1984, p. 302.

5. In 1928 Robert Graves and Laura Riding published *A Pamphlet Against Anthologies*, a 200-page book that, while dated, is very well written and filled with pithy observations that are still pertinent. Here is their paragraph on "taste": "The greater the integrity of the private anthology, particularly when the author is a well-known poet, the more dangerous it is when put on the market: by its publication it appears to be on an act of criticism instead of a mere expression of taste. Taste is the judgment an individual makes of a thing according to its fitness in his private scheme of life. Criticism is the judgment that an individual makes of a thing according to its fitness to itself, its excellence as compared with things like itself, regardless of its application to his private scheme of life. With taste, a poem is good because it is liked; with criticism, it is good because it is good. Now, it is not objectionable for a person who has not sufficient originality to make his own criticism to accept another's; for criticism, unlike taste, which is arbitrary opinion, can be tested. The criticism of one person thus accepted can become another person's taste. But for one person to accept another's taste deprives the former of self-respect. Our charge against anthologies is, then, that they have robbed the poetry-reading public of self-respect."

6. I am indebted to Jerome Rothenberg's *Revolution of the Word* (Seabury Press, New York, 1974— now out of print) for a mapping of American avant-garde poetry between the two world wars. Some of these writers also appear in the Rothenberg/Quasha *America a Prophecy* anthology (Random House, New York, 1973—also out of print), which displays an even larger dimension of poetic activity. The current teaching anthologies offer little or no indication that the poetic spirit is originally, and essentially, bound up with song, dance, and ritual, and that for tribal societies it is communal and central to the life view of all involved.

7. I have focused on American poets in this regard because while NAMP makes gestures to Canadian, Irish, and Australian poetry, the anthology is essentially about American poetry with English poetry presented as a kind of "curtailing angle" around American writing. I should point out, however, that the NAMP gives no indication of any innovative non-American based poetry after Lawrence, Bunting, and MacDiarmid. A more complete "omission list" would have to include such non-American poets as Peter Redgrove, Jeremy Prynne, Allen Fisher, Pierre Joris, Daphne Marlatt, Steve McCaffrey, BP Nichol, Roy Fisher, Ian Hamilton Finlay, Tom Raworth, Edward Brathwaite, and Kofi Awoonor, among others.

8. Hugh Kenner's remarks on the New Criticism in his "The Making of the Modernist Canon" (*Mazes*, North Point Press, San Francisco, 1989, p. 38) contextualize O'Clair's classroom activities: "It was in 1947, under Marshall McLuhan's informal tutelage, that I first became aware of my own century. Such a lag was perhaps possible only in Canada. By then an American movement called the New Criticism was enjoying its heyday. Like most critical stirrings on this self-improving continent, it was almost wholly a classroom movement. Stressing as it did Wit, Tension, and Irony, it enabled teachers to say classroom things about certain kinds of poems. Donne was a handy poet for its purposes; so was Eliot; so, too, was the post-1916 Yeats. Thus Eliot and the later Yeats became living poets, and a few Americans such as Richard Eberhart, also a few Englishmen, e.g., William Empson. The Pound *of Mauberley* was (barely) part of the canon, 1920 having been Pound's brief moment of being almost like Eliot, tentative and an ironist. But when Pound was working in his normal way, by lapidary *statement*, New Critics could find nothing whatsoever to say about him. Since 'Being-able-to-say-about' is a pedagogic criterion, he was largely absent from a canon pedagogues were defining. So was Williams, and wholly. What can Wit, Tension, Irony enable you to say about 'The Red Wheelbarrow'? 'So much depends...' says the poem, and seems to *mean* it; for a New Critic that was too naive for words. I can still see Marshall chucking aside a mint copy of *Paterson I*, with the words 'pretty feeble.'"

9. "The Making of the Modernist Canon," pp. 31–34.

10. Allen's anthology was updated, with the help of George Butterick, as *The Post-Moderns* (Grove Press, New York, 1982). Rothenberg argues in a review of the new version (*Sulfur* #6, 1983, pp. 181–90), that it is not successful. Not only are a number of significant individual poets left out, but according to Rothenberg many of the new "alternative poetic strategies..." "Concrete & Visual Poetry, The New Performance Poetry, The 2nd and 3rd Generation New York School, The New Black Poetry, Indian Poetry, Latino Poetry, The 'Language' Poets, and The Poem in Prose: The 'New Sentence' (R. Silliman)" are not included.

ADDENDUM, 2001

In 1994, Norton published *Postmodern American Poetry*, edited by Paul Hoover, with short selections of 104 poets, only a few of which are in the book that is the subject of my 1989 polemic. The *Postmodern* anthology might appear to redeem Norton from some of its chronic refusal, over many years, to acknowledge and include innovative/experimental American poetry in its widely disseminated anthologies that determine what many undergraduate college students will read. However, it seems to me that the *Postmodern* anthology is a token gesture. It is only when Norton brings out a large, general anthology that in a nontoken way includes "postmodern poetry" that my "Gospel" will become irrelevant to contemporary poetics.

INTRODUCTION TO THE FINAL ISSUE OF *SULFUR* MAGAZINE

I had been talking with Jerome Rothenberg and Robert Kelly, among others, about the need for another *Caterpillar*-like magazine that would engage multiple aspects of innovative contemporary poetry in the context of international modernism. Because the California Institute of Technology is primarily dedicated to, and known for, research in science and engineering, I proposed in 1981, while Dreyfuss Poet in Residence and Lecturer in Creative Writing, that a literary magazine, sponsored by the Humanities Division, would draw attention to the humanities at Cal Tech. (I did so in somewhat the same spirit that Charles Olson, when rector, proposed to other faculty members at Black Mountain College in 1953 that a magazine might effectively advertise the nature of the college's program.) Roger Noll, an economist who was then Director of the Humanities Division at Cal Tech, liked my idea and arranged with President Goldberger for *Sulfur* to be supported initially for five years.

The word "sulfur" evokes the sulfur, a butterfly with black-bordered orange and yellow wings. On one level, the magazine is an evolution of *Caterpillar* (a magazine I founded and edited twenty issues of from 1967 to 1973). On other levels, the word denotes alchemical initiational combustion, and excited or inflamed language. The word was also attractive to me because it had not been used before as a literary magazine title. There is an extended note on the word at the beginning of *Sulfur* #24.

The magazine originally appeared three times a year but became a biannual in 1988. Its more than 11,000 pages of material have included around 800 contributors, some 200 of which are foreign writers and artists. I began *Sulfur* with Robert Kelly as the sole contributing editor. Kelly disappeared due to a misunderstanding after the first issue appeared, and by the third issue, Michael Palmer, Rothenberg, and Eliot Weinberger had become contributing editors. Throughout *Sulfur*'s run, Caryl Eshleman has been the managing editor; she took over the magazine's design from Barbara Martin with #37. She was also in charge of

This essay was written for the final issue of *Sulfur* Magazine, #45/46, Spring 2000.

copyediting, proofreading, and she often read manuscripts and worked with author revisions. In short, her contribution was essential.

Over the years the masthead grew to its current sixteen members. Nearly all of this group have stayed on from the time they came aboard, and all, in one way or another, have contributed actively to what *Sulfur* has become (in contrast to the lists of well-known names that often decorate literary magazine mastheads). *Sulfur* is not, and has never been, a movement magazine. I invited people to join on the basis of believing that they were very good at their chosen focus, and took the chance that while there would be real disagreements among us (see #20 and #22 for the Language Poetry controversy), we had enough in common and were all sufficiently united against "official verse culture" (effectively examined by Charles Bernstein in #10) to be able to work together.

The magazine came close to being derailed on two occasions. In 1983, I was informed by President Goldberger that there was a crisis based on the following incident: he had been using discretionary funds from the Weingart Foundation in Pasadena to support *Sulfur*. At one point he proudly showed the Weingart Board of Trustees a copy of #4, which included twenty-two Paul Blackburn poems. One of these elderly trustees opened the magazine to Blackburn's "Birds chirp listlessly in the heat" and read it aloud to those assembled. They were outraged, and told Goldberger that *Sulfur* was pornographic. Not only did they not want their "discretionary" funds used to support the magazine, they wanted Cal Tech's name removed too. Goldberger told me that as much as he disagreed with this reaction, he had to honor it because of the Weingart Foundation's huge yearly donations to Cal Tech (mainly in the science area, I recall, but it should be mentioned that this foundation also funded a yearly "Humanities Conference" on campus). Goldberger, quite honorably I felt, offered to make good on his original five-year funding commitment via other sources, so *Sulfur* could continue either on its own for a few years or until it attracted a new sponsor. While the Blackburn poem is genuinely shocking, it is hardly pornographic by current standards. That a single poem by this shy, unassertive poet was sufficient to nearly eliminate a literary magazine on grounds of censorship in 1983 should keep us all alert to the fact that while things seem to change, on another level, they remain stuck, and the same.

Sulfur #9, which appeared shortly after the Weingart incident, was one of the two issues without a sponsoring organization. Issues #10 through #15 (1984–1986) were sponsored by the Writers' program in the UCLA Extension Program. In 1986, Karen Costello, who made the connection possible, left the program and the new director decided that *Sulfur's* "office benefits" imposed too much of a burden on the program's budget. Thus #16 was published out of our home in West Los Angeles. In 1986, when I became a professor in the English Department at Eastern Michigan University, I brought *Sulfur* with me. From #17 on, EMU provided me with release time (one course per semester), a part-time graduate assistant, and "office benefits." These "benefits" have not included money for production, promotion, nor payments to authors and contributing editors. While the magazine's subscribers (around 700 at this point) and bookstore sales had offset some of these expenses, from the mid-1980s to 1996, the rest of the deficit was made up by thirteen grants from the National Endowment for the Arts. When we failed to get a grant in the last round of literary magazine support, we seriously considered ending *Sulfur,* but we did not want to be put out of business by the NEA. We have done issues #37 through #45/#46 on a reduced basis, cutting down the magazine's size and press run (which meant dropping distributors, which were costing us money), and stopping contributor payments. We are ending *Sulfur* now because we feel that the magazine has realized its initial purposes as much as is possible. I will turn sixty-five shortly and feel it is time to turn my focus solely on my own writing.

In regard to editing and content: associate editors regularly sent me their own work, or the work of others. More often than not, I published this work. When I was divided over such contributions (or material sent directly by would-be contributors), I sent it to three associate editors and abided by majority decision. This policy enabled work to get into the magazine via other editors—in particular, Palmer and Weinberger—through "lateral entry." It avoided many of the problems that occur with large editorial boards where a number of people vote on everything. Group editorial consensus tends to weed out the eccentric and the complex, filling issues with material that puzzles or offends no one.

While we occasionally published a piece of fiction when it seemed appropriate, for the most part we steered clear of fiction and drama, as it was not possible, given size restraints, to edit such material in a responsible way. The range of *Sulfur's* interests in poetry, poetics, and some tangential fields made it difficult to keep issues under 200 pages. The amount of good material always determined the size of an issue; very little was held over for future issues. Here are our main focuses:

1. Translations of contemporary foreign-language poets and new translations of untranslated (or poorly translated) older works. We usually checked the accuracy of the work of unknown translators. Literary magazines that restrict themselves to a national literature deprive themselves of the international network of information and cross-fertilization that is at the heart of twentieth-century world poetry.

2. Archival materials—unpublished, significant writings—by earlier writers, in *Sulfur's* case including Ezra Pound, William Carlos Williams, Hart Crane, Mina Loy, Basil Bunting, Lorine Niedecker, George Oppen, Charles Olson, Edward Dahlberg, and Francis Boldereff. Writers sometimes misevaluate or abandon significant works that if not destroyed end up in archival collections at university libraries (a great service to the literary community would be to have a checklist of all American archival holdings; the range and depth would astonish everyone). In the same spirit in which living poets share international affiliations, the living are also connected to, and continue to learn from, the "great dead." To include writers of the past as a dimension of the present openly affirms such affiliations.

3. The inclusion of several unknown and usually young poets in each issue. An effective literary magazine gives the impression that anyone, with the right goods, can be a part of it, and that when you turn a page you may find a poem by Karen Kelley or Dan Featherston facing one by Gary Snyder or Adrienne Rich. If the work of the "great dead" is to be included, then the work of the talented and untested should have a place too. A novice can learn something about his own efforts by scrutinizing them in a context with mature writers. Four of *Sulfur's* authors—Jed Rasula, Eliot Weinberger, August Kleinzahler, and John Yau—received General Electric Younger Writers' Awards in the 1980s.

4. Commentary, including poetics, notes, and book reviews (of a polemical as well as nondisputational nature). A crucial difference between a literary magazine and an anthology is that magazines comment on what is being published. Journals that do not publish reviews (or only publish pastel appreciations) evade revealing, and defending, a specific aesthetic viewpoint and become collection plates into which any contribution can be dropped. Certain aspects of poetry hone themselves on conflict and strife, and a literary magazine is an ideal site for the contestation of differing views.

5. Resource materials. Depending on the editor, and the availability, resource materials can vary widely. If poetry is the woof of a magazine, nonpoetic source material might be the warp. The idea here is that vital writing is always dependent upon materials outside of its own discipline for the renewal and deepening of content, of extending what might be called "the cleared ground of the art." Originality depends not only on voicing and technique, but on making writing responsible for previously excluded (and repressed) materials and experience. In *Sulfur*'s case, such materials included art, art criticism, archetypal psychology, anthropology, archeology, and political commentary.

These five areas of attention (along with poetry and prose by well-known American poets) made up what could be thought of as *Sulfur*'s personality. In a typical 225-page issue, there might be forty to sixty pages of commentary, several translation and art sections, and one or two archival or resource sections. Weinberger edited a special issue (#33), "Into The Past." Marjorie Perloff and Jenny Penberthy did a special issue on Anglophone Poetry and Poetics Outside the US and UK (#44). James Clifford edited and translated much of a large section on Michel Leiris (#15). Rachel Blau DuPlessis edited three presentations of George Oppen's working papers (in #25, 26, and 27). Jerry Glenn edited a large section of and on Paul Celan (#11). Caryl and I put together a group of responses to the tragic death of Ana Mendieta (#22), and with Gyula Kodolanyi, I co-translated and edited a section on Hungarian poetry (#21). Smaller sections were done on Blackburn (#4), Antonin Artaud (#9), Porfirio diDonna (#19), East German poetry (#27), Peruvian photography (#34), and the Vancouver Robin Blaser conference (#37). *Sulfur* #32 (at 352 pages, the largest single issue) was filled with work and edited sections by the masthead. Caryl and I also worked with *Sulfur*'s various art editors: John Yau, Pamela Wye, and Roberto Tejada. Over 600 paintings, drawings, photographs, and sculptures were reproduced in the magazine (and on the covers), in most cases with essays or notes.

The background against which *Sulfur* proposed itself is anchored in the Dionysian 1960s. As crazy as the period was, with its blissful and horrendous wave bands compounded of revolution, war, and mindful and mindless introspection, it was the richest period for American poetry since the 1920s. Many of the poets of my generation experienced visionary and political internationalism as a multifoliate force spinning itself out in translations, alternative presses and magazines, enthusiastic college audiences, Vietnam War protest, traditional magics, and a heady confidence articulated by Norman O. Brown at the end of his brilliant 1966 *Love's Body:* "The antimony between mind and body, word and deed, speech and silence, overcome. Everything is only a metaphor; there is only poetry." In fact, I'm sure that I am not alone in believing during the late 1960s that an American poetry based in international modernism, and signaled by Don Allen's "the new American poetry" but not restricted to his perimeters, might become the dominant poetry of the 1970s— in other words, that a world-aware, responsible avant-garde might overcome and peripheralize decades of dominant official verse culture. After all, the impact of the work of Charles Olson was equal in its own way to that of Francis Bacon, so why shouldn't Olson occupy a place in poetry equal to that of Bacon in painting?

Dionysian excess has, built within its boundary explosions, formlessness, violence, and despair. Dionysus must, at some point in his turmoil, find the hand of brother Apollo and swing with him, or be churned to flotsam. For me, there has always been a loose, sinister synchronicity between the crash of hippydom and popular culture (the Manson murders in Los Angeles, the debacle of the Rolling Stones' Altamont concert) and Olson's death in 1970, preceded by Robert Duncan's withdrawal and refusal to publish for the next fifteen years. The '70s flipped over, the energy dispersed.

Two obvious trends of the 1970s and 1980s were the ubiquitous spread of creative writing degree programs and Language Poetry. Of equal magnitude, but less discussed, was the development of a number of poets in their forties, fifties, and sixties. Women poets re/visioned not only the American canon but the heretofore unacknowledged patriarchal government of the history of poetry. There appeared a host of minority-oriented poetries: African-American, Indian, Chicano, gay, lesbian, performance, and many mixes, involving music and libretti, chants, and sound texts. What was once upon a time a Right and a Left Bank (the cooked vs. raw distinction, suspect even in the '60s) became an archipelago of sites.

One reason that Olson has not become a Bacon-like presence is that American (and English) poetry has depended upon academic sanction and support. What was true for Whitman, shunned by most of the "men of letters" of his time, is still true for almost all poets today. Students buy text anthologies and read poetry because it is part of the curriculum. Doctors and lawyers do not, in any noticeable sense, but many, in a very noticeable way, collect paintings—and not merely because wealth is involved, but because paintings (and most novels, plays, and films) offer more surface than poetry. They demand a less active response. One has to work hard to get anything out of *The Cantos*, *The Wasteland*, or *The Maximus Poems*. In such works, there is no plot, or color field to provide an entrance level that can be bypassed by the "ideal observer" or just relaxed into.

By creating a "poet–professor" middle class, the writing programs have played into the hands of poetry's traditional enemies: education and entertainment. The slams and open-mike readings are offsprings of, or reactions to, the creative writing class and courses based on Norton anthologies. It is wonderful for students to have contact with writers, but I continue to believe that such contact should not take place in workshops dominated by student work and response. All of a student's time in literature should be involved with getting a small percentage of it under his belt, and coming to terms with what, in my view, poetry is really about: the extending of human consciousness, making conscious the unconscious, creating a symbolic consciousness that in its finest moments overcomes the dualities in which the human world is cruelly and eternally, it seems, enmeshed.

While *Sulfur* has attempted to not support work that smacks of the creative writing workshops, we have published many Language Poets. An interesting anthology of Language Poetry, in fact, could be assembled from what has appeared in *Sulfur*'s pages. Charles Bernstein is one of our correspondents, and other *Sulfur* editors are associated to varying degrees with the movement. I regard Language Poetry as a significant part of contemporary poetry but not as its primary force of focus (I don't think there is one; I think there are a couple dozen major figures today, and that they make up a crazy quilt of emphases and directions).

Sulfur's primary ambition, as I see it, has been to keep the field open and complex, with archival and contemporary writing, along with commentary, generating a multigenerational interplay. Besides advancing the work of a number of poets in their thirties and forties, the magazine has supported a range of those whose work has either held its significance or deepened during the 1980s and '90s. Along with certain *Sulfur* editors, such a range would include Robin Blaser, Adrienne Rich, Jackson Mac Low, Gary Snyder, Gerrit Lansing, Amiri Baraka, Philip Lamantia, Ron Padgett, Robert Duncan, Barbara Guest, and Gustaf Sobin.

For this last issue, I solicited work from 150 past contributors. In the case of artists, when it was possible, I simply asked for recent material. In the case of writers, I asked for unpublished things that they felt represented them well at the present time. No attempt was made to elicit testimonials. I asked everyone to try to hold their contribution to two *Sulfur* pages. I think it is a gala issue, and that in spite of some omissions (mainly due to death and disappearances), it projects a constellation that is true to *Sulfur*'s overall image.

D. H. Lawrence once wrote: "Living, I want to depart to where I am." As it has been able to, *Sulfur* has carried forth the ore in such a thought.

January 2000

XV

from *Juniper Fuse:*
Upper Paleolithic Imagination &
The Construction of the Underworld

(2003)

FOR CARYL

Lespinasse, 1974: We carried our dinner outside to the stone table

on the landing by the door to our second floor Bouyssou apartment.

The farm was on a rise which sloped down through an apple orchard.

When we sat down to eat, well before sunset, we had for entertain-

ment an extraordinary sky. Clouds would come floating over the

woods, spreading out over us. Puff collisions, Mickey Mouse ears,

gargoyles shredding, turrets, vales, mammoth apparitions densifying

and disintegrating as they appeared. Many reminded us of the images

we were trying to discern on the cave walls. To sit at that stone

table—what an experience—to be in love there, at one of the most

vital times in our many years together. Much of what happened—

the "event aspects"—during our first spring and summer in the

Dordogne is now as dispersed as the clouds we used to watch—

yet it billows in us, an inclusive cloud whose heart is ours.

Wicks made of quarter-inch juniper branches were used in many of the 130 hand lamps found in Lascaux.

Over the cave, a tall juniper had fallen, lifting up with its roots a large mass of earth and creating a pit, soon entangled with brambles. On September 8, 1940, Marcel Ravidat (a young garage hand from nearby Montignac) was drawn to the pit by his barking dog, caught in the undergrowth. While cutting the dog out, he discovered a dead donkey and under it, a vertical shaft. On September 12, with his friend Jacques Marsal, Ravidat returned. Working with his knife, head first, he dug down some 20 feet, at which point he tumbled into the cave.

Juniper as the wick of the cave!

Since the Upper Paleolithic, wick has become fuse as the conveyor of ignition for electrical purposes, as well as for shells and bombs.

Juniper Fuse envisions and examines some of the origins and developments of imagination recorded in cave wall imagery (for the most part in southwestern France)[1] during the last European Ice Age, roughly between 40,000 and 10,000 years ago. It looks at theories proposed by others, as well as my own two-part thesis that considers why such imagery sparked when and where it did. The metaphorical unfolding that can be traced back to a 30,000 year-old Aurignacian engraving of a horse head and neck—across which a vulva of equal size was superimposed—startles with the same refreshed energy as Allen Ginsberg's "hydrogen jukebox."

To follow poetry back to Cro-Magnon metaphors not only hits real bedrock—a genuine back wall—but gains a connection to the continuum during which imagination first flourished. My growing awareness of the caves led to the recognition that, as an artist, I belong to a pretradition that includes the earliest nights and days of soul-making.

This book is also an attempt to answer the first question that the science writer Alexander Marshack fired at me when he walked into our kitchen in the French Dordogne in the spring of 1974:

"What is a *poet* doing in the caves?"

In 1955, Charles Olson wrote two letters to the young poet Ed Dorn later revised as *A Bibliography on America for Ed Dorn*. I read this compilation in the late 1960s. At one point, Olson argued:

> PRIMARY DOCUMENTS. And to hook on here is
> a lifetime of assiduity. Best thing to do is *to dig one*
> *thing or place or man* until you yourself know more abt
> that than is possible to any other man. It doesn't matter
> whether it's Barbed Wire or Pemmican or Paterson or Iowa.
> But *exhaust* it. Saturate it. Beat it.
> > And then U KNOW
> everything else very fast: one saturation job (it might
> take 14 years). And you're in, forever.[2]

His admonition is to Dorn as a novice, and rings with a certitude that at sixty-four I can only partially share. But it planted a seed in me for the writing of this book. My aim is not to know more than "is possible to any other man," but to make use of a pluralistic approach that may result in a fuller "reading" of Upper Paleolithic imagination than archeological or literary approaches alone might yield. I don't want to engage the caves in an ahistorical void or to strip mine them for "poetic" materials. Among other things, I want to incorporate their imagery into poetry as a primary antecedent dimension, in effect opening a trap door in poetry's floor onto these unbounded but evocative gestures. As a poet's book, *Juniper Fuse* is an attempt to reclaim the caves of the Dordogne and the Pyrénées for poets as geo-mythical sites in which early intimations of what we call "muse" may have been experienced. Poetry itself is questioned throughout this book: How can I make use of its strategies to engage materials that have no historical frame or recorded language?

Ice Age imagery, sealed off for thousands of years, reemerges as a nearly disintegrated Atlantis in the twentieth century, offering a basis for the "hidden wealth" attributed by different cultures to the underworld. In a century rife with alienation and hopelessness, Upper Paleolithic imagination implies that we belong to an undifferentiated paradise, a primordial underworld of unchanging perpetuity.

Before leaving for France in 1973, I attempted to bring my writing to a close in the following summation:

> Yorunomado closed the left hand of my book.
> From this point on, he said,
> your work leads on into the earth.[3]

In retrospect, "the left hand of my book" becomes the first half of my life, and "on into the earth" points to our 1974 discovery of the Ice Age underworld.

✹

After my wife Caryl and I began to visit the caves in the Les Eyzies area, our then neighbor, the translator Helen Lane, loaned us her cave book collection and I found something of equal importance in regard to anything I might write: No poet had taken on the Upper Paleolithic to perform what Olson called a "saturation job." There was the novelist and essayist Georges Bataille's 1955 monograph and that was it.[4] Henry Miller and Ezra Pound seem to have known of the existence of the painted caves discovered at the turn of the century, but neither of them, to my knowledge, visited caves or wrote about them.[5] T. S. Eliot appears to have visited a cave in the Pyrénées—Niaux, Hugh Kenner conjectures[6]—and on the basis of what he saw there he determined that "art never improves." In his essay "Tradition and the Individual Talent" he writes:

> [The poet] must be quite aware of the obvious fact that art never improves, but that the material of art is never quite the same. He must be aware that the mind of Europe—the mind of his own country—a mind which he learns in time to be much more important than his own private mind—is a mind which changes, and that this change is a development which abandons nothing en route, which does not superannuate either Shakespeare, or Homer, or the rock drawings of the Magdalenian draughtsmen.

At about the same time Bataille was visiting Lascaux nightly (after crowds of tourists went home) for his monograph, Olson was reading Henry Fairfield Osborne's *Men of the Old Stone Age* and Gertrude Levy's *Gate of Horn*, taking notes and writing lectures for what he hoped would be an Institute in the New Sciences of Man at Black Mountain College, with the archaic as its basis.[7] This institute never materialized, nor did Olson work up his notes and lectures into a book or use them to extend the range of his epic, *The Maximus Poems*, into the Upper Paleolithic: However, in a 1946 poem, "La Préface," he struck a profoundly dissonant chord for our times with:

My name is NO RACE   address
Buchenwald   new Altamira cave[8]

Olson's presentation of Buchenwald and Altamira (shadowed by Odysseus' response to the Cyclops' question), with space rather than a verb between the two nouns, presents the reader with an overwhelming question: What do these two nouns have in common? The answer that I find suggests that the astonishing ancientness of the human creative impulse, which was discovered in this most inhuman century, may somehow offset total despair. Olson's choice of Altamira is slightly inaccurate for my meaning as it was discovered in 1879 (although its antiquity was not officially recognized until 1902). However, the majority of the known Upper Paleolithic caves were discovered between 1900 and 1940 (the year that Lascaux was tumbled into). This represents a staggering synchronicity and argues *contra* Adorno that there can be poetry after Auschwitz. Jerome Rothenberg pulls Adorno's statement inside out in his long poem "Khurbn," written after visits to what is left of the death camps in the 1980s: "After Auschwitz there is only poetry."[9]

The Upper Paleolithic's resurfacing can be thought of as a retrieval of depth, of a bottomlessness that is not simply absence but one complexed with hidden presence and invisible connections. While cave stone might well be thought of as the *tabula rasa* par excellence, caves themselves are hardly *tabula rasas*: Each has its own character. For some, the caves' sensory isolational atmosphere is experienced as spirit-filled, even as hallucinogenic. For example, grotesque and hybrid cave images suggest a fusion between early consciousness and subterranean "entities." It is as if the soul of an all-devouring monster earth could be contacted in cavern dark as a living and fathomless reservoir of psychic force.

We see our present world of vanishing species not only against what we know of the immense and diverse biomass of Pleistocene Europe, but also against the end-Pleistocene extinctions that eerily forecast our own. While climatic change, unaffected by humans, appears to have played a major role in early extinctions, there is credible evidence that from the late Upper Paleolithic on, especially in the New World, extinctions have been increasingly human-induced. So I'm haunted by the rock shelter's name where our ancient and direct ancestors' skeletons were first discovered: Abri du Cro-Magnon, or shelter of the Big Hole People. It seems that over the centuries our "big holeness" has increased in proportion to our domination of the earth. Today it is as if species are disappearing into and through an "us" that lacks a communal will to arrest their vanishing.

As one might expect, studies of Upper Paleolithic image-making have been written by archeologists, in scholarly, objective prose, based on field-work, and often framed by a single theory to account for the art. However, the archeologist Margaret W. Conkey, along with certain colleagues, writes articles that examine the way Upper Paleolithic images have been used to exaggerate or to disguise the complexity of this ever-deepening field. She has also scrutinized gender issues as they involve the presentation of female imagery. Her writing attempts to establish what she calls "a new archeological integrity." She calls into question the matter of "objectivity" and the tendency for archeologists to keep the past in the past. "Undoubtedly," she writes, "it is extremely challenging for archeologists to make inferences about what an artifact or image 'meant' to its creators and their contemporaries. Some of us recognize that certainly this is never an 'objective' enterprise distinct from the questions and concerns of the present."[10]

In the late 1970s, I found that cave imagery is an inseparable mix of psychic constructs and perceptive observations. That is, there are "fantastic" animals as well as realistic ones. There are not only human figures representing men and women whose social roles cannot be determined, but others, with bird masks, bison heads, and peculiar wounds, that evoke an interior world, in some cases shamanism. Instead of solely employing rational documentation (as have the archeologists), it struck me that this "inseparable mix" might be approached using poetic imagination as well as thorough fieldwork and research. In other words, in the spirit that I served the cave images as observer, to ask them to serve my imagination, so as to translate them not back into their own original unknown-to-us context, but forward into my own idiom.

Thus in the writing of *Juniper Fuse* I sought to be open to what I thought about and fantasized while in the caves or while meditating on their image environments—to create my own truth as to what they mean, respecting imagination as one of a plurality of conflicting powers. I also sought to be a careful observer, and to reflect on what others have written, photographed, and drawn. Sometimes a section is all poetry, sometimes all prose—at other times it is a shifting combination like a Calder mobile, with poetry turning into prose, prose turning into poetry.

I brought to bear on what I have come to call "Upper Paleolithic Imagination & the Construction of the Underworld" a range of thinkers outside of archeology proper. While I studied the work of the Abbés Breuil and Glory, Annette Laming, André Leroi-Gourhan, S. Giedion, Max Raphael, Paolo Graziosi, Alexander Marshack, Jean Clottes, Margaret W. Conkey, and Paul Bahn, I also read C. G. Jung, Sandor Ferenczi, Geza Róheim, Mikhail Bakhtin, Weston LaBarre, Charles Olson, N. O. Brown, Kenneth Grant, James Hillman, Hans Peter Duerr, and Maxine Sheets-Johnstone. I sought to match my pluralistic approach with varying styles. *Juniper Fuse* is an anatomy, composed of poetry, prose poetry, essays, lectures, notes, dreams, and visual reproductions.

❧

My thinking concerning the origin and elaboration of cave image making began with a 1970s intuition, while in Combarelles, that it was motivated by a crisis in which Upper Paleolithic people began to separate the animal out of their about-to-be human heads and to project it onto cave walls (as well as onto a variety of portable tools and weapons often made out of the animals themselves). In other words, that the liberation of what might be called autonomous imagination came from within as a projective response on the part of those struggling to differentiate themselves from, while being deeply bonded to, the animal.

To arrange the bones of a slaughtered horse, say, in proper anatomical position might have been both atonement for having killed and hope for the horse's regeneration. To my understanding, such a ritual—which Weston LaBarre proposes to be the oldest of which we have any knowledge[11]—was insufficient to appease a dawning psychic hunger for coming to terms with what was at least a triple bind of feeling superior (on the basis of weapons and tools), equal, and inferior to the animal. After Cro-Magnon people discovered that a tool could produce lines on a wall and that by curving or jumbling them something evoking a creature could be formed, they had the opportunity to bring the animal under their scrutiny into miniature. Which is also to suggest that as their ambivalences concerning the animal became unbearably concentrated, the observed animal imploded, and with the aid of a wall or a piece of antler its spectral double could be drawn forth.

The separating out of the animal as a formative function of Cro-Magnon imagination indicates, on a daily, practical level, the increasing separation between human and animal domains. I conjecture that this separation was brought about in part by action-at-a-distance weapons (the spear, the spear-thrower, the harpoon, and probably the bow and arrow).[12] Shamanism, or what might be more accurately termed proto-shamanism, may have come into being as a reactive swerve from this separation continuum, to rebind being human to the fantasy of that paradise that did not exist until the separation was sensed.

While overlapping and intermingling of animal forms typical of cave imagery certainly evokes the historic shamanic paradise of direct communication between animals and humans, or otherworlds/underworlds and earth, the strongest evidence for shamanic trance activity is the hybrid or grotesque animal/human forms positioned in relation to one or many animal forms in such caves as Les Trois Frères, Lascaux, Gabillou, Pech-Merle, Cougnac, Combarelles, and Chauvet.

As we come forward in time, the animal-headed figures become gods in human form with animals as consorts or antagonists. The so-called

"Fall" is hardly a singular event, as depicted in the *Bible*, but rather a multiphasic expulsion that took on increasingly paradisical depth (and loss) as human beings became more self-conscious.

Since historic rock art is often made to empower a particular site, or is a response to a ritual performed there, it is reasonable to suggest that compositions clearly depicting a psychic reality (such as the "scene" in the Lascaux Shaft)—in comparison to the more widespread realistic animal outlines that would seem to represent an observational reality—were done in conjunction with shamanic activity. Barbara MacLeod's recent sensory isolation experiences in Mayan caves suggest that some of the hybrid or grotesque Cro-Magnon images are the result of an interaction between a quester and what MacLeod has called the "entity" of the cave.[13] And while it is fair to assume that a realistically depicted horse outline is contingent upon careful observation of horses, we cannot rule out the possibility that such a horse, while not grotesque, was a shaman's animal familiar or helping spirit, presented in a naturalistic way. The fact that there are no landscape or hunting scenes per se in Upper Paleolithic cave imagery leaves all figures open to magical interpretations. Deep caves especially would be ideal locations for the experiencing of symbolic death and regenerative vision. Such transformations—fundamental to world historic shamanism—may have roots in the separating-out-of-the-animal and the proto-shamanic rebinding of man to animal that, as I see it, underlie the imaginative turmoil of the Cro-Magnon people.[14]

What psychologically did these people bring with them into the caves? What did the caves offer them as interactive materials?

Based on the thinking of a number of mythologically and psychoanalytically oriented writers (such as Freud, Melanie Klein, Róheim, Ferenczi, and Brown), one can propose that cave exploration in the Upper Paleolithic was stimulated by regressive fantasies concerning the insides of the mother's body; that our distant ancestors, like historical people everywhere, may well have associated fissures, holes, cavern corridors and tunnels with female sexual organs; and that these same people furthermore withdrew into themselves as dreamers, forming cavelike dream wombs out of their own bodies. Since both caves and dreams as we know them are charged with uterine sensations and fantasies, might they not then too have had a metaphorical relationship? For example: To be in a cave with its wondrous topography of "insides," at once organlike *and* alien, is certainly like being in a dream. Dreaming, in which a godlike dreamer watches a dream-self venture into a psychic landscape, unsure of his fate, at the constant mercy of blocks, shifting itineraries, and bizarre openings, is like being in a cave. Cave insides were marvelous and forbidding partially because of what they dramatized, or even magnetized, in the insides (body and soul) of the person groping through those cavernous innards.

Cro-Magnon hand lamps made certain aspects of wall contours suggest animal and human anatomy. A significant number of engravings, paintings, and wall sculptures employ natural formations. In Font-de-Gaume, a horizontal ripple in a wall that curves down into a cluster of fluted draperies is turned into a painted horse's dorsal line, rump, and springing rear legs. In Combarelles, a stag lowering its head while drinking is positioned so that the tongue touches a widening fissure in the wall. In the Combel section of Pech-Merle, ochre disks have been painted around a stalactitic "breast." And in Le Portel, a tiny belling stag is painted on the ceiling of a tight cul-de-sac in such a way that to view it one must scrunch backward on one's back, head craned back in the same position as the stag's.

It may have seemed to these early explorers that animals (and, less often, humans) were partially embedded in, or emerging through, such walls, and that such presences only needed the assistance of some manmade lines to be completely present. As the animal was sighted partly submerged in stone, imagination, reinforced by actual modeling or engraving, brought forth its form. If a wall was "with animal," then some Cro-Magnon midwifery could help it to give birth.

While some areas of caves appear to have been spontaneously marked, others seem to have involved team planning, including the collecting, mixing, and heating of pigments, the making of burins and brushes (or dabbing pads), and even in a few cases the construction of scaffolds. Pollen analysis in Fontanet suggests that a small group of people entered the cave and spent a few nights there, making some images and sleeping on grass cushions. In such caves as Cougnac and Pech-Merle, paintings have had new elements added to them; on the basis of recent solid radiocarbon dating, there appear to be thousands of years between one stage and another. The aesthetic range extends from spontaneous poking and scratchings, possibly done in the dark by children, to complex, friezelike palimpsests, involving different belief systems, worked over by "technicians of the sacred" and their apprentices.

The earliest proto-images include small cup-shaped cavities (or cupules), and wandering, crisscrossing lines (which at Rouffignac are so mixed in with cave bear claw scrapings that the thought occurs that the bears might have started the whole image process!). I agree with Maxine Sheets-Johnstone that such markings need not have had a referential focus (such as hunting or fertility) to have been felt as magical, and that much proto-image gesturing was probably done out of an impulsive desire to participate, as she puts it, in "the transforming powers of insides."[15] It is also possible that in quests involving prolonged isolation in a cave, marks on walls were a spontaneous expression between the quester and the cave itself.

"To explore is to penetrate; the world is the inside of mother,"[16] Brown writes in *Love's Body*. If we follow out the psychic implications of penetrating and exploring, we might imagine finding a Cro-Magnon adolescent gouging a hole in the wall of a cave's terminal chamber. By gouging a small cavity in the limestone this person would symbolically be feminizing the surface of the wall but would also be facing an uninvadable impasse.

The simple but extraordinary solution to this impasse was to abandon penetration *into* for cutting a line across the otherwise unyielding matroclinic matter. Engraving especially was a remarkable solution as it allowed for a shallow surface penetration at the same time that it opened up a surface area for a laterally extending line. Once the line turned, a shape in nature was suggested; when it formed an enclosure, not only were insides and bodies at hand, but also the hole-making impasse had been converted into a successful hole outline.

At the point where the line became referential (a curve, say, suggesting an animal's rump or head), a range of intentional possibilities must have come into play, such as the desire to make a number of lines look right or conform to one's memory of a shape. I want to emphasize here, however, that the crucial move enabling the image projection and drawing skill to merge was the deflection of a stymied head-on penetration. The hole that had become a line was a fundamental metaphoric transformation.

〰

If the cave was charged with a dreamlike womb atmosphere, we can imagine that the person crawling into it, groping from one unknown object to the next, perhaps in total darkness, entered fantasies in which he or she played a fetal role and sought, in some fashion, to be reborn. Implicit here is the idea that the birth from one's mother is not a complete or the real birth, and that the real or second birth involves something more than merely continuing to exist. Those who do not attempt to realize their symbolic fetal role risk moving from substitute womb to substitute womb all their lives, and interment of the dead can be thought of as the final stop in these changes of residence. Yet like the cave, earth burial implies that there are two mothers: one's flesh-and-blood mother to whose insides one can never physically regress, and one's transpersonal or cosmogonic mother who, as long as one is alive, may provide the conditions for a second or fully realized birth.

The transformation of regressive penetration into the forming of self-conceived images is one of the ways this second birth is brought about. A person engraving the image of a bison on a cave wall could be said to be realizing him- or herself within the Great Mother, or to be giving birth to himself. Drawing upon the bacteriologist Hans Zinsser's words to Hart Crane, one could say that this engraver has loosed himself within a pattern's mastery that he himself has conceived, and can yield to.[17]

The release implicit in such transformations may account for the waves of energy that subtly ripple through many large compositions of friezes. Animals and animal parts are often superimposed as if passing behind, through, and before each other with no sense of contradiction or subordination. There is no background, no frame. While often at a considerable remove from the sunlit earth of fauna and flora, the imagery is coextensive with it. Only occasionally is there any hint of vertical or horizontal grids that subsequent lines must take into consideration. No ascendant/descendant duality. Commenting on what he defines as revolutionary Romantic imagination, Northrop Frye seems to be addressing this Cro-Magnon "release":

Poetic thinking, being mythical, does not distinguish or create antithesis: it goes on and on, linking analogy to analogy, identity to identity, and containing, without trying to refute, all oppositions and objections. This means, not that it is merely facile or liquid thinking without form, but that it is the dialectic of love: it treats whatever it encounters as another form of itself.[18]

❧

In the late 1970s, Alexander Marshack showed Caryl and me a photo of an incised ox rib from an Acheulean dig near Bordeaux. The astonishing thing was that between 200,000 and 300,000 years ago a hominid appears to have made a curving slash in the bone (referred to by Marshack as a "core meander"), and then to have placed this cutting instrument on the end of the slash and made another curving cut (referred to as a "branch meander").[19] This act was repeated several times. This is hardly an image, but it certainly is as *readable* (with the help of a microscope) as the cupules and meanders, made much later, that can be thought of as proto-images. Whoever made these meanders was, in a subliminal way, creating history (thinking here of "history" in the Charles Olson derived sense of "istorin, to find out for oneself," in which I put the stress on "out," or exit for the self).[20]

Taking a lead from the caves and the terms Marshack used, I attempted to find a way to branch out in my poetry while keeping a core at work within the meandering. I sought a focused movement forward through material that would keep open to associative sidetracks. Like someone exploring a cave, I wanted to be able to probe any opening regardless of where it might lead. As each cave has its own shape and character, so I believed a poem could end up being a display of its core and branch meanders. Later, I read Anton Ehrenzweig's commentary, in *The Hidden Order of Art*,[21] on the relation of the maze to the creative search, and realized that my approach to core and branch meandering was a way of schematizing the labyrinth I entered when I started to work on a poem.

As one sees *into* a shifting field, there is a desire to see through it. One risks finding that what one is writing is absurd, which of course stops the process in its tracks. However, seeing through what one is writing is the critical aspect of poetic thinking that along with inspiration (or subconscious input) offers imagination its potential wholeness, its dyad of synthesis and melee, the will to cohere in conjunction with the desire to ramify.

In caves I associated *seeing into* with aesthetic appreciation and historical contextualization; *seeing through* with grasping what the images signified to those who made and originally saw them. *Seeing into* and *seeing through* combined into a winding window. Because of the labyrinthine associative field created by unexpected and provocative images, they often wind out of sight before a *seeing through* can take place.

This fascinating and frustrating interplay held for assemblies of images in a particular cave, as well as for isolated compositions. Inching along walls and through tunnels, sometimes on my knees or waddling, occasionally on my belly, the cave and my mind became a synesthetic "salad" of splitting overlays. Sensations and associations amassed and crumbled, bent and extended, died then flashed again, in ways that made me feel I was being processed through them rather than the other way around. Standing before large compositions in which the realistic, the fantastic, and the unreadable are in overlapping juxtaposition, I have felt myself drawn into a vortex of shifting planes which afforded no place for a perspective or a terminal.[22]

The chronological unfolding of *Juniper Fuse* also has cavelike aspects. I never followed a recipe, and I worked hard not to constrict the writing into an elaboration of a single intuition or thesis. I wanted to make this book as multifoliate as the image-making it is focused on. As poems and essays developed, with one segment making the next possible in a nonnarrative way, so did the manuscript move out of itself, from year to year, with no end in sight until the spring of 1997 when at long last I gained permission to climb down into the Lascaux Shaft and view its extraordinary "scene" with my own eyes. I realized standing there that I was not only at the end of Lascaux, but very near the end of the investigation I had started shortly after Caryl and I, thanks to H. L. Movius, Jr., visited Lascaux for the first time in the summer of 1974.

As should be clear from my approach set forth in this introduction, *Juniper Fuse* is not an overview of Upper Paleolithic "art." I wrote about those caves and images that moved me imaginatively and about which I had something special to say. There is a great deal of material on Lascaux here (shifting perceptions spread out over more than two decades) along with a significant amount on Combarelles, Le Tuc d'Audoubert, Montespan, Pech Merle (especially the Combel section), Bernifal, "Venus" figures and statuettes, Aurignacian engraved blocks, the Abri du Cro-Magnon, and the hybrid figures to be found in Cougnac, Les Trois Frères, and Gabillou. I have received the Upper Paleolithic in this book as it thrusts into, and is shadowed by, my twentieth century. I have also included work on more ancient materials (Neanderthal skulls, slabs, and the Drachenloch assemblages) as well as on more recent ones (Mesolithic, Babylonian, and Greek figures and myths), for both are, either as roots tunneling under or shoots budding above, mysterious outgrowths of the Paleolithic rootstock.

※

I believe that we make images not simply because we are creatures who seek to loose ourselves within a pattern's mastery, but that the making of images is one of the means by which we become human. In this sense, to be human is to realize that one is a metaphor, and to be a metaphor is to be grotesque (initially of the grotto). While it is understandable to think that we stand on blind Homer's and Shakespeare's shoulders, it is perhaps more accurate to say that we stand on a depth in them that was struck hundreds of generations before them by those Upper Paleolithic men, women, and children who made the truly incredible breakthrough from no image of the world to *an* image. The cathedrals and churches in which humankind passively sits today, listening to watered-down statements based on utterances of visionaries and ecstatics, were, before being in effect turned inside out, active underground "sanctuaries" or "incubational pits."[23] There people created the first electrifying outlines of animals while performing rites of passage, commemorations of the dead, rituals to insure fertility, and just messing around.

At the point imaginative depth is evoked, soul becomes involved. With the Greeks in mind, James Hillman writes: "When we use the word *underworld*, we are referring to a wholly psychic perspective, where one's entire mode of being has been desubstantialized, killed of natural life, and yet is in every shape and sense... the exact replica of natural life."[24] Behind such a definition is the Upper Paleolithic underworld: animal forms removed from their flesh and blood. These simulacra propose that the soul is always partly hidden or submerged, because the weight of reality lies in a realm we cannot completely conceive. As Cro-Magnon people killed, ate, wore, and tooled animals, they must have felt like parasitic spectres as well as beings who were both "familiar" and "other" to the animal.

Previously I spoke of the contours in the wall itself that gave rise to some engravings and paintings. Such imagery could be thought of as containing the figure's emergent, or retreating, essence. Attempting to understand how early consciousness managed to make the nearly invisible visible, I thought of a moment in a prose work by Rainer Maria Rilke called "An Experience." After leaning against a small tree in the Duino Castle garden by the sea, and having suddenly been filled with the most delicate of vibrations that he could not physically explain, Rilke "asked himself what was happening to him and almost immediately found an expression which satisfied him, as he said aloud to himself that he had reached the other side of nature."[25]

Is it possible that the "place" Rilke reached in the interior or nightside of the tree was a "place" that Cro-Magnon people looked out from? If it were, it would suggest that the locus of projection was sensed as inside the material the surface of which was being painted or engraved. Of course they must have had an intimate relationship with the surface of a wall to be able to pick up, by a flickering flame, the contour that implied the potential presence of a figure. Such people could be said to have seen from the "other side of Nature" as well as outwardly, to have had no fixed boundary or "reality principle" within the fluidity of the imaginal and the observational.

Thus the double separation—from the animal, from mother—endured by our ancient forebears may not only have taken them to the wall but allowed them an encompassing access behind the wall's undulating surface as ghosts of their own potential. Do we today look at images that once were the rounding out of an outwardly directed, interior gaze, "the movement of a self in the rock"? Are Upper Paleolithic images for us the worm casts of this presence?

"The descent beckons..."[26]

1999–2002

NOTES

Juniper Fuse: Upper Paleolithic Imagination & the Construction of the Underworld, Wesleyan University Press, 2003, was researched and written between 1974 and 1999. "The Back Wall of the Imagination / The Juniper Fuse Project," an essay, is to be found in *Archaic Design*, Black Widow Press, 2007. Some of the poems in *The Grindstone of Rapport*, which originally appeared in some of my Black Sparrow Press books, were incorporated into *Juniper Fuse*. They are:

Hades in Manganese

Our Lady of the Three-pronged Devil

The Death of Bill Evans (appears in "Interface II: 'Fracture,'" an essay in *Juniper Fuse*, reprinted here)

Notes on a Visit to Le Tuc d'Auboubert

Like Violets, He Said

from Matrix, Blower

The Cemeteries of Paradise

1. The global Upper Paleolithic is wrapped, as it were, in historical gauze. All our words for continents, countries, regions, areas, sites, tools, weapons, techniques, and aesthetics are historically imposed, more often than not, by modern history. While this is obvious, it is a slippery matter: Many a subliminal association has linked "France" to "the origin of art." In earlier drafts of this book I had used the word "art" to refer to parietal and portable imagery. Because "art" today implies transcendent values while cutting itself off from utilitarian, magical, and occult activities, I have dropped it, feeling more at home with "imagery" and "imagination"—except when referring to "cave art theory," for the most part worked out before such archeologists as Margaret W. Conkey, Olga Soffer, and Silvia Tomaskova began to challenge the applicability of the word. Their current thinking on this matter is to be found in *Beyond Art*, Memoirs of the California Academy of Science, #23, San Francisco, 1997.

2. Charles Olson, *Additional Prose*, Four Seasons Foundation, Bolinas, California, 1974, p. 11.

3. Clayton Eshleman, *Coils*, Black Sparrow Press, Los Angeles, 1973, p. 147.

4. Georges Bataille, *Lascaux, or The Birth of Art*, Skira, New York, 1955. Bataille associates ancient man, including Neanderthal, with work (tool-making) and prohibitions. Cro-Magnon, or in Bataille's phrase, "Lascaux man," breaks with the past, inaugurating the world of play and transgression. Bataille considers Lascaux to have been decorated during the Aurignacian period, around 30,000 B.P., that is, Before the Present or 1950, when absolute radiocarbon dates were first obtained. For Bataille, 30,000 B.P. is curiously at once the dawn and the pinnacle of prehistoric art. While his dating and theoretical approach are not relevant today, Bataille's description of the cave itself (interspersed with excellent color photography by Hans Hinz and Claudio Emmer) is well written and moving. Bataille places the "art" of Lascaux in a wider context, including the concepts of taboo, sacrifice, and sexuality, in *Eroticism* (City Lights, San Francisco, 1986).

5. Miller's stirring evocation of the prehistoric Dordogne occurs in his book on Greece, *The Colossus of Maroussi* (New Directions, New York, 1958, pp. 4–5). He seems to have known about the decorated caves, but I have been unable to find any evidence that he visited any of them:

A few months before the war broke out I decided to take a long vacation. I had long wanted to visit the valley of the Dordogne, for one thing. So I packed my valise and took the train for Rocamadour where I arrived early one morning about sun up, the moon still gleaming brightly. It was a stroke of genius on my part to make the tour of the Dordogne region before plunging into the bright and hoary world of Greece. Just to glimpse the black, mysterious river at Domme from the beautiful bluff at the edge of town is something to be grateful for all one's life. To me this river, this country, belong to the poet, Rainer Maria Rilke. It is not French, not Austrian, not European even: it is the country of enchantment which the poets have staked out and which they alone may lay claim to. It is the nearest thing to Paradise this side of Greece. Let us call it the Frenchman's paradise, by way of making a concession. Actually it must have been paradise for many thousands of years. I believe it must have been so for Cro-Magnon man, despite the fossilized evidence of the great caves which point to a condition of life rather bewildering and terrifying. I believe that the Cro-Magnon man settled here because he was extremely intelligent and had a highly developed sense of beauty. I believe that in him the religious sense was already highly developed and that it flourished here even if he lived like an animal in the depths of the caves. I believe that this great peaceful region of France will always be a sacred spot for man and that when the cities have killed off the poets this will be the refuge and the cradle of the poets to come. I repeat, it was most important for me to have seen the Dordogne: it gives me hope for the future of the race, for the future of the earth itself. France may one day exist no more, but the Dordogne will live on just as dreams live on and nourish the souls of man.

Based on his notebooks kept during a walking tour of southwestern France in 1912 (*A Walking Tour in Southern France/Ezra Pound among the Troubadours,* New Directions, New York, 1992), we know that Pound passed through towns that put him within walking distance of a few of the caves discovered around the turn of the century.

6. Hugh Kenner writes: "The exchange value of the pound sterling in 1919 made that a good summer for the impecunious to travel, and Ezra and Dorothy after five years cooped up in England, met Tom Eliot near Giraut de Bornelh's birthplace, Excideuil. The three headed south, the Pounds finally to Montségur but Eliot on a divagation of his own to inspect nearby cave drawings. That may have been at the Grotte de Niaux. We are to imagine him, rucksacked, deep inside a mountain, individual talent confronted by the Mind of Europe, satisfying himself that art never improves ('but the material of art'—here, bison 'd'un pureté de trait étonnante' drawn with magnesium oxide in bison grease—'is never quite the same'), while 20 kilometers eastward by crows' flight the Pounds, fortified with chocolate, were climbing the southwest face of Montségur to the white walls that ride its summit like a stone ship." (*The Pound Era,* University of California Press, Berkeley, 1971, pp. 333–334). Kenner also mentions that Picasso visited Altamira in 1902.

7. For Olson's lectures and notes, see *Olson* #10, the Journal of the Charles Olson Archives, University of Connecticut Library, Storrs, 1978.

8. "La Préface," *The Collected Poems of Charles Olson*, University of California Press, 1987.

9. Jerome Rothenberg, *Khurbn & Other Poems*, New Directions, New York, 1989, p. 14.

In 1980, Gary Snyder wrote to me:

The '50s–'80s was the discovery of the depths of Far Eastern religious thought for Occidentals. The '90s should be the period of the beginning of the discovery of the actual shape of early Homo Sapiens consciousness: for both Occidental and Oriental seekers. A profound new step. Knowing more of the Paleolithic imagination is to know the "Paleo Ecology" of our own minds. Planetwide human mental health in the twenty-first century may depend on arriving at these understandings. For it is in the deep mind that wilderness and the unconsciousness become one, and in some half understood but very profound way, our relation to the outer ecologies seems conditioned by our inner ecologies. This is a metaphor, but it is also literal.

10. "Making Things Meaningful: Approaches to the Interpretation of the Ice Age Imagery of Europe," in *Meaning in the Visual Arts: Views from the Outside*, Institute for Advanced Studies, Princeton, New Jersey, 1995, p. 61.

11. Weston LaBarre, *Muelos/A Stone Age Superstition About Sexuality*, Columbia University Press, New York, 1984, p. 1.

12. In *The Creative Explosion* (Harper & Row, New York, 1982, pp. 50–51), John E. Pfeiffer writes:

Using a spear alone, it is rarely possible to kill a large animal unless you are close enough and fast enough to make repeated thrusts. Equipped with spear-throwers, Australian aborigines today can hit a target, say a kangaroo, three out of four times from more than 100 feet away, and kill from 30 to 50 feet.

The bow and arrow was something else again, another world when it came to advanced design and hunting efficiency. It may have come into its own with longer seasonal camping, when local game may have been scarcer and more difficult to hunt. Not only did it provide greater range and power, but it also increased the possibility of stealth and surprise. To hurl a spear you must spring out of your hiding place, move forward, and swing your arms and shoulders to achieve maximum momentum. With a bow and arrow you stay put, practically motionless, shooting from your stationary, concealed position. This considerably raises the odds favoring a successful ambush, especially since it can all be done silently and invisibly, and you can take a second or third shot if you miss the first time.

There is some question about who invented this weapon. The earliest known bow dates back some 8,000 years to a site in Denmark, but direct proof of arrows is more ancient. A pair of shafts has been preserved in 10,000-year-old water-logged deposits, also in Denmark, with tanged arrowheads still in place; and, perhaps two millenniums older in northern Germany, a cache of some 100 pine shafts was found, most of them slotted for arrowhead insertion at one end and notched at the other with a bowstring groove. But a cave in south-eastern Spain, a Solutrean site, has yielded a collection of flint points which if mixed in with a collection of American Indian points known to be arrowheads would be accepted without question as the real thing. So it would surprise no one if future evidence shows that the bow and arrow is 17,000 years old.

The invention of power-amplifying devices represented an industrial revolution, and one of the most important signs of the cultural explosion. It was the beginning of a new coming of age, a pulling away from our fellow species.

Concerning Upper Paleolithic depiction of arrows: André Leroi-Gourhan notes that on a pebble from Colombière the belly of an engraved rhinoceros appears to have been struck by three arrows (*Treasures of Prehistoric Art*, Abrams, New York, 1967, p. 484). It is possible that some of the many strokes, or barbed signs, painted or engraved on or around animal images, could represent arrows.

Anthony Appiah, reviewing John Reader's *Africa: A Biography* (Knopf, New York, 1998), in the December 17, 1998, *New York Review of Books*, mentions that Reader reports the discovery of fifty-nine skeletons near Wadi Halfa, dated at 14,000 B.P., many of which had projectile points embedded in their bones.

In his essay "Wars, Arms, Rams, Mars" (*Facing Apocalypse*, Spring Books, Dallas, 1987), James Hillman distinguishes between military and nuclear imaginations: "Mars moves in close, hand-to-hand, Mars *propior* and *propinquus*. Bellona is a fury, the blood-dimmed tide, the red fog of intense immediacy. No distance. The nuclear imagination, in contrast, invents at ever greater distances—intercontinental, the bottom of the sea, outer space."

The quantum leap in concept and technology signaled by a taut bowstring and humming arrow has, in our century, widened the distance between assailant and object beyond visibility, beyond continents. The motionless archer behind cover has become a finger on a computer.

13. See the section "Cave Art Theory" for a quotation from MacLeod's unpublished paper, written for "Advanced Non-Ordinary Reality," taught by Henry Selby, Anthropology Department, University of Texas, Austin, Fall 1980.

14. The basis for dualism may lie in such separation and rebinding. Body is the result of separation, soul of rebinding. In the Upper Paleolithic, boundaries between wild and tribal areas may have instigated time versus eternity. Boundary seems to me to be the primal quake whose aftershocks are content and form.

15. "On Paleolithic Cave Art," from *The Roots of Thinking*, Temple University Press, Philadelphia, 1990, p. 242.

16. *Love's Body*, Random House, New York, 1966, p. 36.

17. The passage paraphrased is from "Havana Rose," in *The Poems of Hart Crane*, Liveright, New York, 1986, p. 201:

And during the wait over dinner at La Diana,
the Doctor had said—who was American also—
"You cannot heed the negative—, so might go on
to underserved doom...must therefore loose yourself
within a pattern's mastery that you can conceive, that

you can yield to—by which also you

win and gain that mastery and happiness which

is your own from birth."

18. *A Study of English Romanticism*, The University of Chicago Press, Chicago, 1968, pp. 121–122.

19. Alexander Marshack, "Exploring the Mind of Ice Age Man," *National Geographic*, Washington, DC, January 1975, p. 81.

20. Charles Olson, *The Maximus Poems*, University of California Press, Berkeley, 1983, p. 249.

21. *The Hidden Order of Art*, University of California Press, Berkeley, 1971, pp. 35–37.

22. My susceptibility to "a vortex of shifting planes" may be linked to hallucinogenic experiences—not involving stimulants—in Kyoto, 1963. Nightly, for weeks, right before falling asleep on a futon I would hear a bell ding, seemingly in my forehead, after which there would be a loud thud, as if someone had slammed a window down next door (an impossibility, since the Japanese houses in our neighborhood did not have Western windows). Then, as if part of this "schedule," upon falling asleep, I would hurtle through a winding tunnel only slightly larger than my body (a portent of the caves to come?). Each time in this tunnel, I would anticipate my father's face at, or as, the tunnel's end, something I never reached.

Subjects participating in controlled hallucinogen testing report that as they move deeper into trance, a rotating tunnel often surrounds them, the sides of which are marked by lattices of squares.

J. D. Lewis-Williams and T. A. Dowson identify the "tunnel" experience as the third stage, resulting in trance, of the altering of consciousness. They propose that the first stage involves seeing entoptic forms (dots, zigzags, grids, meandering lines), and that the second stage turns these simple shapes into potentially ikonic forms (e.g. a shimmering band of light becomes a snake). They view this three-stage alteration as the neurological process by which shamans enter trance. Basing their work on nineteenth and twentieth century Bushman and Coso (South African) rock art, which they allege is shamanistic, they propose that this "neurological bridge affords some access to the Upper Paleolithic." Some access, possibly (though the three-stage alteration seems highly formulaic). More recently, having teamed up with Jean Clottes, Lewis-Williams argues that the making of rock art, including the Ice Age cave imagery, "was largely, but not exclusively, associated with institutionalized, ritualized altered states of consciousness, a central feature of shamanism." This assertion now takes on the blanket force of a single theory for such image-making, and in that way evokes older, now rejected, single theories (such as the hunting hypothesis, or "art for art's sake") that tended to explain away rather than open up this realm in which nothing can be absolutely verified. Trance is not the sole possession of shamans (as my Kyoto experience taught me), nor is there any evidence whatsoever that all (or even most) Ice Age image-making was done in a state of trance.

For Lewis-Williams and Dowson's work, see "The Signs of All Times," *Current Anthropology*, April 1988. For the Clottes/Lewis-Williams work, see *The Shamans of Prehistory*, Abrams, 1998, and "The mind in the cave—the cave in the mind: altered consciousness in the Upper Paleolithic," *Anthropology of Consciousness* 9 (1).

For a collection of papers contesting Clottes' and Lewis-Williams's claims, see *The Concept of Shamanism: Uses and Abuses*, ed. Francfort and Hamayon, Bibliotheca Shamanistica, Budapest, 2002.

23. For "incubational pits," see Barbara G. Walker's *The Woman's Encyclopedia of Myths and Secrets*, Harper & Row, New York, 1983, pp. 2–3.

24. James Hillman, *The Dream and the Underworld*, Harper & Row, New York, 1979, p. 46.

25. Rainer Maria Rilke, "An Experience," *Selected Writings/Prose*, New Directions, New York, 1960.

26. William Carlos Williams, *Paterson*, Book Two, Part III: A few lines later, Williams proposes that the depths are "inhabited by hordes heretofore unrealized." That certainly expresses my experience upon first visiting the Ice Age caves.

ADDENDUM, 2008

In 2002, the Italian scholar Massimo Bacigalupo published a selection of *The Cantos*, from Ezra Pound's manuscripts, typescripts, and magazine publications. In this selection he included the following poem, apparently a rejected version of what is now Canto II. Robert Creeley who, with his wife Penelope, joined us as a guest lecturer on our 2004 cave tour in the Dordogne, sent me this draft in the winter of 2005:

> Dissatisfaction of chaos, inadequacy of arrangements,
> At les Eyzies, nameless drawer of panther,
> So I in narrow cave, secret scratched on a wall,
> And the last reader, with handshake of departing sun
> drifts from sorrowful horizon, patient thus far, now impatient
> e tu lettor, with little candle long after,
> have pushed past the ruined castle, past the underbrush
> > tangled and netted
> past the ant-hive, in the narrow dark of the crevice
> On the damp rock, is my panther, my aurochs scratched
> > in obscurity.

While this fragment appears to be undated, it is probably a response to Pound's walking tour through the Dordogne in 1912. The engravings in the Combarelles cave outside of Les Eyzies were discovered in 1901 and it is probably this cave that Pound visited and responded to. I think his "panther" is the beautifully engraved lioness in the second section of the cave. Pound mentions that the cave is "narrow," and since Combarelles is indeed quite narrow, this is another reason for believing that Pound was there.

INTERFACE II: "FRACTURE"

There are only a handful of primary incidents in life, incidents powerful enough to create cracks or boundary lines that we'll often enter and follow for years before another crucial event pounds us deeper or reorients us to a new map. As we approach these events, omens appear everywhere, the world becomes dangerously magical, as if we had called the gods, and the gods were now answering.

In October 1980, Caryl and I rented a stone cottage, reached only by a dirt road, near Les Eyzies. On October 9th, news of the death of the jazz pianist Bill Evans reached us: Evans was fifty-one. Even though his playing never affected me as deeply as Bud Powell's, I was moved and disturbed by this news.

That afternoon we picked up a young couple who were hitchhiking in the rain. It turned out that they were staying in the man's parents' summer home a few kilometers away. They invited us to look for wild mushrooms with them the following afternoon.

After several hours of tramping around in the woods, we had gathered a couple of pounds of *cèpes*. Crossing a field on the way back to the car, we stopped a farmer on his tractor to inquire if everything we had gathered was edible. While Caryl and the Parisian couple spoke with him (and were informed that over half of what we had picked were *faux cèpes*—fake *cèpes* that when pressed firmly turn blue—and are poisonous), I wandered back to a scene we had passed that fascinated me. Next to several large, mostly eaten *Amanita muscaria* were three field slugs, vibrating on their backs. There was no way to tell if the slugs were in agony or ecstasy. As I stared at them, Diane Arbus's photograph "Jewish Giant" crossed my mind.

The next morning I woke up and wrote "The Death of Bill Evans." The poem disturbed me so much that I decided not to show it to Caryl, to whom I usually show everything I write. I sensed that I was moving toward something that would hurt me, not out of self-destructiveness, but as if I had been moved "on track" toward a harmed and initiated state. For five years I had been asking for a vision of Paleolithic imagination. Was such a vision now on the threshold of manifesting itself?

Three inch caramel-colored field slug
on its back, vibrating
by the scraps of a big *Amanita muscaria.*

It has eaten more than its size
and now its true size in visionary trance
makes me sad of my size—

I can never eat enough of a higher order
to trick the interior leper to the door,
banish him—but what would remain if I were to become pure?

Can't see the wound for the scars,
a small boy composed of scabs is staring into
the corner of his anatomy—where walls and floor end
he figures he ends, so he wears his end
like glasses before his eyes,
beckoned into the snow he will be beaten
by children he thought were his friends,
the implication of his hurt is so dark
it will scab over to be rescabbed the next time,
and he will grow not by an internal urge to mature
but by scabbings until, grown big, he will be the size of an adult
and his face will look like a pebbly gourd.
He will stay inside the little house I have built for him, in which to
    stand he must stoop.

        The death of Bill Evans
makes me ask: what tortured him so?
Why did a man capable of astonishingly beautiful piano playing
feed his leper hero wine?
Or is the leper an excuse to modulate suffering just enough to keep
one's warmth and danger at exactly the right odds?
Eat Amanita-filled slug, I hear my death angel say,
put into yourself living poison in order to know how the taste of a
    wound

that is bottomless, thus pure, and because pure, receptive to infection,
once infected, open to purity, endlessly draining both,
a wound in which you live like a slob and like a king,
in which you hurt yourself because you really don't care,
in which you care so much that you can't always keep caring,
so you say Fuck it
and the gourd-faced leper, misinterpreting his rot
for Dionysian exuberance, seems to drink
or makes a certain sucking motion with the mouth area of his head.[1]

✴

On the evening of October 11th, we invited the Parisian couple over for
dinner, including the edible *cèpes*. Afterward, I drove them home. They
invited me in for a glass of prune brandy and mentioned that they would
be returning to Paris the following morning. They also informed me that
they had a cave on their property. I explained that I was only interested in
caves with prehistoric decoration, but they were so insistent that I agreed
to visit it. A little after midnight, with one flashlight between us, we
walked into the woods and crawled down a more-or-less vertical cave, per-
haps fifty yards deep, consisting of three chambers with two bottleneck
passageways. There was really nothing to see in the cave, and an hour later
we emerged, covered with mud.

As I was pulling myself up through the last bottleneck, I felt a sharp
sensation in my left ankle, which apparently had gotten twisted in a
crevice, but the sensation was of having been bitten. Once outside, I was
limping—my ankle felt sprained.

I thought of asking if I could stay at the couple's house all night, but
there was no way to contact Caryl—no phones—and I had felt increasing-
ly uncomfortable with the man. While we were having our brandy, he had
pointed out a wood mask lodged in the loft window of a barn facing the
house. He said it was a devil's mask, and then went onto talk about how
much he hated his father. I was his father's age.

I got into the car and started home on the narrow, single-lane road. On
a wide curve a cramp shot up through my left calf, apparently stimulated
by the injured ankle. I lost control for a moment, and the car swerved into
a ditch to the left (to the right of the road was a fifty-foot ravine that was

the graveyard of several tourist cars). Because my foot was pressed in spasm to the floorboard, when I smashed into a boulder in the ditch, my ankle broke in three places.

〜

Until the next morning, when I figured I would be discovered by a local farmer, there was nothing to do but stay in the car and try to make sense out of what had happened. It soon began to rain violently and lightning crackled around the car.

I thought back to when I began to write poetry in 1958. The main thing that kept me going was a blind belief that if I worked through the sexism, self-hate, bodilessness, soullessness, and suffocated human relationships that encrusted my background, I could tear down the "House of Eshleman" and lay out a new foundation in its place.

Then, in 1969, on my back, naked, under the scrutinizing eyes of my Reichian therapist, Dr. Sidney Handelman, clothed, on a chair beside me, I was lured into a baby-like game: He leaned over me making baby faces and sounds—I responded, and soon we were gurgling at each other. A desire to suck his nose broke through my play, and I told him so. Gently, he wrapped his forefinger in the edge of the sheet covering my cot and offered it to me. Grateful for any surrogate, I rolled onto my side in order to take it into my mouth. Suddenly Handelman pulled his finger out of the sheet, shifted back in the chair and reversed his expression. He was now regarding me from a throne of domination. Then in a tentative, contemptuous way, he again offered me the "bandaged nipple." I felt a rustling above my anus—something rushed up my spine—I struck at him. He managed to get his finger out when I locked my teeth on the sheet and went wild. In a rage I tore the sheet apart before passing out. When I came to, I felt—and have felt ever since—that I had lost ten pounds of dirty linoleum that had been wound about my organs.

The following week, Handelman asked me how old I was when my mother ceased to nurse me. I didn't know. A few years after my mother died (in 1970), I discovered a diary that she had kept for the year of my birth, 1935. She wrote there that her milk had dried up when I was six months old.

A couple of years before the car accident, I had told this story to an Indian Yogi. To my surprise, he acted as if it were an ancient Yogic "working." He told me that the doctor was lucky, that "had you bitten into his finger, he would have died—because your doctor had succeeded in bringing all your poison into your teeth. You were a cobra at that moment, and you will be protected by that moment for the rest of your life."

As I mulled over all this in the ditch, long greenish lightning shadows raked their paws over the car's hood. I recalled Wilhelm Reich's vision of "cosmic superimposition"[2] in which two streams of energy merge and fuse. I saw that cave pulling me into its field of energy, as if my "cobra experience" had made me vulnerable to it. The Yogi had told me that had I bitten into Handelman's finger I would have killed him. Well, the cave "bit" me, and I was subsequently nearly killed. Had my release of breast-denied frustration come with a karmic price?

Several people, including James Hillman, had warned me: You must be very careful when you are trying to induct prehistoric archetypes; Hillman, in particular, had explained that unlike Greek archetypes, which we can examine today as the discrete and complementary structures of Greek myths, prehistoric archetypes seem to us far less differentiated. This could mean that specific structures were not yet delineated so as to take on distinct characteristics of the mind. Yet we need to remember that cultures that recognize "spirits" (West African, Haiti, circumpolar and South Seas) are also able to differentiate them, and name them as distinct entities.

After my accident, I began to see prehistoric psychic activity as a swamp-like churning in which creative and destructive forces were entwined in such a way that a person seeking to know them could hardly tell them apart. To enter the prehistoric cave of one's own mind then, to seek one's mind before birth, as it were, would be to enter a realm of darkness under the rule of possibly a single massive core. I envisioned this core as amoebic, as an energy flow and restricting membrane that had been activated by the much earlier catastrophic separation between animal and hominid. The membrane would represent the earlier unity still in agony over being disturbed, while the energy flow would represent the multifoliate desire of differentiation set in motion by the evolutionary branching.

Certain experiences are too big, too complex, too loaded for us to see through them as they are going through us. Such appears to be a human limitation, and one that is responsible for countless irrational and abusive responses. Yet it has also led to a great deal of the world's art. Art is, in this sense, the great second chance. What was unrealizable within the experience itself can possibly be realized in imagination.

Cid Corman on Japanese Noh drama:

Nothing happens in these plays: everything, in a sense, has already happened: now, on the stage, comes the realization. Which is, at the same time, a most accurate sense of what the theatre, in fact, is.[3]

On one level, in writing "The Death of Bill Evans," I was making an attempt to get off the sinister "track" that picking up the hitchhikers had set in motion. One could say that I realized the vibrating slugs in imagination by transforming them into my own interior leper. This figure, with this face "like a pebbly gourd," evokes the alchemical *vilifigura*, associated with the *nigredo* or blackness with which transformational projects begin. In *Novices: A Study of Poetic Apprenticeship*, I wrote:

The desire to write poetry leads first to seeing the *vilifigura*, the reviled face, the shame of your own face. To embrace your soul may be to experience the extent to which you despise your soul, the extent to which whatever this soul is feels despised—for what have you actively asked of it before? Isn't it true that it has been left in the corner for years, collecting dust like a castaway doll? Loathing itself, its first motion upon suddenly being awakened may be to claw out at the one who had disturbed its remorseful holding pattern.[4]

In recontacting the *vilifigura* in the form of an internal leper, I had become a novice again, burdened with memories of abuse as a child. But if the figure of the interior leper took me backward, it was also a comment on the present: the rediscovery of my own monstrosity while studying the grotesqueness of hybrid cave image. So while on one level the poem responded to the previous day's events, on another level it flushed out a load of new material that in effect propelled me forward along the "track." It was as if the gods were saying: We'll help you out on this prehistoric project and, in exchange, we will take something from you, and our "help" will ultimately depend on your transforming the loss into an imaginative gain.

I had been told that Bill Evans shot heroin into his fingertips, having exhausted the veins in his arm, an extraordinary masochism, which led to the pun "hero wine," and, at the poem's end, to the Dionysian confusion. The interior leper tries to drink but since he is mouthless (he has grown not by ingesting nourishment but by scabbing over again and again), he can only make "a sucking motion with the mouth area of his head." Given my recollection of breast-denied frustration in the ditch, I have to consider myself here as an infant making sucking motions with no breast to suckle. Psychically speaking, this deprivation would seem to be the origin of the interior leper formation who subsequently "grew" through abuse. To some extent, I was creating in the poem my own undifferentiated complex stimulated not only by Bill Evans's death and the vibrating slugs but by the anomalous images in the caves.

Hillman refers to Hecate as a "dark angel," whose associations with the underworld include "sniffing dogs and bitchery, dark moons, ghosts, garbage, and poisons."[5] My "death angel" instructed me to "Eat Amanita-filled slug," a "living poison," in order to get to the bottomlessness of a "wound" that was at once "pure" and "infected." At this point in the poem, the focus on the *vilifigura*-like leper shifts to the *masa confusa*, or obscure material, that the figure must assimilate. This bottomless, pure, and infected wound evokes the womb as well as the womblike caves in which, since very early times, initiates are said to "die" in order to be reborn. Strangely but logically, the death angel seems to be telling me that I must do several things as a kind of constellated act: Imagine the birth of the interior leper, eat garbage, and enter an initiational process in a womblike cave, one in which the opposition evoked by "pure" and "infected" will be dissolved. As if following an occult recipe, I then ate possibly poisonous mushrooms and crawled to the bottom of a "wild" cave, which clawed out at me as I attempted to emerge. Once out, covered with mud, symbolically I had "Amanita-filled slug" all over me. I was also limping, "marked." Now the angel knew where to strike. Imprisoned in the ditch, "stewing" in the confines of the events, I recalled the "cobra experience." Feeling stupid for having added another scab layer to the interior leper, and at the same time blessed for having been handed a rich, black mass of material, I sat with my "wound," a "slob" and a "king."

1982

FOOTNOTES:

1. "The Death of Bill Evans," *Fracture*.
2. Reich's presentation of "cosmic superimposition" can be found in *Cosmic Superimposition* (Orgone Institute Press, Rangely, 1951). For a solid view of Reich's life and work, see *Fury on Earth / A Biography of Wilhelm Reich* by Myron Sharaf (St. Martin's Press, NYC, 1983).
3. *origin*, Second Series, October 1961, p. 64.
4. *Novices: A Study of Poetic Apprenticeship*, the opening section of *Companion Spider*, p. 8.
5. James Hillman, *The Dream and the Underworld*, p. 49.

XVI

An Alchemist with One Eye on Fire

(2006)

N. O. Brown: "The central feature of the human situation is the existence of the unconscious, the existence of a reality of which we are unconscious." Poetry, then, is about the extending of human consciousness, making conscious the unconscious, creating a symbolic consciousness that in its finest moments overcomes all the dualities in which the human world is cruelly and eternally, it seems, enmeshed.

Part of being fully human is to realize that one is a metaphor. To be a metaphor is to be hybrid, or as Arthur Rimbaud put it, to have a "marvelous body." The first poets were those Upper Paleolithic people who, apprehending that their brothers and sisters were separating the animal out of their heads, and projecting it onto cave walls, attempted to rebond with the animal. These proto-shamans depicted themselves with animal and bird heads, creating a grotesque (initially of the grotto) in which there was symbolic communication between the new human and the old animal realms. Under Rimbaud chasing black and white moons during a Paris hashish session is a young Cro-Magnon dreaming of fiery horses zooming in and out of the sky in a cave somewhere in what would become southwestern France thousands of years later.

In the work of certain poets—William Blake, Lautréamont, H.D., Hart Crane, Antonin Artaud, and Allen Ginsberg come immediately to mind—an archaic and symbolic reality is present. In Artaud's case, the shamanic elements are particularly striking. His vision quests to northern Mexico and southwestern Ireland, use of a magic dagger and cane, loss of identity, possession by doubles, appearing to die during electroshock, glossolalia, spitting, the projection of magical daughters from his own body, and his imaginative resurrection in the Rodez asylum, have more to do with shamanism than with the lives of nineteenth- and twentieth-century "men of letters." What is devastatingly absent in the Artaud scenario is a supporting community. Artaud is a Kafka man, putting himself through a

---

This essay was originally a talk written for the May 2002 International Poetry Conference at the Bibliothèque Nationale Mitterand in Paris.

transfiguring self-initiation to discover, stage by stage (until the final two years of his life), that he was increasingly regarded by his fellow men as an obnoxious and dangerous pariah.

We live in the age of the death of eternity, the age of mortal sky, ocean, and earth, with such caves as Lascaux, Niaux, and Chauvet today appearing to be the cemeteries of the Cro-Magnon paradise. From the Tang Dynasty to Modernism, poets, in spite of the never-ending terror of so-called "mother nature," have sought refuge in a vision of the impermanent permanent. In spite of their almost weightless impermanence, they have felt that their writing was underwritten by "something" that would always be, call it gods, eternal recurrence, or the chain of being. Today, wilderness and nature at large have become increasingly insular. Mother nature has become man's problem child—we must now take care of her. And the nuclear bomb is not the only repository for contemporary terror. In 2002, Adrienne Rich wrote me: "I think that modernity itself drives people into terror and hence into presumed certitudes of tribalism, fundamentalism, their concomitant patriarchalism, and even suicidalism (I think of Ariel Sharon as a kind of suicide bomber for his nation, which he is willing to destroy rather than to accept a non-military solution)."

At the turn of the twentieth century, American poetry, with the compelling exceptions of Walt Whitman and Emily Dickinson, was still filled with Victorian decorum and was a poetry of taste, on extremely limited subjects, written almost exclusively by white males. At the millennium, this picture has changed radically: written by African-American, Asian, Chicano, as well as white heterosexual and declared homosexual men and women, American poetry, as a composite force, has become more representative of humanity.

This democratization of poetry must be evaluated in the light of some three hundred undergraduate and graduate university degree programs offering majors in writing poetry and fiction. This system is now producing thousands of talented but unoriginal writers, most of whom would not be writing at all if it were not for jobs. Once upon a time, there was a "left bank" and a "right bank" in our poetry: the innovative vs. the traditional.

Today the writing scene resembles a blizzard on an archipelago of sites. Not only has the laudable democratization of poetry been compromised by being brick-layered into the academy but with few exceptions there is a lack of strong "signature" and a tacit affirmation of the bourgeois status quo, the politics of no politics.

It is as if a new purgatory, a postmodernist DMZ has insinuated itself between the poet and the events of the world. This purgatory is multifaceted and loaded with funhouse mirrors. While it is scrambled with lies, distortions, and the unreported, it is also permeated with global information on a scale undreamed of before the Vietnam War. During the Gulf War, "impersonal force" was presented as a video game, intercut with information-screened press conferences. Today main stream reportage has suppressed the havoc we are wreaking on Iraq. So one goes online to view cadavers in Baghdad morgues.

Exposed to the non-information avalanche generated throughout a country whose interventionist tentacles are coiling about all parts of the globe, the tendency of many poets of all ilks (especially those with a job at stake) is to preoccupy themselves with word games, displays of self-sensitivity, or pastiches of entertaining asides. In the official verse culture backed by *The New Yorker, The New York Review of Books, The Nation*, and *The New York Times* (magazines and newspapers which often engage current events, history and culture from a liberal point of view), poetry reviews and contributions are determined by taste, precious intellectuality, and a conservative old boys club (which includes old girls). X may be exposed but only under certain conditions and in certain decorous ways. There is still something in the Puritan shallows of the American editor that says: do not attempt to investigate. And do not propose material that does not elicit a knee-jerk reaction, but does require a thoughtful (and often not immediate) response.

What might a responsible avant-garde in poetry today include?

1] Radical, investigational writing that is raw, often wayward, in process; poetry as an intervention within culture against static forms of knowledge, schooled conceptions, clichéd formulations.

2] Writing that evinces a thoughtful awareness of racism, imperialism, ecological issues, disasters, and wars.

3] Multiple levels of language—the arcane, the idiomatic, the erudite, the vulgar, the scientific; relentless probing; say anything; not just "free speech" but *freed* speech.

4] Transgression, opening up of the sealed sexual strong rooms; inspection of occult systems for psychic networks; the archaic and the tribal viewed as part of everyone's fate.

5] Treating boundaries like stage scenery.

I look out of my workroom window: redbud tree, neighbor's garage, church parking lot, gray Michigan winter sky. Bland, peaceful. When I first drafted this essay in 2002, I saw an Afghani woman in full body veil sitting on a bridge in Kabul, begging. She was in a Taliban frame, one constructed in large part by the CIA which helped create Osama Bin Laden. After bombed Afghanistan reverted back to warlord-controlled regionalism, as the second act in the same play, "mission accomplished" Iraq has become a cemetery for at least 40,000 of its citizens, under a rain of 500-pound bombs and 127 tons of depleted uranium munitions. What the Bush administration would have Americans believe was a double reaction to the 9/11 assault now appears to have been in planning stages for not only years but as a program of global domination (taking over from England, now our junior neo-colonial partner) set forth at the end of World War II.

As a citizen of a country that has supported such terrorists as the Nicaraguan Contras, UNITA in Angola, the mujahedeen in Afghanistan, Cuban CIA agents in Miami, and the governments of El Salvador, Guatemala, and Chile, the American poet reaps and suffers the rewards of American terrorism, which are part of his spectre, his anti-imaginative blockage, whether he acknowledges such or not. All of us are connected to the rubble of Fallujah by a poisoned umbilicus.

Unlike poets in China, Iran, and Nigeria, I can still say anything I want to say (for a while at least). This is not only suspect freedom—it renders my situation absurd. I am like a maniac allowed to wander about screaming "fire" in a theater of the deaf. Am I a traitor? Certainly not. I am not committed to the overthrow of anyone or anything. I remind myself mostly of a late-nineteenth-century alchemist mixing and cooking my potions in a Prague apartment—an alchemist with one eye on fire from what he knows is going on outside his laboratory.

As a middle-class American, I am overexposed to the front side of our avuncular top-hatted Uncle Sam. Much of the world has a different view of Sam than I do. Iraqis, Serbs, Laotians, Vietnamese, Cambodians, and Panamanians, for example, see a skeletal backside wired with DU, cluster bombs, dioxin, sarin, napalm (most recently used in Fallujah), and hydrogen cyanide. I know what I see and I keep both sides of Sam's body in mind as I continue to work on myself, to learn, and to love. I show nearly everything that I write to my wife, Caryl. She reads it, tells me what she thinks. Intelligent and honest, she knows my writing well and sometimes detects its flaws. After we talk, I do more work and make more flaws! This exchange is one of the reasons that, at sixty-nine, I continue to write— poetry as a space that two people can enter and relate through. A small world. But no smaller than the human universe, which is a match flicker in cosmic night.

Where is poetry going today? To hell, as usual—not to Christian Hell, but to the underworld, to our pre-Christian unconscious, which is pagan and polytheistic. Poetry's perpetual direction is its way of ensouling events, of seeking the doubleness in events, the event's hidden or contradictory meaning. The first poets, facing the incomprehensible division between what would become culture and wilderness, taught themselves how to span it and thus, momentarily, to be whole in a way that humankind could not be whole before it became aware of its differences from animals.

American poets today, facing the possibly comprehensible mindset of neocon conquest, *amor-fati*, and the need to find out for oneself, must assimilate such vectors and figure out ways to articulate them. If we cannot accomplish this, then our distinction may become that of being the generation to have lived at a time in which the origins and the end of poetry became discernable.

I continue to regard poetry as a form in which the realities of the spirit can be tested by critical intelligence, a form in which the blackness in the heart of man can be confronted, in which affirmation is only viable when it survives repeated immersions in negation—in short, a form that can be made responsible for all the poet knows about himself and his world.

2004

XVII

from *Archaic Design*

(2007)

For nearly fifty years, I have been translating the poetry of César Vallejo. His writing has become the keelson in the ship of poetry I have attempted to construct. Here I would like to offer an overview of my lifelong evolving relationship with Vallejo and with translation, and to evoke some of the experiences that have come out of it. Finally, I would like to say what this companionship has meant to me, as a poet and as a human being.

While I was a student at Indiana University in 1957, a painter friend, Bill Paden, gave me a copy of the New Directions 1944 *Latin American Poetry* anthology. I was particularly impressed with the poetry of Pablo Neruda and César Vallejo. While I was able to make sense of Neruda's Latin American surrealism by comparing it to its French prototypes, Vallejo was something else: he had a unique imagination and a highly complicated style, and his images seemed to work on several levels. He wrote bitterly about Peruvian provincial life and passionately about the Spanish Civil War. I decided at that time to read Neruda first and, other than a few poems from his first book, hold off Vallejo for later.

I then discovered that Angel Flores had translated all of Neruda's *Residencia en la tierra*, and upon comparing his versions with those of H.R. Hays and Dudley Fitts in the anthology, I was intrigued by the differences. Without knowing any Spanish, I began to tinker with the versions. Doing so got me to thinking about going to Mexico City, which was then featured in the literary news as a mecca for the Beats and their followers. At the beginning of the summer of 1959, with a pocket Spanish–English dictionary and two hundred dollars, I hitchhiked to Mexico. The following summer, in order to improve my Spanish, I returned to Mexico, rented a

This essay appeared as an Afterword in my translation of *The Complete Poetry of César Vallejo*, University of California Press, 2007.

room in the back of a butcher's home in Chapala, and spent the summer reading Neruda's poetry, as well as writing most of the poems that were to appear in my first book, *Mexico & North*, in 1962.

In 1960, I edited three issues of the English Department-sponsored literary tri-quarterly, *Folio*, where I printed some Neruda versions I had done with friends in Mexico City, and four Vallejo versions, co-translated with another graduate student, Maureen Lahey. Discovering the poetry of Neruda and Vallejo made me realize that poetry was an international phenomenon and that North American poetry was but one part of it. As a young aspiring poet, I had a hunch that I would learn something about poetry by translating it that I would not learn solely from reading poetry written in English.

I finished a Master's Degree in 1961, and took a job with the University of Maryland's Far Eastern Division teaching literature to military personnel stationed in Japan, Taiwan, and Korea. Before leaving, almost as an afterthought, I packed the copy of *Poesía de America #5: Homenaje a César Vallejo* that I had found in a Mexico City bookstore.

The following year, my first wife, Barbara, and I moved to Kyoto on the advice of the poet Gary Snyder who was studying Zen Buddhism there. For the next two years I studied and wrote, making a living teaching English as a Second Language at various Japanese companies. In 1962, having completed a small collection of Neruda translations (published in San Francisco by George Hitchcock's Amber House Press as *Residence on Earth*), I decided to investigate the Vallejo poems in the Mexican journal.

The first poem I tried to read, from *Poemas humanos*, was "Me viene, hay días, una gana ubérrima, política..." It was as if a hand of wet sand came out of the original and "quicked" me in—I was quicksanded, in over my head. Or was it a spar Vallejo threw me? In this poem, Vallejo was claiming that he desired to love, and that his desire for desire led him to imagine all sorts of "interhuman" acts, like kissing a singer's muffler, or kissing a deaf man on his cranial murmur. He wanted to help everyone achieve his goal, no matter what it was, even to help the killer kill—and he wanted to be good to himself in everything. These were thoughts that, had I had them myself, I would either have dismissed or so immediately repressed that they would have evaporated. But now I realized that there was a whole wailing cathedral of desires, half-desires, mad desires, anti-desires, all of which, in the Vallejo poem, seemed caught on the edge of no desire. And if so, what brought about these bizarre desires? The need to flee his body? His inability to act on desire? A terrible need to intercede in everyone's acts? I did not know, but trying to read him made me feel that I was in the presence of a mile-thick spirit. So I kept at it.

Soon I decided that I should not just try to read the eighty-nine poems in *Poemas humanos*, but I should also try to translate them. To do that meant an awesome commitment of psyche as well as time. In committing myself to such a project, was I evading the hard work of trying to find my way in poetry of my own? Or could I think of working on Vallejo as a way of working on myself? Possibly. But much of what he wrote seemed obscure to me. Did that mean my Spanish was so inadequate that I simply could not make sense of Vallejo's language? Or was it a combination of those things, plus my having tapped into something that was coherent, and instructive, but on a level I had yet to plumb?

In the afternoon I would ride my motorcycle downtown and work on translations in the Yorunomado coffee shop. I would always sit by the carp pond on the patio. There I discovered the following words of Vallejo: "And where is the other flank of this cry of pain if, to estimate it as a whole, it breaks now from the bed of a man?" In that line I saw Vallejo in a birth bed, not knowing how to give birth, an impression that led me to a whole other realization: that artistic bearing and fruition were physical as well as mental, a matter of one's total energy. Both in translating and in working on my own poems, I felt a terrific resistance, as if every attempt I made to advance was met by a force that pushed me back. It was as if through Vallejo I had made contact with a negative impaction in my being, a nebulous depth charge that I had been carrying around with me for many years. For most of 1963 and the first half of 1964, everything I saw and felt clustered about this feeling; it seemed to dwell in a phrase from the *I Ching*, "the darkening of the light," as well as in the Kyoto sky, gray and overcast, yet mysteriously luminous.

I also began to have violent and morbid fantasies that seemed provoked by the combination of translating and writing. More and more I had the feeling that I was struggling with a man as well as a text, and that this struggle was a matter of my becoming or failing to become a poet. The man I was struggling with did not want his words changed from one language to another. I also realized that in working on Vallejo's *Poemas humanos* I had ceased to be what I was before coming to Kyoto, that I now had a glimpse of another life, a life I was to create for myself, and that this other man I was struggling with was also the old Clayton who was resisting change. The old Clayton wanted to continue living in his white Presbyterian world of "light"—not really light but the "light" of man associated with day/clarity/good and woman associated with night/opaqueness/bad. The darkness that was beginning to spread through my sensibility could be viewed as the breaking up of the belief in male supremacy that had generated much of that "light."

In the last half of "The Book of Yorunomado," the only poem of my own I completed to any satisfaction while living in Japan, I envisioned myself as a kind of angel-less Jacob wrestling with a figure who possessed a language, the meaning of which I was attempting to wrest away. I lose the struggle and find myself on a *seppuku* platform in medieval Japan, being condemned by Vallejo (now playing the role of a *karo*, or overlord) to disembowel myself. I do so, cutting my ties to the "given life," and releasing a visionary figure of the imagination, named Yorunomado (in honor of my working place), who had until that point been chained to an altar in my solar plexus. In early 1964, the fruit of my struggle with Vallejo was not a successful linguistic translation, but an imaginative advance in which a third figure had emerged from my intercourse with the text. Yorunomado then became another guide in the ten-year process of developing a "creative life," recorded in my book-length poem, *Coils* (1973).

I was close to completing a first draft of the *Poemas humanos* in March 1963 when I had a very strange experience. After translating all afternoon in the Yorunomado coffee cafe, I motorcycled over to the pottery manufacturer where I taught English conversation once a week. Whenever I had things to carry on the cycle, I would strap them with a bungee cord to the platform behind the seat. That evening when I left the company, I strapped on the poem-filled notebook, my dictionary, and a copy of the Spanish book. It was now dark and the alley was poorly lit. I had gone a half block when I heard a voice cry in Japanese: "Hey, you dropped something!" I stopped and swerved around to find the platform empty—even the bungee cord was gone! I retraced my path on foot—nothing. I looked for the person who had called out. No one was there. While I was walking around in the dark, a large skinny dog began to follow me. I was reminded of the Mexican pariah dogs and that association gave an eerie identity to this dog. Was it Peruvian? Was it—Vallejo? I went back the next morning to search in daylight, and of course there was no trace of the notebook. So I had to start all over again.

If I had turned Vallejo into a challenging mentor from the past, I had also found a living mentor, as complicated in his own way as Vallejo himself: he was Cid Corman, a poet, editor (of *Origin* magazine and books), and translator, who had taken up residence in Kyoto. I began to visit him weekly, in the evening, at the Muse coffee shop downtown. Corman, who was eleven years my senior, seemed to like me, but he did not like the kind of self-involved poetry that I was trying to write. Since, especially in *Origin*, he presented an impressive vision of what poetry could be on an international scale, I found myself in the impossible situation of wanting to address the forces erupting in me and also wanting to write poems that might make their way into his magazine. Thus while testing myself against Vallejo's Spanish, I was also working with a Corman raven on my shoulder staring critically at what I was struggling to articulate. At times the tension between Vallejo and Corman was almost unbearable. These figures who were offering me their vision of the creative also seemed to be dragging me under. I was hearing things, having terrifying nightmares and suffering unexplainable headaches.

In the following year, I completed three more drafts of *Human Poems*. Cid went over the second and third drafts and to him I owe a special debt, not only for the time he put in on the manuscript but also for what I learned from him about the art of translation.

Before talking with Cid about translation, I thought that the goal of a translating project was to take a literal draft and interpret everything that was not acceptable English. By interpret, I mean: to monkey with words, phrases, punctuation, line breaks, even stanza breaks, turning the literal into something that was not an original poem in English but—and here is the rub—something that because of the liberties taken was also not accurate to the original itself. Ben Belitt's Neruda translations or Robert Lowell's *Imitations* come to mind as interpretative translations. Corman taught me to respect the original at every point, to check everything (including words that I thought I knew), to research arcane and archaic words, and to invent English words for coined words—in other words, to aim for a translation that was absolutely accurate and up to the performance level of the original (at times, quite incompatible goals). I learned to keep a notebook of my thoughts and variations on what I was translating, so I could keep this material separate, for every translator has impulses to fill in, pad out, and make something "strong" that in a more literal mode would fall flat—in short, to pump up or explain a word instead of translating it. By reinterpreting, the translator implies that he knows more than the original text does, that, in effect, his mind is superior to its mind. The "native text" becomes raw material for the colonizer–translator to educate and reform.

During these years of undergoing a double apprenticeship—to poetry and to translation—I was so psychically opened up by Vallejo that I had to find ways to keep my fantasies out of the translation. One way was to redirect them into my poetry, as I did with my poem "The Book of Yorunomado." While in Paris in 1973, I visited Vallejo's tomb in the Montparnasse cemetery and imagined my relationship to him and to his work in a poem, "At The Tomb of Vallejo." Upon completing the revision of a translation of *Poemas humanos* in 1977, I developed a culminative fantasia of my years with this poet called "The Name Encanyoned River," a title based on a line that Vallejo had crossed out in one of these poems. Finally, beginning with the 1977 revision, I added detailed notes to my Vallejo collections that commented on crossed-out material as well as arcane and coined words. Thus, I was able to excavate and employ the psychic turmoil of my Kyoto life, all the while keeping the translation of a body of work contoured with its own unadulterated chasms.

Poemas humanos is made up of poems left by Vallejo at the time of his death, in April 1938, in a heavily hand-corrected typescript. When his widow Georgette published them in 1939 there were many errors and the poems were presented out of chronological order. These errors were repeated and amplified in subsequent editions, many of which were pirated because Georgette would not cooperate with publishers. By the spring of 1965, now back in Bloomington, I was working from four textually differing editions of *Poemas humanos*, having seen neither the first edition nor the worksheets.

Instead of shaping up as I worked along, the whole project was becoming a nightmare. Now I was having dreams in which Vallejo's corpse, wearing muddy shoes, was laid out in bed between Barbara and me. By this time I had gotten in touch with Georgette Vallejo and explained that I did not see how I could complete the translation effectively unless I came to Peru and examined the worksheets. I hired a lawyer to draw up a contract and mailed it to her along with samples from my fourth draft. I received one reply from her in which she did not respond to any of my requests. But I was determined to go, and with Barbara several months pregnant, we left in August 1965, with just a few hundred dollars.

Once in Lima, we moved into a small apartment next to a grade school playground on Domingo Orué in Miraflores, the district where Georgette Vallejo also lived. Georgette was a small, wiry, middle-class French woman in her late fifties. Supported by the Peruvian government, she lived rather spartanly, yet not uncomfortably, in an apartment appointed with pre-Incan pottery and weavings. I was in a very delicate position with her, because I not only needed to see the first edition and the worksheets, but I also needed her permission before I could get a publishing contract. I had not been in her apartment for fifteen minutes when she told me that my translations were full of "howlers," that Vallejo was untranslatable (she was at this time working on a French translation of his poetry), and that neither the first edition nor the worksheets were available to be studied.

The months that followed were stressful and cheerless. I had been hired as editor of a new bilingual literary magazine, to be called *Quena*, at the Peruvian North American Cultural Institute. Because I was working for the Institute (which turned out to be an annex of the American Embassy in Lima), most of the Peruvian writers and critics whom I met thought I was an American spy. Only when I turned in the three hundred page manuscript for the first issue of *Quena* did I realize what the Institute represented. My boss told me that translations I had included of Javier Heraud could not be published in the magazine because, although the poems themselves were not political, their author, after visiting Cuba, had joined a guerrilla movement in the Peruvian jungle and had been killed by the army. Since his name was linked with Cuba and revolution, my boss told me, the Institute did not want to be involved. I refused to take the translations out of the manuscript and was fired.

At the end of 1965 I met Maureen Ahern, an American with a Ph.D. from San Marcos University, who was then married and living with her family on a chicken farm in Cieneguilla, about twenty miles outside Lima. Maureen agreed to read through the sixth and seventh drafts of my Vallejo manuscript with me (and she would later facilitate the manuscript's first publication after I had left Peru). Her husband, Johnny, worked in Lima, and once a week he would give me a ride to their place as he drove home from work. Maureen and I would work together all of the following day, and I would ride back to Lima with Johnny the next morning. This arrangement was ideal, but it remains indissociable in my mind from a near tragedy that marked my year in Peru. On one of the evenings that I would normally have gone to Maureen's, her husband was unavailable and I stayed home. That night—it was the week after my son Matthew was born—Barbara began to hemorrhage. After attempting to staunch the flow I realized that if I did not get her to a hospital immediately she was going to bleed to death. I raced out of our apartment and ran through the halls of the building across the street, screaming for help. A door opened, a doctor came out, we bundled her into the back of his Volkswagen and sped to the nearest clinic. We saved her life, barely—but I shudder to think what might have happened had I gone to Cieneguilla as planned.

One afternoon someone knocked on our door, and I opened it to be told by a stranger that Georgette Vallejo wanted to see me in her apartment that evening. When I arrived, I found there a small group of Peruvian writers and intellectuals, such as Javier Sologuren, Carlos Germán Belli, and Emilio Adolfo Westphalen. Georgette explained she had assembled everyone to try to determine what poems I could be given permission to translate. This turned out to be a ridiculous and impossible task, with these luminaries arguing for hours over why X poem could be translated and Y poem could not. At one point, when they all agreed that a particular poem could absolutely not be translated, Georgette cried out, "but I just translated that poem into French!" Nothing was resolved, and after the writers left, I found myself despondently sitting with Georgette.

She asked me if I would like a *pisco*, and brought out a bottle. We began drinking, and I recalled that the editor of Perú Nuevo, a press that had published a pirated edition of *Poemas humanos*, had told me that Georgette and César had never been formally married, and because of this Georgette had no legal control over the estate. I think I blurted out: "Well, I really don't need your permission it turns out, as Gustavo Valcárcel told me you and Vallejo were never actually married!" At this point, she jumped up, ran to the bedroom, and began bringing out shoeboxes of memorabilia, looking for the marriage certificate. She couldn't find it. But the next morning, of course, she was furious over my confrontation. I never saw her again.

When Barbara and I returned to the States in the spring of 1966 and moved to New York City, Grove Press expressed interest in the translation. I prepared a seventh draft, and after having it checked by readers, Dick Seaver, then the senior editor at Grove, offered me a contract—contingent upon Mme. Vallejo's signature. I wrote to Maureen and asked her if there was anything she could do. She offered to go and meet Georgette. Over the next six months, Maureen must have seen Georgette almost weekly, and she did this while taking care of her kids, teaching full-time, battling illness, and trying to save a floundering marriage.

Seaver was also working on Georgette, sending letter after letter to convince her that the translation Grove wished to publish was not the one I had sent her from Bloomington in 1964. Maureen and Johnny were inviting her out to the farm for holiday weekends and sending her back home with chickens and eggs. Since Seaver was getting nowhere, Maureen eventually had to mention that she was a friend of mine and that she had worked on the translation. Georgette protested that she had been betrayed and once again it looked as if everything was off.

But Maureen kept after her and one day, Américo Ferrari, a Peruvian scholar who had written on Vallejo (and worked with Georgette on her French edition of Vallejo's poetry), appeared in the Grove offices and told Seaver that Mme. Vallejo had asked him to check the translation. Apparently he wrote her that it was publishable for a week or so later she wrote Seaver that she would sign a contract if Grove would include the following clause: when and if she found a better translation, Grove would have to destroy mine and publish the other. Seaver told me that he had had it with her.

I wrote again to Maureen, telling her that unless a signed contract were sent to Grove within a month, the whole project would be off. Maureen continued to plead with Georgette, who finally said that if Johnny would type up the contract she wanted, she would sign it. He did, she signed it, and a few weeks later Seaver called to tell me that while it was not their contract, Grove found it acceptable and their lawyer had determined it was legal. He wrote Mme. Vallejo, enclosing her part of the advance. Subsequently, Maureen wrote that Georgette had called to complain that she had never intended to sign a legal contract; she considered the contract Johnny had typed up "only a gesture," that she accepted so that Maureen would not be "upset." Grove went ahead anyway, and *Human Poems* was published in the spring of 1968.

❦

I ended my Introduction to the Grove Edition of *Human Poems* with the words: "My work is done." I must have forgotten that I had begun several drafts of a translation of Vallejo's sheaf of poems on the Spanish Civil War, *España, aparte de mi este caliz*, with Octavio Corvalán, a Professor in the Spanish Department at Indiana University, when I was living in Bloomington in 1965. By starting this new translation project, and leaving it unfinished, I had unconsciously prolonged my relationship with Vallejo.

In 1970, I took a job at the new California Institute of the Arts outside Los Angeles, and my present wife, Caryl, and I moved to the San Fernando Valley. There I returned to *España*, made a new draft, and once again found myself looking for someone to check it. I was introduced to José Rubia Barcia, a Spanish poet and essayist in exile since the Spanish Civil War, who had been teaching at UCLA for years. While going over the draft with Barcia, I was so impressed with his honesty, scrupulosity, and literary intelligence that I suggested we work together as co-translators.

Grove Press published our completed translation of *Spain, Take This Cup from Me* in 1974. While José and I were working on the these poems I showed him the 1968 translation of *Human Poems*, which he carefully went over, penciling in the margins around two thousand queries and suggestions for changes. He felt that what I had accomplished was meaningful but that we could do a better job working together. We worked from roughly

1972 to 1977. The University of California Press brought out *César Vallejo: The Complete Posthumous Poetry* in 1978, including what had previously been called *Human Poems* along with *Spain, Take This Cup from Me*.

Over the years, initially stimulated by Vallejo, I had developed an affinity for a poetry that went for the whole, a poetry that attempted to become responsible for all the poet knows about himself and his world. I saw Vallejo, Arthur Rimbaud, Antonin Artaud, Aimé Césaire, and Vladimir Holan as examples of these poetics. All inducted and ordered materials from the subconscious as well as from those untoward regions of human experience that defy rational explanation. Instead of conducting the orchestra of the living, they were conducting the orchestra's pit.

In 1988 I arranged with Paragon House in NYC to bring out a selection of my translations and co-translations of these poets, to be called *Conductors of the Pit*. When making the Vallejo selection I got involved, once again, in revising previous versions, this time the ones that I had done with José. Some of these changes today strike me as less effective than the Eshleman/Barcia translations they were based on, and I have again, and now clearly for the last time, revised this work. But I do understand my dilemma: given the contextual density of Vallejo's European poetry, there are often multiple denotative word choices, and no matter how closely I have tried to adhere to a rendering of what I thought Vallejo had written, I have found over the years that my own imagination has played tricks on me. At the same time I have often had to invent words and phrases to attempt to match Vallejo's originality, and these back-and-forth movements, between adherence to standard Spanish and the matching of the coined and arcane, have occasionally become confused. And in continuing to read Vallejo scholarship over the years, from time to time I have picked up an interpretation of a particular word that has made me rethink my translation of it.

Up until the late 1980s all of my translational attention to Vallejo had been confined to the European poetry, written between 1923 and 1938. However, I had been circling around his second book, *Trilce* (1922), for many years, realizing in the 1960s and 70s that since it was a much more difficult book to translate than *Poemas humanos*, I should leave it alone. In 1988 I decided that if I could work with a Peruvian, a translation of *Trilce* could be attempted, so I teamed up with Julio Ortega (one of the few

Peruvian writers in Lima in the 1960s who did not think I was a spy!), and we decided to do it together. We worked out a first draft of the book in the fall of 1989. Caryl and I moved to Boston for a month, and every morning I took a bus into Providence, and climbed the hill to Julio's office at Brown University where we would work for several hours. Once back in Michigan, I went over our work and realized that I often had questions about several words in a single line. While Julio would occasionally respond to my queries, it was clear by the end of 1990 that he had decided I should finish *Trilce* on my own and by then I needed his, or someone's help, even more than I had needed it in the beginning. There are still many words in this book that have gone uncommented upon in Vallejo scholarship (or have been wildly guessed at), and while critics can generalize and address Vallejo in terms of themes and preoccupations, a translator must go at him word by word, revealing all of his choices in English without being able to dodge a single one. This process is especially tricky in the case of *Trilce*, with its intentionally misspelled words (often revealing secondary puns), neologisms, and arcane and archaic words.

At this point I contacted Américo Ferrari who had inspected my manuscript at Grove Press in the late 1960s and who was now teaching translation at a university in Geneva. Ferrari had brought out an edition of - Vallejo's *Obra Poética Completa* in 1988, and I figured he knew more about Vallejo's poetry than anyone. He agreed to respond to my questions; I would write in English and he in Spanish. Ferrari was willing to go to the library and research words he thought he was familiar with but that my questions led him to doubt. We had a wonderful exchange and about two years later, after translating up to thirty versions of the most complex poems, I had something that I thought was publishable. Marsilio Publishers brought out a bilingual edition of *Trilce*, with an Introduction by Ferrari, in 1992. When it went out of print, Wesleyan University Press brought out a second edition, with around one hundred word changes, in 2000.

Once more I felt that my involvement with Vallejo had come to an end. The only poetry of his that I had not translated was *Los heraldos negros* (1918), his first book, which had always struck me as more conventional by far than *Trilce* or the European poetry. Much of it is rhymed verse which presents, in translation, its own problems: a sonnet is a little engine of sound and sense, and if you rhyme it in translation, you inevitably have to change some or much of its meaning. If you translate it for meaning alone, there is a chance that you will end up with atonal free verse.

But as Michael Corleone says midway through *Godfather III*, "just when you think you're out, they pull you back in!" In 2003 I began to realize that all of the years I had put in on this body of work had brought me very close to a "Complete Poetry of César Vallejo," and that it would be appropriate to review all of my previous translations, and to add to them a version of *Los heraldos negros*. Once I began to work on *The Black Heralds*, I found the poems in it more interesting than I had originally thought, and since they were relatively easy to render, I took some pleasure in what could be thought of as strolling on a level playing field rather than climbing a vertical wall. When I could rhyme certain words in a sonnet and not change the meaning, I did so, and I constantly made myself aware of sound possibilities, attempting to make the translations sound as rich in English as I could without distorting Vallejo's intentions. Efraín Kristal, a Latin American scholar at UCLA who has recently edited a Spanish edition of *Los heraldos negros*, went over my third draft and made some very useful suggestions. José Cerna-Bazán, a Vallejo scholar from northern Peru now at Carleton College in Minnesota, has inspected my *Trilce* version word for word and proposed around a hundred changes, many of which I have accepted. Assuming that Vallejo is not writing poems in his Montparnasse tomb, I now should be able to make the statement that my work is done stick.

With an overview in mind, it is worth noting that Vallejo's poetic development is quite unusual. Coming from the conventional, if well-written and passionate, rhymed verse in *Los heraldos negros*, the reader is completely unprepared for *Trilce*, which is still the most dense, abstract, and transgression-driven collection of poetry in the Spanish language. For Vallejo to have gone beyond *Trilce*, in the experimental sense, would have involved his own version of the made-up language one finds at the end of Huidobro's *Altazor*. On one level, then, Vallejo took a step back from *Trilce* in his European poetry, but not as far back as the writing of *Los heraldos*

negros. In moving from Lima to Paris, the poet hit the aesthetic honey head of the European colonial world at the moment it was being rocked by political revolution in Russia. Given the non-sequitur shifts in *Trilce*'s composition, it is possible to imagine Vallejo forming some sort of relationship with French Surrealism (the first Manifesto having appeared a year after he arrived). However, Vallejo had nothing but contempt for Surrealism, which he seems to have regarded pretty much as Artaud did: as an amusing parlor game, more concerned with pleasure and freedom than with suffering and moral struggle.

Vallejo's development in his post-Peruvian poetry involves taking on an ontological abyss which might be briefly described as follows: Man is a sadness-exuding mammal, self-contradictory, perpetually immature, equally deserving of hatred, affection, and indifference, whose anger breaks any wholeness into warring fragments. This anger's only redeeming quality is that it is, paradoxically, a weapon of the poor, nearly always impotent against the military resources of the rich. Man is in flight from himself: what once was an expulsion from paradise has become a flight from self, as the worlds of colonial culture and colonized oppressiveness intersect. At the core of life's fullness is death, the "never" we fail to penetrate, "always" and "never" being the infinite extensions of "yes" and "no." Sorrow is the defining tone of human existence. Poetry thus becomes the imaginative expression of the inability to resolve the contradictions of man as an animal, divorced from nature as well as from any sustaining faith and caught up in the trivia of socialized life.

I have thought more about poetry while translating Vallejo than while reading anyone else. Influence through translation is different from influence through reading masters in one's own tongue. I am creating an American version out of a Spanish text, and if Vallejo is to enter my own poetry he must do so via what I have already, as a translator, turned him into. This is, in the long run, very close to being influenced by myself, or better, *by a self I have created to mine*. In this way, I do not feel that my poetry reflects Vallejo's. He taught me that ambivalence and contradiction are facets of metaphoric probing, and he gave me permission to try anything in my quest for an authentic alternative world in poetry.

Human Poems redefines the "political" poem. With one or two exceptions, the poems in this collection have no political position or agenda in the traditional sense. Yet they are directly sympathetic, in a way that does not remind us of other poetries, with the human situation I have briefly described above. In fact, they are so permeated by Vallejo's own suffering as it is wedded to that of other people, that it is as if the dualisms of colonial/colonized, rich and poor, become fused at a level where the human animal, aware of his fate, is embraced in all his absurd fallibility. Whitman's adhesive bond with others comes to mind, but Whitman used his "democratic vista" to express an idealism that is foreign to the world Vallejo saw around him growing up in Peru, and to the even darker world he encountered as a poor man in Paris, where his already marginal existence imploded before the horrors of the Spanish Civil War.

I think the key lesson Vallejo holds today may be that of a poet learning how to become imprisoned, as it were, in global life as a whole, and in each moment in particular. All his poetry, including the blistering Eros that opens up a breach in the wall separating mother and lover in *Trilce*, urges the poet to confront his own destiny and to stew in what is happening to him—and to also believe that his bewildering situation is significant. To be bound to, or imprisoned in, the present, includes confronting not only life as it really is but also psyche as it really is not—weighing all affirmation against, in an American's case, our imperial obsessions and our own intrinsic dark.

Ypsilanti, March–August, 2005

"Bacon at Pompidou"[1]

Bacon's studio: volcanic midden.

1935: an animal pawing up into a garden—sensation probing interior decoration.

...*at the Base of a Crucifixion*—the crucifixion itself: Europe, 1944.

Figures like larvae spawned in concentration camps.

The inhuman as the exhaust of the grotesque.

Bacon's roller rink starts up in the 1945 *Figure in a Landscape*—the orange ground in the '40s (rust–fire–blood exotica) essentially his studio. The world put into a stained box. An ex-interior decorator working in a slaughterhouse.

Bacon's flesh: plaster-tarred, cream-tinted, pink smoke bodies. Black ham snowing through debris-littered skin.

Evoking T.S. Eliot's:
"Withered root of knots of hair
Slitted below and gashed with eyes,
This oval O cropped out with teeth:
The sickle motion from the thighs."

Bed as crib sweating with primal abuse.

White bandage-like arrows, cupidic caricature.

Head II (1949): lower teeth become a tiny white hand attempting to reach palate.

Bacon's screaming mouths are mute, frozen, open manholes. They appear almost without heads, as if the body's toothed sewer can manifest in any of its members.

"The street caved in like a syphilitic's nose"
                    —Mayakofsky

Executives in tub-like cribs with apple-shaped open mouths. Eden-inverts. As if one could sink one's teeth into the Pope's solid, apple-shaped scream.

Eisenstein at Nuremberg.

But Popes do not scream or suffer Jewish genocide. These Popes are Bacon-projected, holy sadism pinned to a throne, or immersed in a uterine bath.

Painting as snail trail, a painter's mental excrement.

The painter as nebbish in tennis shoes, a chump, a comma parked without sentence.

The limits of Bacon's commitment to his own experience: no scenes of flagellation, cocksucking.

Muted buggery, naked lunch *sur l'herbe*.

Man in Blue (1952): corporational hives as imperial saloons.

Bacon's bravura: unceasing deconstruction/titillation of calligraphic grace.

Dog about to vomit into a gutter grate: Hecate before her mirror.

Van Gogh holds his blackened cock, pissing an aster into the bloody surf of a Bacon basin.

Bacon's titles rhyme his figural ambiguity.

Muriel Belcher, battered Medusa with red bulb clown nose.

Human baboon taffy barber pole.

Looks like mastodon bones form the Bacon roller rink around the base of the right-hand panel of *Crucifixion* (1962).

The strife in de-elegantizing.

The lure of beauty in remembered sadism.

Deft Pope crinoline meringue under a blood-stucco shawl, 1965. I sense the horrors of Vietnam in the Pope's exploded face.

Legless Pope on a motorized throne navigating the floor of a closed department store.

Henrietta Morae's flaccid, swollen, wild-boar visage.

Can anyone look hard at this century for a minute without turning away?

Overheard on the Bacon phone: the ongoing party on the *Lusitania*.

Does Bacon study police photos? He never fully renounces decorative elegance. Example: the man chewing into another man (in the 1967 *Sweeney Agonistes*) has vanilla ice cream buttocks.

Bacon's males, penile heads plastered-down with black hair, often excrete deformed shadows.

No end to the pulling down of the hunting blind of history.

Man as a Dionysian junk bond.

Polypus of two men mirrored with an arched forearm jamming in the anvil.

George Dyer as a Hitlerian triskelion boxer revolving along a scarlet beam.

The more coherent the more unstable.

Swastika of male flesh opening a black umbrella.

Figure in Motion (1976): thigh-arm, peeled to the rose of its violet bone, jutting out and out, charred. Not even death will stop it. An eye opening in the stump.

Realism in underwear at the end.

NOTES:

1. Based on notebook entries made at the 2000 Bacon Retrospective at Pompidou, Paris. This piece has appeared in *House Organ*, *T-L-E* (Paris), and *Everwhat* (Zasterle Press, La Laguna-Tenerife, Canary Islands, 2003).

Antonin Artaud's final period (1945–1948), which involved a complex interpenetration of drawing and writing, may be viewed as the successful culmination of his 1930s concept of a Theater of Cruelty. This evolution had three stages. The first project failed to materialize because Artaud was dependent upon the financial support of others for a spectacle that remained sketchy even for him. In the second state, this theater abandoned its projected space in outer ceremony and took up residence in Artaud's own mind and body, becoming a psychotic shadow drama he could neither control nor share. The third and final stage began in the Rodez asylum in 1945 when, after more than a year and a half of electroshock sessions, Artaud began to draw in a way that completely engaged him—which probably saved him from future shock treatments. His Theater of Cruelty was then realized in the one-on-one exchanges between Artaud and his sitters for the post-Rodez portraits. Artaud's commentary and incantations often scattered through such portraits link them to the daily notebook entries in which writing and drawing vie for space, and to those texts with incantational nonsense syllables unpredictably inserted in veering, witty tirades.[1]

Eliminating playwright and script, the original Theatre of Cruelty was to be directed by "a kind of unique Creator to whom will fall the double responsibility of the spectacle and the action." It was to be immediate (no spectacle was to be staged twice), gestural (physically articulated signs; actors as hieroglyphs), and dangerous—threatening the identities and bodies of both participants and spectators. Defining cruelty as a kind of charged rigor ("Everything arranged to a hair in a fulminating order"), Artaud proposed that the barrier between stage and performer should be obliterated, with the spectators placed at the center in a bare, undecorated building. Language, including screams, was to be used as percussive marking. This Theater of Cruelty was to evoke the plague, and be up to the forces of life at large, with the actor "an inspired ghost radiating affective powers."

Sources for this theatrical vision included Balinese dance, Marx Brothers films, Lucas van Leyden's painting *The Daughters of Lot*, the

Conquest of Mexico, and Artaud's psychic dead-end, exacerbated by drug addiction, which he described throughout the 1920s and early-to-mid-1930s as one of total exhaustion, "acidic burning in the limbs, muscles twisted and as cut through to ribbons," an inability to think, and a paralyzing sense of non-existence. As an organism in a constant state of self-destruction and self-reconstruction, the Theater of Cruelty was a phantasmagoric elaboration of Artaud's own life. In spite of being, as he put it, "not dead, but separated," he produced during this period nearly two dozen film scenarios and books which masterfully charted his predicament.[2]

Artaud completely cracked in the fall of 1937, becoming his own deliriously paranoid double, Antonéo Arlaud. He spent the next eight years and eight months in five insane asylums. At Ville Evrard, the interns recorded their amazement at the ferocious energy with which he would fight the demons he claimed surrounded him day and night. He believed that the interns as well as his friends in Paris were infested with Doubles, who were Initiates. They invaded him at night attempting to steal his semen and excrement, dictated letters in his hand, and spied on him, stealing and possessing his thoughts before he could make them conscious.

This last dilemma evokes Artaud's 1923 correspondence with Jacques Riviére in which he protested against someone or some thing intercepting his thoughts. What had been invisible forces in 1923 had, by 1939, taken on identities in a Theater of Cruelty conceived and performed by and in the body and mind of Artaud/Arlaud. The beginning of Artaud's regeneration seemed to take place at this time. Although he still believed that his thoughts were being robbed, he was identifying the robbers as fantasy formations and assigning them names: Astral, Flat-nosed Pliers, Those Born of Sweat, and Cigul the Incarnation of Evil. At this time, Artaud was a savage parody of a creator/director/dancer, a one-man gestural theater, whirling about his intern-spectators, screaming, indeed a true "inspired ghost radiating affective powers."

After Artaud's 1943 transfer to the asylum at Rodez, much of his demon-fighting energy was channeled into sound experiments: condensing syllables, grunting, humming, praying out loud while eating, and declaiming in a range of sonorous, monotonous, and full tones. In hindsight, one can see that these eruptions were leading to the vocal writing of 1946–47. However, Gaston Ferdière, the doctor in charge of Artaud at

Rodez, detested his patient's "happenings" and, in a cruel attempt to redirect Artaud's energy, put him through fifty-one electroshock sessions.

In January 1945, Artaud began to draw on large sheets of paper, using pencils, crayons, and colored chalks. He also funneled his Ville Evrard cast of Doubles into a multi-prismed Catholic drama in the notebooks he began keeping. Near the end of 1945, he began to draw as well as to write in the notebooks, initially depicting bulbous, rigid, naked human figures tattooed with spots.[3]

The drawings on large sheets done between January and September in 1945 are tentative and tensionless, with human bodies, protozoa, and tubular sponges putting forth pseudopods, adrift like loose molecules in an unstable, psychic fluid. The first of the hermaphroditic totem poles and wheeled cannons appear, along with thin columns of syllables.

Over the next several months, Artaud experimented with various layouts and ways of constructing figures. The drawings are playful at times, and include tiny figures strapped to tables, wheeled penis-cannons, cartoonish women holding huge scythes whose handles are penises, free-floating spread-eagled imps, envelopes turning into torso-like machines, and tubes, cylinders, and bubbles. Artaud's first fully articulated drawing, "The Totem" (December 1945), is an assertively-reworked, smudged, mutilated, faceless, spindle-shaped female who will reappear in later writings as "the strangled totem," and "the innate totem."

From February 1946 on, until his release from Rodez the following May, Artaud's drawings become increasingly bold and slashing. His first self-portrait (the last drawing to be completed before his release) scathingly captures the asylum's assault in a face cut through with sores and scars, and measled with black spots. One eye is glazed, dead, the other starkly watchful, and aware. This is probably the drawing that Artaud's one doctor friend, Jean Dequeker, watched him rework for several days, "shattering pencil after pencil, suffering the internal throes of his own exorcism."

Once free of Rodez, and based in a clinic outside of Paris, Artaud turned a derelict pavilion into his workshop. By the end of his life (less than two years later), he had intestinal cancer, but his actual death may have been brought about by an overdose of chloral hydrate; the damp, dirty walls of this last "theater" were smeared with blood; his worktable, his pounding stump, and the head of his bed were gouged with knife holes.[4]

Artaud would draw standing before a table, making noises, and often pressing his pencil point into the part of his head that corresponded to the part of the sitter's head that he was depicting. The sitter was forbidden to move, but allowed to talk. Artaud made dots by crushing his pencil lead into the paper; his strokes were so violent that he sometimes tore the paper, at others so insistent that the drawing took on an anthracitic gleam. Paul Thévenin—Artaud's dearest friend, sitter, and editor—told Stephen Barber that sitting for Artaud was like being flayed alive.

Glancing back to the original Theater of Cruelty, we can see how faithful Artaud was to his all-embracing project. He compressed its grandiosity into a one-on-one face-to-face combat: the creator–director became a creator–drawer, the spectators a single, targeted sitter. Identities and bodies were still threatened; no performance was restaged; doubles were everywhere—in Artaud's sense of himself as a demonized, electro-shock punctured body and its idealized opposite, a virginal, organless body always in the process of being achieved. The paper on which he drew was at once a receptive support and a betraying subjectile that he was forever harrowing. The completed portraits—dappled with moldy and vital flesh, crawling with wiry agitations on the verge of becoming writing, and animated with inner forces that appeared to be redefining the skull—were the sitters' doubles. Or if, as Artaud believed, his friends had been replaced by Doubles, these portraits could be thought of as Artaud's capturing of the sitters' real faces marked by the counterfeiting phantoms. If portrait drawing enabled him to engage the spectator in a full nelson of psychic impingement, his texts and the thousands of notebook pages served to redouble the sitter/spectator into an audience of reader/viewers.

In Artaud's last period, every position taken to attack its opposite must, in turn, be rejected and attacked. Writing at once protects yet attacks the drawing, as drawing attacks yet protects the writing. In the texts the same ambivalence occurs between the incantations and the tirades. Based on nothing, a vertiginous, revolving movement cuts like a band saw through the paper as well as through Artaud's maternal language. The containing wall for these anti-positions is that they are at the mercy of a no longer repressed but still infantile consciousness. At the same time that Artaud sends out volleys of sparks, he regrinds his obsessions.

It had taken nearly two decades of rejection, abuse, and internal may-hem for Artaud to grasp that the only site at which he could exercise his faculties at large was one where he could completely control the unfold-ing of an event.[5] His Stations of the Cross, as it were, now look satanical-ly and meaningfully planned. He had tried to project an unrealizable Theater of Cruelty onto a new kind of stage, but it boomeranged at him and imploded. Rather than silencing or totally destroying him, the implo-sion populated his inner wasteland with saint-quality demons and willy-nilly placed him in the hands of that doctor who fried him alive for twen-ty months. Artaud's terrible saga evokes the poet Kenneth Rexroth's stanza about the knob cone pine, "whose cones / Endure unopened on the branches, at last / To grow embedded in the wood, waiting for fire / To open them and reseed the burned forest." Opened by fire, Artaud revealed "being's disease, the syphilis of its infinity."

NOTES:

1. For the portraits, see *Antonin Artaud: Dessins et portraits*, with essays by Paule Thévenin and Jacques Derrida, Gallimard, Paris, 1986. More available in the USA is *Antonin Artaud: Words on Paper*, edited by Margit Rowell, The Museum of Modern Art, NYC, 1996, with useful supplementary material on the drawings. Some of the notebook pages with drawings are reproduced in *Dessins et portraits*; there are eight pages from such notebooks reproduced in *Sulfur #9* (1984). Selections from Artaud's writing from 1945 until his death in 1948 may be found in *Watchfiends & Rack Screams*, translated by Clayton Eshleman, with Bernard Bador, Exact Change, Boston, 1995. This paper was originally presented as part of a panel dis-cussion on Artaud's writing and drawing at the Drawing Center in NYC, October 11, 1996, in conjunc-tion with the exhibition of Artaud's drawings at MOMA. Organized by Sylvère Lotringer, the panel also included Jacques Derrida, Margit Rowell, Nancy Spero, and Gayatri Spivak. A slightly edited version of the paper first appeared in *Grand Street* magazine; a full version appeared in *Rain Taxi*.

2. For Artaud's writings from the 1920s and '30s, see *Antonin Artaud: Selected Writings*, translated by Helen Weaver, with a substantial introduction by Susan Sontag, FSG, NYC, 1976 (now a University of California Press paperback). For some of Artaud's film scenarios in English, see *Tulane Drama Review (TDR) #33*. Another scenario, "The Spurt of Blood," appeared in *TDR #22*. "The Philospher's Stone, a mime play," is presented in *TDR #27*.

3. Previous to the 1945 Rodez drawings, Artaud produced two series of *sorts* ("spells") in 1937 and 1939. The first ones, sent from Dublin, retain the appearance of letters, with diagrams, marks, and holes burned through the paper, transforming the message—usually a curse on the recipient—into a visual hex. The second series, sent from the Ville Evrard asylum, is more elaborate: torn into burned, shield-like shapes, the sheets are heavily marked with crayons and colored inks, clearly visual works rather than dec-orated messages. Paul Thévenin has catalogued seven, but there were undoubtedly more. These "spells" were Artaud's first attempts to antiphonally charge writing visually. In a 1947 text, "Ten years that the lan-guage is gone" (my English version to be found in *Conductors of the Pit*, Soft Skull, Brooklyn, 2005), he states that since 1939 he has not written without drawing, indicating that the second series of "spells" marks the beginning of his extraordinary final period.

4. For Artaud's life in and outside of Paris after his release from Rodez, see Paul Thévenin's "Letter on Artaud," *TDR #27*, and three recent books by Stephen Barber, *Antonin Artaud: Blows and Bombs*, 1993, *Weapons of Liberation*, 1996 (both published by Faber and Faber in London), and *The Screaming Body* (Creation Books, 1999, London).

5. Artaud also gave three public performances in Paris in 1947. On January 13, at the Vieux-Colombier, as a declaration to Paris that he, as "Artaud le mômo," had indeed returned, the poet faced a packed audience of some 900 people, some of whom were audibly hostile. During the first part of his program, Artaud's voice repeatedly broke, and he kept misplacing his papers. Unnerved by the antagonistic atmosphere, he then abandoned his prepared text, and for the next two hours, between screams and gaps of silence, dramatically described his asylum incarceration and electro-shock torture (the closest thing in American letters to Artaud's Vieux-Colombier performance is probably Charles Olson's four-hour improvised reading at Berkeley in 1965). Artaud considered the evening a failure, and in a heated exchange with André Breton stated that for the kind of language he was trying to create, a theatrical medium was inadequate.

When the Galerie Pierre offered to exhibit his drawings in July of the same year, Artaud seized upon the occasion to do two performances over which he could exert a directorial degree of control. The events would be by invitation only, and to avoid the physical pressure he experienced at Vieux-Colombier, he invited two young friends (who had assisted in his release from Rodez) to read texts he would select for them. The opening event was marred by nervousness on the part of the readers, so Artaud aimed at even greater control over the closing event. He chose to read one text himself, and exhaustively rehearsed Roger Blin and Colette Thomas who read with him. Surrounded by Artaud's drawings and a small, enthusiastic audience, it was by far the most successful of these Paris performances. Yet Artaud left the Gallery Pierre that night exasperated, and told his friend Jacques Prevel: "For me, it was a disappointment. To have made all those people understand what I was doing, I would have had to have killed them."

In effect, any audience beyond a single, accepted individual was impossible for Artaud, in part because of his fury over his nearly nine year incarceration (behind which was the total rejection of his Theater of Cruelty project in Paris in the 1930s), and in part because verbal manifestation per se had become suspect. Anything short of a transcendental physical manifestation in which, as he put it, would "shit blood through my navel," was hopelessly inadequate. It is under these circumstances that I have proposed that the only realization of the Theater of Cruelty project was in the one-on-one portrait drawing context, where Artaud was able to "perform" in a way that made him eager to invite new sitters for sessions up to the end of 1947 (after which he was too weak to take on any artwork other than a few drawings which did not involve sitters).

Andrew Joron graduated from the University of California at Berkeley with a B.A. in "History and Philosophy of Science," and spent the early part of his writing career infusing poetic avant-garde techniques with science fiction. Most of his poems in the 1980s were published in science-fiction magazines and anthologies. With the 1992 collection, *Science Fiction*, published by the surrealist Pantograph Press, he signaled his leave taking from science fiction. His first mature book, *The Removes* (Hard Press, 1999) synthesized surrealism and language poetry. This collection was followed in 2003 by *Fathom* (Black Square Editions, and beautifully designed by Jeff Clark at Quemadura), which was well received and widely reviewed (it was selected by the *Village Voice* as one of the "Top 25 Books of 2003"). From 1982 to 1988, Joron published and edited *Velocities: A Magazine of Speculative Poetry*. Brought up in a German-speaking household in Stuttgart, he has also translated the German Utopian Marxist philosopher Ernst Bloch's *Literary Essays* (Stanford University Press, 1998).

In Joron's poetry, words appear to carry, as if cargo, half-stowed, half-visible, sister and brother words. Discovering such cargo and setting it forth can determine the direction, or spread, of a poem. For example (from *The Removes*):

> Enter *here*
> Inter *here*
> —turn among
> the torn, the Entire.

I introduced Andrew Joron's reading at Eastern Michigan University on October 12, 2005. He read with Jeff Clark. This piece, along with introductions to Clark, Christine Hume, and Will Alexander, appeared in *American Poetry Review*.

Or this longer passage from *Fathom:*

> Now, *cloak*
> Approaches *clock* like a prayer.
>
> Hued, as in air; hewed, as in stone.
>
> Where bells of
>   *dissonance* are still
> Half-submerged in *distance*.
>
> Where the quickening of *eyes* equals *ice*.

As one who has spent many years studying the earliest art of mankind, in particular the Ice Age cave art in southwestern France, I find that Joron's method here evokes one way in which Cro-Magnon hand lamps, some 20,000 years ago, appear to have made aspects of wall contours suggest animal and human anatomy. A significant number of engravings, paintings, and wall sculptures employ natural formations. In the way that Joron discovers words possessing word shadows, it may have seemed to these early explorers that animals (and, less often, humans) were partially embedded in, or emerging through, such walls, and that such presences only needed the assistance of some man-made lines to be completely present. If a wall was "with animal," then some Cro-Magnon midwifery could help it give birth.

In a way that beautifully parallels the ancient emergence of something from nothing, or an image from no image at all, Joron defines the first mark as "an arc sinking upward, crowded with sensations," and stone as "curv[ing] thought toward the drinking of its shadow." His poem "Mazed Interior" in *Fathom* is, in part, an original meditation on what might be called "the construction of the underworld."

I also want to point out the way that Joron's constantly interrupted syntax, and fragmentary clauses, break off where the imaginal density quits. No explanations here, and no narrative in a conventional sense. Rather, reading a Joron poem is like watching an orb-weaving spider weave a web, a labyrinthine process, as he says, "imprisoned in liberties." His tense and flexible line breaks and positionings recall the taut yet airy stanzas of the late Gustaf Sobin. In a recent meditation entitled "Language as a Ghost Condensate," Joron sets forth the idea of a poetics poised between order and chaos, a position that for a change seems really cutting edge. He writes: "Poetic 'lines of force' point toward uninhabited wildernesses within language, toward removes of irreducible meaning—so that a poetic impulse will cause the system of language to exceed its own boundary conditions, and to undergo a phase transition toward the Unsayable."

A GLOSS OF HART CRANE'S "LACHRYMAE CHRISTI"

The title: "Lachrymae Christi" (The Tears of Christ) is a dryish pale golden wine, made from the grapes grown along the southern slope of Mount Vesuvius in southwest Italy in the state of Campania. The Neapolitans claim that the Saviour, looking down one day on the citadel of wickedness that Naples had become, shed a tear which fell on Mount Vesuvius, where a vine sprang up (the wine has nothing in common with the sweet dessert wine from Málaga, Spain, by the same name). Thus, both Christ and Dionysus, as dying/reviving gods are summoned in the title, which also implies resurrection.

Embedded in the title as well is a sense in which Christ's blood and suffering are to be transformed into Dionysian celebration.

> Whitely, while benzine
> Rinsings from the moon
> Dissolve all but the windows of the mills
> (Inside the sure machinery
> Is still
> And curdled only where a sill
> Sluices its one unyielding smile)

Stanza one: "Benzine" is a key word for the entire poem. As a volatile flammable distillate it not only conjures fermentation and distillation, but fire, and ignites a long fuse that will burn through the poem to contact the "tinder" in the one line fifth stanza and then burst into flame in the seventh, as "lattices of flame." Whitely (that is, purely, blankly, and voidly), the moon cleanses the world of human industry—almost. Even though the building (a mill evoking grinding labor) is dissolved, the lower part of the window still smiles evilly at the speaker—a smile that will not yield to "the benzine rinsings." Note the double rhyme in this phrase, which must have appealed to Crane and possibly, sound-wise, led him to the juxtaposition.

This piece appeared in the online magazine *Fascicle*.

Immaculate venom binds
The fox's teeth, and swart
Thorns freshen on the year's
First blood. From flanks unfended,
Twanged red perfidies of spring
Are trillion on the hill.

Stanza two: While this process is going on, spring comes forth, yet it is under the control of "whitely" (suggesting that an unknowable blankness, or abyss, enfolds everything, including the moon). The purification and void implied in the first stanza are picked up now in "immaculate venom." The fox is not evil, but from the lamb's viewpoint, with its "unfended flanks," it is deadly. As flowers burst forth, so does the blood of carnivorous consumption, life feeding on life. There seems to be something perfidious (treacherous) about this, or let's say betrayal seems to be sewn into the nature of things. "Perfidious" starts a chain reaction, picked up in stanza #3 by "perjuries," converted to "penitence" and "perpetual" in stanza #4, and then transformed into "perfect" in stanza #8, the five "p" words underscoring the transformation underway.

And the nights opening
Chant pyramids,—
Anoint with innocence,—recall
To music and retrieve what perjuries
Had galvanized the eyes.

Stanza three: Yet spring and night continue to open, expand, and the speaker can suddenly see through all the way back to Egypt, to the pyramids. The night makes him feel innocent again; it cleanses his eyes of the perjuries imposed on him (thus the night is effecting the speaker as the moon was said to effect the mills). Here "galvanized" probably denotes "coated," as iron or steel can be coated with zinc, rather than "stimulated."

While chime
Beneath and all around
Distilling clemencies,—worms'

Inaudible whistle, tunneling
Not penitence
But song, as these
Perpetual fountains, vines,—

Stanza four: The speaker is also aware of worms, evoking aerated earth, as well as the transience of the flesh. The worms are whistle-shaped; their tunneling is a kind of singing, and what their action implies is not repentance or moral remorse, but celebration. The proper response to death and betrayal is transformation, renewal. The perjury that had galvanized/coated the eyes must erupt as a perpetual fountain, or the adopting of a viewpoint in which all is sensed as flowing, in which destruction and immolation are, at the same time, rebirth. Life and death are dyadic, a kind of circular causation.

Thy Nazarene and tinder eyes.

Stanza five: The one line fifth stanza creates a midway pause in the poem. At this point a lot of material accumulates and coalesces. Christ on the cross is to be transformed into Dionysus or, to put it slightly different, the tears (remorse, sorrow, sufferings) of Christ are to be consumed in the livingdying god of poetry and wine, Dionysus, the inventor of vine culture. Joseph Campbell writes, "Dionysus, known like Shiva as the Cosmic Dancer, is both the bull torn apart and the lion tearing." The birth of Dionysus is also pertinent here: Father Zeus appeared in his true form as lightning, killing Dionysus's mother, Semele, and causing the god's premature birth (and the need on Zeus's part to shelter the infant in his thigh until his subsequent rebirth). Both Dionysus and Christ are symbolically killed and eaten yet resurrected gods of bread and wine; a significant resemblance between the fate of Dionysus and Osiris links Dionysus in the poem to pyramids and sphinxes. Dionysus is also, besides vines, a god of trees (note "slender boughs" in stanza #8). While he dies a violent death, there is no evidence I know of that he was burnt at the stake or on a pyre (as was Hercules). Dionysus was dismembered but not burned, so Crane's vision of him as being burned at the stake appears to be his own invention. This is also true about Christ; mauled and crucified, he was not in the Gospels set on fire.

The Nazarene's tender eyes are "tinder eyes," inflammable, kindling in effect.

> (Let sphinxes from the ripe
> Borage of death have cleared my tongue
> Once again; vermin and rod
> No longer bind. Some sentient cloud
> Of tears flocks through the tendoned loam:
> Betrayed stones slowly speak.)

Stanza six: While the sixth stanza takes place, the Nazarene is set on fire by Crane and begins to transform into a blazing Dionysus (who does not fully appear until the last stanza). "Let" here means unbound, I believe, or released.

"The ripe borage of death" = death envisioned as medicinally fertile. I wonder if the Egyptians had borage (the sentence implies they did). The hybrid sphinx (evoking Dionysus and Christ at the moment they fuse) emerges from a demulcent herb (capable of soothing an inflamed membrane). I understand that borage is also used in the preparation of a cordial.

"Vermin" (related to the worms above) and "rod" (flagellation associated with the penitence above) "No longer bind" plays off the venom that binds the fox's teeth in the 2nd stanza.

Now instead of worms, "a sentient cloud / of tears flocks" (stanza #2 lamb flanks recalled) "through the tendoned" (or now human) "loam," or earth. Why were the stones "betrayed?" Perhaps because until this minute they were not envisioned as participants in a cosmo-poetic resurrection?

> Names peeling from Thine eyes
> And their undimming lattices of flame,
> Spell out in palm and pain
> Compulsion of the year, O Nazarene.

Stanza 7: Back to the god's eyes, which are now peeling/pealing, as bells peal, with names (Adonis, Attis, Dionysus, Christ, etc.)—with each name carrying its own "undimming [lattice] of flame" (recalling the burning of viniculture and creeping vines). These names "Spell out in palm" (the spiked palms of the Nazarene, also the palm tree, thus Dionysus-associated). "Compulsion of the year" = the driven cycling of nature, relentless, without freedom to deviate, that all living things suffer, Dionysus and Nazarene here as man.

> Lean long from sable, slender boughs,
> Unstanched and luminous. And as the nights
> Strike from Thee perfect spheres,
> Lift up in lilac-emerald breath the grail
> Of earth again—

Stanza #8: "Sable," like "swart" (stanza #2) = black; the "boughs" that the burning figure leans from are blackened (possibly from past burnings as well). They become the "riven stakes" (possibly from vineyards) in stanza #9. As a transformation of the moon with its rinsings/cleansings this figure is now aflow with fire, that is, he is "unstaunched" (not cauterized or checked but "luminous," light-giving). The nights that previously opened to pyramids now strike an ethereal harmony (Pythagoras' vision, produced by planetary motion—"harmony of the spheres" I assume is being alluded to here). The "perfect spheres" suggests dew and grapes, as well as sweat (borage is also a diaphoretic). "Perfect," the culmination of the "p" flotilla, also suggests that the word itself has reached a state of grace.

Then the "breath" of the "earth," embodied in the blazing god, is proposed to consist of lilacs and emeralds (plants and gems). The "grail" is no longer associated solely with Christ (from which he ate the Last Supper, in which his blood was collected, or in other versions, from which he drank wine at the Last Supper). The "grail" now belongs to Dionysus, or to a Dionysian perspective in art. "Again" implies that this is a cyclic, perhaps yearly/seasonal ceremony. The god is thus blessing the fruitfulness of the earth as he burns, with the lifting up of the grail, another trope for resurrection/transformation.

> Thy face
> From charred and riven stakes. O
> Dionysus, Thy
> Unmangled target smile.

Stanza nine: "O Nazarene" (stanza #5) is now "O Dionysus," as if the god now looks down at the speaker (though his eyes have been twice acknowledged). The lack of a verb here is significant. After "Thy face," I think we are to pause, as if the verb missing is covered by such a pause. Note that "O" is set by itself at the end of this line, punning on zero as well as the roundness of the target to appear two lines later. The last line presents us with a god whose face is filled with arrows but who is still smiling. This "unmangled... smile" is set against the unyielding sill smile in stanza #1. The "twanged red perfidies" (stanza #2) may play into the target also, as a twang is the sharp release of a bowstring, and to twang is to release an arrow (a minor point, perhaps, but "twanged" is so odd that one seeks to account for it).

The dovetailing drive of the poem seems to be one in which the negative suffering-for-others qualities of what we might call "the Christ complex" are to be not substituted, but subsumed, assimilated into the positive, celebratory qualities of the "Dionysus complex." If I am to be torn apart, the poet seems to be saying, I want to sing as I break or burn; I do not want to go down in penitence. This transformation is synchronized with the appearance of spring, though it is worth pointing out that spring is also seen as one aspect of a venom-bound natural cycle. Since Crane prays for this transformation (in the command "Lift up..."), we can assume that the poem is self-reflective of his own life and creative problems. There is a strong implication running through the text that his own tendency has been to take as personal, as directed at him, the venom, perfidies, perjuries, and betrayals that are part of the havoc of his life. By casting his speaking self against the great cycles of natural life and mythological imagination, it is as if Crane would depersonalize these negative forces and transform them into the compulsive pain of being part of life at large. The absolutely extraordinary last line, we should note, does not present a Dionysus made whole, or a figure who has simply been purified by fire— rather, in the word "target" are gathered all the arrows, all the agonies evoked at various points in the poem, so that the smile we encounter is one that carries in its surrounding flesh the cruel and horrifying contradictions of life and yet is somehow "unmangled," whole. One might say that this is a truly honest smile because it is offered not in evasion or simplistic transformation of the speaker's multifoliate sufferings.

NOTE:

Over the years I have written several poems about Hart Crane, and in a couple of them I have invented conversations with him. The longest of these pieces is "At the Speed of Wine" (see p. 96 in this volume). A shorter "conversation," which took place on the patio of Hotel Centenaire, in Les Eyzies, in the French Dordogne, on July 20–21, 1985, has the following exchange, which seems pertinent to this Gloss:

He paused long enough for me to ask: your Dionysus, with a Nazarene core, is a full company of bit parts as he flames and sparks at the stake. In what sense is his "target smile" "unmangled?"

"The 'I' must go unpruned and be allowed to elaborate its tendrils. Since I could not 'shoulder the curse of sundered parentage,' I sought a hermaphroditic grafting. I refused my parents' nature in favor of a vision that included crucifixion *and* pagan multiplicity. Dionysus never was mangled—his being takes place in parts, or minute orders, 'divine particulars,' yet 'the bottom of the sea is cruel.' For the Protestant, always under curfew, the underworld is infested with criminal elements, thuds of Capone, Manson butt-raped as a child whose later martial hysteria wrote its 'helter-skelter' in living flesh. As a Protestant, I was always on that 'sundered' leash when I went down into the image hive, but that was part of my vision too: to wander under Dionysus and to suffer Dionysus in the flesh. Because of this, I allowed my sense of line to be governed by Tate and Winters. Only the voicings rising in writing, I know now, are not estrangements. Winters often visits me in this place. In death his soul has become mellow and most open. I see him wandering a nearby vale, chewing peyote, reading Artaud, his flesh neatly stacked on his skull..."

Not long ago in an issue of the politically liberal *New York Review of Books*, the poet/reviewer Charles Simic praised as a major achievement a poem by the then Poet Laureate Billy Collins which basically expressed Collins's "sensitive" surprise that cows actually moo. In a separate article, Simic dismissed Robert Duncan's inspired confrontation of the American destruction of Vietnam in 1967 in his poem "Uprising" as "worthless." This downgrading of Duncan's imaginative engagement with power, and the extolling of Collins's work, which is hardly even sophisticated entertainment, sadly exemplifies much of what is supported these days by editors, reviewers, and judges as endorsable American poetry.

Some years ago, in *Sulfur #10*, Charles Bernstein defined the officially sanctioned verse of our time as characterized by "a restricted vocabulary, neutral and univocal tone in the guise of voice or persona, grammar-book syntax, received conceits, static and unitary form." This definition is still good today, some twenty years later. In the academic writing programs, the post-confessional and language poetries of the 1970s have fused to produce, in the main, a poetry that is an abstract display of self-sensitivity, the new "official verse." Such programs produce hundreds of young writers each year eager to be accepted, get jobs, and win prizes (virtually the only way a poet can get a first book published today is by winning a contest judged in most cases by a well-known conventional writer; poetry editors who actually edit hardly exist any longer, especially in the service of first books). To my knowledge, few writing programs back a genuinely international viewpoint, exposing novices, for example, to the range of materials one finds in the two volumes of *Poems for the Millennium* (ed. by Jerome Rothenberg and Pierre Joris). More commonly, student–poets are taught material by the same names that reappear with deadly regularity as featured writers at summer retreats, as judges, as grant recipients and as those invited to festivals as keynote speakers.

The extent that Harold Bloom's pronouncements have had a direct effect on contemporary American poetry is hard to determine, but given the extent that poetry readership is oriented to critical admonition, a case can be made that Bloom's and Helen Vendler's failure to back the innovative push at the end of World War II—I mainly have in mind here such poets as Louis Zukofsky, Charles Olson, Robert Duncan, Muriel Rukeyser, George Oppen, and Jackson Mac Low—has skewed readership to several generations of basically conventional writers. While Bloom has brought his considerable erudition to bear on Blake and Shakespeare, his role in the evaluation of several decades of American poetry can be summed up in a statement he made on the poetry of Jay Wright: "His most characteristic art returns always to that commodious lyricism I associate with American poetry at its most celebratory, in Whitman, in Stevens, in Crane, in Ashbery."

Bloom's primary position is that we are at the tail end of a great English tradition, with Wallace Stevens as the last major Romantic figure, trailed by John Ashbery as his radiant ghost. The implication of Bloom's position is that English language poetry has culminated and that what is occurring now, or has been for the past one hundred years, with the above-cited exceptions, is a belated and fractured caricature of it. Such thinking is Koranic, as far as I am concerned, in as much as it treats a great complete tradition (five hundred years of English poetry) as the Koran is treated by its disciples: as a sacred incomparable text. The upshot of such a position is to tell the young poet that he would be better off doing something else, that all his language tits are dry. There is a powerfully-repressed Urizenic poet in Bloom that must account for some of the respect given to his pontifications. Of course if the young poet can be defeated by the likes of Harold Bloom, he would clearly be better off doing something other than writing poetry.

Ever since I discovered the poetry of César Vallejo in the late 1950s, I have intuited that poetry is at a very early stage in its potential unfolding. The depth of "I" has only been superficially explored. Ego consciousness is inadequate to write innovative poetry. Rather than the Freudian hierarchical model, a kind of totem pole consisting of super-ego, ego, and unconscious, I would propose the antiphonal swing of the bicameral mind, which in a contemporary way, relates to shamanism, the most archaic mental travel. While the idea of poetry as a spiral flow, with simultaneous interpenetrations of what we call perception, intuition, feeling, and imagination, is too demanding for most writers, I think it may be one key in enabling a poet to write a poetry that is responsible for all of his experience.

Many poetries prized in any particular decade perform conventional pieties and thus unwittingly bolster the position of someone like Bloom. Given what the American government has been doing throughout the world from the end of World War II on, the American subconscious, into which news spatters daily, is now, more than ever, a roily swamp, at once chaotic and irrationally organized. The fate of American Indians and African-Americans is at the base of this complex. There is a whole new poetry to be written by Americans that pits our present-day national and international situation against these poisoned historical cores.

There are, in 2006, a significant number of poets doing inventive work in their mature years and young poets who look as if they are capable of contributing a fresh body of work. The first names who come to mind in this regard are Adrienne Rich, Robin Blaser, Gary Snyder, Jerome Rothenberg, Jayne Cortez, Robert Kelly, Rachel Blau du Plessis, Ron Silliman, Ron Padgett, Paul Hoover, Nathaniel Mackey, Michael Palmer, Lindsay Hill, John Olson, Pierre Joris, Andrew Joron, Forrest Gander, Will Alexander, Wang Ping, Christine Hume, Linh Dinh, Jeff Clark, Cathy Wagner, Susan Briante, Kristin Prevallet, and Ariana Reines.

I should also mention the poetry of the late Tory Dent and Gustaf Sobin, and the extraordinary English poet, Peter Redgrove, who died at 71 in June 2003, whose writing is hardly known here. In France, the poet Michel Deguy continues to expound a multifaceted, philosophical poetics (a recent translation of a major Deguy work, *Recumbents*, by Wilson Baldridge, received the 2006 PEN Poetry Translation Award). Recently, I discovered the writing of the Spanish transplant, Gerardo Deniz, who has lived in Mexico City for many years (in Monica de la Torres' fine translation, *poemas / poems*). Also recently Joannes Göransson sent me his translation of a young Swedish poet, Aase Berg (*Remainland*), some of whose linguistic deftness evokes the late poetry of Paul Celan.

Civil poetry in the 20th century is associated with the poetry of Pier Paolo Pasolini. In his Foreword to a selection of Pasolini poems translated by Norman MacAfee (Vintage, 1982), Enzo Siciliano writes: "Civil poetry is poetry in which abstract subject matter—'moral' and 'religious' in Dante's case, and as we know, these can also instantly turn 'political'—becomes fused with an entirely personal sensibility, which absorbs every detail, every shading of inspiration into itself and into the transformation of its content into poetic language."

Without the qualifying clause, Siciliano's statement could refer to Stevens or Ashbery as well as to the Pasolini of "Gramsci's Ashes" (recently retranslated by Michelle Cliff in *NO: A Journal of the Arts #4*). As I see it, the "fusion" involves the figure of the writer against the ground of society. Or the figure of the writer as a kind of moving target in relentless evasion of those forces society uses to disarticulate him: self-censorship as well as editorial censorship, the shying away from materials that disturb a predictable and aesthetically-acceptable response.

For example, I wanted, in my poem "The Assault," to get the possible government conspiracy on 9/11 into the poetic record. Beyond that, I seek to build an atmosphere of political awareness into much of what I write— to write a civil poetry as a citizen–writer, something I have done for several decades. I want a sense of my own time, on a national/international register, to permeate my language. One way that the American poem can remain human, in a social sense, as our government expands its imperialist domination in the world (and space) is for the poet to assimilate and imagine the monstrous interventionist framework within which, as a tiny and impotent god, he mixes his "potions" and proceeds. Siciliano's "fusion" also involves, in my sense of it, not only a porous mixing of perceived and imagined materials, but keeping an experimental poetics intact when addressing civil concerns. The European poetry of César Vallejo reverberates with a social awareness contoured and spiked with associationally arresting metaphors.

In the fall of 2004, I spent a month at the Rockefeller Study Center on Lake Como, Italy, studying a large reproduction of Hieronymus Bosch's triptych, *The Garden of Earthly Delights*, the most challenging painting I have studied. My 50-page improvisations on the triptych, in prose and poetry, tip it, at points, into the 21st century so that, for example, the American assault on Fallujah is there as a disaster of Bosch's Apocalypse. In a section called "Improvisation off the Force of Bosch," I sense the presence of Bush and Rumsfeld in the apocalyptic mayhem to be found in the triptych's right-hand panel:

The intoxications of immortality light up the switchboards when
    someone is murdered.
The furnaces of immortality are fed with the bodies of people
    who look a little different than us.
How does this work, Donald Rumsfeld?
Does your Reaper retreat an inch for each sixteen-year-old Iraqi
    boy snipered while out looking for food?
Men in power are living pyramids of slaughtered others.
Bush is a Babelesque pyramid of blood-scummed steps.
The discrepancy
between the literal suit and psychic veracity is nasty to
    contemplate.
Imagine a flea with a howitzer shadow
or a worm whose shade is a nuclear blaze.

Reading these lines today, I realize that "living pyramids of slaughtered others" evokes the tortured body piles of Abu Ghraib.

Being caught up in an agenda can be as undermining to imagination as self-censorship. Traditionally, so-called "political poetry" tends to express a formed, and thus predictable, viewpoint that the writer locks in place as a poem. Such in effect displaces an imaginative openness to spontaneity and notions, images, associations that come up during writing. If I am going to use George Bush in a poem I have to figure out ways to imagine him and to absorb him into my sensibility. This is close to thinking of him as a text that must be translated. Bush creates his own reality (at odds with what we might call real reality) which millions of Americans induct at the same time its repercussions undermine their lives. Bush's "language" is the collision between what he proposes to be and what he actually legitimizes.

Or let me put the problem this way: how to get Colin Powell's language odor into the poem? How layer the lies, the distorted research, the sighs and implications, the black uncle in a My Lai stained uniform, his heil-thin integrity, his good duped intentions, the extent to which slavery is still in his saliva—how ladle all of this, not into proclamation, but into the poem's very climate, into its feelers, its tonalities?

Visually, Botero's recent bringing of tortured Iraqis in the Abu-Ghraib prison into his invented pantheon of the obese (which is starting to look like "real reality" in America) strikes me as a valid example of such translation. And of course, for several decades, until his death in 2004, Leon Golub had been envisioning American power as the dirty work carried out by mercenaries and "white squads" in Central America.

Another of the responsibilities of the poet is to believe that writing remains significant, that significance is not the enemy. The enemy is the eternal game of sticking our heads in the sand and pretending not to know what is going on. In an essay in *American Letters and Commentary*, Ann Lauterbach stated that her response to 9/11 was to stop watching television—a doubly curious statement, since mainstream television has stopped watching life as we know it to be. 9/11 opened up not merely a can of worms but a silo of hydras, and the event itself should drive every artist crazy with curiosity not only about the "official" account of the destruction of the World Trade Center but about what has been done in our name to make *them*, apparently, *assault* us. I think these are the initial commands. One then might ask: why do we now have people in our government who would sacrifice thousands of American and Afghan and Iraqi lives for greedy, global ambitions the repercussions of which they themselves do not understand? I think that one has to face such commands and to risk being overwhelmed by what one finds out during one's investigations. Then one must assimilate them, and, as Vallejo writes, "see if they fit in one's own size."

It is wrong to believe that an event like 9/11 provides justification for a poetry that avoids meaning, or to believe that 9/11 changed the world just because it happened to us. Of course those directly impacted by the assault on the WTC and the Pentagon must grieve and work through their grief, but the rest of us should not feel sorry for ourselves. If anything 9/11 should make us investigate our foreign policy of the past fifty years. Relevant to the Middle East: over the past twenty years, we have shot down Libyan and Iranian planes, bombed Beirut, created a Vietnam situation for the Russians in Afghanistan, aided both Iran and Iraq during their war in the 1980s so as to maximize the damage each side could inflict on the other, bombed Iraq, imposed grueling sanctions upon its population, blown up a pharmaceutical plant in Sudan (that as I understand it provided half of that impoverished nation's medicine), established a hi-tech military presence in Islam's holiest land, Saudi Arabia, and given ten million dollars a day to Israel. The quality of life in Palestine has been so ruined that it is no wonder that many of the humiliated and the abject young there, as well as the educated, can only think of themselves as ammunition.

9/11 aside (if that is possible, at this time), responsibility has to involve responsible innovation, a poetry that pushes into the known and the unknown, making not non-sequitur nonsense but uncommon sense. Wyndham Lewis's view of the basis of art is still true: that of clearing new ground in consciousness. Blake's "Without contraries there is no progression" likewise still holds. Unless poets stave off and admit at the same time, keeping open to the beauty and the horror of the world while remaining available to what their perceptivity and subconscious provide them with, one is pretty much left with an unending "official verse culture." Here I think of a statement by Paul Tillich: "A life process is the more powerful, the more non-being it can include in its self-affirmation, without being destroyed by it." Affirmation is only viable when it survives repeated immersions in negation. At the point one says: "I am an American artist," one finds oneself facing the news in which what is true and what is untrue, what is necessary and what is human, blur into an almost imponderable palimpsest. Such is outer negation with its acidic rivulets of guilt. Inner negation, far more complex, plays the abyss off against one's own hedged gestation and decay.

Poets do not lack an audience because what they write is difficult and demanding—they lack an audience because the poetry that is published and reviewed in mass media publications is often superficial and seldom innovative. People who read *The New Yorker* for its terrific investigative reports, its witty movie reviews, and its often excellent fiction, must find much of the poetry in its pages boring, rococo entertainment. My notion here is that very few readers of complex fiction and commentary seek out poetry because they have a limited view of what it can be, based on examples or reviews of it in publications like *The New Yorker, The New York Review of Books, The New York Times,* or *The Nation*—which often publish sophisticated and pertinent material in other areas they address but not poetry.

In response to my complaint about the pathetic poetry reviewing policy of *The New York Review of Books*, a young poet friend wrote to me: "But who reads it for poetry reviews?"

Indeed, since there is so little real news there, as far as poetry goes. This raises the question, however, of what to read for news of or incisive commentary on complex collections of contemporary poetry. First-rate poetry magazines today, like *New American Writing* and *No: A Journal of the Arts*, do not publish reviews. *The American Poetry Review*, with its huge circulation, publishes some commentary on books and authors, but no reviews. Ron Silliman's blog and John Trantor's online *Jacket* magazine (based in Australia) review a range of books, including contemporary poetry. Silliman's Argus-eyed daily also includes whatever dance, music, and films the editor is attending to, and his daily bulletins and commentaries remind me more of an arts newspaper than a journal. While I find things to gripe about in the way that Silliman categorizes, extols, and dismisses (he tends to peck about the edges of contemporary poetry, sniffing out small issues to dispute or affirm, rather than offering in-depth perspectives on accomplished and demanding works) his blog is the best vehicle we have at this point for news on what is new. And he is a more engaged editor than John Trantor. While I appreciate the international range of *Jacket*, the magazine lacks an argued vision of poetry as well as a core group of savvy reviewers. Saying this I recall the excitement with which I would open new issues of *Kulchur* in the 1960s, eager to see what Gilbert Sorrentino or Leroi Jones had to say in their pungent reviews, which included bristling polemic as well as praise.

Earlier I spoke of the increased irrational turmoil in all of our minds. There is palpable guilt everywhere, and we poets must make ourselves conscious of it. If we feel that we must express it, we should work such out in our poetry and not thoughtlessly take it out on others in vicious literary commentary. Not too long ago, Peter Campion, in *Poetry* magazine, ended a trashing of Jeff Clark's book, *Music and Suicide*, with the following: "Clark writes and publishes these poems for the same reason that Kim Jong Il shoots missiles over Japan: simply because he can." It is of course outrageous that *Poetry* would publish such crap, in which a writer with whom the critic disagrees is compared to a Stalinist dictator. Of course, who knows, Mr. Campion might say the same thing under any circumstances. But the times are ripe for a lot of projected, misplaced bile...

We might ask, with Nietzsche: "Are we forced to be conquerors because we no longer have a country we want to remain in?"

Writing on Henri Michaux's art in 1977, Octavio Paz stated: "His paintings are not so much windows that allow us to see another reality as they are holes and openings made by powers on the other side." At seventy now, I continue to work on accessing one kind of the language I hear in dreams, a kind of magnificent nonsense, non-English English which, in the dream, makes perfect uncommon sense! Such language is super-egoless, and potentially the presence of that "other side" that Michaux seems to have visualized. I believe this language relates to the language-twisting of shamans, and that it is still writhing, in our subconscious, on the ground floor of poetry. However, like all dreams, it does not transfer directly, effectively, into writing. The dream mind is a rapt spectator which does not reflect on the meaning of what it is beholding or hearing. The same can probably be said about shamanic trance. Thus, if in trance, the poet has to keep a shit-detector active, a bird's-eye critical view, that injects invention with responsibility.

When not dreaming these days, the American artist is confronted by a plethora of new information daily on the misdeeds of the Bush administration at home and abroad. Unlike the Vietnam era, there are no artistic mobilization units like "Angry Arts." One is on one's own. To really follow the news as the writers Eliot Weinberger and Mark Crispin Miller have done is a fulltime job. Aesthetically, one of the most vexing aspects of the present administration is that an artist is forced to give up a lot of traditionally creative time just to keep up on new revelations about the war, torture, renditions, the Patriot Act and the 2004 national election (with probable voting irregularities in 2008 now on the horizon), or to disregard this political nightmare completely, and subsequently live as an artist in one's own little bubble. And if one does not go the bubble route, the more roguery one uncovers or tunes in to, the more one may confront extreme emotions of rage, despair, and bafflement. The news has become an unfollowable roadmap of facts crisscrossing opinions. For every uncovered so-called "fact" one suspects there is a host of supporting and contradictory ones in the shadows. I realize that one reason that I have written poems about art and artists over the past decade is that, complex as Bosch, Caravaggio, and Golub may be, one is at least on firm ground facing their imaginative elaborations.

It would now seem that with the 20th-century re-discovery of the Ice Age painted caves in Europe, we have made contact with what could be thought of as the back wall of image-making which, especially in its hybrid aspects, evokes mental travel and thus the roots of poetry. While it is possible that there are even older imaginative materials in Africa and Australia, the chances are that researchers will not uncover on these continents the ancient creative range and quality to be found in such caves as Lascaux and Chauvet. While it is thrilling to know where one is ultimately based as an artist, it is equally horrifying to realize that one may also be witnessing the ecological destruction of the fundament that made art possible in the first place. As these massive vectors shift into place and cross, a disturbance in my mind challenges the convictions that I held as a young man: that the most meaningful way I knew of to deal with myself and with the world was to explore poetry and to write it. This is not a back-handed way of suggesting that poetry or art at large is dead, but a recognition that I may be of the first generation to be witness to one of the recuperations of the roots of culture *and* to the devastations that may make culture as we know it today a thing of the past. Rather than resonating with the magnificent aurochses of Lascaux, the abyss that opens before us today declares itself through the potential extinction of frogs and honey bees, and the accompanying sensations of the empty and lifeless space that humankind has always suspected fueled depth and its analogues of loss.

TRANSLATIONS

XVIII

Arthur Rimbaud, *The Drunken Boat*   *

Pulled as I was down phlegmatic Rivers,
Suddenly—no longer a barge for towers!
Whooping Redskins with emptied quivers
Had nailed them naked to painted posts!

Contemptuous? Of every kind of crew:
Carriers of English cotton or Flemish wheat.
The moment my shrieking towers were subdued,
The Rivers let me plunge to open sea.

Amidst the furious slaps of racing tides,
I, last winter, blunter than children's brains,
I ran! No untied Peninsula's
Been trounced by a more triumphant din!

The tempest blessed my sea-born awakenings.
Lighter than cork, I skipped across rollers called
The eternal loop-the-loops of victims, ten nights,
Without missing the simpleton stares of lamps!

Sweeter than tart apple flesh to kids,
The green water probed my pine hull
And of the stains of blue wines and vomit
It scoured me, scattering rudder and grapnel.

From then on, I bathed in the Poem of the Sea,
Star-infused, lactescent, devouring
The verdant blue; where, ghastly and ravished
Flotsam, a rapt drowned man at times descends;

Where, tinting instantly the bluicities, deliriums
And slow rhythms under the day's rutilations,

Stronger than alcohol, vaster than our lyres,
The bitter russets of love ferment!

I know the sky split with lightning, and the undertows
And the currents and the waterspouts; I know the evening,
The Dawn as glorious as an entire nation of doves,
And I've seen sometimes what man thought he saw!

I've seen the sun low, spotted with mystic horrors,
Raying forth long violet coagulations,
like actors in prehistoric plays the whitecaps
Flickering into the distance their shutter shudders!

I've dreamed of the green night with dazzled snows,
A kiss rising through the seas' eyes in slow motion,
The circulatory flow of outrageous saps,
And the bilious blue arousals of singer phosphors!

I've followed, for months on end, swells
Like exploding stables, battering the reefs,
Never dreaming that the Marys' luminescent feet
Could force a muzzle onto wheezing Oceans!

I've struck, are you aware, incredible Floridas
Comingling with flowers the eyes of panthers in the skins
Of men! Rainbows arched like bridle-reins
Below seas' horizons, taut to glaucous herds!

I've seen enormous swamps fermenting, weirs
Where in the reeds a whole Leviathan rots!
Cave-ins of water in the midst of standing calms,
The distances cataracting toward the abysses!

Glaciers, pearly waves, suns of silver, molten skies!
Hideous wrecks in the slime of fuscous gulfs

Where gigantic snakes devoured by bugs
Drop from twisted trees, squirting black perfumes!

I would've liked to show children these dorados
Of the blue wave, these gold, these singing fish.
—Flower foam cradled my berthless driftings
And at times I was winged by ineffable winds.

Sometimes, a martyr weary of poles and zones,
The very sea whose sobbing made my churning sweet
Proffered her yellow suckered shadow flowers
And I held there, like a woman on her knees...

Almost an island, tossing off my wales
The squabbles and dung of gossipy blond-eyed birds.
And so I scudded, while through my frayed
Cordage drowned sailors sank sleepwards, back first!

But now, a boat lost under the hair of coves,
Flung by the hurricane into birdless ether,
I whose carcass, drunk on water, no Monitor
Or Hanseatic schooner would've fished out;

Free, fuming, risen from violet mists,
I who pierced the reddening sky like a wall
Bearing exquisite jam for genuine poets—
Solar lichen and azure snot;

Who ran, speckled with electric lunules,
A crazy plank, by black sea horses escorted,
When the Julys with cudgel blows were crushing
The ultramarine skies into burning funnels;

I who trembled, hearing, at fifty leagues, the whimpers
Of Behemoth rutting and turgid Maelstroms,

Eternal spinner of blue immobilities,
I miss the Europe of age-worn parapets!

I've seen astral archipelagos! and isles
Whose raving skies open wide to the voyager:
—In those bottomless nights do you sleep, are you exiled,
A million golden birds, O Force of the future?—

But, truly, I've wept too much! Dawns are harrowing.
Each moon is atrocious, each sun bitter:
Acrid love has swollen me with inebriating torpors.
O let my keel burst! O let me be gone to the sea!

If there is one Europe I long for,
It's a chill, black puddle where, at the scented end of day,
A squatting child, utterly forlorn,
Releases a boat fragile as a butterfly in May.

No longer will I, bathed in your languors, O waves,
Slip into the wakes of cotton carriers,
Nor cut across the arrogance of flags and streamers,
Nor swim below the prison hulks' horrific stares.

1871

XIX

from **Pablo Neruda's**
Residence on Earth I and II

*

SINGLE GENTLEMAN

The young homosexuals and the amorous girls,
the gaunt widows suffering from delirious insomnia,
the young wives thirty hours pregnant,
the raucous cats criss-crossing my garden in the dark—
like a necklace of throbbing sexual oysters
they encircle my solitary house
like enemies set up against my soul,
like conspirators in pajamas
exchanging countersigns of long thick kisses.

Radiant summer directs the lovers
in identical melancholy regiments
made up of fat, skinny, gay and sorrowful pairs:
under the elegant cocopalms, by the ocean and the moon,
there's a steady life of trousers and skirts,
a rustle of caressed silk stockings
and feminine breasts twinkling like eyes.

The petty employee, after a lot of bitching,
a week of boredom, the novels read in bed at night
has once and for all seduced his neighbor.
He escorts her to the wretched movies
where heroes are colts or impassioned princes,
and he fingers her sweet downy legs
with damp hot hands that stink of cigarettes.

The seducer's late afternoons and the nights of couples
join like double sheets to bury me,
and the hours after lunch when the male students,
the co-eds and the priests masturbate,
and animals openly hump,
and the bees smell of blood, and flies buzz angrily,

and cousins play peculiar games with their girl cousins,
and the doctors glare furiously at the husband of the young patient,
and the morning hours when the professor, absent-mindedly,
fulfills his conjugal duty and then sits down to breakfast,
and even more, the adulterers, who truly make love to each other
upon beds high and long as ocean liners:
securely, eternally, I am surrounded by
this great breathing forest entangled
with huge flowers like mouths and false teeth
and black roots shaped like fingernails and shoes.

Residence on Earth I, 1933

There are lonely cemeteries,
tombs full of bones with no sound,
the heart passing through a tunnel
blackness, blackness, blackness,
as if in a shipwreck we die inward,
as if drowning in our hearts,
as if falling from our skin down to our soul.

There are cadavers,
there are feet of cold, clammy slabs,
there is death in the bones
like a pure sound,
like a bark with no dog,
wafting from certain bells, from certain tombs,
increasing in the humidity like weeping or rain.

I see, alone, at times,
coffins set sail
weighing anchor with pallid souls, women with dead tresses,
bakers white as angels,
pensive girls married to accountants,
coffins ascending the vertical river of the dead,
the royal purple river,
upward, sails swollen by the sound of death,
swollen by the silent sound of death.

To what is loud and clear death comes
like a shoe with no foot, a suit with no man,
comes knocking with a ring without stone or finger,
comes shrieking with no mouth, no tongue, no throat.
Yet her steps echo
and her clothing rustles, silent, like a tree.

I don't know, I recognize very little, I hardly see,
but I think her song is the color of moist violets,
of violets used to the earth,
for the face of death is green,
and the look of death is green,
with the prickly dampness of a violet leaf
and its solemn color of exasperated winter.

But death also moves through the world dressed as a broom,
licking the floor looking for souls,
death is in the broom,
is the tongue of death looking for the dead,
the needle of death looking for thread.

Death is in cots:
in sluggish mattresses, in black blankets
she lives stretched out, and suddenly blows:
she blows a dark sound that swells the sheets,
and there are beds sailing to a port
where she is waiting, dressed as an admiral.

Residence on Earth II, 1935

It happens that I am tired of being a man.
It happens that I enter tailorshops and movies
shriveled, numb, like a felt swan
circling a pond of origin and ash.

The smell of barbershops makes me howl.
All I want is a respite from stones and from wool,
all I want is to see no establishments, no gardens,
no merchandise, no eyeglasses, no elevators.

It happens that I am tired of my feet and my fingernails,
and my hair and my shadow.
It happens that I am tired of being a man.

Still it would be delicious
to scare an accountant with a cut lily,
or to kill a nun with a blow to the ear.
It would be beautiful
to sidle through the streets with an obscene knife
yelling until I froze to death.

I don't want to go on being a root in the dark,
vacillating, extended, shivering with sleep,
downward, in the moist guts of the earth,
absorbing and thinking, eating everyday.

I don't want all all these afflictions.
I don't want to continue being root and tomb,
solely underground, a bodega of corpses,
frozen stiff, dying from anguish.

That's why Monday blazes like gasoline
when it sees me coming with my jailbird face,

and it yowls in passing like a wounded wheel,
taking steps of hot blood into the night.

And it shoves me into certain corners, into certain humid houses,
into hospitals where bones jut from the window,
into certain shoe stores that smell of vinegar,
into streets as frightening as fissures.

There are sulphur-colored birds and horrible intestines
hanging from the doors of houses that I hate,
there are false teeth forgotten in a coffeepot,
there are mirrors
that should have wept from shame and terror,
there are umbrellas everywhere, and poison, and navels.

I walk along calmly, with eyes, with shoes,
with fury, completely out of it,
I pass, I cross offices and orthopedic shops,
and courtyards where washing is hanging from a wire:
underwear, towels and shirts that weep
sluggish splotchy tears.

Residence on Earth II, 1935

ODE WITH A LAMENT

Oh girl among roses, oh pressure of doves,
oh garrison of fish and rosebushes,
your soul is a bottle full of thirsty salt
and a bell full of grapes is your skin.

I have nothing, alas, to give you but fingernails
or eyelashes or molten pianos,
or dreams frothing from my heart,
dust dreams racing like black horsemen,
dreams full of velocity and misfortune.

Looking at ash-colored horses and yellow dogs,
I can only love you with poppies and kisses,
with garlands drenched by the rain.
I can only love you with waves at my back,
between vague blows of sulphur and brooding water,
swimming against the cemeteries flowing down certain rivers
with wet fodder growing over the sad plaster tombs,
swimming across submerged hearts
and the pallid birth certificates of unburied children.

There is so much death, so many funerals
in my abandoned passions, my desolate kisses,
there is a water falling on my head,
while my hair grows,
a water like time, a black unchained water
with a nocturnal voice, with a cry
of birds in the rain, with an interminable
shadow of damp wings protecting my bones:
while I dress, while
interminably I stare at myself in mirrors, in windowpanes,
I hear someone pursue me calling me
sobbing in a voice rotted by time.

You are standing on the earth, filled
with lightning and teeth.
You spread kisses and murder ants.
You weep from health, from onions, from bees,
from a burning alphabet.
You are like a blue and green sword
and undulate to my touch like a river.

Come to my soul dressed in white, with a bunch
of blood-smeared roses, and goblets of ashes,
come with an apple and a horse
for here there is a dark parlour, a broken candelabrum,
some warped chairs waiting for winter,
and a pigeon dead, with a number.

Residence on Earth II, 1935

Erect like a cherry tree without bark or blossoms,
particular, ignited, with saliva and veins,
and fingers, and testicles,
I watch a girl of paper and moon,
horizontal, trembling and breathing and white,
and her nipples like two separate codes,
and the rosebush uniting her thighs where
her vulva of nocturnal eyelashes winks.

Pallid, overflowing,
I feel words submerge in my mouth,
words like drowned children,
and onward and onward and ships sprouting teeth,
and waters and latitude like burned forests.

I'll arrange her like a sword or a mirror,
and I'll open her timorous legs until I die,
and I'll bite her ears and her veins,
and I'll make her retreat with eyes closed
in a river dense with green semen.

I will inundate her with poppies and lightningbolts,
will truss her in knees, in lips, in needles,
will enter her with inches of bawling epidermis,
with criminal pressure and soaked hair.

I'll make her flee escaping through fingernails and gasps
toward never, toward nothing,
climbing up viscous marrow and oxygen,
clutching memories and reasons
like a single hand, like a severed finger
brandishing a fingernail of helpless salt.

She must run sleeping down roads of skin
in a country of ashen gum and ashes,
fighting with knives, and bedsheets, and ants,
and with eyes that fall upon her like corpses,
and with drops of black matter slithering
like blind fish or bullets of jelled water.

Residence on Earth II, 1935

SEXUAL WATER

Tumbling in big solitary drops,
in tooth-like drops,
in big thick drops of marmalade and blood,
tumbling in big drops,
the water falls,
like a sword in drops,
like a ripping river of glass,
falls biting,
striking the axis of symmetry, sticking to the soul's seams,
breaking abandoned things, saturating the darkness.

It is only a breath, more humid than sobs,
a liquid, a sweat, a nameless oil,
a sharp movement,
forming, thickening,
the water falls,
in big slow drops,
towards its sea, towards its dry ocean,
towards its waterless wave.

I see a spacious summer, a death rattle leaving a granary,
bodegas, cicadas,
thronging masses, stimulants,
bedrooms, girls
sleeping with their hands upon their hearts,
dreaming of bandits, of conflagrations,
I see ships,
I see trees of marrow
bristling like rabid cats,
I see blood, daggers and women's hose,
and men's hair,
I see beds, see corridors where a virgin shrieks,
I see blankets and organs and hotels.

I see the stealthy dreams,
I admit the final days,
also the origins, also the memories,
like an eyelid horrendously raised by force
I am looking.

And then there is this sound:
a red noise of bones,
meat fastening to meat,
and yellow legs like conjoining ears of corn.
I listen in the crossfire of kisses,
listen, jolted between gasps and wails.
I am watching, hearing,
with half my soul at sea and half my soul on land,
and with both halves of my soul I watch the world.

And although it closes my eyes and utterly covers my heart,
I see a deaf water fall,
in big deaf drops.
Like a hurricane of gelatin,
like a cataract of jellyfish and sperm.
I see a turbid rainbow flow.
I see its waters crossing at the bone.

Residence on Earth II, 1935

XX

from **César Vallejo's**
Trilce and *Human Poems*

*

Who's making all that racket, and not even letting   *
the islands that linger make a will.

A little more consideration
as it will be late, early,
and easier to assay
the guano, the simple fecapital ponk   **
a brackish gannet
toasts unintentionally,
in the insular heart, to each hyaloid
     squall.

A little more consideration,
and liquid muck, six in the evening
     OF THE MOST GRANDIOSE B-FLATS

And the peninsula raises up
from behind, muzziled, imperturbable   *
on the fatal balance line.

Trilce, 1922

VI

The suit I wore tomorrow
my laundress has not laundered it:
she used to launder it in her Otilian veins,
in the gush of her heart, and today I don't
have to wonder if I left
the suit muddy with injustice.

*

Now that there's no one who goes to the waters,
the linen for feathering
fledges in my underlining, and all the things
on the nightstand from so much what'll become of me,
all don't feel mine
at my side.
          They remained her property,
lustred, sealed with her olive-skinned goodness.

*

And if only I knew she'd come back;
and if only I knew what morning she'd come in
to hand me my laundered clothes, my own that
laundress of the soul. What morning she'd come in
satisfied, tawny berry of handiwork, happy
to prove that yes she does know, that yes she can
          HOW COULD SHE NOT!
blue and iron all the chaoses.

*

Trilce, 1922

VIII

    Tomorrow that other day, some-
time I might find for the saltatory power,   *
eternal entrance.

    Tomorrow someday,
it would be the shop plated
with a pair of pericardia, paired
carnivores in rut.

    Could very well take root all this.
But one tomorrow without tomorrow,
between the rings of which we become widowers,
a margin of mirror there will be
where I run through my own front
until the echo is lost
and I'm left with my front toward my back.

Trilce, 1922

X

The pristine and last stone of groundless
fortune, has just died
with soul and all, October bedroom and pregnant.
Of three months of absent and ten of sweet.
How destiny,
mitered monodactyl, laughs.

How at the rear conjunctions of contraries
destroy all hope. How under every avatar's lineage
the number always shows up.

How whales cut doves to fit.
How these in turn leave their beak
cubed as a third wing.
How we saddleframe, facing monotonous croups.

Ten months are towed toward the tenth,
toward another beyond.
Two at least are still in diapers.
And the three months of absence.
And the nine of gestation.

There's not even any violence.
The patient raises up
and seated enpeacocks tranquil nosegays.

Trilce, 1922

XXXII

 999 calories.
Roombbb... Hulllablll llust... ster   *
Serpenteenic **e** of the sweet roll vendor   *
engyrafted to the eardrum.   *

 Lucky are the ices. But no.
Lucky that which moves neither more nor less.
Lucky the golden mean.

 1,000 calories.
The gringo firmament looks blue
and chuckles up its hocker. The razzed
sun sets and scrambles the brains
even of the coldest.

 It mimics the bogeyman: Weeeeeetrozzz......
the tender railcar, rolling from thirst,
that runs up to the beach.

 Air, air! Ice!
If at least the calor (——Better
            I say nothing.

 And even the very pen
with which I write finally cracks up.

 Thirty-three trillion three hundred thirty-
three calories.

Trilce, 1922

We struggle to thread ourselves through a needle's eye,
face to face, hell-bent on winning.   *
The fourth angle of the circle ammoniafies almost.   *
Female is continued the male, on the basis
of probable breasts, and precisely
on the basis of how much does not flower.

Are you that way, Venus de Milo?
You hardly act crippled, pullulating
enwombed in the plenary arms
of existence,
of this existence that neverthelessez   *
perpetual imperfection.
Venus de Milo, whose cut-off, increate
arm swings round and tries to elbow
across greening stuttering pebbles,
ortive nautili, recently crawling
evens, immortal on the eves of.
Lassoer of imminences, lassoer
of the parenthesis.

Refuse, all of you, to set foot
on the double security of Harmony.
Truly refuse symmetry.
Intervene in the conflict
of points that contend
in the most rutty of jousts
for the leap through the needle's eye!

So now I feel my little finger
in excess on my left. I see it and think
it shouldn't be me, or at least that it's
in a place where it shouldn't be.

And it inspires me with rage and alarms me
and there is no way out of it, except by
imagining that today is Thursday.

Make way for the new odd number
                            potent with orphanhood!

Trilce, 1922

And we'll get up when we feel
like it, even though mama all luminosity
rouses us with melodious
and charming maternal anger.
We'll laugh in secret about this,
biting the edge of the warm vicuña
quilts—and don't do that to me!

Fumes from thatched huts—ah bunch
of scamps!—rising early to play
with bluish, bluing kites,
and, copping grinders and stones, they'd
pungently incite us with cow dung,
                        to draw us out
into the baby air that doesn't know its letters yet,
to struggle over the strings.

Another time you'll want to pasture
between your omphaloid hollows
                        avid caverns,
                ninth months,
                        my drop curtains.
Or you'll want to accompany the elders
to unplug the tap of a dusk,
so that all the water slipping away by night
surges during the day.

And you arrive dying of laughter,
and at the musical lunch,
popped roasted corn, flour with lard,
with lard,
you tease the decubital peasant
who today once again forgets to say buenos días,

those días of his, buenos with the b of barrens,
that keep backfiring for the poor guy
through the dentilabial
v that holds vigil in him.

Trilce, 1922

The highest points craterized, the points
of love, of capital being, I drink, I fast, I ab-
sorb heroin for the sorrow, for the languid
throb and against all correction.

Can I say that they've betrayed us? No.
That all were good? Neither. But
good will exists there, no doubt,
and above all, being so.

And so what who loves himself so! I seek myself
in my own design which was to be a work
of mine, in vain: nothing managed to be free.

And yet, who pushes me.
I bet I don't dare shut the fifth window.
And the role of loving oneself and persisting, close to the
hours and to what is undue.

And this and that.

Trilce, 1922

Tonight I get down from my horse,
before the door of the house, where
I said farewell with the cock's crowing.
It is shut and no one responds.

The stone bench on which mama gave birth
to my older brother, so he could saddle
backs I had ridden bare,
through lanes, past hedges, a village boy;
the bench on which I left my heartsick childhood
yellowing in the sun ... And this mourning
that frames the portal?

God in alien peace,
the beast sneezes, as if calling too;
noses about, prodding the cobbles. Then doubts,
whinnies,
his ears all ears.

Papa must be up praying, and perhaps
he will think I am late.
My sisters, humming their simple,
bubblish illusions,
preparing for the approaching holy day,
and now it's almost here.
I wait, I wait, my heart
an egg at its moment, that gets blocked.

Large family that we left
not long ago, no one awake now, and not even a candle
placed on the altar so that we might return.

I call again, and nothing.
We fall silent and begin to sob, and the animal
whinnies, keeps on whinnying.

They're all sleeping forever,
and so nicely, that at last
my horse dead-tired starts nodding
in his turn, and half-asleep, with each pardon, says
it's all right, everything is quite all right.

Trilce, 1922

Mother, tomorrow I am going to Santiago,
to dip myself in your blessing and in your tears.
I am taking on my disillusions and the rosy
sore of my pointless tasks.

Your arch of astonishment will await me,
the tonsured columns of your longings
that exhaust life. The patio will await me,
the downstairs corridor with its tori and festive   *
pie edgings. My tutorial armchair will await me,
that solid bigjawed piece of dynastic
leather, forever grumbling at the great-great-grandchild
rumps, from strap to strand.

I am sifting my purest affections.
I am axling—don't you hear the plummet gasping?   *
            —don't you hear the reveilles champing?   *
I am molding your love formula
for all the hollows of this ground.
Oh if only tacit volantes were available
for all the most distant ribbons,
for all the most diverse appointments.

There, there, immortal dead one. There, there.
Under the double arches of your blood, where
one can only pass on tiptoes, even my father
to go through there,
humblest himself until less than half a man,   *
until being the first child that you had.

There, there, immortal dead one.
In the colonnade of your bones
which not even sobs can topple,

and in whose side not even Destiny could intrude
even one of his fingers.

    There, there, immortal dead one.
There, there.

Trilce, 1922

You're all dead.

What a strange way of being dead. Anyone would say you aren't. But, truly, you're all dead.

You float nothingly behind that membrane that, pendant from zenith to nadir, comes and goes from dusk to dusk, vibrating before the sonorous box of a wound that hurts none of you. Verily, I say unto you, then, that life is in the mirror, and that you are the original, death.

While the wave goes, while the wave comes, with what impunity does one stay dead. Only when the waters crash against facing banks, folding and doubling, do you then transfigure yourselves and believing you are dying, perceive the sixth string that no longer is yours.

You're all dead, not having lived before ever. Anyone would say that, not existing now, in another time you might have. But, verily, you are the cadavers of a life that never was. A sad fate. The not having been but always dead. Being a dry leaf, without ever having been green. Orphanhood of orphanhoods.

How ever, the dead are not, cannot be cadavers of a life they have not yet lived. They always died of life.

You're all dead.

Trilce, 1922

BLACK STONE ON A WHITE STONE

I will die in Paris in a downpour,
a day which I can already remember.
I will die in Paris—and I don't budge—
maybe a Thursday, like today, in autumn.

Thursday it will be, because today, Thursday,
as I prose these lines, I have forced on
my humeri and, never like today, have I turned,
with all my journey, to see myself alone.

César Vallejo has died, they beat him,
all of them, without him doing anything to them;
they gave it to him hard with a stick and hard

likewise with a rope; witnesses are
the Thursdays and the humerus bones,
the loneliness, the rain, the roads...

Human Poems, 1939

And don't say another word to me,
since one can kill perfectly,
now that, sweating ink,
one does what one can, don't say another ...

We will, gentlemen, see each other again with apples;
late the creature will pass,
the expression of Aristotle armed
with great hearts of wood,
that of Heraclitus grafted on that of Marx,
that of the gentle sounding coarsely ...
This is what was well narrated by my throat:
one can kill perfectly.

Gentlemen,
sirs, we will see each other again without packages;
until then I demand, I shall demand of my frailty
the accent of the day, that,
as I see it, was already awaiting me in my bed.
And I demand of my hat the accursed analogy of memory,
since, at times, I assume successfully my wept immensity,
since, at times, I drown in my neighbor's voice
and endure
counting on kernels the years,
brushing my clothes to the tune of a corpse
or sitting up drunk in my coffin...

Human Poems, 1939

Today I like life much less,
but I always like to live: I've often said it.
I almost touched the part of my whole and restrained myself
with a shot in the tongue behind my word.

Today I touch my chin in retreat
and in these momentary trousers I tell myself:
So much life and never!
So many years and always my weeks! ...
My parents buried with their stone
and their sad stiffening that has not ended;
full-length brothers, my brothers,
and, finally, my being standing and in a vest.

I like life enormously,
but, of course,
with my beloved death and my café
and looking at the leafy chestnut trees of Paris
and saying:
This is an eye, that one too, this a forehead, that one too... And
    repeating:
So much life and never does the tune fail me!
So many years and always, always, always!

I said vest, said
whole, part, yearning, said almost, to avoid crying.
For it is true that I suffered in that hospital close by
and it is good and it is bad to have watched
from below up my organism.

I would like to live always, even flat on my belly,
because, as I was saying and I say it again,
so much life and never! And so many years,
and always, much always, always always!

Human Poems, 1939

EPISTLE TO THE PASSERSBY

I resume my day of a rabbit,
my night of an elephant in repose.

And, within myself, I say:
this is my immensity in the raw, in jugfuls,
this is my grateful weight, that sought me below as a pecker;
this is my arm
that on its own refused to be a wing,
these are my sacred writings,
these my alarmed cullions.   *

A lugubrious island will illuminate me continental,
while the capitol leans on my innermost collapse
and the lance-filled assembly brings to a close my parade.

But when I die
of life and not of time,
when my two suitcases come to two,
this will be my stomach in which my lamp fit in pieces,
this that head that atoned for the circular torment in my steps,
these those worms that my heart counted one by one,
this will be my solidary body
over which the individual soul keeps watch; this will be
my navehall in which I killed my innate lice,   *
this my thing thing, my dreadful thing.

Meanwhile, convulsively, harshly,
my restraint convalesces,
suffering like I suffer the direct language of the lion;
and, because I have existed between two brick powers,
I myself convalesce, smiling at my lips.

Human Poems, 1939

Considering coldly, impartially,
that man is sad, coughs and, nevertheless,
takes pleasure in his reddened chest;
that the only thing he does is to be made up
of days;
that he is a gloomy mammal and combs his hair...

Considering
that man proceeds softly from work
and reverberates boss, sounds employee;
that the diagram of time
is a constant diorama on his medals
and, half-open, his eyes have studied,
since distant times,
his famished mass formula...

Understanding without effort
that man pauses, occasionally, thinking,
as if wanting to cry,
and, subject to lying down like an object,
becomes a good carpenter, sweats, kills
and then sings, eats lunch, buttons himself up ...

Considering too
that man is truly an animal
and, nevertheless, upon turning, hits my head with his sadness ...

Examining, finally,
his discordant parts, his toilet,
his desperation, upon finishing his atrocious day, erasing it ...

Understanding
that he knows I love him,
that I hate him with affection and, in short, am indifferent to him...

Considering his general documents
and scrutinizing with a magnifying glass that certificate
that proves he was born very tiny...

I make a gesture to him,
he approaches,
I hug him, and it moves me.
What's the difference! It moves me... moves me...

Human Poems, 1939

Idle on a stone,
unemployed,
scroungy, horrifying,
at the bank of the Seine, he comes and goes.
Conscience then sprouts from the river,
with the petiole and outlines of the greedy tree;
from the river rises and falls the city, made of embraced wolves.

The idle one sees it coming and going,
monumental, carrying his fastings on his concave head,
on his chest his purest lice
and below
his little sound, that of his pelvis,
silent between two big decisions,
and below,
further below,
a paperscrap, a nail, a match...

This is, workers, that man
who in his work sweated from inside out,
who today sweats from outside in his secretion of rejected blood!
Cannon caster, who knows how many claws are steel,
weaver who knows the positive threads of his veins,
mason of the pyramids,
builder of descents through serene
columns, through triumphant failures,
idle individual among thirty million idle,
wandering multitudes,
what a leap is portrayed in his heel
and what smoke from his fasting mouth, and how
his waist incises, edge to edge, his brutal tool, idle,
and what an idea of a painful valve in his cheekbone!

Likewise idle the iron before the furnace,
idle the seeds with their submissive synthesis in the air,
idle the linked petroleums,
idle in its authentic apostrophes the light,
idle without growth the laurels,
idle on one foot the mobile waters
and even the earth itself, idle from stupor before this lockout,
what a leap is portrayed in his tendons!
what a transmission his hundred steps start up!
how the motor in his ankle screeches!
how the clock grumbles, wandering impatiently in his back!
how he hears the owners knock back
the shot that he lacks, comrades,
and the bread getting into the wrong saliva,
and, hearing it, feeling it, in plural, humanly,
how lightening nails
its headless force into his head!
and what they do, below, then, aie!
further below, comrades,
the dirtypaperscrap, the nail, the match,
the little sound, the stallion louse!   *

Human Poems, 1939

Sincere and utterly Peruvian mechanics
that of the reddened hill!
Soil theoretical and practical!
Intelligent furrows: example; the monolith and its retinue!
Potato fields, barley fields, alfalfa fields, good things!
Cultivations which integrate an astonishing hierarchy of tools
and which integrate with wind the lowings,
the waters with their deaf antiquity!

Quaternary maize, with opposed birthdays,
I hear through my feet how they move away,
I smell them return when the earth
clashes with the sky's technique!
Abruptly molecule! Terse atom!

Oh human fields!
Solar and nutritious absence of the sea,
and oceanic feeling for everything!
Oh climates found within gold, ready!
Oh intellectual field of cordilleras,
with religion, with fields, with ducklings!
Pachyderms in prose when passing
and in poetry when stopping!
Rodents who peer with judicial feeling all around!
Oh my life's patriotic asses!
Vicuña, national
and graceful descendant of my ape!
Oh light hardly a mirror from shadow,
which is life with the period and, with the line, dust
and that is why I revere, climbing through the idea to my skeleton!

Harvest in the epoch of the spread pepper tree,   *
of the lantern hung from a human temple

and of the one unhung from the magnificent barret!
Poultry-yard angels,
birds by a slipup of the cockscomb!
Cavess or cavy to be eaten fried
with the hot bird pepper from the templed valleys!
(Condors? Screw the condors!)
Christian logs by the grace of
a happy trunk and a competent stalk!
Family of lichens,
species in basalt formation that I
respect
from this most modest paper!
Four operations, I subtract you
to save the oak and sink it in sterling!
Slopes caught in the act!
Tearful Auchenia, my own souls!
Sierra of my Peru, Peru of the world,
and Peru at the foot of the globe: I adhere!
Morning stars if I aromatize you
burning coca leaves in this skull,
and zenithal ones, if I uncover,
with one hat doff, my ten temples!
Arm sowing, get down and on foot!
Rain based on noon,
under the tile roof where indefatigable
altitude gnaws
and the turtle dove cuts her trill in three!
Rotation of modern afternoons
and delicate archaeological daybreaks.
Indian after man and before him!
I understand all of it on two flutes
and I make myself understood on a quena!
As for the others, they can jerk me off!...

Human Poems, 1939

My chest wants and does not want its color,
through whose rough paths I go, I cry with a stick,
try to be happy, cry in my hand,
remember, write
and rivet a tear into my cheekbone.

Evil wants its red, good its red reddened
by the suspended ax,
by the trot of the wing flying on foot,
and man does not want, sensitively
does not want this;
he does not want to be lying down
in his soul, horn throbs in his temples,
the bimanous, the very brutish, the very philosophical.

Thus, I am almost not, I collapse
from the plow with which I succor my soul
and almost, in proportion, almost exalt myself.
To know why this dog dogs life,
why I cry, why,
big-browed, inept, fickle, I was born
screaming;
to know it, to comprehend it
to the sound of a competent alphabet
would be to suffer for an ingrate.

And no! No! No! Neither scheme, nor ornament!
Anguish, yes, with a yes firm and frenetic,
coriaceous, rapacious, want and does not want, sky and pecker;

anguish, yes, with all my zipper.
Struggle between two sobs, theft of a sole chance,
painless path on which I endure in clogs
the velocity of walking blind.

Human Poems, 1939

Alfonso: you are looking at me, I see,   *
from the implacable plane where
the lineal always, the lineal nevers, dwell
(That night, you slept, between your dream
and my dream, on rue de Riboutté)
Palpably,
your unforgettable cholo hears you walk
in Paris, he feels you go silent on the phone
and it is your last act's turn on the wire
to test its weight, to drink
to the depths, to me, to you.

    I still
buy "du vin, du lait, comptant les sous"
under my overcoat, so that my soul will not see me,
under my overcoat that one, dear Alfonso,
and under the simple ray of my compound temple;
I still suffer, and you, not now, never again, brother!
(I have been told that in your centuries of pain,
beloved being,
beloved to be,
you made zeros of wood. Is that true?)

    In the "boîte de nuit," where you played tangos,
your indignant child playing out his heart,
escorting yourself, crying
for yourself and for your enormous resemblance to your shadow,
Monsieur Fourgat, the owner, has aged.
To let him know? To tell him about it? No more,
Alfonso; that's it, not now!

    Hôtel des Écoles is open as always
and they still buy tangerines;

but I suffer, like I say,
sweetly, remembering
what we both suffered, in both of our deaths,
in the opening of the double tomb,
of that other tomb with your being,
and of this mahogany one with your to be;
I suffer, drinking a glass of you, Silva,
a glass to straighten me out, as we used to say,
and afterward, we'll see what happens...

This is the other toast, among three,
solemn, diverse
in wine, in world, in glass, the one that we raised
more than once to the body
and, less than once, to the mind.
Today is even more different;
today I suffer bitterly sweet,
I drink your blood as to Christ the hard,
I eat your bone as to Christ the soft,
because I love you, two by two, Alfonso,
and could almost say so, eternally.

Human Poems, 1939

Professor of sobbing—I said to a tree—
staff of quicksilver, rumorous
linden, at the bank of the Marne, a good student
is reading in your deck of cards, in your dead foliage,
between the evident water and the false sun,
his three of hearts, his queen of diamonds.

Rector of the chapters of heaven,
of the burning fly, of the manual calm there is in asses;
rector of deep ignorance, a bad student
is reading in your deck of cards, in your dead foliage,
the hunger for reason that maddens him
and the thirst for dementia that drives him mad.

Technician of shouts, conscious tree, strong,
fluvial, double, solar, double, fanatic,
connoisseur of cardinal roses, totally
embedded, until drawing blood, in stingers, a student
is reading in your deck of cards, in your dead foliage,
his precocious, telluric, volcanic, king of spades.

Oh professor, from having been so ignorant!
oh rector, from trembling so much in the air!
oh technician, from so much bending over!
Oh linden, oh murmurous staff by the Marne!

Human Poems, 1939

I want to write, but out comes foam,
I want to say so much and I mire;
there is no spoken cipher which is not a sum,
there is no written pyramid, without a core.

I want to write, but I feel like a puma;
I want to laurel myself, but I stew in onions.
There is no spoken coughv, which doesn't come to brume,   *
there is no god nor son of god, without progression.

For that, then, let's go eat grass,
the flesh of sobs, the fruit of wails,
our melancholy soul canned.

Let's go! Let's go! I'm struck;
let's go drink that already drunk,
raven, let's go fecundate your mate.

Human Poems, 1939

AND, unfortunately,
pain grows in the world all the time,
grows thirty minutes a second, step by step,
and the nature of the pain, is twice the pain
and the condition of the martyrdom, carnivorous, voracious,
is twice the pain
and the function of the purest grass, twice
the pain
and the good of being, our dolor doubled.

Never, human men,
was there so much pain in the chest, in the lapel, in the wallet,
in the glass, in the butcher's shop, in arithmetic!
Never so much painful affection,
never did the distance charge so close,
never did the fire ever
play better its role of dead cold!
Never, Mr. Minister of Health, was health
more mortal,
did the migraine extract so much forehead from the forehead!
Did the cabinet have in its drawer, pain,
the heart, in its drawer, pain,
the lizard, in its drawer, pain.

Misfortune grows, brother men,
faster than the machine, at ten machines, and grows
with Rousseau's livestock, with our beards;
evil grows for reasons we know not
and is a flood with its own liquids,
its own mud and its own solid cloud!
Suffering inverts positions, it acts
in that the aqueous humor is vertical
to the pavement,

the eye is seen and this ear heard,
and this ear sounds nine strokes at the hour
of lightning, and nine guffaws
at the hour of wheat, and nine female sounds
at the hour of weeping, and nine canticles
at the hour of hunger, and nine thunderclaps
and nine lashes, minus a scream.

    The pain grabs us, brother men,
from behind, in profile,
and drives us wild in the movies,
nails us to the gramophones,
· unnails us in bed, falls perpendicularly
onto our tickets, our letters,
and it is very serious to suffer, one might pray ...
For as a result
of the pain, there are some
who are born, others grow, others die,
and others who are born and do not die, others
who die, without having been born, and others
who neither are born nor die (the majority)
And likewise as a result
of suffering, I am sad
up to my head, and sadder down to my ankle,
from seeing bread, crucified, the turnip,
bloodied,
the onion, crying,
cereal, in general, flour,
salt, made dust, water, fleeing,
wine, an ecce-homo,
such pallid snow, such an arduent sun!
How, human brothers,
not to tell you that I can no longer stand it and
can no longer stand so much drawer,
so much minute, so much
lizard and so much

★

inversion, so much distance and so much thirst for thirst!
Mr. Minister of Health: what to do?
Ah! unfortunately, human men,
there is, brothers, much too much to do.

Human Poems, 1939

There are days, there comes to me an exuberant, political hunger
to desire, to kiss tenderness on both cheeks,
and there comes to me from afar a demonstrative
desire, another desire to love, willingly or by force,
whoever hates me, whoever tears up his paper, the little boy,
the woman who weeps for the man who was weeping,
the king of wine, the slave of water,
whoever hid in his wrath,
whoever sweats, whoever passes by, whoever shakes his person in my soul.
And I desire, therefore, to adjust
the braid of whoever talks to me; the soldier's hair;
the light of the great; the greatness of the child.
I desire to iron directly
a handkerchief for whoever is unable to cry
and, when I am sad or happiness aches me,
to mend the children and the geniuses.

I desire to help the good one become a little bad
and I have an urge to be seated
to the right of the left-handed, and to respond to the mute,
trying to be useful to him
as I can, and likewise I desire very much
to wash the cripple's foot,
and to help my one-eyed neighbor sleep.

Ah to desire, this one, mine, this one, the world's,
interhuman and parochial, mature!
It comes perfectly timed,
from the foundation, from the public groin,
and, coming from afar, makes me hunger to kiss
the singer's muffler,
and whoever suffers, to kiss him on his frying pan,

the deaf man, fearlessly, on his cranial murmur;
whoever gives me what I forgot in my breast,
on his Dante, on his Chaplin, on his shoulders.

I desire, finally,
when I'm at the celebrated edge of violence
or my heart full of chest, I would desire
to help whoever smiles laugh,
to put a little bird right on the evildoer's nape,
to take care of the sick annoying them,
to buy from the vendor,
to help the killer kill—a terrible thing—
and I would desire to be good to myself
in everything.

Human Poems, 1939

THE SOUL THAT SUFFERED
FROM BEING ITS BODY

You suffer from an endocrine gland, it's obvious,
or, perhaps,
suffer from me, from my tacit, stark sagacity.
You endure the diaphanous anthropoid, over there, nearby,
where the tenebrous darkness is.
You revolve around the sun, grabbing on to your soul,
extending your corporal Juans
and adjusting your collar; that's obvious.
You know what aches you,
what leaps on your rump,
what descends through you by rope to the ground.
You, poor man, you live; don't deny it,
if you die; don't deny it,
if you die from your age, ay, and from your epoch.
And, even if you cry, you drink,
and, even if you bleed, you nourish your hybrid eyetooth,
your wistful candle and your private parts.
You suffer, you endure and again you suffer horribly,
miserable ape,
Darwin's lad,
bailiff spying on me, most atrocious microbe.
And you know this so well,
that you ignore it, bursting into tears.
You, then, were born; that
too is obvious at a distance, poor devil and shut up,
and you put up with the street fate gave you
and you question your navel: where? how?

My friend, you are completely,
up to your hair, in the year thirty-eight,
Nicolas or Santiago, someone or other,
either with yourself or with your abortion or with
me

and captive in your enormous freedom,
dragged on by your autonomous Hercules...
But if you calculate on your fingers up to two,
it's worse; don't deny it, little brother.

You say no? You say yes, but no?
Poor ape!... Gimme your paw!... No. Your hand, I meant.
To your health! Keep suffering!

Human Poems, 1939

The day is about to come; wind
up your arm, look for yourself under
the mattress, stand once more
on your head, so as to walk straight.
The day is about to come, put on your coat.

The day is about to come; grip
your large intestine tightly in your hand, reflect,
before meditating, for it is horrible
when misfortune befalls one
and one's tooth falls out completely.

You have to eat, but, I tell myself,
do not grieve, for grief and graveside
sobbing do not belong to the poor;
patch yourself, remember,
trust in your white thread, smoke, call roll
on your chain and keep it behind your portrait.
The day is about to come, put on your soul.

The day is about to come; they go by,
they've opened up an eye in the hotel,
lashing it, beating it with one of your mirrors...
You're trembling? It is the remote state of the forehead
and the recent nation of the stomach.
They're still snoring... What a universe is stolen by this snore!
What state your pores are in, on judging it!
With so many twos, ay! how alone you are!
The day is about to come, put on your dream.

The day is about to come, I repeat
through the oral organ of your silence
and it is urgent to take the left with hunger

and to take the right with thirst; in any case,
abstain from being poor among the rich,
poke
your cold, for my warmth is one with it, beloved victim.
The day is about to come, put on your body.

The day is about to come;
the morning, the sea, the meteor, go
in pursuit of your weariness, with banners,
and, because of your classic pride, the hyenas
count their steps in time with the ass,
the female baker thinks about you,
the butcher thinks about you, palpating
the cleaver in which the steel
and the iron and the metal are prisoners; never forget
that during Mass there are no friends,
The day is about to come, put on your sun.

The day is coming; double
your breath, triple
your rancorous goodness
and scorn fear, connections and affectation,
for you, as one can observe in your crotch, the evil one
being aie! immortal,
have dreamed tonight that you were living
on nothing and dying from everything...

Human Poems, 1939

SERMON ON DEATH

And, finally, passing now into the domain of death,
which acts as squadron, former bracket,
paragraph and key, huge hand and dieresis,
for what the Assyrian desk? for what the Christian pulpit,
the intense tug of Vandal furniture
or, even less, this proparoxytonic retreat?

Is it in order to end,
tomorrow, as a prototype of phallic display,
as diabetes and in a white chamber pot,
as a geometric face, as a dead man,
that sermon and almonds become necessary,
that there are literally too many potatoes
and this watery specter in which gold blazes
and in which the price of snow burns?
Is it for this, that we die so much?
Only to die,
must we die each instant?
And the paragraph that I write?
And the deistic bracket that I raise on high?
And the squadron in which my helmet failed?
And the key which fits all doors?
And the forensic dieresis, the hand,
my potato and my flesh and my contradiction under the bedsheet?

Out of my mind, out of my wolvum, out of   *
my lamb, out of my sensible horsessence!
Desk, yes, my whole life long; pulpit,
likewise, my whole death long!
Sermon on barbarism: these papers;
proparoxytonic retreat: this skin.

In this way, cognitive, auriferous, thick-armed,
I will defend my catch in two moments,
with my voice and also with my larynx,
and of the physical smell with which I pray
and of the instinct for immobility with which I walk,
I will be proud while I'm alive—it must be said;
my horseflies will swell with pride,
because, at the center, I am, and to the right,
likewise, and, to the left, equally.

Human Poems, 1939

XXI

from **Aimé Césaire's**
The Miraculous Weapons,
Solar Throat Slashed,
Lost Body, and Ferraments

*

POEM FOR THE DAWN

the mettles of vivid flesh
with summers spread from the cerebral cortex
have flogged the contours of the earth
the Rhamphorhynchi in the sarcasm of their tails take to the wind
the wind which has no more sword
the wind no more now than a pole to gather
   the fruit of all seasons of the sky
hands open
hands green
for the beautiful feasts of anhydrid functions
delightful dusks will snow onto the lopped hands of breathing memories
behold
in the rhagades of our lips of a desperate Orinoco
the blissful tenderness of islands rocked by the adolescent breast of the
   sources of the sea
and in the air and the ever reborn bread of muscular efforts
the dawn irresistible open under the leaf
claritous as the thorny pluck of belladonnas

The Miraculous Weapons, 1946

oh surge without number without dust harbinger of each vinous word
surge and my chest salted by the coves of ancient days and the young
color
tender on the breasts of the sky and of women electric with what
diamonds

eruptive forces trace your orbs
telepathic communications resume across recalcitrant matter
messages of love strayed to the four corners of the world return to us
rekindled
by the carrier pigeons of sidereal traffic

as for me I have nothing to fear I am from before Adam I do not come
under the same lion
nor under the same tree I am from a different hot and a different cold
oh my childhood of firefly milk and reptile quivering

but already the vigil was straining toward the star and the postern and we
were racing
across an arched sea incredibly planted with shipwrecked sterns
toward a shore where I was welcomed by a rustic people penetrators of
forests with wrought-iron
boughs in their hands—the comradely sleep on the jetty—the blue dog
of metamorphosis
the white bear of icebergs and Your truly wild disappearance
tropical as an apparition of a nocturnal wolf at high noon

The Miraculous Weapons, 1946

PERDITION

we will strike the new air with our armor-plated heads
we will strike the sun with our wide-open palms
we will strike the soil with the bare foot of our voices
the male flowers will sleep in coves of mirrors
and even the armor of trilobites
will sink in the half-light of forever
over tender breasts swollen with lodes of milk
and will we not cross the porch
the porch of perditions?
a vigorous road with veiny jaunders
tepid
where the buffaloes of irrepressible angers bound
runs
full-tilting the ripe tornados
in the tolling balisiers of crepuscular riches   *

The Miraculous Weapons, 1946

The great machete blow of red pleasure right in the face there was blood
and that tree called flamboyant and which never deserves this name
more than just before a cyclone or pillaged cities the new blood the
red reason all words in all tongues which mean to die of thirst and
alone when dying tasted like bread and the earth and the sea like
ancestors and this bird shrieking at me not to surrender and the
patience of screams at each detour of my tongue

the finest arch and it is a spurt of blood
the finest arch and it is a lilac ring about the eye
the finest arch and it is called night
and the anarchistic beauty of your arms made into a cross
and the eucharistic beauty—and how it blazes—of your sex in the name
of which I hailed the barrage with my violent lips

there was the beauty of minutes which are marked-down trinkets from
the bazaar of cruelty the sun of minutes and their pretty wolf snouts
which hunger drives out of the woods the red cross of minutes
which are moray eels on their way toward breeding grounds and the
seasons and the immense fragilities of the sea which is an insane bird
nailed dead on the gateway of carriage crossed lands there were to
the point of fear as with the July report of toads of hope and of
despair pruned from the stars over waters right where the fusion of
days guaranteed by borax justifies the gestant watchwoman the for-
nications of grass not to be observed without precaution the copu-
lations of water reflected by the mirror of magi the marine beasts to
be taken in the trough of pleasure the assaults of vocables all gun
ports smoking in order to celebrate the birth of the male heir simul-
taneously with the apparition of sidereal prairies on the flank of vol-
canic scrotums

scolopendra scolopendra
until the eyelid of dunes over forbidden cities struck by the anger of God
solopendra scolopendra
until the crackling and ponderous defeat which drives dwarf cities to take
    command of the fieriest horses when in the thick of the sand they raise
their portcullis over the unknown forces of the deluge
scolopendra scolopendra
crest crest cyma unfurl unfurl as a sword as a cove as a village
asleep on its leg-like pilings and on saphenas of tired water
in a moment there will be a rout of silos sniffed close up
chance pit face of a mounted condottiere armored in artesian puddles and
    the little spoons of libertine roads
face of wind
lemur and uterine face with fingers dug into coins and chemical nomen-
    clature
and the flesh will turn over its great plantain leaves which the wind of
    dives outside the stars signalling the backward march of the night's
    wounds toward the deserts of childhood will pretend to read
in an instant there will be blood shed where the glowworms pull their lit-
    tle electric lamp-chains to celebrate the Compitalia   *
and the childish tricks of the alphabet of spasms which constitutes the
    great boughs of heresy or complicity
there will be the indifference of the ocean liners of silence that furrow
day and night the cataracts of the catastrophe in the proximity of wise
    human temples in transhumance
and the sea will roll back its tiny falcon eyelids and you will try to grasp
    the moment the great feudal lord will ride though its fief at the speed
    of fine gold of desire along the neuron roads look at the birdie if it
    has not swallowed the stole the great king bewildered in the hall full
    of stories will adore his very pure hands his hands raised in the cor-
    ner of the disaster then the sea will once again be on pins and nee-
    dles be sure to sing so as not to extinguish the morals which are the
    obsidianal coin of cities deprived of water and sleep then the sea will

very softly spill the beans and the birds will very softly sing in the sea-saws of salt the Congolese lullaby which the tough old troopers made me unlearn but which the very pious sea of cranial boxes preserves on its ritual leaves

scolopendra scolopendra

until the cavalcades sow their wild oats in the salt meadows of abysses their ears filled with human humming rich in prehistory

scolopendra scolopendra

as long as we do not reach the stone without a dialect the leaf without a dungeon the frail water without a femur the serous peritoneum of springhead evenings

The Miraculous Weapons, 1946

PROPHECY

there where adventure remains clear-sighted
where women radiate language
where death in the hand is beautiful like a milk season bird
where the tunnel gathers from its own genuflexion a profusion of wild
    plums fiercer than caterpillars
where the agile wonder leaves no stone nor fire unturned

there where the vigorous night bleeds a speed of pure vegetation

where the bees of the stars sting the sky with a hive more ardent than the
    night
where the noise of my heels fills space and raises the face of time
    backwards
where the rainbow of my speech is charged to unite tomorrow with hope
    and the infant with the queen,

for having insulted my masters bitten the sultan's men
for having cried in the wilderness
for having screamed at my jailers
for having begged from the jackals and the hyenas shepherds of caravans

I watch
the smoke rushes like a mustang to the front of the stage briefly hems its
    lava with its fragile peacock tail then tearing its shirt suddenly opens
    its chest and I watch it dissolve little by little into British isles into
    islets into jagged rocks in the limpid sea of the air
where my mug
my revolt
    my name
        prophetically bathe

The Miraculous Weapons, 1946

oh mountain oh dolomites bird heart in my childlike hands
oh icebergs oh ghosts old gods sealed in full glory
and even if around a three stone fire crowned with a quivering
circle of tipulas
a pond for the drowned renews itself
province of the dead you strike in vain against the rotation of highways
where the spectacle passes from the level of green flames to the edge of
malefice
velocity fight with me I wear the solar tiara
gong multiply the prison whose animal fights experience
the voices of men preserved in the petrifaction of millennial forests

my dear let's bend with the geological veins

Solar Throat Slashed, 1948

Too bad for you men who don't notice that my eyes remember
   slings and black flags
    which murder with each blink of my lashes

Too bad for you men who do not see who do not see anything
not even the gorgeous railway signals formed
under my eyelids by red and black discs of
the coral snake that my munificence coils in my tears

Too bad for you men who do not see that in the depth of the reticule
where chance deposited our eyes
there is, waiting, a buffalo sunk to the very hilt of the swamp's eyes

Too bad for you men who do not see that you cannot stop me from
building for him plenty
of egg-headed islands out of the flagrant sky
under the calm ferocity of the immense geranium of our sun.

Solar Throat Slashed, 1948

BLUES OF THE RAIN

Aguacero   *
beautiful musician
unclothed at the foot of a tree
amidst the lost harmonies
close to our defeated memories
amidst our hands of defeat
and a people of alien strength
we let our eyes hang low
and untying
the tether of a natal anguish
we sobbed.

Solar Throat Slashed, 1948

EX-VOTO FOR A SHIPWRECK

Hélé helélé the King is a great king
let his majesty deign to look up my anus to see
if it contains diamonds
let his majesty deign to explore my mouth to see
how many carats it contains
laugh tom-tom
laugh tom-tom
I carry the king's litter
I roll out the king's rug
I am the king's rug
I carry scrofula for the king
I am the king's parasol
laugh laugh tom-toms of the kraals
tom-toms of mines that laugh up their shafts
sacred tom-toms laughing about your rat and hyena teeth
right in the missionaries' faces
tom-toms of the forest
tom-toms of the desert
weep tom-tom
weep tom-tom
burned down to the impetuous silence of our shoreless tears
and roll
roll softly no longer than a speck of coal
the pure carbon duration of our endless major pangs
roll roll heavy speechless deliriums
russet lions without manes
tom-toms which protect my three souls my brain my heart my liver
hard tom-toms which very loudly uphold my star wind dwelling over
the blasted rock of my black head
and you brother tom-tom for whom sometimes all day long I keep a word
now hot now cool in my mouth like the little known taste of vengeance
tom-toms of the Kalahari
tom-toms of Good Hope that cap the cape with your threats

O tom-tom of Zululand
Tom-tom of Shaka
tom, tom, tom
tom, tom, tom
King our mountains are mares in heat caught in the full convulsion of bad blood
King our plains are rivers vexed by the supplies of putrefactions drifting in from the sea and your caravels
King our stones are lamps burning with a hope widowed from its dragon
King our trees are the unfolded shape taken by a flame too big for our hearts too weak for a dungeon
Laugh laugh then tom-toms of Kaffraria
like the scorpion's beautiful question mark
drawn in pollen on the canvas of the sky and of our brains at midnight
like the quiver of a sea reptile charmed by the anticipation of bad weather
of the little upside down laugh of the sea in the sunken ship's gorgeous portholes

Solar Throat Slashed, 1948

YOUR HAIR

Wouldn't you have taken it bombarded by lateritic blood
for a beautiful stripped tree
the invincible and spacious cockcrowing already in invincible departure
toward
—one imagines—a witches' sabbath of splendor and cities

Undulating innocent
all the juices rising in the lust of the earth
all the poisons distilled by the nocturnal alembics in the involucres of
the malvaceae
all the thundering of the saponaria
are like these discordant words written by the flames of pyres
over the sublime oriflammes of your revolt

Your hair
ingenuous flames licking a rare heart
the forest will remember the water and the sapwood
as I too remember the compassionate snouts
of big rivers that stumble around like blind men
the forest remembers that the last word can only be
the flaming cry of the bird of ruins in the bowl of the storm

Innocent who goes there
forget to remember
that the baobab is our tree
that it barely waves arms so dwarfed
that you would take it for an imbecilic giant
and you
inhabited by my insolence my tombs my twisters
mane bundle of lianas violent hope of the shipwrecked
sleep softly by the meticulous trunk of my embrace my
woman
my citadel

Solar Throat Slashed, 1948

THE WHEEL

The wheel is man's most beautiful and only discovery
there is the sun which turns
there is the earth which turns
there is your face turning on the axle of your neck when you cry
but you minutes won't you wind on your spindle for living
the lapped up blood
the art of suffering sharpened to tree stumps by the knives of winter
the doe drunk from not drinking
which on the unexpected wellcurb presents me with your
face of a dismasted schooner
your face
like a village asleep at the bottom of a lake
which is reborn to daylight from the grass and from the year
germinates

Solar Throat Slashed, 1948

ALL THE WAY FROM AKKAD, FROM ELAM, FROM SUMER

Awakener, uprooter
Suffered breath, hastener breath
Master of the three paths, you are facing a man who has walked a lot.
All the way from Elam. From Akkad. From Sumer.
Master the three paths, you are facing a man who has carried a lot.
All the way from Elam. From Akkad. From Sumer.
I have carried the commandant's body. I have carried the commandant's railroad. I have carried the commandant's locomotive, the commandant's cotton. On my wooly head which works so fine without a little cushion I have carried God, the machine, the road—the God of the commandant. Master of the three paths I have carried under the sun, I have carried in the fog I have carried over the ember shards of legionary ants. I have carried the parasol I have carried the explosives I have carried the iron-collar. All the way from Akkad. From Elam. From Sumer.
Master of the three paths, Master of the three channels, for once only the first time since Akkad since Elam since Sumer may you grant that—my muzzle apparently more tanned than the calluses on my feet but in reality softer than the raven's scrupulous beak and as if draped in bitter folds provided by my borrowed grey skin (a livery that men force onto me every winter)—I advance across the dead leaves with my little sorcerer steps

toward where the inexhaustible injunction of men thrown to the knotted sneers of the hurricane threatens triumphantly.
All the way from Elam from Akkad from Sumer.

Solar Throat Slashed, 1948

AT THE LOCKS OF THE VOID

In the foreground and in longitudinal flight a dried up brook drowsy roller of obsidian pebbles. In the rear a not exactly tranquil architecture of torn down burgs of eroded mountains on whose glimpsed phantom serpents chariots a cat's-eye and alarming constellations are born. It is a strange firefly cake hurled into the grey face of time, a vast scree of shards of ikons and of blazons of lice in the beard of Saturn. On the right very curiously standing against the squamous wall of crucified butterflies wings open in majesty a gigantic bottle whose very long gold neck drinks a drop of blood from the clouds. As for me I'm no longer thirsty. It gives me pleasure to think of the world undone like an old copra mattress like an old voodoo necklace like the perfume of a felled peccary. I'm no longer thirsty.

> through the shaken sky
> through the exploded stars
> through the tutelary silence
> from very far from beyond myself I come toward you
> woman sprung from a beautiful alburnum
> and your eyes wounds barely closing
> on your modesty from having been born.

It is I singing with a voice still caught in the babbling of elements. It is pleasant to be a piece of wood a cork a drop of water in the torrential waters of the end and of the new beginning. It is pleasant to doze off in the shattered heart of things. In no sense am I any longer thirsty. My sword made from a shark tooth smile is becoming terribly useless. My mace is very obviously out of season and out of bounds. The rain is falling. It is a crisscross of rubble, it is an incredible sowing of the invisible with first-rate ties, it is a branchwork of syphilis, it is the diagram of a brandy bender, it is a conspiracy of dodders, it is the nightmare's head impaled on the lance point of a crazed mob.

I advance to the region of blue lakes. I advance to the region of sulphur springs.

I advance to my crateriform mouth toward which have I struggled enough? What do I have to throw away? Everything by God everything. I am stark naked. I've thrown everything away. My genealogy. My widow. My companions. I await the boiling. I await the wingbeat of the great seminal albatross supposed to make a new man of me. I await the immense tap, the vertiginous slap which will consecrate me as a knight of a Plutonian order.

And suddenly it is the outpour of great rivers
it is the friendship in the eyes of toucans
it is the fulminatory erection of virgin mountains
I am invested. Europe patrols my veins like
a pack of filariae at the stroke of midnight.

Europe cast iron explosion
Europe low tunnel oozing a bloody dew
Europe old dog Europe worm-drawn carriage
Europe peeling tattoo Europe your name is a raucous
clucking and a muffled shock

I unfold my handkerchief it is a flag
I have donned my beautiful skin
I have adjusted my beautiful clawed paws

Ancient name
I hereby join all that powders the sky with its insolence all that is loyal and fraternal all that has the courage to be eternally new all that knows how to yield its heart to the fire all that has the strength to emerge from an inexhaustible sap all that is calm and self-assured all that is not you considerable hiccup

Solar Throat Slashed, 1948

This is the word that sustains me
and smacks against my brass carcass
where in the garret of rust the moon devours
the barbarous bones
of the cowardly prowling beasts of the lie

Barbarity
of the rudimentary language
and our faces beautiful like the true surgical power
of negation

Barbarity
of the dead circulating in the veins of the earth
who at times come and break their heads against the walls of our ears
and the screams of revolt never heard
which turn in tune with musical tones

Barbarity
the single article
barbarity the horned lizard
barbarity the white amphisbaena
barbarity I the spitting cobra
awakening from my putrefying flesh
suddenly a flying gecko
suddenly a fringed gecko
and I adhere so well to the very loci of strength
that to forget me you must
cast the hairy flesh of your chests to the dogs

Solar Throat Slashed, 1948

ELEGY

The hibiscus that is nothing other than a burst eye
from which hangs the thread of a long gaze the trumpets of the chalice
vines,
the huge black sabers of flamboyants the twilight that is an ever jingling
bunch of keys,
the areca palms that are nonchalant suns never setting because pierced
through and through by a pin which the addlebrained lands
never hesitate to jab all the way in
to their hearts, the terrifying souklyans, Orion   *
the ecstatic butterfly that magical pollens
crucified on the gate of trembling nights,
the beautiful black curls of canafistulas that are very proud
mulatto women whose necks tremble a bit under the guillotine,

and do not be surprised if at night I moan more heavily
or if my hands strangle more secretly
it is the herd of old sufferings which toward my smell
black and red
scolopendra-like
stretches its head and with the still soft and clumsy
insistence of its muzzle
searches more deeply for my heart
then it is no use for me to press my heart against yours
nor to lose myself in the foliage of your arms
the herd finds it
and very solemnly
in a manner always new
licks it
amorously
until the first blood savagely appears
on the abrupt open claws of
DISASTER

Lost Body, 1949

NURSERY RHYME

It is this fine film on the swirls of the cloudy wine of the sea
it is this great rearing of the horses of the earth
halted at the last moment on a gasp of the chasm
it is this black sand which roughs itself up on the hiccup of the abyss
it is this stubborn serpent's crawling out the shipwreck
this mouthful of stars revomited into a cake of fireflies
this stone on the ocean tugging with its drool
at a trembling hand for passing birds
here Sun and Moon
form the two cleverly engaged toothed wheels .
of a Time ferocious in grinding us
it is this wretchedness
         these droppings
         this sob of coral reefs
it is alighting from the memorable sky
down onto the lure of our hearts red at dawn
this beak of prey breaking the unwelcoming chest
                 cage
                 and
                 quagmire
It is this kestrel which hovering blazons the noon sky of our black hearts
      this abducting
      this slacking
      this dumping

      this earth

Ferraments, 1960

BEAT IT NIGHT DOG

the sea ebbed untouched from the blood of giant octopuses stranded on
the sands
in the landscape which deteriorates always to be reworked I search
for the memory of a tide for a water flower for a rumor of fury
but too many tracks confuse their caravans
too many evil suns impale their rancor on the trees
too many deceitful portulans are sucked down
into the always diverging crest lines
from high ants polishers of skeletons
    from this impetuous silence from the mouth of this sand
will nothing surge forth other than the dried forest's blighted tops

rage of an unwonted solstice ignited lurid at the so faltering barbarous
limit of the sea
beat it night dog beat it
sudden and absolute at my temples
      you hold between your fangs a bleeding

flesh I recognize only too well

Ferraments, 1960

If my thought borrows the wings of the menfenil   *
oh faces it is clear
you are prey for my claws

      and I I am prey
for the beak of the wind of doubt of the soot
of night oh cinder denser toward the heart
and this hiccup of nails driven in by the seasons

for there is this hurt
Here Lies at the height of myself
spread out in a big pool the hidden one with no undertow
when the voracious day robbed me of my odor

about this blood of mine you will say
that always at the threshold of its bitter gallop it tripped
that more just before God than their correct mouths
my lie

before his distraught face soared with a thousand
infantes out of the high sea plunging flush with the bulwarks
shaken by the original black sobbing of brambles

Ferraments, 1960

FANGS

It is no pigment powder
nor myrrh
pensive odor nor delectation
but flower of blood flush with the skin
map of blood map of the blood
bled raw sweated raw skinned raw
nor tree cut to a white thrust
but blood which rises in the tree of flesh
by catches by crimes
          No remittance
—straight up along the stones
             straight up along the bones—for
copper weight shackle weight heart weight
venoms caravaners of the bite
at the tepid edge of fangs

Ferraments, 1960

LIMINAL VAMPIRE

An atrocious light appears
from the Occident to the Orient counter-current
the howling of the mastiffs of the fog vouches
for the City according to the plenary Fear waving like flags galore
ten thousand sticky tongues and the viscous parade between two nights
at first of all the sumptuous beasts vomited from putrefactions

but under the brambly advance of the venom
they prevailed their eyes intact at the most fragile point
of the unpardonable image
of the memorable vision of a world to be built
of the brotherhood that cannot but come
however awkwardly

sniffing at the foot of the tree of life
black rats cardinals of the lie mingled with
the unicorn of racial hatred
on the other end of the line the inquisitor's ear

then the sewer water makes a terrific leap
from the whole untold journey of hoped for birds
Enough that words turn into a cassava of dust
as if into deer flesh the mud
clamped its claws over the stars

Ferraments, 1960

MY PROFOUND DAY'S CLEAR PASSAGE

in the spice open sea
there is steady this thickness like an acidic season a poisonous
tower that one finally does not hear anymore because never
never does it fall back in drops fissuring with a fragment the wall which
waits patient

there is this awesome vertical whose name fidelity fixes me skinned
to the whirling pommel of the double-edged glaive
of which I am only the affable cross guard in time and which
each drop of my blood vainly strives to cleave

nevertheless it is not easy to draw the map of the battle-
ground a clearing shifting each time from where remorse
bestrews me every time more savage toward the loyal
face of constellations

to howl at the aroused forest's edge unbreakable into bars
forged in vigilance and twisted by madness
to howl at the unavowed sources of great rivers at the nonmemorable
maternities at the never sucked breasts of fabulous beasts

the awakening is in torpor at the peremptory foot of palm trees
frigid women tightly girdled who forever and from very high
fan themselves

surely there is me as a great serpent of the bogs which
the sun's trident aping itself nails and which nameless
frightened bifid at the very edge of a ruptured night crawls
fragilely avid avid for a tenuous milk

Ferraments, 1960

CORPSE OF A FRENZY

the memory of a road
rising very steeply in bamboo shade
the cane juice that invents itself always new
and the odor of hog plums

the little skirts of the sea
the seasons of childhood
the parasol of grandleaf seagrapes
        have been left below

at the curve I turn around I look over the shoulder
of my past it is full of always not immediately comprehensible
magical and anguishing blows of breadfruit
falling and rolling down into ravines where no one finds them

catastrophe made for itself a too high perched throne
out of the delirium of the destroyed city it is my burned down life

        Grief will you never
stop expecting our howling
I dreamed face twisted
mouth bitter I dreamed about all the impurities of my blood
and the ghosts roamed about with each of my gestures
at the indentation of fate

        never mind it is a weakness

let my heart keep vigil
a prisoner who alone in his cell inexplicably survives the evidence of fate
ferocious taciturn
at the very bottom a lamp lit from his horrible wound

Ferraments, 1960

XXII

Three texts by Antonin Artaud   *

We have never been able to write without triggering an incarnation of the soul, but it was already formed, and not by us, when we entered into poetry.

The poet who writes is concerned with the Word and the Word has its laws. It is in the poet's unconscious to believe automatically in these laws. He believed himself to be free and he is not free.

There is something behind his head, around the ears of his thought. Something is budding in his nape, where it existed even before he began. He is the son of his works, perhaps, but his works are not of him, for what there is of himself in his poetry was put there not by him, but by the unconscious producer of life who chose him as its poet and whom he himself did not choose. And who has never been well disposed toward him.

I don't want to be the poet of my poet, of that alter ego that wanted to appoint me poet, but the poet creator, in rebellion against the ego and the self. And I remember the ancient rebellion against the forms that advanced against me.

It is through the revolt against the ego and the self that I rid myself of all the evil incarnations of the Word which were never anything more for man than a compromise of cowardice and of illusion and who knows what abject fornication between cowardice and illusion. And I don't want a word that comes from who knows what astral libido that was totally conscious of the formations of my desire in myself.

There is in the forms of the human Word some predatory operation, some predatory self-consumption in which the poet, focusing on the object, sees himself eaten by that object.

A crime weighs on the Word made flesh, but the crime is in having admitted it. Libido is animal thought and it was the animals who, one day, were changed into men.

𝔀

The word produced by men is the idea of an invert buried by the animal reflexes of things and who, through the martyrdom of time and of things, has forgotten that the word was invented.

The invert is a man who eats his self and expects his self to nourish him, he seeks his mother in his self and wants to keep her for himself. The primitive crime of incest is the enemy of poetry and the killer of immaculate poetry.

𝔀

I don't want to eat my poem, but I want to give my heart to my poem and what is my heart to my poem. My heart is what isn't me. To give one's self to one's poem is also to risk being raped by it. And if I am Virgin for my poem, it should remain virgin for me.

𝔀

I am that forgotten poet, who one day saw himself fall into matter, and the matter will not devour me, not me.

I don't want those aging reflexes, the product of an ancient incest due to an animal ignorance of the Virgin law of life. Ego and self are those catastrophic states of being in which Living Man allows himself to be imprisoned by the forms of himself that he perceives. To love the ego is to love a corpse, and the law of the Virgin is infinity. The unconscious producer of ourselves is that of an ancient copulator who indulges in the basest of magics and who has discovered a magic in the infamy of endlessly reducing oneself to oneself in order to make a word emerge from a cadaver. The libido is the definition of that cadaverous desire and fallen man is an inverted criminal.

✺

I am that primitive made unhappy by the inexpiable horror of things. I don't want to reproduce myself in things, but I want things to be produced by me. I don't want an idea of the ego in my poem and I don't want to recognize myself in it.

✺

My heart is that eternal Rose that grew from the magic power of the initial Cross. The one who crucified himself in Himself and for Himself never came back to himself. Never, for this himself through which he sacrificed Himself he also offered to Life after having himself forced it to become the being of his own life.

✺

I want forever only to be that poet who sacrificed himself in the Kabbala of the self to the immaculate conception of things.

—Rodez, 1944

The anchored spirit,
screwed into me
by the psycho-
lubricious thrust
of the sky
is the one who thinks
every temptation,
every desire,
every inhibition.

o dedi   *
o dada orzoura
o dou zoura
a dada skizi

o kaya
o kaya pontoura
o ponoura
a pena
poni

It's the penetral spider veil,
the female onor fur
of either-or the sail,
the anal plate of anayor.

(You lift nothing from it, god,
because it's me.
You never lifted anything of this order from me.
I'm writing it here for the first time,
I'm finding it for the first time.)

Not the membrane of the chasm,
nor the member omitted from this jism,
issued from a depredation,

but an old bag,   *
outside membrane,
outside of there where it's hard or soft.

B'now passed through the hard and soft,
spread out this old bag in palm,
pulled, stretched like a palm
of hand
bloodless from keeping rigid,
black, violet
from stretching to soft.

But what then in the end, you, the madman?

Me?

This tongue between four gums,

this meat between two knees,

this piece of hole
for madmen.

Yet precisely not for madmen.
For respectable men,
whom a delirium to belch everywhere planes,

and who from this belch
made the leaf,

listen closely:
made the leaf
of the beginning of generations
in the palmate old bag of my holes,
mine.

Which holes, holes of what?

Of soul, of spirit, of me, and of being;
but in the place where no one gives a shit,
father, mother, Artaud and artoo.

In the humus of the plot with wheels,
in the breathing humus of the plot
of this void,
between hard and soft.

Black, violet,
rigid,
recreant
and that's all.

Which means that there is a bone,
where
                    god
sat down on the poet,
in order to sack the ingestion
of his lines,
like the head farts
that he wheedles out of him through his cunt,

that he would wheedle out of him from the bottom of the ages,
down to the bottom of his cunt hole,

and it's not a cunt prank
that he plays on him in this way,
it's the prank of the whole earth
against whoever has balls
in his cunt.

And if you don't get the image,
—and that's what I hear you saying
in a circle,
that you don't get the image
which is at the bottom
of my cunt hole,—

it's because you don't know the bottom,
not of things,
but of my cunt,
mine,
although since the bottom of the ages
you've all been lapping there in a circle
as if badmouthing an alienage,
plotting an incarceration to death.

> **ge re ghi**
> **regheghi**
> **geghena**
> **e reghena**
> **a gegha**
> **riri**

Between the ass and the shirt,
between the gism and the under-bet,
between the member and the let down,
between the membrane and the blade,
between the slat and the ceiling,

between the sperm and the explosion,
'tween the fishbone and 'tween the slime,
between the ass and everyone's
                    seizure
of the high-pressure trap
of an ejaculation death rattle
is neither a point
nor a stone

burst dead at the foot of a bound

nor the severed member of a soul
(the soul is no more than an old saw)
but the terrifying suspension
of a breath of alienation

raped, clipped, completely sucked off
by all the insolent riff-raff
of all the turd-buggered
who had no other grub
                    in order to live
                    than to gobble
                    Artaud
                    mômo
                    there, where one can fuck sooner
                    than me
                    and the other get hard higher
                    than me
                    in myself
if he has taken care to put his head
on the curvature of that bone

located between anus and sex,

                    of that hoed bone that I say

in the filth
of a paradise
whose first dupe on earth
was not father nor mother
who diddled you in this den
       but
       I
screwed into my madness.

And what seized hold of me
that I too rolled my life there?
       ME,
       NOTHING, *nothing*.
Because I,
       I am there,
       I'm there
and it is life
that rolls its obscene palm there.

       Ok.
       And afterward?

       Afterward? Afterward?
       The old Artaud
       is buried

in the chimney hole
he owes to his cold gum
to the day when he was killed!

       And afterward?
       Afterward?
       Afterward!
He is this unframed hole
that life wanted to frame.
Because he is not a hole

              but a nose
that always knew all too well to sniff
the wind of the apocalyptic
              head
which they suck on his clenched ass,
and that Artaud's ass is good
for pimps in Miserere.

And you too you have your gum,
your right gum buried,
              god,

you too your gum is cold
for an infinity of years
since you sent me your innate ass
to see if I was going to be born
              at last
since the time you were waiting for me
while scraping
my absentee belly.

              menendi anenbi
              embenda
              tarch inemptle
              o marchti rombi
              tarch paiolt
              a tinemptle
              orch pendui
              o patendi
              a merchit
              orch torpch
              ta urchpt orchpt
              ta tro taurch

campli
ko ti aunch
a ti aunch
aungbli

Artaud the Mômo, 1947

TO HAVE DONE WITH
THE JUDGMENT OF GOD   *

kré	Everything must	**puc te**
kré	be arranged	**puk te**
pek	to a hair	**li le**
kre	in a fulminating	**pek ti le**
e	order.	**kruk**
pte		

I learned yesterday

(you must think that I'm very slow, or perhaps it is only a false rumor,
some of the dirty gossip that is peddled between the sink and the
latrines at the hour when the buckets are filled with meals once again
regurgitated),

I learned yesterday

about one of the most sensational official practices of the American pub-
lic schools

which no doubt make that country consider itself at the head of progress.

Apparently, among the examinations or tests that a child has to undergo
on entering a public school for the first time is the one called the sem-
inal liquid or sperm test,

which consists of asking this newly-enrolled child for a little of his sperm
in order to put it into a glass jar

and of thereby keeping it ready for all the attempts at artificial insemina-
tion which might eventually take place.

For more and more the Americans find that they lack manpower and
children,

that is, not workers

but soldiers,

and at all costs and by all possible means they want to make and manu-
facture soldiers

in view of all the planetary wars which might subsequently take place,

and which would be destined to *demonstrate* by the crushing virtues of
force

the superexcellence of American products,

and the fruits of American sweat in all the fields of activity and potential
dynamism of force.

Because there must be production,

nature must be replaced wherever it can be replaced by every possible
means of activity,

a major field must be found for human inertia,

the worker must be kept busy at something,

new fields of activity must be created,

where all the false manufactured products,

all the ignoble synthetic ersatzes will finally reign,

where beautiful true nature has nothing to do,

and must give up its place once and for all and shamefully to all the tri-
umphant replacement products,

where sperm from all the artificial insemination factories

will work miracles

to produce armies and battleships.

No more fruit, no more trees, no more vegetables, no more plants phar-
maceutical or not and consequently no more food,

but synthetic products to repletion,

in vapors,

in special humors of the atmosphere, on particular axes of atmospheres
drawn by force and by synthesis from the resistance of a nature that has
never known anything about war except fear.

And long live war, right?

For by doing this, it is war, isn't it, that the Americans have prepared for
and that they prepare for thus step by step.

To defend this insane machining against all the competition which would
inevitably break out on all sides,

there must be soldiers, armies, airplanes, battleships,

therefore this sperm

which the American governments have apparently had the nerve to
consider.

For we have more than one enemy

and one who watches us, kid,

us, the born capitalists,

and among these enemies

Stalin's Russia

which is not short of armed men either.

All this is very fine,

but I did not know that the Americans were such a warlike people.

To fight you must receive blows

and perhaps I have seen many Americans at war

but in front of them they always had incommensurable armies of tanks,
planes, battleships .

serving as a shield.

I saw a lot of machines fight

but I saw only in the infinite
                    rear
the men who drove them.
Confronted by a people who make their horses, oxen and donkeys eat the
    last tons of true morphine which may be left to them in order to
    replace it with ersatz smoke,
I prefer the people who eat right out of the earth the delirium that gave
    birth to them,
I am speaking of the Tarahumaras
who eat Peyote straight from the soil
while it is born,
and who kill the sun in order to establish the kingdom of black night,
and who split the cross so that the spaces of space will never again meet
    or cross.

In this way you will hear the dance of the TUTUGURI.

TUTUGURI: THE RITE OF THE BLACK SUN

And below, as at the bottom of the bitter,
cruelly desperate slope of the heart,
the circle of six crosses opens,
       far below,
as if embedded in the mother earth,
disembedded from the filthy embrace of the mother
       who slobbers,

The earth of black coal
is the only humid spot
in this cleft of rock.

The Rite is that the new sun passes through seven points before explod-
   ing at the earth's orifice.

And there are six men,
one for each sun,
and a seventh man
who is the sun completely
       raw
dressed in black and red flesh.

Now, this seventh man
is a horse,
a horse with a man leading him.

But it is the horse
that is the sun
and not the man.

On the rending of a drum and of a long, peculiar
trumpet,
the six men
who were lying down,
rolled up flush with the ground,

spring up successively like sunflowers,
not suns at all
but turning soils,
lotuses of water,
and to each upspring
corresponds the increasingly gloomy and *repressed*
        gong
        of the drum
until suddenly we see coming in full gallop, at vertiginous speed,
the last sun,
the first man,
the black horse with a
        man naked,
        absolutely naked
        and *virgin*
        on it.

Having gamboled, they advance following circular meanders
and the horse of bloody meat panics
and caracoles without stopping
on the top of its rock
until the six men
have finished encircling
completely
the six crosses.

Now, the major tone of the Rite is precisely
        THE ABOLITION OF THE CROSS.

Having finished turning
they uproot
the earthen crosses
and the man naked
on the horse
raises high
an immense horseshoe
which he has tempered in a cut of his blood.

RESEARCH ON FECALITY

There where it smells of shit
it smells of being.
Man could very well have avoided shitting,
and kept his anal pocket closed,
but he chose to shit
like he could've chosen to live
instead of consenting to live dead.

The fact is that in order not to make caca,
he would've had to consent
not to be,
but he could not resolve to lose
        being,
in other words to die alive.

There is in being
something particularly tempting for man
and that something is precisely
        CACA
      (Roarings here.)

In order to exist you need only let yourself go to be,
but to live,
you must be somebody,
to be somebody,
you must have a BONE,
not be afraid of showing the bone,
and of losing meat on the way.

Man has always preferred meat
to the earth of bones.
The fact is there was only earth and bone wood,
and he had to earn his meat,
there was only iron and fire,

and no shit,
and man was afraid of losing shit
or rather he *desired* shit
and, for that, sacrificed blood.

In order to have shit,
in other words meat,
where there was only blood
and the scrap iron of bones
and where there was no question of earning being
but where there was one of losing life.

> **o reche modo**
> **to edire**
> **di za**
> **tau dari**
> **do padera coco**

There, man withdrew and fled.

Then the beasts ate him.

It was not a rape,
he lent himself to the obscene meal.

He found it tasty,
even he himself learned
to play the beast
and to eat rat
daintily.

And where does this filthy abasement come from?

From the fact that the world is not yet formed,
or from the fact that man has only a faint idea of the world
which he wants to keep forever?

That comes from the fact that man
one fine day,
stopped
        the idea of the world.

Two roads were offered to him:
that of the infinite outside,
that of the infinitesimal inside.

And he chose the infinitesimal inside.
Where it is only a question of squeezing
the rat,
the tongue,
the anus
or the glans.

And god, god himself hastened the movement.

Is god a being?
If he is it is made of shit.
if he is not
he's not.
Now, he is not,
but like the void which advances with all its forms
of which the most perfect representation
is the march of an incalculable group of crab lice.

"You are mad, Mr. Artaud, and the Mass?"

I abjure baptism and the Mass.
There is no human act
which, on the internal erotic plane,
is more pernicious than the descent
of so-called Jesus Christ
onto the altars.

No one will believe me
and from here I see the public shrugging its shoulders
but the named christ is no other than he
who facing the crab louse god
consented to live without a body,
while an army of men
descended from a cross,
where god believed he had long ago nailed them,
rebelled,
and, cased in iron,
in blood,
in fire, and bones,
advances, reviling the Invisible
in order to end GOD'S JUDGMENT there.

TO RAISE THE QUESTION OF...

What is serious
is that we know
that after the order
of this world
there is another.

Which is it?

We do not know.

The number and order of possible suppositions in this domain
is precisely
infinity!

And what is infinity?

We do not exactly know!

It is a word
we employ
to indicate
the opening
of our consciousness
towards an immeasurable
possibility,
indefatigable and immeasurable.

And what exactly of consciousness?

We do not exactly know.

It is nothingness.

A nothingness
we employ
to indicate
when we do not know something
from what side
we do not know it
and we say
then
consciousness,
from the side of consciousness,
but there are a hundred thousand other sides.

So what?

It seems that consciousness
is in us
linked
to sexual desire
and hunger;

but it could
very well
not be
linked to them.

It is said
it can be said,
there are those who say
that consciousness
is an appetite,
the appetite for life;

and immediately
beside the appetite for life,
is the appetite for food
which comes immediately to mind;

as though there were not people who eat
without any kind of appetite;
and who are hungry.

For that also
occurs
to be hungry
without appetite;

so what?

So

the space of possibility
was given me one day
like a loud fart
that I will let;

but neither the space,
nor the possibility,
I didn't know exactly what they were,

and I didn't feel the need to think about it,

they were words
invented to define things
which existed
or did not exist
confronted by
the pressing urgency
of a need:
that of abolishing the idea,
the idea and its myth,
and of enthroning in its place
the thundering manifestation
of this explosive necessity:

to dilate the body of my internal night,
of the internal nothingness
of my self

which is night,
nothingness,
irreflection,

but which is an explosive assertion
that there is
something
to make way for:

my body.

And really
reduce my body to
this stinking gas?
To say that I have a body
because I have a stinking gas
which forms
inside me?

I don't know
but
I do know that
        space,
        time,
        dimension,
        becoming,
        the future,
        the hereafter,
        being,
        non-being,
        the self
        the non-self,

are nothing to me;
but there is one thing
which is something,
only one thing
which is something,
and I feel it
because it wants to
COME OUT:
the presence
of my corporal
pain,

the menacing,
never tiring
presence
of my
body;

however much I am pressed with questions
and deny all questions,
there is a point
where I find myself forced
to say no,
            NO

then
to negation;

and this point,
it's when I'm pressed,

when I am squeezed out
and am milked
until the departure
within me

of food,
of my food
and its milk,

and what remains?

That I am suffocated;

and I don't know if it is an action
but by pressing me thus with questions
even to the absence
and the nothingness
of the question
I was pressed
even to the suffocation
within me
of the idea of body
and of being a body,

and it is then that I smelled the obscene

and that I farted
out of folly
and out of excess
and out of revolt
of my suffocation.

The fact is that I was pressed
right up to my body
and right up to the body

**and it is then
that I shattered everything
because my body
it is never to be touched.**

CONCLUSION

—And what has been your purpose, Mr. Artaud, in this radio broadcast?

—In principle to denounce a certain number of officially consecrated and acknowledged social filths:
1° this emission of infantile sperm given free of charge by children with a view to the artificial insemination of fetuses still to be born
that will see the light of the day in a century or more.

2° To denounce, in this same American people who occupy the entire surface of the former Indian continent, a revival of the warlike imperialism of ancient America which caused the pre-Columbian Indians to be despised by all precedent mankind.

3° —You are expressing here, Mr. Artaud, some very bizarre things.

4° —Yes, I am saying something bizarre,
the fact is that the pre-Columbian Indians were contrary to whatever one might have believed, a strangely civilized people
who had in fact known a form of civilization based on the exclusive principle of cruelty.

5° —And do you know exactly what cruelty is?

6° —Just like that, no, I don't know.

7° —Cruelty, it's to extirpate through the blood and as far as the blood-god, the bestial risk of unconscious human animality, wherever it may be encountered.

8° —Man, when he is not held back, is an erotic animal,
he has within him an inspired tremor,
a sort of pulsation

producing innumerable beasts which are the form the ancient terrestrial
   peoples universally attributed to god.
That made what is called a spirit.
Now, this spirit which came from the American Indians is reappearing a
   little bit everywhere today in scientific guise which serves only to reveal
   this spirit's morbid infectious hold, the salient state of vice, but a vice
   pullulating with diseases,
for, laugh as much as you wish,
what have been called microbes
                  is in fact god,
and do you know what the Americans and the Russians make their atoms
   with?
They make them with the microbes of god.

—You are raving, Mr. Artaud.
You are mad.

—I am not raving.
I'm not mad.
I'm telling you that microbes have been reinvented in order to impose a
   new idea of god.

A new way has been found to make god come out again and to catch him
   in the act of his microbial noxiousness.
It's to nail him in the heart,
there where men love him best,
in the form of sickly sexuality,
in that sinister guise of morbid cruelty which he dons in the hours when
   it pleases him as it does now to tetanize and madden humanity.

He uses the spirit of purity of a consciousness that has remained ingenu-
   ous like mine to asphyxiate it with all the false appearances which he
   spreads universally through the spaces and it is thus that Artaud the
   Mômo can appear to be hallucinating.

—What do you mean, Mr. Artaud?

—I mean that I have found a way to have done once and for all with this
   monkey.
and that if nobody believes anymore in god everybody believes more and
   more in man.

And it is man that we must now decide to emasculate.

—How so?
             How so?

From whatever angle one approaches you you are mad, mad enough to
   tie down.

—By having him undergo once more but for the last time an autopsy in
   order to remake his anatomy.
I say, in order to remake his anatomy.
Man is sick because he is badly constructed.
We must decide to strip him in order to scratch out this animalcule which
   makes him itch to death,

          god,
          and with god
          his organs.

For tie me down if you want to,
but there is nothing more useless than an organ.

When you have given him a body without organs,
then you will have delivered him from all his automatisms and restored
   him to his true liberty.

Then you will teach him again to dance inside out
as in the delirium of dance halls
and that inside out will be his true side out.

XXIII

Miklós Radnóti, *Seventh Eclogue*   *

Do you see? Evening falls, fringed with barbed wire,
the hacked-out oak fence and barracks waver, sucked up by dusk.
The framework of our captivity is undone by a hesitant gaze
and the mind alone—the mind alone—knows the tautness of the wire.
Do you see, dearest, imagination here can free itself only this way.
By dreaming, that beautiful liberator, our broken bodies are unleashed,
in that moment the prison camp starts home!
In rags, heads shaved, snoring, the prisoners fly
from Serbia's blind heights to the hiding homelands.
The *hiding* homelands? O is our home still there?
Maybe no bomb touched it? Might it *be*, as when we were drafted?
The one groaning on my right, the one sprawling on my left,
    will they return home?
Tell me, is there still a homeland where this hexameter will be
    understood?

Without accent marks, feeling out line after line,
here, in the dusk, I write this poem just as I live,
blindly, a caterpillar inching my way on the paper.
Flashlight, book, everything taken away by the Lagar guards,
and there's no mail—only fog settles on our barracks.
Among false rumors and worms, here in the mountains live
Frenchmen, Poles, loud Italians, Serbian separatists, and brooding Jews,
a chopped up, fevered body, still living one life,
waiting for good news, woman's beautiful word, free human fate,
waiting for the end that drops into dense twilight, for the *miracle*.

I am lying on a plank, a captive animal among worms,
the fleas' assault starts up again, but the army of flies are at rest.
It is night, one day shorter again, you see,
and, one day shorter, life. The camp is sleeping. The landscape

lit by the moon. In its light, the wire is again taut.
One can see through the window, cast on the wall,
shadows of armed guards passing among the night sounds.

The camp is sleeping, do you see, dearest, dreams are rustling,
a startled man snorts, tosses about in his tight space,
already back to sleep, his face radiates. Only I sit up awake,
I feel a half-smoked cigarette in my mouth instead of the taste of your kiss,
and sleep, the comforter, does not come,
for I cannot die nor live without you anymore.

Lagar Heidenau, in the mountains
above Žagubica, July 1944.

XXIV

from **Michel Deguy's, Acts, Figurations, and Couplings**

*

I call *muse* the seesaw of the sky, the wind transshipper at *his* volition of our views, this tinting when I open with the cat my eyes a slit, the one who caressed the cat; *muse*, the profusion that works range in uncompletable concerto sequences, in reiterated poems, in Indian file, flattened, and classified piled up on canvases, on stones, on wood, on music paper, in Linnaeus's octavos, Aristotle's glass cases, files

I call *muse* the pain that they cause me, the moon sun jugglery, *muse* the voyage to the south of the earth where frozen lakes are bordered by flamingos pink as the painted nails of the fan of twilight, the moon and its cortege of ponds when nuptially it crosses the bridge of the earth similar to Chile from one extreme to the other, *muse* the cranes the black bull an owl passed the swans, the most southern town where I was which called itself *Porvenir*, the pubis bird, the sea horse was rotting under the dextrogyre cross of gulls, *muse* the voyage, Tierra del Fuego like a cloud at the end of *Punta-Arenas* Street, the royal hand of the sea, the airplane like an elegant eye, the patience of Noah necessary to greet the daylong curtsy of the Magellan Sea, the cloud with which the sky veiled its love and the portico of colors through which it passed, on return the Patagonian shore like a cock

muse the moral voyage where dreams are daydreams and courage growing in one's back, the poetic exactitude of the earth crossing one's mind, the Pampa night disclosing the distance, womanless table at which each doubts if he will speak, this platform of calm at a certain depth in the torment, the patience of colors that help us make our choice, the humus tablecloth put away each morning, the vale one must descend

mist to sand

the phlegmatic homonymy in the language that is gioconda like the famous effigy, the hospitable paronomasia similar to the jigsaw puzzle abandoned by the children, the acceptance where everything reposes in genitive ambiguity, the always original erosion which draws Spanish and Portuguese out of Latin *muse* the tender brain where everything escapes, the shortage granted to the storyteller, the audacity to which grammar lends itself, *muse* my confidence in not willing thinking, the migratory responses, the equality which falls like snow on the "slightest events," that everything is true including "the deceitful tenderness in the farewell"

muse that the climbing be climbing in the body and the descent descent in the body, *muse* once again the strange soul and the conditions, the poems that we read at the dentist's, tapping a foot to cover the blood, at the display of chance the poems that resist the leafing pulse; *muse* the meal that is always *served there* in this tale of *Beauty and the Beast* where we live, for "he went down into the garden and found the meal prepared"

I call *muse* Venice the porches Negroes in ribbons Venice of the gondolaed nails where the stranger turns around like the one arriving in Venice led to the visible by a miracle the plaza like a square of players the things that look at each other for the visible is a human concern

muse the equal filling up of all places, that rich frieze of the strait equal to our straightened eyes, the spacious liberty of free space, that every parvis every esplanade every terrace every stoop "clears" so as to show, this discrete multiplicity that allows us to enter and to leave, to go away, to approach, "I'm not disturbing you," *muse* this void

muse the history of the muses, the chronic testimonies, every birth a fairy a bedside located under nine gifts of irrefutable provincial godmothers, history now this collage of *news* and the inclined plane of inventions, the utterly surprising coming of Philoctetes or of Joyce, the unforeseeable gesture of Achilles or of Tintoretto

Ting tint Orée Auray tent forest stentor Aretino Parrot Tyndareus Paindoré Tintoretto

the excessive promise of names, the namelessness of still hidden species which wait their turn to rise to the clearing of men

I summon this tardy wedding that must be waked, this festival absence whose fire down there supports our virgin lamps, *muse* therefore her advent, her prefiguration with guinea fowl gilded grey jerks

the delicate grafts of memory in the night, the legend of a word, *muse* likewise the enemy, the hate that crumples the interview, this handful of fake bones and grimaces, this solid alloy of derma and humour that pursues far from me the relationship between densities, the indifference to my death, the slowness of men in transforming their element into a law, the frigidity of happiness for knowledge, all the configurations of hiatuses, of props, of breaks in the involuntary edifice of the stay, the petrified shoulder of the hand that writes *mene tekel upharsin*

Acts, 1966

The water loves only the sky
It wants to see (It overturns
At every pause) Only the sky
It looks for no other proof

How many dead how many living
In their "hole" in their jail
Have desired desire that which is there
The spacious contracting of the Three
Where the tree is the dark precursor

Like the edges of a wave of a wave thus
We the relatives of a daughter a lover and in the same
Way there is a science of this labile wave in the same
Analysis of the soul our emptiness What happens
To the cry uttered a thousand seconds ago a thousand years

Think it through   There really must
Be a poem there
Such as for this hour and this sort of contagion
Of what one doesn't know in what way comparable from porch to
porch

This hum of evening of bank of return
It touches a greater number of men
In that case   Begin   Advance one word then another
Still   Walk   Release your hands   Get
The Pacific in on it—the last antiphrasis
The most vast $\frac{3}{5}$ths of the earth to reduce

That he can sit down that is peace
Among the others like Pasternak
With the dogs facing with feet of rain

Host writing the sounds with the dogs
   Admitted on the tiled floor
   While the desire to survive does not cease

Figurations, 1969

ETC.

The 10-pointer moon, an amazon, or this old ubiquitous head waiter who wanders around our month, bending over our tables like a legend, bald here, but full of himself, napkin over shoulder

over there an oestricultivatress, more visible from here than the Punjab, she goes from one cloister to another, the gates cut our faces, she is without meridian, we put her in charge of our telecommunications, our invariant

sublime tessera which regularly fragments, her phases guarantee hospitality, from North to South we exchange quarters of the moon, our sons recognize each other

for the last time the common moon for the last time to tell us that, of an amazon or of a head waiter, or her apparition among the trees for Eustace etc., for the last time this game—or must we *delete when appropriate* and leave only

"The volume of the moon is fifty times smaller than that of the earth, from which it is at an average distance of 175,000 miles"

neither a clairvoyant nor a Hausfreund nor a visitor nor a cervida nor Nuktiphaès peri gaian alômenon allotrion phôs

isn't she the mute on Brecht's roof, the lucid extra whose ruse undresses us?

on her tacit nail don't we deposit our words without a word from her in exchange against all the others   her silence makes us confess, we offer her bathtubs, swing mirrors, jewels, a hecatomb of lexicons   she patronizes the poetry business

silver reserve at
the capital of every township, counterpart of our translations deposited
ostensible nonnegotiable like a zenith she guarantees our treaties and
backs up every debt

for the last time I warn you, what
is happening since we have approached her ... This absent thing which is
nothing lends herself to everything, white turntable of names and of
meanings, this emphyteutic thing untransferable completely present, un-
nameable, she passes, over in silence but insignificant and so there
it's her

moon there and at that distance—
accessible today but unapproachable always for terrestrials—exceeding all
naming   her fate touches our foreheads and the most demented things
that we talkative ones say don't suit her badly

fingernail barque
chastity lunule unicorn billhook huntress stable dune anagram of anul

her reappearances distend glossaries she respins the wheel of prayers of
wonderful talks we all have to go through it no combination is to be struck
out there is no word that does not file past appropriate no word not a coin
tossed onto her touchstone
"There are more things in heaven etc." That means something? That
since things are not all on the same level, those least within hand's reach
are models that none of them are simply within hand's reach:

but they tierify rarify rise up to the stars distancing less and less sure
up to the crown of numbers (and on the other hand hiding in opacity set-
tling between the antipodes keeping compact) more and more indifferent
in their astronomic exposition detached "inevitable" idols inducting the
litany of languages:

By the stars by the forests and by Acheron honored
Diana in the high the mid and the low world presides

And her horses her dogs her Eumenides she guides
So as to light up to hunt to create death and horror

. . . .

Her strong flames and grievances fires nets and fetters
Moon Diana Hecate in heaven earth and hell
Adorning questing hindering our Gods us and our shadows

for the last time we are required to focus on the rapport between
the scarab and the sun

                    (the unconscious sham of philosophy pre-
tending to believe that perception saw the moon setting "two hundred
steps away" (?) let us note rather the aberrant symptom on her lips of a
repressed secret which speaks transvestite, in rags among us flattened
vestige of the ancient figure, waiting for her Jodelian blaze to wash her
features,

                    for in the antique version the
moon the sun, no "error of the senses" observed them sleeping under the
stars at the town's end in the area reserved for nomads)

                    for
the last time rather we are summoned to concentrate on the sun as a
scarab, on the scarab as a sun, since it has never been a case of bad judg-
ment, of a confused optical ignorance to patiently await the advent of cor-
recting science

                    but a mystical triangle like that of
the omphalus and the iliac crests, the sun the eye the scarab equidistant
incommensurable summits: the difference contracted from the beginning
into a figure between the eye and the scarab, between the sun and the eye,
between the sun and the scarab, the silence of this infinity has something
to emphasize

O resemblance adopted country
Your faces don't resemble and which thus resemble
The volume of the sea is explicit about itself
A blackbird enchants his territory

The body will be spoken through the body:
Hair (like an uprush of blood
from a bone crossbow)

. . .

silence

   school of silence the ears stop the hearing tingles asleep no the
eye does not take itself to be the most interesting subject its tutor eman-
cipates it at this moment: the 10-pointer moon redoubled within its own
halo like an icon frame surges between the trees of the hunt

                   silence

my friends ("my friends")

        why give in to the mutism of the moon,
loss in the eye which reappears lower between the talkative lips summon-
ing all the languages in the world before her anonymity like the icon-bear-
ing bifurcated stag mobile bush between the branches, the moon's silence
authorizes all words reed baskets metals flutes painters of inexhaustible
signs like baths in which she doesn't even get her feet wet, Madame Sphinx
without a question the round breast confused with her face and thus with-
out response and wordless is it a coffee bean a Φ a sexual organ a Θ the
moon prowls like something that one cannot remember, what is closest,
the mammary jogger remember that there is something

         and when we arrive on
her sunlit "ground," then *to moon to land*—already the hesitation regarding
the metaphor trembles—we bring our words, we'll find there our pumices
our relief recurring our fictions as everywhere reinjecting a big man with
a little one, fitting our animal spirits into her cavities (*"the formal cause of
drunkenness consists in the superabundant quantity and in the quality of warm
and humid vapors, which rise from the substance of the wine, which upon filling*

the brain and its ventricles and spreading thence to the origin of the nerves and touching their passages, excite in man the sleep of drunkenness keeping the animal spirits bound, attached and deadened through their humidity")

we'll get into the brain in about the same epoch landing thus on our two satellites skull and moon

but still set in their interval unable to turn over by ourselves alive the glove of soul skin

metaphoring everything at our approach occidentals perhaps (formerly in Amazonia the same transport nomination the same questions about race and incarnation and the immortal breath a conquest trading salt and blood)

to speak my friends as if we were never to meet again, in such a way that seeing each other again would be useless, posthumously from here, of such things because we never will see each other again

Figurations, 1969

I have looked at you as Christ, imagine, Veronica and they separated each with the scalped face of the other
Their *thou* does not date from this conventional poem

Moored to this beauty so close to you, the shopsign of hair banging around as if in a street of birth, my eyes tumified me

The bandage of nights will drain me, I will scatter your ashes; will shoo away your curves, your figure of an inverted "muse" in this found out young woman who was seeking poetry among the very men who usurp it, your age of an inverse ignorant muse reincarnated older in every age
the linen shreds of night heal me, your face dies away, your teeth bridle me less each morning since this morning

And what were we talking about among the others, everyone pretending that beauty was self-evident, like your skin looking very beautiful (like a piece of work) goes about itself among this pretensive we

    (Frost on the finished bone structure, your greyish-brown
      forehead,
    The blue headband of eyes at mid-face,
    Temples versant and walls incunabula over
    The patent mouth and the immortal teeth,
    Trapezoids toward the breasts perhaps, and the drawn back sex)

Tomorrow evening the muteness of our stage whisper dies out, I no longer wear the ringlets of Cathar murmur by my ears

...and of what were we speaking pretending not to fix beauty like an oblique species that our mimed distraction would not bother, or because there no longer is any beauty, or because beauty has to learn equal footing, but allowing stealth to take care of gathering beauty to your side allowing your face to pass behind your collar, your face to continue behind so little wool everywhere invisible, a millimeter of linen forbids your skin which goes up wrists and tibias again to rejoin versants under the wool, to stick to you

And troubled men mechanically invited you, whom your oblique presentation or yourself without make-up like a piece of bark enamored, mayor or president, speaking to not say that you were holding a meeting more open than one of theirs

In spite of the body like Casanova you wanted to know, to learn, to change, but your hair that a gravity in your service spread without respite like a spring across its stone, was betraying you, and the impoverished imagination was catching the wound of your endemic face

The tampon of night, I know, will drain the games injected with you, at last I will try to remind myself that you were without ever having been blue companion from station to station

The strange law to not love, that timidity occults with its likeness, will relax its constraint, and the eclipse total through your image will eclipse in a poem

the hard law to not love leaves our vassalage, migrates in the neighboring compartment, forgets itself in a poem

"I search for my words"

Couplings, 1978

XXV

Sándor Csoóri, *The Visitor's Memories*   *

I left a piece of my head in that smoky-smelling house, there, right there on the milk-burnt plain of the oven-top, with the bread crust tossed to the dog. I arrived, uninvited early in the morning. At first, the waking children merely stared at me from behind the fortifications of their bunched-up quilts: who might I be? what might I want? in what shop did I steal my camomile-yellow shoes? But when I discovered, one by one, their bud-like noses and geranium ears, and before their very eyes did a hairy bear-fist waddle, "grr-grr-grr, my skin is bitten by fleas, the fleas are biting my knees," I saw the little bishops of laughter consecrated by merriment. Their tiny bread-like teeth exploded through the room like popcorn. From the blackened table to the stool, from the stool to earthen floor, down to the sandals tossed under the beds. More! More! Don't take the bear away once you have brought him here (their timid mouths would have said had they expressed themselves).

Out of one eye their mother watched the theater tumbling out of no-where. Instead of cat-flaying excitement, or bear-flaying blood adventure, she noticed marching clouds reined in by the serenity in the children's dilated eyes. She continued sitting on her hatchet-hewed milking stool, drinking her eternal cup of tea. I knew that the sun sets in her liver, that the years support her ramshackle heart with a wooden beam. I also knew that with her blackening dried-plum face, I would appear beneath frosty chandeliers at drink-nursing diplomatic feasts where, wrapped in lettuce, her prematurely-harvested breasts would also be served.

I will arrive at such dinners perhaps by plane, perhaps with iron-plated wings attached to my shoulders, perhaps on the back of a leaf drifting in through an open window, I, the spy for the poor, who is blessed with destroyer eyes and who sees everything. My ironed shirt will be the skin of those who have been sophisticatedly flayed, my Golgothically ticking clock their pounding temples, after those of my father, my mother, and this sister as well, sitting before me, the orphan of a familiar but vanishing story, harboring no impassioned revenge, in tea steam breathing through her children's mouths and surviving through her children's flesh the tribute exacted from her womb.

1977

XXVI

Gyula Kodolányi, *Tract on Rhyme*   *

Eighty daisies. It must mean something that it is exactly eighty and specifically daisies. The geochemical features of the area's soil. Aunt Rosy, yes, she would know. The colors of the flowers growing there depend upon it, that is, what can grow there is determined in advance. Grows, in halos. Feminine numinosity. One for whom images are only set in motion by end-rhymes must be tone-deaf. But it is possible that it is the inches per year of rainfall that carries the most weight. A team of scientists will have to perform a microscopic analysis. We took the daisies to her for her birthday. Others say that we received them from her.

The engineers of the mind, the machinists, are annoyed by additional trains, stunting pilots, and indeterminate daisies. *To measure what cannot be measured.* Pumpkins for bumpkins. Via this odd conjunction, a door opens onto childhood: the sweet smell of warm, steaming pumpkins, the row of orange scooped-out heads on the roof of the shed in the courtyard, in Nagyenyed, in the third head the openings for eyes and mouth are already beginning to grow. Poems with end-rhymes are like child rearing with face-smacks. Something has to thwack because it is impossible to confess emptiness, chaos has to be revenged. Uncle Axel in a two-seated Maxwell.

End-rhyme is not necessary when the whole sentence modulates according to an inner cadence. But such a dance should be almost imperceptible, "in music each redundant sound pains our ears." Yes, the building now houses the local Party Council. "What a bouquet!" Aunt Rosy laughed. We were crying. Why exactly eighty?

A plot of definite size must be divided by the area size each flower needs in order to grow, thinks the faltering layman, attempting to be scientific. Day's eyes, said Aunt Rosy. She loves the petals raying out. The extent of acidity and calcite. Anomaly? Pumpkins for bumpkins, he used to say, stressing the p/s, yet we all understood him. Understood what it meant to him. 16 Hungarian Street (no longer Hungarian Street).

When the sentence "is too musical, it draws attention away from the mental music to the outward music of sounds." Eighty daisies. There *are* rare conjunctions in which end-rhyme continues something, and does not thwack at the end of the line like minestrone against the sides of a kettle.

Rhyme-smiths: kettle menders? Eighty daisies. Without the "a/s" the whole thing would be worthless. Pumpkins for bumpkins: "for" is significant, but even without "for" the phrase is still significant. Pumpkins: bumpkins. It is impossible to invent such a phrase beforehand in an abstract way. The dance is all: the dance of sounds, of hands, of memories. Although they alliterate, there can be no mention of sixty or seventy daisies. Much less of eighty fleabanes. He loves me—he loves me not. With the fortieth "loves me not" we arrive at eighty, but there are not that many numinous, feminine petals on one stem. In other words, La Méthode is useless. Rhyme-menders: kettle smiths?

To reach the plaza one had to ascend the street that went by the College, and beyond the plaza the vineyards appeared: a bunch of grapes, lunch for apes. We obey the command of such rare conjunctions and we are enchanted by the charm of excessive music. In the prose poem the dance of sounds creates a more complex form: in it there is the gesture of human feet, of hands, of gazing eyes, the motion of memories and unthought thoughts. Of the incompatible and the ungraspable. Then lightning strikes and we say: *feminine numinosity.*

It swooped down under the Baja Bridge, my father said.

To make the measurable immeasurable.

1985

XXVII

Bernard Bador, from *Sea Urchin Harakiri* *

Camels pregnant
with flies searching for facetted
fissures.

O forger wells
of bones gone to seed!

High priests
initiated into impotency
pack up the graffiti of C.O.D.
liturgies.

Better to make a hole in the air
than at a blind intersection
to core the bulbs of the Cross.

Acrid,
a spar of rose wreckage skims the second,
a wound of light
on the faded mandala of eyes in ashes.

Behind all this,
a long mauve cry is escaping,
its high note has sliced the petrified biruti.

Stillborn, flies
are swarming
the skin of veiled Vestals.

Soul
hookable
wall.

Sea Urchin Harakiri, 1986

PROGRESS

Jacaranda blindings
heightened by summer's ponderous cymbals.

The melody slinks off to die
under a rolling-mill of potato bugs,
ardent myosoti spouses.

Under the flashings,
faceless sucklings
are flaying the dancers.

The turbulent macaw mutism
is quartered on a wheel of main-jibs
swollen with bear bites.

Tristan Tzara tramples the sacred wells
of the peacock butterflies
scythed by shamrock machetes.

At the call of the termite totems,
pastel blue moray eels
begin to lay tides,
popping sleigh-bells
under the murmuring of heraldic sables.

Ah charisma of deluges!
Hand-to-hand of turgescent mud
into which asphyxiated
walruses are plunging their tusks.

Sea Urchin Harakiri, 1986

A CAPE OF WILD FLIES

Beyond the silent aurochs-haunted forests,
victims give birth to victims,
white she-wolf jaws crush
the black lord's

epileptic sleigh on the powdery
sand of summer, sand
promised to the horse-blood drinkers.
The multiple odyssey under each step!

A hardened rainbow shelters the tarot players
whose fauve oil faces long to crush
the trembling she-mummies
scratching at the surfaceless sheer walls.

Bloodsplashed palettes of eyes.
The fine nerves we entangle in concrete clouds.
After all, the moon does
menstruate on the shadows of our limp

members and bonzai willows dot
the weary fur of our retinas.
Her eyelids hung with deadly nightshade
stuffed bats, her sheets

wet with the blood of virgins,
the royal harpy again and again
yields to the peaty crusades of orgasms.
The juice of marine snails

germinated on Uranus streams
from the sex of icy stones

while witches from the Karpaths
anoint the Countess's vaginal chasm.

In the darkness of underground wash houses,
hordes of infuriated, trilobite-fringed
fledglings immerse themselves in the storm graffiti
chiseled in our limestone lungs.

Sea Urchin Harakiri, 1986

CURDLED SKULLS

The butcher debones the violets
with a suckling's love
for the alpine breast
scattered with curdled skulls

❦

At the sprouting of the first bud
a blue shriek of saws
which the madness of the rake would have liked
to twist around its little prongs

❦

Sound attacked from every side,
codfish rotting in the beds of bishops
mossy with canonical butts

❦

In the flower bed
a slug is urinating on a masochistic spider

❦

Obese women with very delicate joints
dragging about bloated snarling cats
packed with porcupine quills

❦

Tongues vibrating
in the tops of bald trees
fish shadows teeming
with schools of men

❦

Out of breath but smooth with semen
milky spiders
forage in our troubled eyes

❦

The bird comes into you through your eyes
ripping out in beakfuls
the tender shoots of your steps

❦

Sounds shelled on a rosary of barbed wire

❦

Onto the night of curdled eyes
caterpillars
lay
the droppings of our orphan cries

❦

Choked under the mourning caramel
mobs bury themselves
with velvety yells

❦

Covered with antique snow
the pollen of our draw-bridge languages

❦

Music hanged itself
from a tumefied tongue—
in search of the echo
a fly paces up and down

❦

An orchestra conductor in tears
elevates to fire's limits
the lacquered veins of luminous winds

The sun longs for gravedigging waves
but shivers at the sweet swift swish
of the multicolored harp of razors

A capillary breath
marinated in embrace's smut
irrigates
the aurora of the living disguised as the UnDead

Sea Urchin Harakiri, 1986

XXVIII

Milan Exner, *The Eternal Bum in the Heart of Bohemia*

*

ELEGY ON THE ETERNAL BUM
IN THE HEART OF BOHEMIA

Like the rain and clouds on the horizon there are eternals,
look a little lower: an eternal bum is wandering the heart of Bohemia.
Unrecognized, because his cheeks lack make-up, he crosses an intersec-
tion without a stick.
His hair is not braided into a four-plait. His cheeks under a field of
stubble.
You can recognize him, though afterward he cannot be recognized.
He'll buy a cake on the corner and share it with a pigeon and a sparrow
when they're not looking. But just look around—its clear he's
omnipresent.
Like a tree gone wild, he broke through the pavement
and resignedly holds the sun by its pendulum—look, like a bud
with a trident of Neptune's twig. Leaning against a poster,
he says nothing against ties but doesn't wear them. He escapes into a
grayness
like those stratified days of dull silence heaped up
in the heart of Bohemia. He's like the rain and clouds on the horizon.

In spite of being omnipresent, he must cross the Charles Bridge.
But he stumbles over the first statue's shadow. An unfinished word will
break him. And so he will wander, overturned in his waist
like a noonless sunflower. Even the shadow nailed to the post
behind Christ urges him to disturb the peace.
Gulls can be addressed as fish wings. And the Bridge,
as a sidetrack with a fixed number of arms. When the Huns
skirmished here, he realized how much he loved horses.
But after his grandpa was trampled, he stopped eating horse meat.
Later, he forgot all that and here he is again.
To this day he remembers his first sin, in paradise,
with the Tree of Knowledge. What did God know about vitamins!
Explanations are in vain: God was old and for a long time
had not climbed an apple tree. And *exules filii Evae*

lack C and are constipated. So, to this very day,
it's necessary to climb the apple tree of knowledge and to knock with
 a mocking pinkie
on what has grown there. And the sower hath gone, but
he was no sower, merely a prayer. And he did not sow seeds,
he imitated dung. And the peasant hath gathered, but hath not reaped,
he took it to the recycling center. You know, a philosopher at a lens
 grinding mill.

Each pain is too huge to fit in him.
Certainly never in its entirety. He wipes his inflamed ducts solely on his
 lapel
under the fish eye of a dreamless night. Nobody knows where he lives,
but at the stroke of seven you'll notice the city is incomplete without
 him.
He's be sitting on a threshold, leaning against his tiger
which purrs. Welcome everybody, come on in!
In the panoptic herbarium of substitute portraits, there is
every face. A sneered-at idolatry room has lain down whitely
like a tablecloth in the warm sun. A bug is crawling.
Smoke and lead are hanging in the air. From them, like hops,
a fraud of foaming bursting flows. For who of you have
witnessed spring on a sappy galloping mare? It is ridiculous
to think longing could be round!
He once believed his daughter would give birth to
Christ and Buddha, but he cannot believe that the Vltava is
flowing into the Elbe near Melnik! Although the wine is only
half-pure once sipped, he pipes a little bacchanal
on the osier reed he cut in the slums today,
near the frog-bubbling rubbish heap's water hole.
Based on this, he approves some relief for a neighbor's cat
which is hungrier than his own relatives. Voraciously
he eats everything. But the door stiles remind him of
the gallows of Westphalian peace! So he asks to which close are things
drawing and doesn't laugh, although he knows the answer, the definite
 one.

I would say that he shivers in his soul. But he has no soul.
He has only a heart whirled in roe membrane, an animal sense of smell
and an ear inclined toward one of the cardinal points.
He is the naked body of consciousness in the tips of five touch,
he is the bum in the heart of Bohemia.

The most intense odor will not draw his hand to his nose. There's
     nothing
godlike in front of his peace. The sun knocks over the window-box
and shouts for joy in the bottomless watering pot. Under the window
a cactus nightmares its foot. If you kick off your quilt,
the coolness will paralyze you: at 7 A.M., ah, to promenade!
To what can the city's joy be compared when he returns?
But he doesn't return—actually he slept at the edge of
a slum crust, and the city feels like the edge of a cake!
However, it is pleased he does not return to the raisin and almond
enchased in the destroyed half of the Old Town Hall's front wall
so as to strew, with a pigeon shaker, for the poultry gathered at
the holy tower of Tyn. Where an extortionist pulls
the stays of an accordion. And the pigeon king holds a banquet.
Again, as if he forgot, he touches his breast pocket
to take hold of a little book. But he gave up reading (after his fifth PhD).
Only in a newspaper, clutched tightly to the printer's ink,
does he sometimes wrap his dryness. What would you expect? He
     breathes
with only half of his lungs, eats half, and does not drink at all!
Water he's hidden in his hump. A saint? No—he's a camel!
He admires donkeys for their stubbornness and patience.
Otherwise, he's a man-hen. It roots in ashes and scratches in dung,
looking askance with distrustful eye. It has wings but
at best flaps over a neighboring fence. Death, in the form of
a malicious cyclist, will run it down. Among animals
he pardons the following: the mentioned donkey,
the elephant, the boar, the cat and the dolphin—and sometimes
the carcass-eating vulture and the human child. Concerning turtles,
     he hates their armor,

snails their spiral shell, giraffes their long necks stolen from swans.
Concerning men, their excessive humanity and concerning himself,
   his chronic colds.
When I say he cannot be recognized, it's true, but only
half. When he smiles at a child, you recognize him.
When he smiles at himself, you recognize him. When he smiles
not moving his eyebrows, that's him—he doesn't see you!

The eternal bum in the heart of Bohemia! When brother sun heats up
   the wall,
he's like a kid. He huddles into himself and breathes.
Nothing can disturb him. When pedestrians pass the sanatorium,
he sees a garden. Suspiciously, he touches the vertical ditches
a whip has irritated into the air. Instead of horses, he hitches up
four frogs and a Siamese twin. Then he heads toward a beach
where the air is sucked down into disposable cups.
Torrid air. The pavement chirps. A cricket shouted into
the heat of a staircase cut from a single oak. So what...
The greatest poets are the least accomplished, their poems look like
digressions. He uncrutched speech but will not run—
his feet pulled out from under him, he'll make no attempt to find
the reader with his finger. Look! Snow is sprinkling the Tower,
a tale sticks its hairy paw into the astrological clock. He will not give up
his sight for a single week of eyes! Nothing can make him speak
in parables or quote someone, or dawdle over wise tablets.
He just looks that way! He makes a path so that
an ant can continue carrying its beam. But he will not make one
so that a man can drag his cross into his siesta!
Later, you will see him being led away, without a rope,
he'll be back tomorrow. The city will recognize him with joy.
It will lean from its windows and beam and beam at him.
The eternal bum in the heart of Bohemia! Come spring he will distrib-
   ute from his pockets

all his tiny marbles even though he does not believe in the approaching
   summer.
Of course, why should he! He's the eternal bum in the heart of Bohemia.

The perishable values are firmly anchored in time.
Imperishable ones are out of time. But as there is nothing
out of time, everything is perishable. Yes, everything will perish
and it is worth everything to live this perishable life, a life
anchored in time. That is why he loves animals so much,
and trees and children too. The child remains in us. And the old man is
with him, until they grow into one. He will let him live
like a little pony at the children's railing.
In his old age he will again rejoice. And death
will be as merciful to him as to a child. And he will understand
and wait. For we *are* children.
He will cover himself up to his chin with a child's featherbed
and fall asleep, balled up like a cat. In the morning,
when the sun lifts into the smog, the bed is empty—
only a tiny cloud pillar is gently soaring! Flying
above the city, which will recognize him with joy.

And then, there is a young one, to whom no angel appeared,
rushing out the door with a pram full of a boy. No one knows
where he came from. And now he no longer toddles
or builds sand castles. Now rowings, now pigeons and now the river
which will speak to the gulls. The city is incomplete without him.
Meanwhile, sitting on the threshold, leaning against his tiger,
he awaits whatever action will come into his panopticon.

ca. 1978

XXIX

Notes on the Translations

NOTES ON THE TRANSLATIONS

ARTHUR RIMBAUD, The Drunken Boat
This translation of "The Drunken Boat" first appeared in *The Gull Wall* (1975). It was reprinted in both editions of *Conductors of the Pit*, the first edition of which (1988) included poetry by Vallejo, Césaire, Artaud, and Vladimir Holan. The second edition (2005), besides Vallejo, Césaire, Holan, and Artaud, included translations of Pablo Neruda, Bernard Bador, Miklós Radnóti, Ferenc Juhász, Sándor Csoóri, and Géza Szöcs. The four Hungarian poets were co-translated with Gyula Kodolányi. The Césaire was co-translated with Annette Smith. Bernard Bador worked with me on the Artaud.

PABLO NERUDA POEMS
These six poems are from the first two volumes of *Residencia en la tierra* (1933, 1935). Neruda was the first poet I translated, and my initial efforts (now considerably revised) were published in 1962 by The Amber House Press. At the end of the 2005 edition of *Conductors of the Pit* there is an essay, "Revising Neruda's *Residencias*."

CÉSAR VALLEJO POEMS
I have been translating and co-translating Vallejo since the late 1950s. Grove Press published my first translation of *Human Poems* in 1968. University of California Press published a substantially revised version of this book, along with *Spain, Take This Cup From Me*, co-translated with José Rubia Barcia, in 1978, as *César Vallejo: The Complete Posthumous Poetry*. Marsilio brought out my translation of *Trilce* in 1992, and Wesleyan University Press reprinted the book in 2000. Revisions of all of this work, along with a new translation of *The Black Heralds*, has been collected in *The Complete Poetry of César Vallejo*, with a Foreword by Mario Vargas Llosa, and an Introduction by Efrain Kristal, published by University of California Press in 2007.

For the twenty-seven Vallejo poems included here, I have restricted commentary to just a few neologisms, archaic, arcane, and obscure words. A much larger section of notes can be found in *The Complete Poetry of César Vallejo*, pp. 621–676.

Trilce I
"Who's making all that racket:" While Vallejo was in the Trujillo jail (November 7, 1920 to February 26, 1921), inmates were taken outside to use the latrines

four times a day. Apparently the guards would coarsely urge them to hurry up. In the first stanza of this poem, it seems that the racket-makers are the guards and that the "islands" are the inmates' turds.

"fecapital:" Based on *tesoro* (treasure), the word *tesórea* is identified by Giovanni Meo Zilio as a neologism incorporating the later part of *estercórea* (excrement), influenced by the guano references in the stanza (as well as by the "islands" in the first).

"ponk:" The Spanish *calabrina*, meaning an intolerable, intense stench, is archaic. If I had used the word "stench," the translation would reflect the common Spanish word *hedor*—thus the necessity, in such cases, of finding archaic English words for their Spanish equivalents.

"muzziled:" The Spanish *abozaleada* is based on *abozalada* ("muzzled"), with an *–ear* infinitive ending substituted for the standard *–ar* ending.

Trilce VI

"Otilian:" The Spanish *otilinas* is based on the first name of Vallejo's lover in Lima (1918–1919), Otilia Villanueva.

"lustred:" The old Spanish word *fratesadas* means "to give a luster to hose after washing them," using a glass or wooden trowel-shaped object.

"tawny berry:" The *capulí* is a bush that yields a flower and dark-yellow berry, appreciated throughout the Peruvian sierra for its delicate, ornamental beauty.

Trilce VIII

"saltatory:" Based on the Greek *hyphállomai*, *hifalto* is a rare, ornithological word for birds that walk by hopping. "Saltatory" is defined as "proceeding or taking place by a leap or leaps, rather than by gradual, orderly steps." On one level, the word identifies the discontinuous, non-sequitur poetics of *Trilce*.

Trilce XXXII

"Roombbb… Hulllablll llust…ster:" While the Spanish sounds (*Rumbbb… Trrraprrr rrach… chaz*) may be read as street noise, the fact that the words *trapa*, *racha*, and *cachaza* seem to be involved, invites me to reconstruct the line making use of English equivalents. With poetry, the challenge is always to translate everything.

"Serpenteenic **e** of the sweet roll vendor:" The "u" (in boldface) of the *biz-cochero's* ("sweet roll vendor's) cry—"*biscochouus*"—unwinds in the air like a serpentin. I change the "u" to an "e" to pick up the sound of "ee" in "serpenteenic," as well as the "ee" in "sweet" (which is echoed in line 13, along with the long "o" in "rolls"—Weeeeeetrozzz).

"Engyrafted:" The Spanish *engirafada* is a neologism fusing *girafa* ("giraffe") with *girar* ("gyrate") and the prefix *en*.

Trilce XXXVI

"hell-bent on winning:" *a las ganadas* is a northern Peruvianism.

"ammoniafies:" The Spanish *amoniácase* (ammoniac, ammonia) turned into a verb. While we have a verb in English ("ammonify"), I do not use it, since none exists in Spanish.

"neverthelessez:" The Spanish *todaviiza* is the adverb *todavía* ("yet, still, nevertheless,") extended/warped into a verb. A few lines later, another adverb, *aunes* ("evens") is treated as a plural noun.

Trilce LXV

"tori:" round moldings ("torus" in the singular). In the same line, *repulgos* could be translated as "borders" or "pie-edgings." I opt for the latter.

"axling:" *Ejeando* is *eje* ("axle") turned into a verb.

"reveilles champing:" This mysterious phrase, *tascar dianas*, might also be translated as "dianas scotching" or, even more dramatically, "bull's-eyes crunching."

"humblest:" According to Meo Zilio, with *humildóse* Vallejo has taken an archaic verb, *humildarse*, and substituted it for the current *humillarse*.

Trilce LXXV

Juan Espejo Asturrizaga (who wrote a memoir of Vallejo's years in Peru) comments that

> on the 27th of April [1921], we left the port of Callao, on the steamer *Aysen*, for Salaverry, arriving on the 30th. At this time, Vallejo had with him in a binder most of the poems that would make up *Trilce*. His friends met us at the Trujillo station. Having just arrived from Lima, where he

had been embroiled in quarrels and agitation, and in a constant flurry of activity, Vallejo was floored by the placid ambience, and immediately seemed to lose once and for all his interest in Trujillo. At the same time, he discovered his old friends asleep on their feet, going through life as if in "slow motion"... The following day he came to my house and read me the poem beginning "You're all dead."

Epistle to the Passersby

"cullions:" In Spanish, *compañones* is an archaic word for "testicles."

"navehall:" Vallejo intentionally misspells *ombligo* ("navel") as *hombligo* (playing off *hombre*—"man"). Since there is no way to pick up the pun in English, I invent my own distortion.

"Idle on a stone..."

"stallion louse" for *piojo padre*. As an adjective, *padre* ("father") is a common augmentative for almost everything e.g., *una vida padre* ("a great life"), *un automóvil padre* ("a great car"). Here the attempt is to translate the act of the lowest parasite being ironically elevated to a role of seminal importance.

Telluric and Magnetic

"pepper tree:" A *molle* is a genus of tropical American trees of the sumac family, known as the pepper tree.

"cavy:" The *cuy* is a short-tailed, rough-haired South American rodent. A *cuya* ("cavess" in my approximation) would be a female *cuy*.

"bird pepper:" The Peruvian *rocoto*, an extraordinarily hot pepper.

"Alfonso: you are looking at me..."

An elegy inspired by the death of Vallejo's close friend from his first days in Paris, Alfonso Silva (1903–1937). Silva was a Peruvian composer and musician who returned to Peru and died in Lima. Vallejo used to accompany him to restaurants where Alfonso would play his violin to pay for their meal.

Intensity and Height

"coughv:" The Spanish *toz* appears to be a neologism, combining *tos* ("cough") with *voz* ("voice").

The Nine Monsters

"arduent:" The Spanish *ardio* appears to be a metaplasm derived from *ardiente* ("ardent") and *arduo* ("arduous").

Sermon on Death

wolvum: The Spanish *lovo* appears to be an intentional misspelling of *lobo* ("wolf"), possibly to link the word to *ovo* ("egg," or "ovum").

AIMÉ CÉSAIRE POEMS

These translations, from four of Césaire's books, come from *Aimé Césaire: The Collected Poetry*, co-translated with Annette Smith, University of California Press, 1983. For part of the poem, "The Thoroughbreds" (from *The Miraculous Weapons*) and the title poem to *Lost Body*, see the essay "At the Locks of the Void: Co-Translating Aimé Césaire," in the prose section of this book.

Perdition

balisier: A wild plantain found in the forests of Martinique that has an unusually shaped bright red flower some liken to an open heart, others to a flame.

The Miraculous Weapons

Compitalia: In Roman religion, the *lares compitales* were the guardians of the crossroads, in whose honor were held the *Laralia*, or *Compitalia*.

Blues of the Rain

Aguacero: The Spanish word means a brief sudden shower or downpour. In the poem "Black Stone on a White Stone," Vallejo claims he will die in one.

Elegy

souklyan: A Dahoman sorcerer who has the ability to leave his skin to carry out evil tasks. The word appears to be derived from *soukou* ("moonless night") and *gnan* ("master") i.e., a master of the moonless night.

...But There Is This Hurt

menfenil: The Caribbean sparrow hawk.

ANTONIN ARTAUD TEXTS

Revolt Against Poetry was written in the Rodez asylum in 1944. My version appeared in the 2005 *Conductors of the Pit* (which contains an additional thirty-five pages of Artaud translations). My gratitude to Deborah Treisman for crucial suggestions in one draft of this translation.

With the continuing publication of volumes in his *Oeuvres complètes* by Gallimard, along with several excellent books on the poet by Stephen Barber (*Blows and Bombs*, 1993; *Weapons of Liberation*, 1996; *The Screaming Body*, 1999; *Artaud: Terminal Curses*, 2008), it is now clear that Antonin Artaud (1896–1948) has two distinct periods, with the shorter second period (1945–1948) containing much more material than the entire first period (1923–1938). About this second period, Barber has written:

> "The last phase of Artaud's work... has suffered from a certain
> marginalization. It is the work of a man newly released from
> nine years in five successive asylums, and has sometimes been
> dismissed summarily. But this last phase is far from a psychosis-
> induced linguistic stalling. More than any other phase of
> Artaud's work, that from the period after his release from Rodez
> conveys a magnificent lucidity and lust for life. Utterly stubborn
> in its torrent of invective and denunciation, it is immensely ver-
> satile in terms of its imagery of the body, and in its linguistic
> experiments."

The Return of Artaud, the Mômo (the first of five sections that make up *Artaud le Mômo*) was written when the poet was living in Ivry outside of Paris, in 1946. *Mômo* is Marseille slang for simpleton, or village idiot. The word may also relate to the Greek god of mockery and raillery, Momus, said by Hesiod to be the son of Sleep and Night, as well as the nocturnal voice of Hermes who in this vision bears in his hand a crotalum in contrast to a caduceus.

"o dedi...:" As early as 1943, Artaud was working out "syllable words" in the Rodez asylum as part of his defense against demons. These "syllable words" begin to appear fairly frequently from 1945 until his death in 1948. Their effect is to

physicalize the writing, giving it a harsh vocality, or, as Susan Sontag has commented, "an unmediated physical presence," and one that contrasts sharply with the veering fantasies and arguments of the text. Such words usually appear in one to three word lines, and seem to be carefully worked out, with repetitions, semi-repetitions, and variations. While some of the words appear to be non-referential, others are plays on Latin or Greek words denoting parts of the human body.

"*old bag*": A much-pondered translation of *carne*, which Harraps defines in the following way: "1. (a) tough meat; (b) old horse; screw. 2. (a) bad-tempered person; (of man) cantankerous brute; (of woman) bitch; (b) wastrel, bad egg; (of woman) slut." The word's appearance in the poem, as *une carne*, seems to register a kind of woman, rather than meat. However, in one of the early drafts for this section, Artaud replaces *viande* ("meat") with *carne* in the line: *cette carne entre deux genoux* ("this *carne* between two knees"), indicating that the word may be a substitute, perhaps in that section alone, for *viande*. It appears to be impossible to translate *carne* in a single word as low-quality or tough meat. One is forced into such words as "gristle" or "mutton," which signal meaning associations that are irrelevant. While "old bag" compromises to some extent the denotative density of *carne*, it plays off "hole" and "palm" in fascinating ways.

To Have Done with the Judgment of God was written in 1947 at the invitation of the Director of Radiodiffusion Française. The performance utilized other readers besides Artaud, and a xylophone, drums, kettledrums, and gongs. On the day before the program was to be broadcast, it was determined to be obscene and was banned. A considerable controversy ensued. A recording of the banned performance is available on a CD (*Antonin Artaud: pour en finir avec le jugement de dieu*, Sub Rosa aural documents SF 92, edited with an introduction by Marc Dachy, Paris, 1995).

These last two Artaud texts appeared in *Watchfiends & Rack Screams: Works from the Final Period*, translated with Bernard Bador, and published by Exact Change in 1995.

MIKLÓS RADNÓTI, Seventh Eclogue
In 1986, supported by a Soros Travel Grant, Caryl Eshleman and I spent a month in Hungary. For several weeks we stayed in the home of Gyula and Maria

Kodolányi in Budapest, where Gyula and I co-translated sixty-five pages of 20th-century Hungarian poetry later published in *Sulfur* #21.

As a Hungarian Jew, Radnóti (1909–1944) was forced into a labor battalion after the country's forced entry into World War II. After having been moved from Serbian mines, exhausted and diseased, the poet was shot by German guards and buried in a mass grave near the city of Gyor, in western Hungary. After the war, the grave was opened and a notebook containing some of his finest poems was found in Radnóti's trenchcoat pocket. With the Kodolányis, Caryl and I visited the cemetary north of Gyor where Radnóti had been reburied. Etched on his tombstone: "I lived in an age so ugly, men killed not only on command, but for pleasure."

MICHEL DEGUY POEMS

Michel Deguy (1930–) is the author of a wide and complex range of books (poems, prose poems, philosophical essays, drama scholarship, etc.) and the Director of *Po&Sie*, an international French journal of poetry and poetics. My translations, done with Michel's help, are from *Given Giving: Selected Poems of Michel Deguy*, University of California Press, 1984, with an introduction by Kenneth Koch, who writes:

> Deguy is interested in how his predecessors [Rimbaud, Eluard, Reverdy] wrote—unexpected transitions, confidence in momentary sensations, willingness to remain unclear—but not in their conclusions. The unconscious, the irrational, isn't the answer. The intellect or, perhaps more precisely, intellectual disciplines, such as psychology and linguistics, come back in his poetry as directions and as points of view and, verbally, as part of the very texture of Deguy's poems. For all their intellectual atmosphere, Deguy's poems suggest that, for him, if anything is the answer, it is the happy—or distressing—confusing mixture of all the complicated thoughts and points of view that delineate his subjects. His poetry proceeds, verbally as well as thematically, by means of hesitations, interruptions, changes. It stops, it diverges; it often has an air of being unfinished—even, one could say, of having gone nowhere, the way a moment goes nowhere, a moment of perception or sensation with all its intermixture of memories, associations, ideas.

SÁNDOR CSOÓRI, The Visitor's Memories

Sándor Csoóri (1930–), born in Zámoly, Transdanubia, is a Hungarian poet who has also written essays and screenplays. As a poet, he is one of the most articulate representatives in Hungary of so-called "Folk Surrealism," a modernist aesthetics that builds on archaic elements in folk art and regards as its forerunners such artists as Béla Bartók and Garcia Lorca. At the same time, Csoóri is an alert and active intellectual, whose essays probe the spiritual and political situation of Hungary, often reflecting on the plight of Hungarian minorities living in Rumania and the Czech Republic. He has often been in political disgrace, with books suspended and writings banned. This prose poem was co-translated with Gyula Kodolányi and most recently appeared in the 2005 *Conductors of the Pit*.

GYULA KODOLÁNYI, Tract on Rhyme

Gyula Kodolányi (1942–) was born and educated in Budapest. He has a long relationship with American poetry, having translated such poets as Robert Duncan, Robert Creeley, and Denise Levertov, and edited a Hungarian anthology of American poetry. He was a founding member of the Hungarian Democratic Forum in 1987, and served as Senior Foreign Policy Advisor to Prime Ministers József Antall and Péter Boross in 1990–1993. His recent projects include a sequence of sonnets on themes by Plotinus, and a series of prose poems called "Intimations." In 2002, he received the József Attila Prize for Literature. "Tract on Rhyme," which I co-translated with him, appeared in *Sulfur* #21.

BERNARD BADOR POEMS

The French post-surrealist poet and collagist Bernard Bador lived for several decades in Los Angeles where I met him in the early 1980s. With his help, I translated forty-four poems from several French collections as *Sea Urchin Harakiri* (with a Postface by Robert Kelly, Panjandrum, 1986). The four poems here are from that collection. In my Introduction to the book, I wrote:

> "In Bador, there is incessant entropic closure. Each stanza is an orphan, an isolate isle, with only possible ties to the one that is found before or after it. Momentary evocations of grandeur are abruptly double-crossed by torture, disembowelment, and abortion. Reading him is like watching little pieces being broken off from stories and collaged in such a way that omnipotency and impotency are like grooved pipes that screw into

each other perfectly. What makes these poems unique is the way that they utilize various surrealist strategies without edging in under the canopy of established surrealist procedure."

Bador is not only of Hungarian ancestry, but a descendant of the noble Báthory family, which not only includes kings and princes but the notorious Erzsébet Báthory, known as "the bloody countess."

MILAN EXNER, Elegy on the Eternal Bum in the Heart of Bohemia

When I was teaching in the Summer Seminar in Frenstat, Czechoslovakia, in the summer of 1977, one of my students, Jan Benda, introduced me to the poetry of Vladimir Holan, which led to my co-translation with Frantisek Galan and Michael Heim of Holan's *A Night with Hamlet*. Benda also brought the poetry of the Czech Milan Exner to my attention, and in the late 1970s we co-translated four poems of Exner's, three of which appeared in Eliot Weinberger's *Montemora*.

Milan Exner was born in Northern Bohemia in 1950. At the time Benda and I were translating him, he was living in Prague. While he had written five collections of poetry and one novel, none were considered acceptable for publication by the state-controlled press. The first of his poems to be published in Czech occurred in the bilingual presentation of "Elegy on the Eternal Bum in the Heart of Bohemia," *Montemora* #7.

Exner is now teaching literary arts at the University of Liberec. In 1998, he published a collection of poems called *Poesie Z* with Torst, in Prague. It included the five single collections mentioned above: *Charles Bridge, Elegies, The Devil According to Darwin, Night of Majesty,* and *The Father of Those who Suffered the Plague.*

IN ADDITION:

I am deeply grateful to Joe Phillips, of Black Widow Press, for offering me this generous amount of pages in which to assemble a Clayton Eshleman Reader. While I am very happy with the selection Joe, my wife Caryl, and I, have come up with, I am also aware that certain works have had to be left out—mainly because of length, but also because a few of them today strike me as being of mixed success. So here is a short list of works that in a gargantuan-sized collection would probably have been included:

The Book of Eternal Death, 1964 (*Double Room* #7, online, 2007, edited by Mark Tursi).

The Book of Niemonjima 1964–65, and Coils, 1972 (*Coils*, Black Sparrow Press, 1973)

The Moistinsplendour (*Caterpillar* #3/4, 1967).

The Tomb of Donald Duck (*Fracture*, Black Sparrow Press, 1982).

My Night with Artaud & Othlor (*From Scratch*, Black Sparrow Press, 1998).

Visions of the Fathers of Lascaux, 1980 (*Juniper Fuse*, Wesleyan University Press, 2003).

Novices: A Study of Poetic Apprenticeship, 1989 (*Companion Spider*, Wesleyan University Press, 2002).

Notes on Charles Olson and the Archaic, 1994 (*Archaic Design*, 2007).

Poems from *i, laminaria*, by Aimé Césaire, co-translated with Annette Smith (*Lyric and Dramatic Poetry 1946–1982*, University Press of Virginia, 1990).

Here Lies, by Antonin Artaud, with Bernard Bador (*Watchfiends & Rack Screams*, Exact Change, 1995).

Notebook of a Return to the Native Land, by Aimé Césaire, co-translated with Annette Smith (Wesleyan University Press, 2001).

A Night with Hamlet, by Vladimir Holan, co-translated with Frantisek Galan and Michael Heim (*Conductors of the Pit*, Soft Skull, 2005)

Spain, Take This Cup from Me, by César Vallejo (*The Complete Poetry of César Vallejo*, University of California Press, 2007).

TITLES FROM BLACK WIDOW PRESS

TRANSLATION SERIES

Chanson Dada: Selected Poems by Tristan Tzara
Translated with an introduction and essay by Lee Harwood.

Approximate Man and Other Writings by Tristan Tzara
Translated and edited by Mary Ann Caws.

Poems of André Breton: A Bilingual Anthology
Translated with essays by Jean-Pierre Cauvin and Mary Ann Caws.

Last Love Poems of Paul Eluard
Translated with an essay by Marilyn Kallet.

Capital of Pain by Paul Eluard
Translated by Mary Ann Caws, Patricia Terry, and Nancy Kline.

Love, Poetry (L'amour la poésie) by Paul Eluard
Translated with an essay by Stuart Kendall.

The Sea and Other Poems by Guillevic
Translated by Patricia Terry. Introduction by Monique Chefdor.

Essential Poems and Writings of Robert Desnos: A Bilingual Anthology
Edited with an introduction and essay by Mary Ann Caws.

Essential Poems and Writings of Joyce Mansour: A Bilingual Anthology
Translated with an introduction by Serge Gavronsky.

Poems of A. O. Barnabooth by Valery Larbaud
Translated by Ron Padgett and Bill Zavatsky.

Eyeseas (Les Ziaux) by Raymond Queneau
Translated with an introduction by Daniela Hurezanu and Stephen Kessler.

Art Poétique by Guillevic *(Forthcoming)*
Translated by Maureen Smith.

Furor and Mystery and Other Writings by René Char *(Forthcoming)*
Edited and translated by Mary Ann Caws and Nancy Kline.

La Fontaine's Bawdy by Jean de la Fontaine *(Forthcoming)*
Translated with an introduction by Norman R. Shapiro.

Inventor of Love by Gherasim Luca *(Forthcoming)*
Translated by Julian and Laura Semilian. Introduction by Andrei Codrescu. Essay by
Petre Răileanu.

The Big Game by Benjamin Péret *(Forthcoming)*
Translated with an introduction by Marilyn Kallet.

I Want No Part in It and Other Writings by Benjamin Péret
Translated with an introduction by James Brook. *(Forthcoming)*

Essential Poems and Writings of Jules Laforgue *(Forthcoming)*
Translated and edited by Patricia Terry.

Preversities: A Jacques Prevert Sampler *(Forthcoming)*
Translated and edited by Norman R. Shapiro.

MODERN POETRY SERIES

An Alchemist with One Eye on Fire by Clayton Eshleman

Archaic Design by Clayton Eshleman

Backscatter: New and Selected Poems by John Olson

Crusader-Woman by Ruxandra Cesereanu
Translated by Adam J. Sorkin. Introduction by Andrei Codrescu.

The Grindstone of Rapport: A Clayton Eshleman Reader
Forty years of poetry, prose, and translations by Clayton Eshleman.

Packing Light: New and Selected Poems by Marilyn Kallet *(Forthcoming)*

Forgiven Submarine by Ruxandra Cesereanu and Andrei Codrescu
(Forthcoming)

Caveat Onus by Dave Brinks *(Forthcoming)*
Complete cycle, four volumes combined.

Fire Exit by Robert Kelly *(Forthcoming)*

NEW POETS SERIES

Signal from Draco: New and Selected Poems by Mebane Robertson

LITERARY THEORY/BIOGRAPHY SERIES

Revolution of the Mind: The Life of André Breton by Mark Polizzotti
Revised and augmented edition. *(Forthcoming)*

WWW.BLACKWIDOWPRESS.COM